Parental Care and the Best Interests of the Child in Muslim Countries

Nadjma Yassari · Lena-Maria Möller
Imen Gallala-Arndt
Editors

Parental Care and the Best Interests of the Child in Muslim Countries

ASSER PRESS

Springer

Editors
Nadjma Yassari
Max Planck Research Group: Changes in God's Law—An Inner Islamic Comparison of Family and Succession Laws
Max Planck Institute for Comparative and International Private Law
Hamburg
Germany

Lena-Maria Möller
Max Planck Research Group: Changes in God's Law—An Inner Islamic Comparison of Family and Succession Laws
Max Planck Institute for Comparative and International Private Law
Hamburg
Germany

Imen Gallala-Arndt
Max Planck Institute for Social Anthropology
Halle
Germany

ISBN 978-94-6265-173-9 ISBN 978-94-6265-174-6 (eBook)
DOI 10.1007/978-94-6265-174-6

Library of Congress Control Number: 2016960773

Published by T.M.C. ASSER PRESS, The Hague, The Netherlands www.asserpress.nl
Produced and distributed for T.M.C. ASSER PRESS by Springer-Verlag Berlin Heidelberg

Printed on acid-free paper

This T.M.C. ASSER PRESS imprint is published by Springer Nature
The registered company is Springer-Verlag GmbH Germany
The registered company address is: Heidelberger Platz 3, 14197 Berlin, Germany

Preface

This volume compiles selected contributions to the workshop 'Parental Care and the Best Interests of the Child in Muslim Countries', which, under the auspices of the Max Planck Research Group 'Changes in God's Law—An Inner Islamic Comparison of Family and Succession Laws', was convened at the Centre Jacques Berque pour les Études en Sciences Humaines et Sociales au Maroc in Rabat, Morocco, 1–5 April 2015. The workshop brought together the members of the Max Planck Working Group on Child Law in Muslim Countries that was established in 2014 to conduct comparative studies on various fields of child law in Muslim countries.

The first project of the Working Group focused on the principle of the best interests of the child and parental care. In recent years, legislatures of many Muslim countries have revised the conventional Islamic rules on child custody. Whereas in the past, rules were oriented on fixed age brackets and the gender of the parent and child, they have increasingly been formulated in favour of the principle of the best interests of the child and/or in favour of the mother through an extension of the custodial time period afforded to her as a matter of law.

Against this background, the principal goals of the workshop were to: (i) trace the incorporation of the principle of the best interests of the child into domestic law; (ii) analyse the reasons for establishing the concept as a fundamental principle in child law; and (iii) identify the ways in which each jurisdiction under review perceives and interprets the best interests of the child in the field of parental care. The overriding research aim was to determine the impact made by the inclusion of the principle of the best interests of the child in Muslim legal systems and, in a second step, to compare the respective results and draw more general conclusions about the dynamics of legal developments in Muslim countries.

Each of the ten chapters collected herein contains a historical perspective on the evolution of domestic rules on parental care and on the introduction and development of the notion of the best interests of the child. Further, the chapters consider social and cultural factors and discuss the particular characteristics of each country before analysing the policies and agendas of national legislatures and other stakeholders which have led them to amend law in a specific direction.

Finally, significant attention has been given to legal practice and the role of the judiciary in interpreting the principle of the best interests of the child.

In addition to the country-specific analyses collected herein, a thematic chapter by Shaheen Sardar Ali and Sajila Sohail Khan explores the public law dimension of children's rights by assessing Muslim state party practice in light of responses to the UN Convention on the Rights of the Child. Moreover, a comparative analysis of the themes explored is presented in the Synopsis at the end of this volume.

The editors wish to thank Baudouin Dupret for hosting the workshop at the Centre Jacques Berque as well as Global Affairs Canada for their valuable support in making those chapters originally written in French accessible to a wider English-speaking audience. We also would like to express our deep gratitude to Tess Chemnitzer, Michael Friedman, Jocasta Godlieb and Shyam Kapila for their continuous assistance in editing and formatting this volume.

Hamburg, Germany
September 2016

Nadjma Yassari
Lena-Maria Möller
Imen Gallala-Arndt

Contents

Editors and Contributors

About the Editors

Nadjma Yassari is the Director of the Max-Planck Research Group "Changes in God's Law—An Inner Islamic Comparison of Family and Succession Laws" at the Max Planck Institute for Comparative and International Private Law in Hamburg. Her main fields of research are national and private international law of Islamic countries, in particular the Arab Middle East, Iran, Afghanistan and Pakistan with a special focus on family and succession law. Nadjma studied law in Austria, France and the United Kingdom. She holds a LL.M. degree from the University of London, School of Oriental and African Studies and a LL.D. from the University of Innsbruck, Austria. In 2000/2001 she spent a year at the University of Damascus in Syria, Faculty of Language. In 2016 she was awarded a postdoctoral degree (Habilitation) from the University of Hamburg.

Lena-Maria Möller is a Senior Research Fellow at the Max Planck Institute for Comparative and International Private Law. She holds an M.A. in Middle East Studies and a Ph.D. in Law. Lena-Maria Möller's research and teaching experience is in Islamic law, Muslim family law in particular, as well as in comparative and private international law. She has held teaching positions at the University of Hamburg, the University of Augsburg, and, most recently, the University of Münster where she served as Visiting Professor of Islamic Law. Currently, Lena-Maria Möller is preparing a postdoctoral research project which explores how contemporary Muslim jurisdictions engage with and frame vague and still undefined legal concepts.

Imen Gallala-Arndt is a Senior Research Fellow in the Department Law and Anthropology at the Max Planck Institute for Social Anthropology. She holds a DEA in Public Law from the University of Tunis Carthage as well as an LL.M. and Ph.D. in Law from the University of Heidelberg. After having worked for the peace process projects at the Max Planck Institute for Comparative and International Public Law in Heidelberg, Imen joined the Max Planck Institute in Hamburg in 2006. From 2009 until 2016 she was a member of the Max Planck Research Group on Family and Succession Law in Islamic Countries. Imen is currently finalizing a postdoc monograph on interfaith marriages in Tunisia, Lebanon and Israel. Imen has published on various legal issues relating to Islamic countries especially constitutional law as well as comparative and international family law.

Contributors

Souhayma Ben Achour is Professor of Private Law at the Faculty of Law and Political Sciences, Université de Tunis El Manar. She holds two DEA in Private International Law and in Private Law from the Université Panthéon-Assas in Paris and the Université Robert Schuman in Strasbourg respectively. In 2003, Souhayma completed her Ph.D. in Law at the Université de Tunis Carthage. Souhayma has held various teaching positions in private law at universities in Tunisia and has published widely on issues of family and succession law in private international law and the impact of religion on Tunisian private international law. More recently, Souhayma's research has also focused on migration trends to and from Tunisia.

Harith Al-Dabbagh is Assistant Professor specialized in Comparative and International Private Law at Université de Montréal. Harith holds an LL.B. (1996) and an LL.M. (1998) from his native Iraq. He completed his DEA in Private Law (2003), in Comparative Law (2006) and his Doctorat en droit (2009) in France. He was previously a lawyer and Assistant Professor at the University of Mosul, Faculty of Law. Harith also served as a contractual Professor at Université de St-Etienne, France. During these years he taught various courses in fundamental private law. Trained in Civil and Comparative Law, his latest works focused on the study of legal pluralism, especially the interaction between secular and religious rules. Before joining the teaching staff at Université de Montréal, Harith led a postdoctoral project within the CRDP regarding the receptivity of Muslim family institutions in Canada and in France. Harith is the author of numerous publications in French and Arabic on Civil Law in the Middle East.

Shaheen Sardar Ali is Professor of Law at University of Warwick, UK and former Vice-Chair of the United Nations Working Group on Arbitrary Detention (2008–2014) as well as a former Member of the International Strategic Advisory Board, Oslo University (2012–2014). She has served as Professor II University of Oslo, Norway, Professor of Law, University of Peshawar, Pakistan, as well as Director Women's Study Centre at the same university. She has served as cabinet Minister for Health, Population Welfare and Women Development, Government of the Khyber Pukhtunkhwa (formerly North West Frontier Province of Pakistan) and Chair of Pakistan's first National Commission on the Status of Women. She served on the Prime Minister's Consultative Committee for Women (Pakistan), and the Senate National Commission of Enquiry on the Status of Women (Pakistan). Professor Ali has published extensively in the areas of Human Rights; in particular, Women and Children's Rights, Islamic Law and Jurisprudence, International Law, and Gender

Studies. Her latest monograph entitled Modern Challenges to Islamic Law (2016) is published in the Law in Context Series by Cambridge University Press.

Jean-Philippe Dequen is a Research Fellow at the Max Planck Institute for European Legal History in Frankfurt. He holds an MRes. in Legal Anthropology from University Paris I Panthéon-Sorbonne, and another in Islamology from the École Pratique des Hautes Études (EPHE), as well as Ph.D. in Law from the School of Oriental and African Studies (SOAS), University of London. His doctoral thesis focused on the evolution of Islamic law within the Indian colonial and postcolonial legal frames. During the course of his Ph.D. Jean-Philippe also taught on Legal Systems of Asia and Africa, as well as on Law and Society in South Asia. His current research focuses on the legal transfer of Common Law within the Subcontinent, and in particular its relation to precolonial legal systems during the early modern period.

Anver M. Emon is Professor and Canada Research Chair in Religion, Pluralism and the Rule of Law, at the University of Toronto, Faculty of Law. Anver's research focuses on premodern and modern Islamic legal history and theory, premodern modes of governance and adjudication, and the role of Shari'a both inside and outside the Muslim world. His general academic interests include topics in law and religion; legal history; and legal philosophy. He teaches in the areas of torts and statutory interpretation, and offers specialized seminars on Islamic legal history, gender and Islamic law, and law and religion. The recipient of numerous research grants, he was named as a 2014 Guggenheim Fellow in the field of law. In addition to publishing numerous articles, Anver is the author of Islamic Natural Law Theories (Oxford University Press, 2010), and Religious Pluralism and Islamic Law: Dhimmis and Others in the Empire of Law (Oxford University Press, 2012), as well as the co-editor of Islamic Law and International Human Rights Law: Searching for Common Ground? (Oxford University Press, 2012). He is the founding editor of Middle East Law and Governance: An Interdisciplinary Journal, and series editor of the Oxford Islamic Legal Studies Series.

Dörthe Engelcke is an early career fellow at the Lichtenberg-Kolleg, the Göttingen Institute for Advanced Study at the University of Göttingen. She received her Ph.D. from St Antony's College, University of Oxford, in 2015. She is the co-winner of the 2016 BRISMES Leigh Douglas Memorial Prize for the best Ph.D. dissertation on a Middle Eastern topic in the Humanities and Social Science awarded by a British University. For the academic year 2014/2015, she was a stipendiary visiting fellow at the Islamic Legal Studies Program at Harvard Law School. During her Ph.D., Dörthe has taught Middle East Politics at Oxford and was a visiting fellow at the German Institute of Global and Area Studies (GIGA) in Hamburg. She holds an MA in Near and Middle Eastern Studies from the School of Oriental and African Studies (SOAS).

Isfandyar Ali Khan is currently Senior Partner of S&K Partnership, a law and policy consulting firm in Peshawar, Pakistan and has been supporting an international consulting firm in Alternative Dispute Resolution (ADR)/Community Based Dispute Resolution (CBDR) Project management in Khyber Pakhtunkhwa (KP) province of Pakistan for the past 2 years. For over 5 years, Isfandyar was associated with Alternate Dispute Resolution Project of IFC/World Bank Group as a Project Officer and was instrumental in supporting development of Karachi Centre for Dispute Resolution (now known as National Centre for Dispute Resolution) and launch of mediation practices in Lahore, Punjab province. Isfandyar is currently serving as Provincial Vice-President (KP) of Pakistan Mediators Association. Prior to joining IFC in 2008, Isfandyar worked as Project Coordinator for UNDP Project in Vientiane, Lao PDR (2006/2007) and Young Professional Officer at UNDP Islamabad in Pakistan (2005/2006). He has worked with Aurat Publication and Information Services Foundation (2005), Peshawar and at law firm, Afridi, Shah and Minallah, Peshawar (2003–2005). Isfandyar has strong interest in Dispute Settlement, Rule of Law, Democracy, Governance, Access to Justice, Human and Child Rights, Investment Climate and Environmental issues.

Sajila Sohail Khan has a master's degree in Public Administration from Peshawar University, Pakistan and a master's degree in Sociology from Warwick University in the United Kingdom. She is a gender and development specialist—particularly in the field of gender, employment and education in which she has more than two decades of experience, at grassroots, policy and implementation levels. Sajila has worked as gender adviser in the Sarhad Rural Support Programme, Khyber Pukhtunkhwa province of Pakistan, United Nations Development Programme, USAID and the International Labour Organization.

Najma Moosa is Professor in the Department of Private Law at the University of the Western Cape in South Africa where she was also the 'first' alumna to receive a master's and doctoral degree in law. She was the first female and black dean of the faculty of law where she served as dean for seven years (2002–2008). She is an alumna of both HER-SA and the American Council on Education (ACE) and has completed two certificated Higher Education leadership programs in the USA where she received mentoring at Wellesley College (2002) and Old Dominion University, Norfolk, Virginia (2005). She has, in the past, been a research fellow at Yale University and SOAS, London and the recipient of many teaching and research awards including the Vice-Chancellor's (University) Distinguished Teaching Award. Najma was also admitted as an Advocate of the High Court of South Africa in 1989 and was a Committee Member in the South African Law Reform Commission Project 59 (Islamic Marriages & Related Matters) from 1999 to 2003. She is currently a National Research Foundation (NRF) rated researcher and her publications, which pertain mainly to Muslim personal law, include the second edition of a book Unveiling the Mind. The Legal Position of Women in Islam—A South African Context (Juta, Cape Town, 2011).

Jasmine Moussa is Assistant Professor of Law at the American University in Cairo (AUC). She teaches Public International Law and the Law of Armed Conflict and International Humanitarian Law. Before joining AUC, Jasmine completed her Ph.D. in Law at the University of Cambridge (Magdalene College) in 2014. She also holds an LL.M. in Public International Law from the London School of Economics and

Political Science and degrees from the American University in Cairo (B.A. in Political Science and Economics and M.A. in International Human Rights Law) as well as an LL.B. from Cairo University. Between 2008 and 2010, she was desk officer for legal affairs, human rights and humanitarian affairs in the cabinet of Egypt's Minister of Foreign Affairs. She has also worked at the legal department and multilateral affairs department of the Ministry. Other engagements include providing legal advice to international non-governmental organizations and think tanks. Jasmine is the author of Competing Fundamentalisms and Egyptian Women's Family Rights: International Law and the Reform of Shari'a-Derived Legislation (Martinus Nijhoff, 2011). From 2012 to 2013, she was co-editor-in-chief of the Cambridge Journal of International and Comparative Law.

Marie-Claude Najm is Agrégée des facultés françaises de droit, Professor at the Faculty of Law and Political Science of Saint-Joseph University (Beirut) and head of the Department of Private Law. She is the Director of the Centre of Legal Studies and Research for the Arab world (CEDROMA), which aims to promote the knowledge of Arab legal systems (Maghreb and Mashrek) within a comparative law approach. Marie-Claude has also served as Visiting Professor at Panthéon-Sorbonne University Paris I (2007–2009), and is a Visiting Professor at Panthéon-Assas University since 2009. Born on April 6th, 1971 in Beirut, Marie-Claude holds law degrees from Panthéon-Assas University (Paris II) and Saint-Joseph University of Beirut as well as a Ph.D. in Private International Law from Panthéon-Assas University (Paris II). Her fields of research are international jurisdiction and conflict of laws, mainly in plural legal systems, and her publications include: Principes directeurs du droit international privé et conflit de civilisations. Relations entre systèmes laïques et systèmes religieux (Dalloz, Paris, 2005); « La Cour de cassation française et la répudiation musulmane, une décennie après l'entrée en vigueur des réformes du droit de la famille au Maroc et en Algérie » (Journal de droit international, Clunet, 2015, p.789); « LEBANON- Country report on Private International Law », Basedow/Rühl/Ferrari/De Miguel (eds.), Encyclopedia of Private International Law, Edward Elgar (2016).

Euis Nurlaelawati is Senior Lecturer in Islamic law at the faculty of Sharia and law, Sunan Kalijaga, State Islamic University (Universitas Islam Negeri/UIN), Jogjakarta. She is also a member of editorial boards of Al Jamiah, Journal of Islamic Studies, UIN Jogjakarta. She has been involved in a number of research projects and her research areas include the development and application of Islamic (family) law in Indonesia, judicial practices, and gender issues. She has published books and articles, including Modernization, Tradition and Identity: The Kompilasi Hukum Islam and Legal Practices in Indonesian Religious Courts, Amsterdam University Press, 2010; 'Managing Familial Issues: Unique Features of Islamic Legal Reform in Indonesia', in Islam in Indonesia: Contrasting Images and Interpretation, Leiden University Press, 2013; 'Training, Appointment and Supervision of Islamic Judges in Indonesia', in Pacific Rim Law and Policy Journal, Vol. 21:1, 2012; 'Muslim Women in Indonesian Religious Courts: Reform, Strategies, and Pronouncement of Divorce', Islamic Law and Society, Vol. 20:3, 2013; Sharia'a-Based Laws in

Indonesia: Legal Position of Women and Children in Banten and West Java, in Islam, Politics, and Change: The Indonesian Experiences after the Fall of Suharto, Leiden University Press, 2016, and the Legal Fate of the Indonesian Muslim Women at Court: Divorce and Child Custody', in Law, Religion and Intolerance in Indonesia, Routledge, 2016.

Ayesha Shahid is a Lecturer in Law at Brunel University London. Her research in the field of international human rights law focuses on gender, migration, and informal employment in the labor market. Her monograph Silent Voices, Untold Stories: Women Domestic Workers in Pakistan and their Struggle for Empowerment has been published by the Oxford University Press in 2010. In Islamic law, her research addresses family law reform in the Muslim world, post-divorce maintenance for Muslim women, and Islamic family law in the West. The third strand of her research looks into the historiography of International law. Currently, she is co-editing a book with Dr. Ignacio De La Rasilla New Approaches to the Islamic History of International Law (Brill, forthcoming 2016). Ayesha is also the Editor of the Journal of Islamic State Practices in International Law (JISPIL). Ayesha has carried out a number of research projects for Asia Foundation, International Labour Organization, Human Rights Commission of Pakistan and Higher Education Commission, Pakistan. She is also a recipient of the Warwick Postgraduate Research Fellowship Award in 2002 and International Research Fellowship award by the Center for Human Rights, Columbia University in 2000 and 2002.

Chapter 1
Egypt

Jasmine Moussa

Abstract This chapter examines the incorporation of the concept of the 'best interests of the child' in contemporary Egyptian legislation and judicial practice, with a particular focus on child custody, visitation and guardianship. Parental care in Egypt is governed by a series of fragmented personal status laws (the only area where religious law has been carried on into modern times) in addition to the Child Law. While the Child Law has referred to the child's interests since 1996, it defers to the personal status laws, which still approach some issues related to child custody, guardianship and visitation as rights of the parents. Moreover, under Egypt's personal status laws, the 'best interests of the child' principle has been interpreted in light of rigid gender roles that posit the mother and female family members as more compassionate nurturers whose role in the child's upbringing is essential in the early years. Achieving the 'best interests of the child' has therefore been synonymous with prolonging the custody period of the mother (and other female family members), while guardianship rests with the father and the agnatic line. Important legal reforms since the year 2000, however, have increasingly solidified the notion of the 'best interests of the child'. These include a reference to the principle in Egypt's 2014 Constitution. Moreover, since 2005, the principle has been interpreted as requiring the child's participation in their own custody arrangements once they reach the age of fifteen. The jurisprudence of the Court of Cassation and the Supreme Constitutional Court further reaffirms the principle, merging the shariʿa rationale for custody arrangements with the best interests principle, and validating the principle in religious terms.

The author is Assistant Professor of Law at the American University in Cairo.

J. Moussa (✉)
American University in Cairo, AUC New Cairo Campus, AUC Avenue,
P.O. Box 74, New Cairo 11835, Egypt
e-mail: jasmine.moussa@aucegypt.edu

N. Yassari et al. (eds.), *Parental Care and the Best Interests of the Child in Muslim Countries*, DOI 10.1007/978-94-6265-174-6_1

Keywords Best interests of the child · Child custody · Guardianship · Egypt · Legal reform · Islamic law · Personal status law

Contents

1.1 Introduction

Although the 'best interests of the child' standard enjoys international consensus as a general principle governing custody arrangements, its exact meaning is highly contested. As a result, the 'best interests' principle is decidedly subjective and may be interpreted differently depending on the cultural context.[1] In practice, applying the 'best interests' standard is left to the discretion of domestic Judges and is therefore a principle whose application differs from one setting to another and from one culture to another.[2]

The first Decree-Law to regulate child custody in Egypt in 1929 gave the Judge discretion to prolong the period of maternal custody beyond the specified ages, if the child's interests so required. Also, since 1952, Egyptian legislation on guardianship has provided that decisions regarding the disposal of a minor's property must take into consideration the minor's interests. Egypt's first child law, adopted in 1996 after Egypt ratified the Convention on the Rights of the Child (CRC), formally incorporated the principle of the best interests of the child as an overarching principle into Egyptian legislation. Article 3 of the law stipulates 'all decisions and procedures relating to children, by whomever initiated and enforced, must give priority to the protection of the child and to the child's interests'.[3] This provision

[1] An-Na'im 1994, p. 62.

[2] Ibid.

[3] Law No. 12 of 1996 Regarding the Promulgation of the Child Law, Official Gazette no. 13*bis* of 28 March 1996. The principle is also incorporated in legislation relevant to juvenile justice and criminal procedure. See Egypt, Consideration of Reports Submitted by States Parties Under Article 44 of the Convention, Committee on the Rights of the Child (11 November 1999), CRC/C/65/Add.9, p. 21, para 53; p. 64, para 194.

was virtually replicated under the new Child Law, Law No. 126 of 2008, with the exception of replacing the term 'child's interests' (*maṣāliḥihi*) with the 'child's *best* interests' (*maṣāliḥihi al-fuḍlā*). Since 1996, Article 7 of the Child Law has stated, 'children enjoy all their rights under the shariʿa, and especially the right to nursing, custody, food, clothing, domicile, visiting their parents and having their wealth administered in accordance with the laws on personal status'. Although custody and guardianship were framed, under this provision, as a right of the child, the Child Law deferred to personal status laws in regulating these issues. In practice, custody, visitation and guardianship were overwhelmingly dealt with as the rights of parents rather than rights of children.

In response to pressure from civil society organisations, Egypt's new Constitution, promulgated in 2014, incorporated the notion of the 'best interests of the child' at the constitutional level for the first time in Egypt's history.[4] The Constitution stipulates in Article 80 that 'the State shall endeavour to achieve the best interests of children in all measures taken against them'. In spite of the clear recognition of the notion of the child's best interests in Egypt's legislation and recently in the Constitution, applying this principle in practice comes up against a number of obstacles. This chapter examines Egyptian legislation governing parental care, particularly guardianship and custody over children, in light of the 'best interests' standard. It begins, in Sect. 1.2, with a general overview of the domestic law framework applicable to personal status issues in Egypt. Section 1.3 examines the provisions of Egypt's legislation regarding parental care, specifically guardianship, child custody, visitation and some special applications regarding matters such as the *kafāla* system and children born outside of wedlock. Section 1.4 investigates the most important legislative reforms, adopted in 2000 and 2005, with particular focus on the incorporation of the 'best interests of the child' principle. Finally, Sect. 1.5 explores the role of the judiciary in interpreting and applying legislation regarding parental care and the 'best interests' principle, with a focus on the Court of Cassation. It also examines the role of the Supreme Constitutional Court in upholding legislative reforms advancing the principle, in spite of constitutional challenges invoking a purported conflict with the Islamic shariʿa.

1.2 General Legal Framework

Personal status law, also known as family law, or *qānūn al-aḥwāl al-shakhṣiyya*, is the law that governs family relations, including marriage, divorce, child custody and successions. It is the only area of law in Egypt that was not displaced by European codes in the nineteenth century. In 1874, Egypt gained administrative and judicial autonomy from the Ottoman Empire. In 1875, Mohamed Qadri Pasha was commissioned by Egypt's Khedive to codify Egypt's personal status law for

[4] Khattāb 2015; Maḥmūd 2014.

Muslims. The resulting compilation of 647 articles, which were based on the teachings of the Hanafi jurisprudential school, was never officially promulgated. However, Hanafi jurisprudence remained the backbone of Egypt's family law.[5]

Simultaneously, Egypt began to codify its laws in accordance with European codes. All commercial, civil, and criminal codes were secularised, leaving only personal status laws under the jurisdiction of the religious authorities. In 1883, a national court system was established applying the *Code Napoléon*, although some effort was made to incorporate Islamic elements. The new code was applied to all areas of law with the exception of personal status matters and endowments (*awqāf*), which were adjudicated by the shariʿa courts.[6] Family law was therefore the only area of law that resisted displacement, surviving attempts at secularisation in the post-colonial period.[7]

Under Egypt's personal status law, each recognised religious group, namely the Muslim majority and the Christian and Jewish minorities, remained governed by the religious personal status laws of their respective communities. This 'plurality of laws,' meant that non-Muslims were granted relative legislative and judicial autonomy; until today, no uniform personal status code exists for all Egyptians, there being instead 'a separate code for almost every one of the fifteen religious communities within Egypt'.[8] This system has its origins in the Islamic law notion that non-Muslim subjects of the 'Islamic state' (*dhimmiyyīn*) enjoy autonomy in their religious and personal affairs.[9] However, this does not apply to a number of personal status issues—namely alimony, child custody and inheritance—which are governed by personal status law for Muslims, irrespective of religion or confession.[10] Muslim personal status law also applies in cases of inter-marriage between different recognised religious communities, or even between the different denominations within the same religious community.[11]

In 1897, the *Egyptian Code of Organisation and Procedure for Family Courts* declared Hanafi law as the official law of the state in matters of personal status, instructing the *quḍāt* (Judges) to apply it when adjudicating on all personal status questions. Since then, most family law codifications and reforms have attempted to mitigate the harsh and formalistic provisions of Hanafi jurisprudence by incorporating the teachings of other jurisprudential schools, particularly the Maliki school.

---

[5] Esposito and DeLong-Bas 2001, p. 47 and 49.

[6] Abu-Odeh 2004, pp. 1081–1083. The capitulations system was an offshoot of the widespread European influence in Egypt and the ensuing legal privileges and concessionary benefits granted to European immigrants. Foreign nationals demanded that they be exempt from Islamic law, which was considered primitive and incapable of regulating complex economic and financial transactions.

[7] See Moussa 2011, p. 5 and 14; Hajjar 2004, pp. 235–236 and 250–252. See also Büchler et al 2010, p. 80.

[8] Berger 2002, p. 558; Berger 2001, p. 88; Berger 2005, p. 402.

[9] Fadel 2012, p. 184.

[10] Guindy 2014.

[11] IslamopediaOnline 2011; Bibāwī 2004, p. 18; Sezgin 2013, p. 144.

In the 1920s, Egypt promulgated two decree-laws, No. 25 of 1920[12] and No. 25 of 1929,[13] which incorporated aspects of Maliki doctrine into Egypt's personal status law. In spite of this, Hanafi jurisprudence maintained a privileged position; where the law was silent on an issue, Judges had to have recourse to the predominant opinion of the Hanafi school. In practice, Judges usually referred to the unofficial codification of Qadri Pasha as the most authoritative compilation of Hanafi jurisprudence. In 2004, however, the law was amended to allow Judges recourse to the stipulations of any of the four sunni jurisprudential schools. This proved instrumental in allowing non-Muslim women to exercise custody over their children in cases of divorce.

A series of other laws have been promulgated that amend or add to the substantive and procedural provisions of Decree-Laws No. 25 of 1920 and No. 25 of 1929. The most significant laws are the following: (1) 1931 Shariʿa Court Regulations[14] (abolished in 1955); (2) Law No. 118 of 1952 on Rules of Guardianship Over Self[15]; (3) Law No. 119 of 1952 on Rules of Guardianship Over Property[16]; (4) Decree-Law No. 44 of 1979 (expanding the grounds of divorce for harm), which was later repealed by the Supreme Constitutional Court on procedural grounds; (5) Law No. 100 of 1985[17] amending Law No. 25 of 1929 (which similarly expanded the grounds of divorce for harm and introduced divorce for discord); (6) Law No. 1 of 2000[18] (modifying court procedures and introducing judicial *khulʿ*); (7) Law No. 10 of 2004[19] (establishing specialised family courts); (8) Law No. 11 of 2004[20] (establishing a Family Insurance Fund to allow litigants to collect court-ordered alimony and child support); and (9) Law No. 4 of 2005[21] amending Decree-Law No. 25 of 1929 (raising the age of maternal custody

[12] Decree-Law No. 25 of 1920 Concerning Maintenance and Some Provisions in Personal Status, Official Gazette no. 61 of 15 July 1920.

[13] Decree-Law No. 25 of 1929 Concerning Provisions in Personal Status, Official Gazette no. 27 of 25 March 1929.

[14] Decree-Law No. 78 of 1931, Shariʿa Court Regulations, Official Gazette (Extraordinary Issue) no. 53 of 30 May 1931.

[15] Law No. 118 of 1952 on Rules of Guardianship Over Self, Official Gazette no. 118*bis* of 4 August 1952.

[16] Law No. 119 of 1952 on Rules of Guardianship Over Property, Official Gazette no. 118*bis* of 4 August 1952.

[17] Law No. 100 of 1985 Amending Certain Rulings of the Laws of Personal Status, Official Gazette no. 27 of 4 July 1985.

[18] Law No. 1 of 2000 Regarding the Promulgation of a Law to Organize Certain Conditions and Procedures in Matters of Personal Status, Official Gazette no. 4*bis* of 29 January 2000.

[19] Law No. 10 of 2004 Regarding the Promulgation of the Family Courts Law, Official Gazette no. 12(a) of 18 March 2004.

[20] Law No. 11 of 2004 Establishing a Family Insurance Fund, Official Gazette no. 12(a) of 18 March 2004. This law was amended by Presidential Decree No. 113 of 2015, Official Gazette no. 46 of 12 November 2015.

[21] Law No. 4 of 2005 Amending Article 20 of Decree-Law No. 25 of 1929 (raising the age of maternal custody), Official Gazette no. 9*bis* of 8 March 2005.

over children).[22] A number of other laws deal with issues of inheritance and testamentary bequests. Family law in Egypt is therefore not based on a single comprehensive and unified code, but rather on a large number of fragmented laws. These have gone beyond Hanafi doctrine to embrace the majority opinions of the other sunni jurisprudential schools, as well as opinions 'attributed to certain early Muslim jurists or to later, but somewhat unorthodox, reformers, or even occasionally in what virtually (but unofficially) amounted to a new exercise of *ijtihad*'.[23]

1.3 Egyptian Legislation on Guardianship and Child Custody

In accordance with Islamic legal doctrine, Egypt's personal status law distinguishes between legal guardianship (*wilāya*) and child custody (*ḥaḍāna*).[24] Issues relating to parental care (both *wilāya* and *ḥaḍāna*) arise mainly in the event of divorce or separation. Since 2000, Egyptian courts have been authorised to apply the laws on child custody applicable to Muslims to all other persons, regardless of their faith.[25]

---

[22] For a detailed discussion, see Moussa 2011, pp. 134–143.

[23] Anderson JND 'Law Reform in the Middle East', reproduced in Liebesny 1975, p. 103.

[24] For a detailed discussion of these two concepts and the relationship between them, see Zahraa and Malek 1998.

[25] Before then, Coptic Christians applied articles 127–128 of the 1938 *Regulations on Personal Status for Coptic Christians*, which granted priority in custody to the mother. However, in cases of divorce, the Regulations provided that custody was to be given to the parent that had been awarded a judicial divorce. This was deemed unconstitutional by the Supreme Constitutional Court in its Case no. 151 for the 20th Judicial Year (6 June 2000), in which it stipulated that: 'Article 127 of the Regulations stipulates that the mother has a superior right to custody of her children during the marriage and after. After the mother, custody passes to the maternal grandmother and then to the paternal grandmother.... Article 128 of the same Regulations provides that "if there is no female relative of the child who has the capacity to act as custodian, custody passes to male relatives, while the father has priority ...". Article 72—which is currently being challenged—stipulates in its first paragraph that: "Custody of children is awarded to the spouse who is granted a divorce, unless the [Clerical] Council awards custody to the other spouse or to whosoever has the right to custody after him/her." These provisions, together, provide that the right to custody belongs first to women who are close of kin or *maḥārim* (too closely related to marry), with priority to the child's mother, whether during the marriage or after. This right does not pass to the child's male relatives, including the father, except when there is no female relative eligible to exercise custody. However, the regulations excluded the "divorced mother" from this rule—according to the challenged text—in the case that the divorce judgment is issued in favor of the child's father. This transfers custody to the father .... The plaintiff challenges this provision ... for discriminating between the citizens of one nation, in a matter that does not relate to the essence of faith, and for breaching the principle of equality in the right to custody—between divorced Muslim women, their husbands and children, on the one hand, and divorced Christian women, their husbands and children on the other. It also squanders the interests of the Christian

Decree-Law No. 25 of 1929 established the mother's custody over her child in cases of divorce until 7 years of age for boys and 9 years for girls. This could be extended to 9 years for boys and 11 years for girls, if the child's interests so required (Article 20). Legal reforms adopted in 1979 extended the age of termination of maternal custody to 10 years for boys and 12 years for girls, subject to possible extension by a Judge. Although this law was repealed by the Supreme Constitutional Court, these age limits were re-enacted in 1985.[26] In 2000 the law was modified again to give more consideration to the child's best interests. However, these reforms were still criticised as inadequate. In 2001, the UN Committee on the Rights of the Child (hereinafter the Committee), established to monitor compliance with the CRC, criticized Egypt's implementation of the best interests of the child principle, particularly in relation to child custody upon the separation of parents. The Committee stated that child custody legislation in Egypt is discriminatory, criticizing the notion that custody is 'determined by the child's age rather than the child's best interests'.[27]

Although this criticism targeted the provisions of Decree-Law No. 25 of 1929, as amended by Law No. 100 of 1985, these provisions have since been amended to better reflect the best interests of the child principle. In particular, in 2005 the age for termination of maternal custody was extended to 15 years for both the boy and girl child, at which point a decision is to be made by a Judge after consulting with the child. Nonetheless, Egypt's personal status legislation is still based on a gendered division of labour between the parents that posits the father as guardian and provider and the mother as caregiver, thereby differentiating between the spouses in terms of their rights and responsibilities *vis-à-vis* their children. It underscores and entrenches the mother's prominent role in childbearing, nursing and child rearing during the early years, while reinforcing the father's role as breadwinner, a principal tenet of shariʿa-derived personal status law. This gendered conception of child custody is also applied and reinforced by the Courts, including the Supreme Constitutional Court. The rationale behind this is the perception that the younger

Footnote 25 (continued)

family, in violation of the provisions of Articles 10 and 40 of the Constitution. Child custody, in its legal essence—and according to this Court's jurisprudence—is *wilāya* for upbringing whose objective is paying attention to the child's needs and to look after his/her affairs in the early period of his/her life, in which he/she cannot dispense with the care of women who have the legal (*sharʿī*) right to raise the child. The origin of this right is the child's interest, which is realized through bringing the child under her wing, as she is more capable of taking care of, directing and preserving him/her, and because ripping the child from her—while she is more compassionate and patient with him/her—is harmful to the child at this critical period of his/her life, in which the child is not yet independent.'

[26] See below, notes 46–47 and accompanying text.

[27] See Concluding observations of the Committee on the Rights of the Child: Egypt (21 February 2001), Committee on the Rights of the Child, 26th Session, UN Doc CRC/C/15/Add.145, p. 7, para 33–34.

child is in need of maternal love and affection, whereas the maturing child is in need of the father's discipline and guidance.[28]

Under Egyptian law, therefore, the child's best interests are considered synonymous with remaining in the custody of the mother and other female family members for the longest duration possible. The younger child arguably requires the emotional nurturing that only a woman is capable of providing.[29] Although the primary sources of Islamic legislation, the Qur'an and sunna (traditions and sayings—or hadiths—of the Prophet Muhammed) contain no clear rules regarding child custody upon the dissolution of marriage,[30] a number of Prophetic hadiths establish the mother's priority in custody over younger children. These hadiths, however, do not establish a particular age at which custody should pass on to the father,[31] which has fuelled calls by feminists to extend the duration of the mother's custody rights. This has had important implications for the development of custody and guardianship legislation.

1.3.1 Guardianship

Legal guardianship primarily belongs to the father even where the children are in the mother's exclusive custody. As legal guardian, the father has the right to 'generally supervise' the child's upbringing and make decisions on the child's behalf (however, the amended child law allows the parent exercising custody to exercise guardianship with respect to decisions relating to the child's education).[32]

As opposed to custody, guardianship belongs to the agnatic line.[33] In the father's absence, or if he is stripped of guardianship rights (e.g. in the event of conviction for particular crimes, including rape),[34] legal guardianship passes on to the paternal grandfather unless the father specifically appoints another legal

[28] See Badran 1996, p. 132; Ḥaḍānat al-aṭfāl 2012. Arguably, such reasoning perpetuates the stereotype of women as necessarily emotional and men as more rational and hence more mentally capable.

[29] Moussa 2011, p. 187.

[30] Büchler et al 2010, p. 81.

[31] Ḥaḍānat al-aṭfāl 2012.

[32] Second Shadow Report of the Egyptian NGOs Coalition on the CEDAW, p. 60; according to article 54 Child Law, 'the educational responsibility of the child shall rest with the parent having custody, and in case of disagreement as to the best interests of the child, any of the concerned parties shall bring such matter to the attention of the President of the Family Court, in his capacity as a judge for temporary affairs, to decide upon the issue taking into consideration the financial situation of the child's legal guardian, without prejudice to the right of the parent having educational responsibility.'

[33] Büchler et al. 2010, p. 82.

[34] Article 2 Law No. 118 of 1952. See below.

guardian (*waṣī*). In certain cases, the Court may appoint a guardian.[35] In this case, Article 12 Law No. 118 of 1952 envisages the possibility of awarding guardianship to the mother.[36] According to Article 27 Law No. 119 of 1952, a guardian has to be just and have full legal capacity. The guardian must also be honest and capable of administering the ward's wealth.

As the child's legal guardian, the father has the right to manage and dispose of the child's property and to act as the marriage guardian. According to Article 18 Law No. 119 of 1952, the father's guardianship rights over his sons and daughters extend until the age of 21. The law severely restricts the guardian's ability to dispose of the child's property, requiring the Courts' permission for transactions of significant value.[37]

The father also has an obligation to provide maintenance for his children. The father's maintenance obligation includes the provision of food, clothing, lodging, education and preparation for adulthood.[38] According to Article 18 *bis*2 Decree-Law No. 25 of 1929 as amended by Law No. 100 of 1985, the father must provide his minor children with maintenance if they do not have their own personal resources until the son reaches the age of fifteen and the girl marries or is able to earn her own income. This may be extended if the son suffers from a handicap or is unable to earn a living, the latter including his choosing to pursue studies.[39] The child's disobedience does not relieve the father of his maintenance obligation. Maintenance is provided according to both the child's needs and the father's means.[40] These provisions are enforced through a special fund within the Nasser Social Bank, under whose terms the father may face imprisonment for failure to comply.[41] The child may therefore take his or her father to court if the latter fails to provide maintenance. The same principles apply where the parents are divorced, in which case the father pays his maintenance dues as child support, even when the children are in the mother's custody. The father is also required to provide a suitable dwelling for the divorced wife and their children as long as they are in her custody. A child born out of wedlock, however, is not entitled to maintenance and has no legal remedy against the biological father unless paternity is established or admitted by the father.[42]

The father's maintenance obligation is based on what is arguably a principal tenet of shari'a-derived personal status law, which relieves the wife of the burden of earning a living to support herself as well as her children, particularly since she

[35] Articles 29–31 Law No. 118 of 1952.

[36] But see Shadow Report of the Egyptian NGOs Coalition on the CEDAW, p. 36.

[37] Articles 5–12, 15, 16 Law No. 119 of 1952; Moussa 2011, p. 184.

[38] Hodkinson 1984, p. 310.

[39] Article 18*bis*2 Decree-Law No. 25 of 1929 as amended by Law No. 100 of 1985.

[40] Ibid.

[41] Law No. 10 of 2004.

[42] Thomason 2008, p. 129.

traditionally bears the brunt of child-rearing. Although the father (husband) is obliged to maintain the wife and the children, the mother (wife) has no such commitment, regardless of her wealth. This notion is presented by Egyptian feminists as one of 'shared' rather than 'equal' responsibility, and it is widely accepted 'as part of a system of interdependence and reciprocity'.[43] However, the law disadvantages mothers who happen to find themselves as the *de facto* provider, whether in the absence of the father or other male guardian, or in cases of circumvention of legislative and judicial orders regarding maintenance.

1.3.1.1 End of *Wilāyat* Loss and Revocation of Guardianship

Egyptian legislation distinguishes between 'guardianship over property' and 'guardianship over the person' of a ward. The issues of eligibility, loss and revocation of guardianship over property are governed by a number of legal provisions. Articles 38–40 of Law No. 119 of 1952 stipulate that the guardian must consider the child's interests in all his or her actions. Pursuant to Law No. 119 of 1952, the period of exercising guardianship over property ends when the minor reaches 21 years of age, unless a competent court decides otherwise (Article 18). The Judge may revoke or limit the *walī*'s guardianship rights if the minor's wealth is in danger, whether this is due to the *walī*'s mishandling or any other reason (Article 21). Guardianship rights are also lost if the *walī* is considered absent or is serving a prison sentence that is longer than 1 year (Article 22). In this case, loss of guardianship is mandatory and is not subject to the Judge's discretion.

Loss or revocation of guardianship over the child's person is governed by Law No. 118 of 1952. According to Article 3, the Judge *may* revoke guardianship or suspend some guardianship rights, in relation to all or a number of the *walī*'s wards, in the following cases: (1) If the *walī* is sentenced to a prison term of hard labour; (2) if the *walī* is convicted of rape, sexual assault, or one of the felonies prohibited under Law No. 68 of 1951 on Combating Prostitution; (3) if the *walī* is convicted more than once of endangering a child's life, unlawful confinement or aggravated assault; (4) if one of the *walī*'s wards is placed in a correctional facility; (5) if the *walī* endangers the ward's health or safety or morals, as a consequence of mistreatment, a bad reputation, alcohol or drug addiction, or lack of care and guidance. Under this last provision, the law does not require prior conviction of the *walī* for any of these acts, leaving the matter to the Judge's discretion.

Revoking guardianship becomes mandatory in a number of cases. The *walī* loses guardianship permanently over *all* his or her wards if he or she is convicted of committing—against any one of them—the crime of rape, sexual assault, or one of the felonies prohibited under Law No. 68 of 1951 on Combating Prostitution. The *walī* also loses guardianship over all his or her wards if they are repeat offenders under Law No. 68 of 1951. Finally, in the case that the *walī* is convicted of

---

[43] Behrouz 2003, p. 1151.

perpetrating any other felony against one of his or her wards, or is convicted for a felony committed by any one of his or her wards, the *walī* loses guardianship over that ward only, unless the court decides otherwise. Revocation of guardianship over the child's person automatically results in loss of guardianship over the child's property, but not vice versa.

1.3.2 Child Custody

Under Egypt's personal status law, child custody is shared consecutively between both parents in the event of dissolution of marriage. This is in line with the shariʿa-based rationale, which posits the mother as better capable of providing love and affection necessary for a younger child's development. There is no consensus among the four sunni jurisprudential schools (the Hanafi, Hanbali, Shafiʿi and Maliki schools) with regard to the age at which custody should be transferred from the mother to the father. Until 1985, mothers retained custody over their children until 7 years of age for boys and 9 years for girls, after which custody would pass to the father. This was in accordance with the teachings of the Hanafi jurisprudential school.[44] On the other hand, the predominant view of the Hanbali school was that the mother retained custody until the age of seven for children of either sex, at which point the child could make a choice with respect to their own custody arrangement, while the Shafiʿi school placed no age limits at all, giving priority to the child's choice. According to Maliki doctrine, the mother retained custody of the son until he reached puberty and of the daughter until marriage. It is arguable that the approach adopted by the Shafiʿi and Hanbali schools most closely reflects the modern notion of the 'best interests of the child'.[45]

Prolonging the duration of the mother's custody became a priority for Egyptian feminists, not on the grounds of the child's best interests, but rather as an important demand of divorced women. A means for achieving this was the adoption of Maliki doctrine. Egyptian feminists, led by then First Lady Jihan Sadat, campaigned to incorporate Maliki doctrine into Egyptian custody legislation. In 1979, President Sadat issued Decree-Law No. 44 of 1979 during parliamentary recess. The law, popularly known as 'Jihan's law', extended the mother's custody over her children in cases of divorce to 10 years for boys and 12 years for girls and granted her the right of residence in the rented conjugal home throughout the period of custody. In 1985, as a result of widespread opposition, the law came before Egypt's Supreme Constitutional Court for review. It was repealed on procedural grounds, namely that there was no constitutional basis for modifying Law No. 25 of 1929 during parliamentary recess by Presidential decree.[46]

---

[44] Badran 1996, p. 132.

[45] Büchler et al. 2010, p. 82.

[46] See Bernard-Maugiron and Dupret 2002, p. 7; Büchler et al. 2010, p. 80.

However, some of the provisions of the 1979 Decree-Law were re-enacted by parliament in 1985. Law No. 100 of 1985 extended maternal custody over the son until 10 years of age and the daughter until 12, during which time the mother would receive a custody payment from the father. Throughout the duration of the mother's custody, the father is obliged to provide an independent residence for the children and their mother. Under this law, maternal custody could be extended through court order until the son reached 15 years of age and until the daughter married, if the court considered this in 'the child's interests'. In cases of custody extended through a judicial decision, the wife is not entitled either to any custody payment from the father or to a residence over the course of the duration as prolonged by the Judge. In 2005, certain provisions of Law No. 100 of 1985 were amended once more, extending maternal custody over both children until the age of 15, at which point a Judge would decide on custody based on the child's preference.[47]

Custody over children is not limited to the child's parents but extends to the whole extended family. According to Article 20 of Law No. 25 of 1929 as amended by Law No. 100 of 1985, in cases where the mother is deceased, or loses custody over the child, the maternal grandmother is awarded custody, followed in line by the paternal grandmother, then full sisters, then half-sisters, and so on. Priority is always given to female family members as long as the child is in the early childhood years. Once the child has passed the legal age, or if there are no women in the family, custody passes on to the father and male agnates from the father's family, then males from the mother's family. If the mother remarries, she loses custody to another family member, in the following order: the maternal grandmother, maternal aunt, paternal grandmother and paternal aunt.

1.3.2.1 Loss, Revocation and Extension of Custody

In cases where the mother loses custody over her child, Article 20 of Law No. 25 of 1929 (as amended) stipulates the order of priorities under which custodians (other than the mother) may exercise custody. However, the law is completely silent on the circumstances that may lead to such loss of maternal custody. Article 20 only provides for the temporary suspension of custody, for a period to be decided by the court, if the custodial parent refuses to implement a judicial decision on visitation.

Although there are no legal provisions on either the conditions for exercising custody or the loss and revocation of custody, courts have applied the relevant principles of Hanafi jurisprudence.[48] These are summarised in Qadri Pasha's com-

[47] See below, Sect. 1.4.

[48] See e.g. Court of Cassation, Case no. 5277 for the 78th Judicial Year (15 June 2009).

pilation, according to which the ability and integrity of the custodian, the security of the child, the custodian's marital status and disparity in religion between the custodian and child are all factors that affect custody. Egypt's courts may also have recourse to religious decrees (or fatwas) from the State religious institutions, but they are not bound by them.[49]

Article 382 of Qadri Pasha's compilation stipulates that in order for a female custodian (including the mother) to be eligible to exercise custody, she must: be free (i.e. not a slave), have reached puberty, enjoy legal capacity, be trustworthy such that the child will not go adrift due to her inattention, be capable of raising and safeguarding the child, not be an apostate, not be married to a 'stranger' (i.e. non-*maḥram*)[50] to the child, and not keep the child in a domicile with those who have an aversion to him/her. These conditions apply to the mother as well as all other female custodians. Article 383 further stipulates that the mother (or other female custodian) automatically loses her right to custody if she marries a 'stranger' (non-*maḥram*) to the child. This is revocable, however, as she may regain custody once she is no longer married to that stranger.

According to Article 381 of Qadri Pasha's compilation, the mother's 'presumptive custody' applies equally to non-Muslim (*dhimmī*) women as it does to Muslim women. However, this priority ends when the child reaches the age of 'religious majority', which is the age at which the child becomes aware of religion and, subsequently, there could be fears that the child's faith may be affected if they become accustomed to a religion other than Islam. This principle was applied by Egypt's courts until 2009, thereby shortening the period of custody for non-Muslim mothers. According to Article 387 of Qadri Pasha's compilation, a female custodian cannot be compelled to exercise custody over the child, unless there is no other female custodian who is also a *maḥram*, and on the condition that she is not married to a non-*maḥram*.

Several conditions also apply to custody of the father or a male relative. In this case too, the custodian must be trustworthy and capable of raising the child. The male custodian's right to custody can therefore be revoked if he is a 'sinner or corrupter or is incapable of raising the child by reason of insanity, dementia or disease'.[51] The father or male custodian's exercise of custody is not affected by marital status.[52] Although lifestyle and morals are not considered among the conditions for a woman's exercise of custody, this could be implied from 'trustworthiness' and capacity to raise the child. Unlike female custodians, the male custodian of a Muslim child must himself be Muslim.

---

[49] Stark 2005, p. 194.

[50] A *maḥram* is a relative who is prohibited from marrying the child.

[51] Khallāf 1938, p. 209 (author's translation).

[52] Stark 2005, p. 194.

1.3.2.2 The Custodial Child's Domicile

With respect to change of domicile, the provisions of Qadri Pasha's compilation are confusing and difficult to reconcile with modern developments in communications and transportation technology. The divorced mother may travel with her child, but only after the waiting period (*ʿidda*) is over. Curiously, Article 392 of the compilation distinguishes between city-to-city, village-to-city, village-to-village and city-to-village travels without stating the reasons for this distinction. It provides that the mother must obtain the father's consent in order to travel with the child from city to city, from village to city, or from village to village, unless the destination city or village is close enough to the father's domicile, such that he can visit the child and return home before dark. In this case, the father's consent is not required. Also, the divorced mother does not need the father's consent to travel with the child to her domicile of origin, provided the marriage contract was concluded there. In the case of a city-to-village travel, on the other hand, the father's consent is *always* required.[53] The principles on change of domicile do not apply to the non-Muslim mother or to female custodians other than the mother, who may not travel at all with the child without the father's consent.[54] Similarly, as long as the child is in the mother's custody, the father may not remove him or her at all from the mother's town of domicile without her consent.

1.3.3 Visitation Rights

Article 20 of Law No. 100 of 1985 also provides that both parents have the right to visit their children upon their mutual agreement (as do the grandparents if the parents are deceased). If the parents fail to reach agreement on the frequency and venue of such visits, the matter may be decided by a Court, on the condition that the visit should not be held in a place that would cause harm to the child, such as a police station. Before the amendments to Law No. 25 of 1929 were adopted by parliament, they were referred to a joint committee composed of members of the parliamentary Constitutional and Legislative Committee and the Committee of Religious Affairs, Social Affairs and Trusts (*awqāf*) for review. The joint committee's report, as well as the law's explanatory memorandum, stipulated that 'the right of parents to see/visit the boy or girl child is a right stipulated by the shariʿa',[55] implying that visitation rights are primarily the right of the parent rather than the child.

[53] Article 392, Qadri Pasha's Compilation.

[54] Stark 2005, p. 194.

[55] ʿAbd al-Ākhir 1985.

The law does not explicitly state that the Court may limit visitation rights if this is contrary to the child's best interests, which is embodied in Article 9 CRC.[56] The law therefore essentially—and consistent with the view of the parliamentary committee—treats child custody and visitation as rights of the divorced parents rather than rights enjoyed by the child, to be regulated according to the child's best interests. This is at odds with the provisions of the CRC as well as the interpretation given by the Committee on the Elimination of All Forms of Discrimination Against Women (CEDAW Committee) to Article 16(f) of the CEDAW, which establishes the equality of the spouses with respect to guardianship, wardship, trusteeship and custody. In interpreting this provision, the CEDAW Committee did not clarify the precise meaning of equality in custody rights; however, it affirmed that 'the best interests of the child shall be the paramount consideration'.[57]

A new draft personal status law prepared in 2010 proposed important amendments in the area of parents' visitation rights. The draft required that, as long as the child was in the mother's custody, the mother or grandfather would be required to accompany the child when visiting his or her father. This proposed amendment would have greatly increased the mother's custody rights, giving her the upper hand in raising the children and influencing them throughout the period of upbringing. However, this would come at the expense of the non-custodial father's right to spend time with the child and possibly the child's interest in maintaining a healthy relationship and direct contact with the father throughout the early childhood years. The proposed draft law was not adopted, due to the overthrow of the ruling regime in February 2011.

1.3.4 Some Special Applications: Children Born Out of Wedlock and Kafāla

Because conceiving out of wedlock is considered contrary to the shari'a, the exercise of custody and guardianship in such cases is not clearly regulated by law. Essentially, a father has no obligations towards a child born out of wedlock. Such a child is seen as belonging exclusively to the mother. Until 2008, no birth certificate could be issued without a father's presence or consent. According to Article 350 of Qadri Pasha's compilation, a father could voluntarily acknowledge paternity over a child of unknown parentage. This would establish paternity, whether the child confirmed it or not (in cases where the child is above the age of discernment) and provided the father is of an age where it is possible to conceive such a child. The father would therefore assume responsibility for the child's maintenance and upbringing. In its decision of 12 May 1976, the Court of Cassation stated that paternity is established 'through the bridal bed' (*bi-l-firāsh*), meaning

[56] Article 9 CRC.

[57] General Recommendation no. 21, CEDAW 1994.

through a valid marriage. The Court opined that paternity is primarily the right of the mother, as it allows her to reverse the stigma of illicit sexual relations and of having a child out of wedlock, but equally the right of the child as it results in 'rights established by law' such as the right to maintenance, nursing, custody and inheritance.[58] In order to enjoy these rights, it must be established that the parents were legally married (and that the child was therefore 'legitimate') at the time of conception. Courts have interpreted this to include children born of customary (unregistered or *'urfī*) marriages[59] as well as of a marriage that is voidable[60] (such as the case of a minor woman marrying without the consent of her marriage guardian).

A high profile case in 2004 prompted changes in the legislative framework relating to children born out of wedlock. In that case, the Judge considered the respondent's refusal to take a DNA paternity test as a presumptive indication that he was indeed the father; hence, the court proclaimed the child to be his.[61] A number of legislative changes ensued. Article 4 Law No. 126 of 2008 stipulates that children have the right to establish kinship to their legitimate parents and to enjoy their care. This right is to be exercised by proving parentage through all available scientific and technological means (which includes DNA testing).

Article 15 of the same law provides that a mother has the right to issue a birth certificate for her child in her own name, although this can only be used 'as a proof of the birth and for no other purposes'. This measure was intended to address the problem of children that are not recognised by their fathers or who have not been conceived through a valid marriage. In April 2015, Social Solidarity Law No. 137 of 2010 was amended by Presidential Decree No. 15 of 2015,[62] allowing women involved in *'urfī* marriages to obtain temporary birth certificates for their children using the name of the purported father, pending a final court decision.[63] In spite of these legal developments, Egypt's laws do not require parents of children born out of wedlock to provide care for their children.[64]

In accordance with Islamic doctrine, Egyptian legislation does not allow adoption, although a system of surrogate care, known as *kafāla,* exists.[65] Article 92 of the bylaws of Law No. 12 of 1996 provides that 'an orphan or a child of unknown parentage, male or female, carries the surname of the guardian family to be attached at the end of his/her first name. This action should be documented in the

58 Court of Cassation, Case no. 28 of the 44th Judicial Year (12 May 1976).

59 See Thomason 2008, p. 123.

60 Court of Cassation, Case no. 10 of the 29th Judicial Year (17 January 1962).

61 Thomason 2008, p. 122.

62 Presidential Decree No. 15 of 2015 Amending Law No. 137 of 2010, Official Gazette no. 10*bis* (b).

63 Talal 2015.

64 Thomason 2008, p. 142.

65 Ibid., p. 126; Article 4 Law No. 126 of 2008 Amending Certain Rulings of the Child Law, the Penal Code and the Civil Status Law, Official Gazette no. 24*bis* of 15 June 2008.

child's file, and it does not to lead to any effects related to adoption.' So, although the *kafāla* system allows a married couple to bring a child to live with them in their home, and hence assume a form of 'guardianship' over the child, providing him or her with maintenance, education and protection, this does not create a legal child-parent relationship and does not produce legal entitlements.[66] The law is silent as to what occurs if the family breaks down and who is to assume guardianship and custody in such a case.

1.4 Notable Legislative Developments

The law and practice related to the 'best interests of the child' changed in the year 2000 then again in 2005 with two important amendments to Egypt's law. Under Article 70 of Law No. 1 of 2000, if a dispute arises between the parents regarding child custody, the public prosecutor may carry out an investigation to discern where the 'best interests of the child' lie and may then grant custody on that basis until a court ruling is issued resolving the matter. In March 2005, Article 20 of Law No. 25 of 1929 as amended by Law No. 100 of 1985 was amended again so as to treat children of both genders equally and to give the mother more extensive custody rights.[67] This was in response to criticism leveled against the 1985 law for discriminating between a girl-child and a boy-child. According to the new law, both children would remain in their mother's custody until they reached 15 years of age. At that point, instead of automatically transferring custody of the boy-child to the father, the Judge would have to question him about his preference. The same would apply to the girl-child, who could now express her preference, at the age of fifteen, with regard to custody. This amendment was based on a fatwa by the Islamic Research Academy (*majma' al-buḥūth al-islamiyya*), the research arm of the official religious institution, Al-Azhar, adopted on 24 April 2003 and reaffirmed in its 47th session on 5 May 2011.[68]

The 2000 and 2005 legislative amendments are particularly significant for a number of reasons. First and foremost, they brought the concept of the 'best interests of the child' to the centre stage. Until these amendments were introduced, the 'best interests of the child' principle was translated as granting custody to the mother in the early childhood years and then transferring it automatically to the father at the age of 'maturity'. It was argued that the Judge may always use his discretion to prolong the mother's custody in cases where the application of the law would lead to a situation that was not in the 'child's

[66] Sayed 2013, pp. 513–514; Muslim Women's Shura Council 2011, p. 6 and 16; Fontes and Wanchic.

[67] Law No. 4 of 2005; Leila 2005.

[68] Ḥaḍānat al-aṭfāl 2012.

best interest'. The legislators' understanding of the 'best interests' principle has since evolved and is now seen as entailing that children spend more time with the mother (until they reach 15 years of age) and then take part in the decision affecting their custody. At that point, neither parent is at an advantage in custody arrangements because of their gender; what matters is the child's preference and what constitutes the 'child's best interests'. The law therefore merges the shariʿa rationale—based on the belief that the interest of the child is best served if he or she spends the early childhood years with a female family member—with the legal concept of the 'best interests of the child'. At age fifteen, the child is arguably old enough to make an informed decision regarding his or her own custody arrangements and may thus choose to remain with either parent. Secondly, the amendments achieve equality in the treatment of boy-children and girl-children, replacing the traditional notion that a girl-child was in need of her mother's affection for a longer period than a boy-child. Moreover, the concept of the parent's custody rights has now been qualified by the principle of the 'best interests of the child.'

In the years following these amendments, the Islamic Research Academy issued a number of other important fatwas. In its 44th session on 29 July 2007, the Academy issued a fatwa stipulating the following: (1) custody may pass to the father after the mother and maternal grandmother; (2) the grandparents have the right to visit the child whether in the presence or absence of the parents; (3) if a parent is awarded visitation rights and fails to visit the child at the agreed time on three consecutive occasions, the Judge has the right to strip that parent of visitation rights; and (4) the child may stay in the non-custodial parent's home during holidays if the custodial parent agrees.[69] These fatwas have not been formalised through any legislative action.

1.5 The Role of the Judiciary in Interpreting and Enforcing the 'Best Interests of the Child' Principle

1.5.1 The Jurisprudence of the Court of Cassation

Judicial decisions have somewhat mitigated the harsh conditions imposed by Hanafi jurisprudence regarding the mother or female custodian's loss of custody. In 1985, the Court of Cassation ruled that a mother's remarriage does not

[69] Ḥaḍānat al-aṭfāl 2012.

necessarily lead to loss of custody. The matter is 'subject to the discretion of the Judge; he may keep the child in her hand if the child's interests necessitate that, in order to avoid the greater harm by committing the lesser'.[70]

Similarly, in 2009 the Court of Cassation reversed a ruling by the Alexandria Appeals Court, which had awarded a previously Coptic man, who had converted to Islam, custody over his 11-year old sons. Both the Court of First Instance and the Court of Appeals had ruled that, since the father had converted to Islam, his minor children now followed the father's new religion. Since the boys had surpassed the age of 7 years, at which they were expected to become aware of their religion, and since there was no Muslim female custodian, the father had priority in exercising custody. The Court of Cassation reversed this ruling, awarding custody to the Coptic mother. The Court reasoned that: (1) under Hanafi jurisprudence, when the child reaches 7 years of age, the mother is no longer *obligated* to exercise custody, but this does not mean she is *prohibited* from exercising it; (2) Hanafi doctrine recognises the priority of a non-Muslim (*kitābī*) woman in exercising custody over her Muslim children as long as she does not perpetrate any acts that jeopardise their religious belonging, such as feeding them pork or wine. The Court added that the Court of Appeals had not given sufficient justification for revoking the Coptic mother's custody (it had not based its reasoning on any evidence that the mother had engaged in actions that would accustom the children to a religion other than Islam); (3) under Hanafi doctrine, the Muslim father may be awarded custody over the non-Muslim mother only if the children have reached an age in which they are capable of distinguishing between religions. The Court held that it was not clear (or rather the lower courts had not established) that this was possible at the age of 7 years. The Court added that, until the child becomes *mukallaf* (i.e. accountable in religious terms), he or she follows either parent in Islam since Islam is the best religion. Sometimes, however, the child may not become *mukallaf* (pubescent, sane) until 15 years of age; (4) a mother, regardless of her religion is more compassionate and more capable of exercising custody. The shariʿa does not rush to revoke the mother's right to custody as long as there is a way to avoid that, as the basis for the mother's right to custody under the shariʿa is her compassion and not her religion; and (5) under Law No. 4 of 2005, custody of the mother is obligatory until the child reaches the age of fifteen.[71]

Although the term 'best interests of the child' does not appear in the decision, it is implied through the Court's reference to the mother's compassion and to Law No. 4 of 2005. Possibly, this decision creates a precedent for dissociating the 'best interests of the child' concept from the parents' faith.[72]

---

70 Court of Cassation, Case no. 75 for the 53rd Judicial Year (19 March 1985).

71 Court of Cassation, Case no. 5277 for the 78th Judicial Year (15 June 2009).

72 IslamopediaOnline 2011.

1.5.2 The Jurisprudence of the Supreme Constitutional Court

Egypt's Supreme Constitutional Court (SCC) has played an indispensable role in interpreting the provisions of Egypt's legislation regarding child custody so as to serve the child's best interest. It has done this through its role as the institution with the authority to interpret Egypt's Constitution and to make determinations regarding the compatibility of Egypt's legislation with the Constitution. In particular, it has employed the reform tool of *ijtihād* (legal reasoning) to interpret personal status laws based on the shariʿa in a manner that meets the evolving needs and values of society. This has allowed it to uphold the constitutionality of important legal reforms in the area of child custody, which have been challenged based on their purported conflict with the shariʿa.

The essence of the SCC's progressive role lies in its interpretation of Article 2 of Egypt's Constitution, which stipulates that 'the principles of the Islamic shariʿa shall be *the* principal source of legislation'. This text is the result of an amendment proposed by President Sadat, replacing the previous formulation of the 1971 Constitution, which provided that the principles of the shariʿa were '*a* principal source of legislation' (i.e. one source among others). Since then, a growing number of challenges to the constitutionality of personal status legislation have been based on a purported conflict with the shariʿa. The provision, introduced to appease Islamic revivalists whose political influence was growing at the time (as part of Sadat's strategy to undermine the political left), has remained in every Egyptian Constitution ever since.

Since 1985, the SCC's jurisprudence has developed a methodical theoretical framework for interpreting Article 2, through which it has upheld progressive legal reforms by employing three tools. First, it has distinguished between immutable aspects of the shariʿa, and other aspects which were left ambiguous in the religious sources and therefore open to *ijtihād* to meet the changing needs of society.[73] This doctrine, enunciated in the SCC's judgment of 4 May 1985, was based on the following reasoning:

> According to the report of the Commission [charged with preparing the Constitutional reform of Article 2], the aim of the new formulation of Article 2 of the Constitution is to 'force the legislator to have recourse to the commands of the shariʿa, to the exclusion of any other source, in order to discover what he is searching for; then, if he does not find there an explicit ruling, he is to employ the shariʿa resources of interpretive effort (*al-ijtihādiyya*) in order to arrive at the proper rules to follow and which do not transgress the foundations and general principles of shariʿa.'[74]

This doctrine became the basis of a series of landmark cases in the 1990s. The first such case, decided in 1993, involved a dispute regarding child custody.

[73] Supreme Constitutional Court, Judgment of 4 May 1985, translation in Arabi 2001, p. 6.
[74] Ibid.

A challenge was brought against the child custody provisions of Law No. 100 of 1985, which had raised the age limit for maternal custody to 10 years for boys and twelve for girls, subject to further judicial extension to 15 years for boys and until marriage for girls. The SCC distinguished between the so-called explicit or formal principles of the shariʿa whose origin and meaning are definitive (*qaṭʿiyyat al-thubūt wa-l-dalāla*) and those that may be the object of interpretive effort (*ijtihād*) to adapt to the changing needs of society (*al-ẓanniyya*). The former, which are directly derived from the religious scriptures (the Qurʾan and the Prophet's hadith—together known as *al-naṣṣ*), take precedence over the latter. The authority of the SCC was 'limited to safeguarding their [i.e. the definitive principles'] implementation and their overruling any other legal rule that contradicts them'.[75]

The SCC declared that the differences in opinion between Islamic scholars regarding the age limit for custody indicated that this issue was one that was subject to *ijtihād* and that—despite the lack of consensus—it could be inferred that determining child custody revolved around furthering the child's benefit and interests. For this reason, the age limit for maternal custody could not be determined by a fixed, inflexible rule which did not take into consideration developments in society, culture and the needs and interests of people. The SCC then asserted that 'these are the origins and roots of the shariʿa, a flexible and non-rigid shariʿa in which *ijtihād* is limited to exerting effort to arrive at a legal opinion in which there is no explicit text (*al-naṣṣ*)—in line with its [the shariʿa's] overall rules (*ḍawābiṭha al-kulliyya*) and in a manner that does not obstruct its goals (*maqāṣidha*)'.[76] It therefore emphasised that *ijtihād* could be employed in matters in which there was no explicit or absolute principle derived from the primary sources of Islamic jurisprudence. Stressing this very narrow scope of application of *ijtihād* is absolutely essential for conferring legitimacy on the SCC's role in interpreting Article 2.

Secondly, the SCC reaffirmed that the shariʿa upholds the ruler's authority and discretion in matters that affect the people's affairs, as long as this is in line with the overall goals of Islamic law (*al-maqāṣid al-sharʿiyya*). It stated that:

> It follows that the ruler (*walī al-amr*) may assess what he perceives to be good for the child and in his/her best interest, keeping into consideration that the child's right to custody does not depend on any claim to it by the person entitled to custody. Safeguarding the child's psychological stability, preventing harm to him/her and rearing him/her are all among the overall goals of Islamic law (*al-maqāṣid al-sharʿiyya*) that cannot be questioned. Waiving the right to custody after it is established does not prevent its restoration. In fact, some scholars have said that the [woman] custodian can be compelled to exercise

75 Supreme Constitutional Court, Judgment of 15 May 1993, translation in Dupret 1997, p. 96.

76 Supreme Constitutional Court, Judgment in Case no. 7 of the 8th Judicial Year (15 May 1993), Al-Jarīda Al-Dustūriyya 5(2), p. 260 and 270-1 (author's translation).

custody – provided she meets all the conditions – whenever this is necessary for safeguarding and preserving the custodial child.[77]

Thirdly, the SCC emphasised that the shari'a seeks to apply the legal rule that serves the interests of people in an evolving society. It asserted that the shari'a principles on custody aim to serve the interests of the child and prevent any harm from befalling him/her. It was on these grounds that the SCC justified prolonging the mother's custody over the child in light of the principle of the child's best interest. The SCC also justified the law's distinction between a girl-child and a boy-child on the grounds of the different 'inherent natures' of the two genders and their differing needs. In detail, the SCC stated:

The legal essence of custody in Islamic law is that it constitutes a guardianship over the upbringing of a child (*wilāya li-l-tarbiya*) whose purpose is to guarantee attention and care for the child and his/her affairs during the early period of the child's life. Its fundamental principle is the child's interest, which is achieved by keeping him/her at the side of the (woman) custodian – who is more entitled to raise him/her – as she is considered better capable of protecting, caring for and safeguarding the child and because tearing the child from her – while she is the most compassionate with the child, the closest to him/her, the most aware of his/her needs and the most patient with the child – is harmful to the child in this critical period of his/her life, in which he/she is not independent in his/her affairs and cannot be entrusted to someone that is not trustworthy, who might eat [i.e. steal] from the child's maintenance, feed the child the bare minimum or look down upon the child. Neither the Islamic shari'a, in its explicit legal principles, nor the laws of the Orthodox Copts, mainly determined by the Holy Bible, establish limits for the age of custody that cannot be surpassed. This is because raising a child is a grave matter, which if affected by a defect even in some aspect, could lead to the loss (straying) of the child. Its range must therefore be limited by what upholds the child's interests and what is more likely to spare him/her harm, considering that custody concerns the child's benefit. Care for the child takes priority over any interest of any other party, even according to those

[77] Ibid., p. 260 (author's translation). In subsequent cases, the SCC went even further to confer legitimacy upon the government and legislature's departure from the reasoning of the established juristic schools. It stated that the shari'a 'does not vest sacredness on the arguments of any Muslim scholar on any affair, i.e. sacredness that precludes revision and reconsideration, even substitution … it is correct to say that the independent reasoning by any one Muslim scholar is not necessarily worthy of being followed than that by any other.' Supreme Constitutional Court, Judgment in Case no. 8 of the 17th Judicial Year (18 May 1996). It later elaborated on this principle in Case no. 82 (1997), in which it stipulated that: 'independent reasoning in indecisive [or discretionary] legal rules … is a right given to Muslim scholars, but the ruler is more entitled thereto so that he can consider each issue individually … with the help of those Muslim scholars, but without being necessarily restricted by the opinions of others. He may give different legal rules after referring to [the Qur'an] and [the sunna] to regulate people's affairs in a certain environment with its special circumstances, considering that the interests to be regarded are those which agree with the objectives of the shari'a, defined in light of their development, since they are unlimited. Thus the ruler, when choosing between two opinions, should consider the easier, unless it is a sin, and not give a legal rule that is hard upon the people, or else he will be contradicting the Qur'anic verse "Allah would not place a burden on you".' Supreme Constitutional Court, Judgement in Case no. 82 of the 17th Judicial year (5 July 1997).

> who state that custody does not arise from the right of the child but also involves the rights of [the custodial woman] to whose care the child is entrusted.[78]

This decision is significant for three reasons. First, the tools developed in this case, which are based on the doctrine declared by the SCC in 1985, were later refined and employed on several occasions to uphold the constitutionality of reforms to personal status law that were challenged on the grounds of conflict with the shariʿa. These included two other cases that specifically addressed child custody (in 1997[79] and 2008). Secondly, the decision clearly establishes the superiority of the child's interests over the interests of the custodian. It establishes the child's rights in custody as independent of the rights of any other party, an issue left ambiguous in the law itself. Thirdly, through this decision, the SCC was able to validate in religious terms the essentially secular concept of the child's best interests.[80] It relied on a broad interpretation of the overall goals of Islamic law to consecrate the principle of the child's best interests, to the extent that it ruled that custody may be restored even after it is waived, and indeed that a custodian may be compelled to exercise custody (against his/her will) if dictated by the child's best interests.

After the 2005 legal reforms, a third constitutional challenge came before the SCC. In that case, the plaintiff was a divorced father who had been awarded custody over his son in 2004, at first instance, for having attained the legal age. The adoption of Law No. 4 of 2005, however, resulted in the overturning of the decision at the appeals stage (as the age limit for the mother's exercise of custody was raised from 12 to 15 years). The plaintiff challenged the constitutionality of the law before the SCC on the grounds of non-conformity with Articles 2 and 9 of the Constitution.[81] The plaintiff argued that Law No. 4 of 2005.

> leads to a disruption and deterioration of the family by placing the reins of the issue in the hands of the woman and the minor. In addition [he claimed that] it contradicts the principle of equality, because it excludes men in an authoritative fashion in favour of women.[82]

Employing the three tools developed in its decision of 3 May 1993 and further elaborated in its subsequent decisions, the SCC dismissed the challenge on the following grounds:

---

[78] Supreme Constitutional Court, Judgment in Case no. 7 of the 8th Judicial Year (15 May 1993), p. 269 (author's translation).

[79] Supreme Constitutional Court Judgment in Case no. 74 of the 17th Judicial Year (1 March 1997), Al-Jarīda Al-Dustūriyya 8, p. 437.

[80] See Büchler et al. 2010, p. 92.

[81] Supreme Constitutional Court, Judgment in Case no. 125 of the 27th Judicial Year (2008), translation in Büchler et al 2010, pp. 87–88. Article 9 of the 1971 Constitution stipulated that: 'the family is the basis of the society founded on religion, morality and patriotism. The State is keen to preserve the genuine character of the Egyptian family—with all values and traditions represented by it—while affirming and promoting this character in the interplay of relations within Egyptian society.'

[82] Ibid.

> The provisions that the [legislature] may not contradict are those that are definitive [or peremptory] under the Islamic shariʿa (*qaṭʿiyya fī thubūtihā wa dalālatihā*). As for issues which are indecisive [or presumptive or discretionary] (*al-aḥkām al-ẓanniyya*), these are characterised as being subject to *ijtihād*, changing with time and place to ensure flexibility and vitality. This *ijtihād* must take place within the framework of the overall roots (*al-uṣūl al-kulliyya*) of Islamic jurisprudence.... Since *ijtihād* in discretionary matters is a right that belongs to the experts of legal reasoning (*ahl al-ijtihād*), then the ruler [or legislator] (*walī al-amr*) is even more entitled thereto...[83]

As in previous cases, the SCC emphasised the difference between definitive or absolute principles, which could not be the object of legal reasoning, and indecisive or discretionary rules, which could be changed and developed through *ijtihād*. It also emphasised the authority of the ruler and legislator to engage in *ijtihād* to achieve the interests of society, as long as this was in conformity with the overall goals of Islamic jurisprudence. Focusing on the rules on child custody, the SCC proceeded to state that:

> It [the *ḥaḍāna* period] is a matter of *ijtihād*, about which the opinions vary. As a consequence, the age [limit] of *ḥaḍāna* shall not be defined with a strict and solid regulation which does not take into consideration changes in time and place, but it requires a degree of flexibility which embraces its [the regulation's] secondary rulings (*al-aḥkām al-farʿiyya*) that are always responsive to development. It would be contradictory to this flexibility, if the legislator constricted himself to [the consideration of] certain opinions and would not deviate from them....[84]

Since the specific rules on child custody were part of the corpus of indecisive, discretionary or presumptive rules that were subject to legal reasoning and *ijtihād*, they were open to interpretation and development in accordance with changes in society. This interpretation opened the door for the subsequent departure from the provisions of the 1985 law and the adoption of a new amendment in 2005, which further raised the age limit for maternal custody. In light of the SCC's jurisprudence, this legislative amendment could be justified as a necessary response to societal changes and developments. The SCC added:

> The legal essence of custody is the child's best interests and the shariʿa does not specify an age-limit for [maternal] custody that cannot be surpassed. The fundamental value is what is necessary to fulfil the child's interests.... Keeping the child in the hands of the (woman) custodian before reaching the mandatory age for custody or after this age – when the child chooses to stay with her – does not deter his father's hands from him or restrict his guardianship in accordance with the shariʿa ... The challenged text was issued in consideration of the overall goals of Islamic law and without contradicting its basic fundamentals, whether related to the determination of the age [limit] of *ḥaḍāna* or the necessity of the minor's choice after reaching the age of fifteen. It [the challenged text] falls within its [the overall goals'] general directions recommending *ijtihād* for provisions, where there are no absolutely definite rulings in terms of immutability and meaning. For

---

[83] Supreme Constitutional Court, Judgment in the Case no. 125 of the 27th Judicial Year (2008), (author's translation).

[84] Supreme Constitutional Court Judgment in Case no. 125 of the 27th Judicial year (2008), translation in Büchler et al. 2010, p. 88.

> these reasons, the claim of this [legislative] text's violation of Article 2 of the Constitution has no ground.[85]

The SCC therefore reasserted that the legal reforms, which were based on the concept of the child's best interests, were in conformity with the 'overall goals of Islamic law' and did not conflict with the shariʿa.

1.6 Conclusion

Egyptian legislative provisions on parental care are based on the shariʿa-derived notion of shared responsibility between the parents. In cases of separation, the mother has priority in exercising custody, followed by other female family members. Ever since the 1920s, extending the duration of the mother's custody has been a priority for Egyptian feminists, not necessarily on the grounds of the child's best interests, but rather as a right of the divorced wife. In 2005, the period of maternal custody was extended until the child reached 15 years of age, at which point he or she could choose which parent to reside with. This signifies that Egyptian legislation considers the 'child's best interests' as synonymous with remaining in the mother's custody for the longest duration possible. The law further departed from previous legislation by allowing children to participate in the custody decision after reaching 15 years, rather than automatically transferring custody to the father. Since the year 2000, the law has stipulated that in cases of custody disputes, the public prosecutor may temporarily award custody based on the child's best interests, pending a final resolution by the court. Egyptian law therefore merges the shariʿa rationale for custody arrangements, based on the belief that the children's interests are best served if they spend their early childhood years with the mother, and the concept of the 'best interests of the child'.

Because the law is silent regarding conditions for loss and revocation of custody, courts have mainly applied the principles of Hanafi jurisprudence, informally codified in the 1875 Qadri Pasha compilation (although since 2000 they have been authorised to apply the principles of any of the four sunni jurisprudential schools). Under the broad terms of Qadri Pasha's compilation, a mother can lose custody based on claims that she is inattentive, untrustworthy or if she marries a 'stranger' to the child. Additionally, under Hanafi jurisprudence the non-Muslim mother's period of presumptive custody is shorter than that of the Muslim mother, ending at the age of religious discernment. However, the Court of Cassation's jurisprudence has departed sharply from these juristic interpretations. Based on a utilitarian argument of 'avoiding the greater evil by committing the lesser', it ruled that a mother's remarriage does not deprive her of custody. It also ruled that a Coptic mother could exercise custody beyond the age of discernment. The Court of Cassation is

---

[85] Ibid.

therefore inclined to narrowly interpret the principles governing the revocation of the mother's custody. Similarly, the SCC has upheld the mother's right to a prolonged period of custody through employing the tools of *ijtihād* and emphasising the ruler's discretion in matters affecting the people's affairs. It has also interpreted the overall goals of the shari'a (*al-maqāṣid al-shar'iyya*) so as to include the promotion of the child's welfare and interests, and it has established the superiority of the child's interests over the interests of the custodian. The SCC was therefore able to restate the concept of the child's best interests in religious terms.

In the area of guardianship over money, ever since the earliest codification in 1952 the validity of the guardians' actions have been measured against the child's interests. The law on revocation of guardianship over the child's person does not explicitly mention the best interests of the child principle. However, it provides a list of cases in which guardianship can be suspended or revoked, with considerable discretion given to the Judge to deprive the *walī* of guardianship rights where the latter jeopardises the ward's health, safety or morals. The law therefore implicitly reflects the principle of the best interests of the child. Nonetheless, the overriding consideration in appointing the guardian is the right of the father followed by the grandfather and the agnatic line, even where the children are in the mother's exclusive custody.

Visitation rights are still construed as the rights of parents. The law does not stipulate that the court may limit visitation rights where it is in the child's best interests to do so. Similarly, the legal provisions related to children born out of wedlock do not centre on the notion of the child's best interests. A child born out of wedlock has no legal rights until paternity is established through either the father's acknowledgment or proof that the parents were legally married at the time of conception. In 2008, mothers were given the right to issue birth certificates in their own name for children born out of wedlock or whose paternity is disputed. This can only be used as a proof of birth and not to create any legal rights. Children in *kafāla* arrangements similarly enjoy no legal entitlements.

While Egypt's 2008 Child Law further formalises the incorporation of the principle of the 'child's best interests' in all measures relating to children, there is still much to be desired in terms of the principle's application in practice. Whether the principle's incorporation in Egypt's 2014 Constitution will lead to its further consolidation and to the amendment of conflicting legislation remains to be seen.

References

'Abd al-Ākhir Ḥ (1985) Taqrīr al-lajna al-mushtaraka min: lajnat al-shu'ūn al-dustūriyya wa-l-tashrī'iyya wa-maktab lajnat al-shu'ūn al-dīniyya wa-l-ijtimā'iyya wa-l-awqāf (annexed to Law No. 100 of 1985), Official Gazette no. 27 of 4 July 1985

Abu-Odeh L (2004) Modernising Muslim Family Law: The Case of Egypt. Vand. J. Transnat'l L. 37:1043–1146

An-Na'im A (1994) Cultural Transformation and Normative Consensus on the Best Interest of the Child. Int J Law Fam 8(1):62–81

Arabi O (2001) The Dawning of the Third Millennium on Shariʿa: Egypt's Law no. 1 of 2000, or Women May Divorce at Will. Arab Law Q 16(1):2–21

Badran M (1996) Feminists, Islam, and Nation: Gender and the Making of Modern Egypt. Princeton UP, Princeton

Bibāwī NL (2004) ʿAdam dustūriyyat qānūn al-aḥwāl al-shakhṣiyya al-muṭabbaq ʿalā al-masīḥiyyīn, Cairo

Behrouz AN (2003) Transforming Islamic Family Law: State Responsibility and the Role of Internal Initiative. Columbia Law Rev 103:1136–1162

Berger M (2001) Public Policy and Islamic Law: The Modern Dhimmī in Contemporary Egyptian Family Law. Islamic Law Soc 8(1):88–136

Berger M (2002) Conflicts Law and Public Policy in Egyptian Family Law: Islamic Law Through the Backdoor. Am J Comp L 50(3):555–594

Berger M (2005) Secularizing Interreligious Law in Egypt. Islamic Law Soc 12(3):394–418

Bernard-Maugiron N, Dupret B (2002) From Jihan to Susanne. Twenty Years of Personal Status Law in Egypt. Recht van de Islam 19:1–19

Büchler A et al (2010) Supreme Constitutional Court of Egypt: A Commented Translation of Egypt's Supreme Constitutional Decision in Case No. 125 of Judicial Year 27 on Child Custody. GAIR-Mitteilungen 79–93. www.rwi.uzh.ch/oe/cimels/publications/GAIR-2010-Mitteilungen-02.pdf. Accessed 1 May 2014

Dupret B (1997) A propos de la constitutionnalité de la sharīʿa: Présentation et traduction de l'arrêt du 26 Mars 1994 (14 Shawwāl 1414) de la Haute Cour Constitutionnelle (al-maḥkama al-dustūriyya al-ʿulyā) égyptienne. Islamic Law Soc 4:91–113

Esposito J, DeLong-Bas N (2001) Women in Muslim Family Law, 2nd edn. Syracuse UP, New York

Fadel MH (2012) Political Liberalism, Islamic Family Law, and Family Law Pluralism. In: Nichols J (ed) Marriage and Divorce in a Multicultural Context: Multi-Tiered Marriage and the Boundaries of Civil Law and Religion. Cambridge University Press, New York, pp 164–199

Fontes A, Wanchic F (n.d.) Beloved Outcasts. Mafhoum 8(4). www.mafhoum.com/press7/187S28_fichiers/adoption0804.htm. Accessed 1 March 2016

Guindy A (2014) Family Status Issues Among Egypt's Copts: A Brief Overview. On Coptic Nationalism. https://copticliterature.wordpress.com/2014/08/23/quest-article-family-status-issues-among-egypts-copts-a-brief-overview/. Accessed 15 March 2014

Ḥaḍānat al-aṭfāl (2012) National Council for Women. www.ncwegypt.com/index.php/ar/docswomen/pslara/282-custogyara. Accessed 13 January 2015

Hajjar L (2004) Domestic Violence and Shari'a: A Comparative Study of Muslim Societies in the Middle East, Africa and Asia. In: Welchman L (ed) Women's Rights and Islamic Family Law: Perspectives on Reform. Zed Books, New York, pp 231–274

Hodkinson K (1984) Muslim Family Law: A Sourcebook. Helm Publishers, London

IslamopediaOnline (2011) Non-Muslims Personal Status Laws. www.islamopediaonline.org/country-profile/egypt/islam-and-legal-system/non-muslims-personal-status-laws. Accessed 15 March 2015

Khallāf ʿA (1938) Aḥkām al-aḥwāl al-shakhṣiyya fī al-sharīʿa al-islāmiyya, 2nd edn. http://sh.rewayat2.com/b7oth/Web/8631/001.htm. Accessed 23 September 2015

Khattāb M (2015) Interview (24 March 2015)

Leila R (2005) More Maternal Rights. Al-Ahram Weekly no. 733. http://weekly.ahram.org.eg/2005/733/eg9.htm. Accessed 1 March 2016

Liebesny HJ (ed) (1975) The Law of the Near and Middle East: Readings, Cases and Materials. State University of New York Press, Albany, pp 103–104

Maḥmūd R (2014) Waḍʿ muṣṭalaḥ al-maṣlaḥa al-fuḍlā li-l-ṭifl fī dustūr 2013 li-awwal marra, Ṣawt al-Umma. www.masress.com/soutelomma/50234

Moussa J (2011) Competing Fundamentalisms and Egyptian Women's Family Rights. Brill Martinus Nijhoff Academic Publishers, Leiden

Muslim Women's Shura Council (2011) Adoption and the Care of Orphan Children: Islam and the Best Interests of the Child. American Society for Muslim Advancement. www.wisemuslimwomen.org/images/activism/Adoption_(August_2011)_Final.pdf. Accessed 1 March 2016

Sayed M (2013) The Kafala of Islamic Law - How to Approach it in the West. In: Essays in Honour of Michael Bogdan. Juristförlaget, Lund

Sezgin Y (2013) Human Rights under State-Enforced Religious Family Laws in Israel, Egypt and India. Cambridge University Press, New York

Stark B (2005) International Family Law: An Introduction. Ashgate, Burlington

Talal O (2015) '20 Years to Prove He Was My Child's Father': Paternity Disputes in Egypt Destroy Lives. Aswat Misriya. http://egyptianstreets.com/2015/12/03/20-years-to-prove-he-was-my-childs-father-paternity-disputes-in-egypt-destroy-lives. Accessed 4 March 2016

Thomason LM (2008) On the Steps of the Mosque: The Legal Rights of Non-Marital Children in Egypt. Hastings Women's Law J 19:121–148

Zahraa M, Malek NA (1998) The Concept of Custody in Islamic Law. Arab Law Q 13(2):155–177

Chapter 2
India

Jean-Philippe Dequen

Abstract Despite India not being a Muslim country, its Muslim citizens are nonetheless governed by Islamic law in matters relating to custody and guardianship through a personal legal system. Irrespective of the large number of Muslims it affects, Muslim personal law remains however a minority law, and it is both administered and fashioned within a secular legal framework inherited from British colonisation. This chapter seeks, through a legal-historical approach, to present the evolution of Islamic guardianship and custody laws in India, particularly in relation to the Guardians and Wards Act of 1890, which still holds force today. After briefly detailing the place of Islamic law within the Indian legal order, it will be shown how the Guardians and Wards Act 1890 has profoundly changed the legal characterisations pertaining to guardianship and custody, which but partially reflect the classical Islamic dichotomy between *wilāya* and *ḥaḍāna*. It is argued that the subsequent 'secular' legal categories of 'guardianship of the person' and 'guardianship of property', upon which Muslim personal law is applied, have had an adverse effect on both the rights of the mother and on the minor's property. Furthermore, it is submitted that the status of Islamic law as a minority law in India has also hindered the enforcement of the notion of the 'best interests of the child'. Although Islamic law has traditionally integrated this concept within its jurisprudential framework, its transformation into Anglo-Muhammadan law within the British Raj has impeded the incorporation and development of the 'best interests of the child' principle within Muslim personal law, especially if compared to the evolution of Hindu personal law or English law in that regard.

Keywords Muslim personal law · Custody and guardianship · India · Legal history · Best interests of the child · Islamic law

The author is a research fellow at the Max Planck Institute for European Legal History, Frankfurt.

J.-P. Dequen (✉)
Max Planck Institute for European Legal History, Hansaallee 41, 60323, Frankfurt am Main, Germany
e-mail: dequen@rg.mpg.de

N. Yassari et al. (eds.), *Parental Care and the Best Interests of the Child in Muslim Countries*, DOI 10.1007/978-94-6265-174-6_2

Contents

2.1 Introduction

India is not per se a Muslim country. It does not recognise Islamic law as a general source of law,[1] and Muslims are but a minority within an otherwise Hindu dominated population.[2] However, despite not being a 'Muslim' jurisdiction, India remains particularly relevant in the analysis of the incorporation of the notion of the 'best interests of the child' vis-à-vis the Islamic legal concepts of *ḥaḍāna* (custody) and *wilāya* (guardianship).

Indeed, with a little over 172 million people, Indian Muslims represent on the one hand the second largest Muslim national community in the world behind that of Indonesia and on par with Pakistan. Hence, the legal framework upon which Indian Muslims settle their disputes relating to custody and guardianship directly impacts over ten per cent of the global Muslim population.[3] On the other hand the

---

[1] The Constitution of India 1950 in its 'Preamble' defines India as a 'sovereign socialist secular democratic republic' (the term 'secular' having been added by section 2 of the Constitution (Forty-second Amendment) Act 1976). The 'Preamble' is considered as an integral part of the Constitution, see *Kesavanda Bharati Sripadagalvaru v. State of Kerala*, AIR 1973 SC 1461.

[2] According to the 2011 Census, Muslims amount to 14.2% of the Indian population, making it the second largest religious community, behind Hindus (79.8%), Census of India, www.censusindia.gov.in/2011census/C-01.html. Accessed 01 November 2015.

[3] Based on an estimate of approximately 1.6 billion Muslims worldwide, who for the most part (73%) reside in Muslim-majority countries, Pew Research Center (Religion & Public life), www.pewforum.org/2012/12/18/global-religious-landscape-muslim. Accessed 27 January 2015.

Indian Sub-Continent, given its long history of Muslim rule, has had a lasting influence on the Islamic legal tradition, which has partly survived through both a colonial and post-colonial personal legal system, whereby Indian Muslims remain governed by Islamic law in specific subject matters (including custody and guardianship) in the absence of superseding statutes of general application. Therefore, the study of *ḥaḍāna* and *wilāya* vis-à-vis the notion of the 'best interests of the child' in India constitutes an important part of any analysis pertaining to Islamic law, both for empirical as well as theoretical reasons and despite the latter's status as a 'minority' law.

Nevertheless, one must bear in mind the specificity of the Indian legal context in regards to Islamic law's 'minority' status, within which the latter is not only influenced by internal debates among Muslim jurists and confronted with the incorporation of international standards but is also subject to an inherent tension with the overarching Indian secular constitutional legal framework.

It is thus necessary to first present the history of the place of Islamic law within the Indian colonial and postcolonial legal orders in order to explain how a secular statute (Guardians and Wards Act 1890) grounds the application of the Islamic norms pertaining to guardianship and custody. The main effect of this architecture has been to apply both *ḥaḍāna* and *wilāya* substantive rules through the non-Islamic legal categories of 'guardianship of the person' and 'guardianship of property', which but partially reflect this classical Islamic legal dichotomy. As such, the incorporation of the notion of the 'Best Interests of the Child' (hereafter BIC) in India has been deeply influenced by the Common Law's own evolution in the matter, where beyond legislative enactments, the influence of the judiciary has played a key role.

2.1.1 Historical Setting: Muslim Personal Law Within the Indian Legal Order

2.1.1.1 The Circumscribed Applicability of Islamic Law to Family Matters: The Invention of Muslim Personal Law

Despite the deposition of the last Mughal emperor in 1858, the status of India as *Dār al-Islām*, irrespective of its non-Muslim government in the form of the British Raj, remained an open question for both British authorities and Muslim elites.[4] Indeed, Islamic law had remained the generally applicable law in most parts of the country, as it had been the policy of the East India Company—continued under the Crown's direct rule—for different communities to be administered by their own

---

[4] See Guenther 1999, Ghose 2014.

laws in the absence of general statutes. As such, Indian Muslims remained governed according to the Islamic legal framework, despite the latter's domain shrinking from that of a general legal system to a set of special laws.[5] The field of application of Muslim law, as well as its potential conflict with customary law, was however settled and embedded through the Muslim Personal Law (Shariat) Application Act 1937 (hereafter the Shariat Act).[6]

2.1.1.2 The Sources of Muslim Personal Law

The sources of Muslim personal law (hereafter MPL) fluctuated throughout the 19th century. Whereas Hastings had envisaged the *Qu'rān* as its sole basis,[7] later regulations would be more vague so as to encompass a greater diversity of

[5] The personal legal system in India is deemed to have originated in Warren Hasting's 1772 'Plan for the administration of justice', whereby Hindu and Muslim laws would apply to their respective communities in matters 'regarding marriage, inheritance, caste and other religious usages and institutions' (see Monckton Jones 1918, p. 324). Henceforth, Islamic criminal and contract laws were quickly superseded by general statutes such as the Indian Penal Code 1860 and the Indian Contract Act 1872. Even within the scope of the aforementioned subject matters regarding family relations, Muslim law was sometimes set aside in favour of the English concept of 'Justice Equity and Good Conscience' introduced by section 60 and 93 of the Regulations for the Administration of Justice in the Courts of Dewanee Adaulut 1781 (see Giunchi 2010), albeit only in the absence or vagueness of any personal legal rule (see section 9 of Regulation VII of 1832, and *Moonshee Buzloor Ruheem v. Shumsoonissa Begum* (1867) 11 MIA 551). Custom could also override Muslim law if the former was both duly recognised according to English legal standards (see Sinha 1976; also *Muhammad Ismael v. Lale Sheomukh* (1913) 17 Calcutta Weekly Notes 97; and section 112 of Government of India Act 1915 (5 & 6 Geo 5 C 61)) as well as provided for by a series of local or personal statutes (for instance the Punjab Laws Act 1872, the Oudh Laws Act 1876, and the Cutchi Memons Act 1920 among others).

[6] Whilst repealing the multiple statutes allowing Islamic law's suppletive nature vis-à-vis customary law (section 6), the Act entrenches Muslim law's imperative character in regards to matters of guardianship. Section 2 thus states: '[n]otwithstanding any custom or usage to the contrary, in all questions (save questions relating to agricultural land) regarding … guardianship … the rule of decision in cases where the parties are Muslims shall be the Muslim Personal Law (Shariat)'. Guardianship must here be construed following the Guardians and Wards Act 1890 (section 4(2)) as encompassing both guardianship of a person (thus custody) and/or of the latter's property. It is worth mentioning that this Act does not apply in Goa where the Portuguese Civil Code 1867 has never been repealed (see the Goa, Daman And Diu (Administration) Act 1962), nor to the 'Renoncants' of Pondicherry (see the Pondicherry (Extension of Laws) Act 1968); finally Muslim personal law's overriding character vis-à-vis customary law in Jammu and Kashmir has only recently been entrenched through the Jammu and Kashmir Muslim Personal Law (Shariat) Application Act 2007.

[7] See Monckton Jones 1918, p. 324.

bases in line with different juristic schools.[8] Although the existence of a dual judicial system within British controlled territories[9] and the subsequent presence of law officers in *mufaṣṣal* territories allowed for a wider variety of interpretations and decisions in the first half of the 19th century, their progressive dismissal, as well as the standardisation, and the hierarchal organisation of the British Indian judicial apparatus have greatly impeded Muslim law's pluralistic nature in favour of authoritative textual references whose interpretation was also subject to the doctrine of *stare decisis* and the precedents of the Privy Council.[10]

The fact that predominantly non-Muslim judges now had to apply Islamic legal provisions, and the necessity of greater legal certainty as to the latter, became a growing concern among colonial authorities, illustrated by Lord Macaulay's famous speech in the House of Commons:

> We do not mean that all the people of India should live under the same law; far from it ... whether we assimilate those systems or not, let us ascertain them, let us digest them .... Our principle is simply this – uniformity where you can have it – diversity where you must have it – but in all cases certainty.[11]

As such, compendiums of Muslim law were progressively translated and held authoritative value in front of State jurisdictions.[12] In parallel, the non-State legal

---

[8] Regulation IV of 1793 subsequently uses the term 'Muhammadan laws' as to include both a greater variety of traditions (*ḥadīth*) as well as to allow the incorporation of custom. Judicial decisions also progressively took into account the litigant's own sect and juristic school as the basis of their ruling, hence forgoing Hanafi law's general application (as was the case under the Mughals) and hence the progressive recognition of both Shi'i law (see *Rajah Deedar Hosseen v. Zuhooroon Nissa* (1841) 2 Moo IA 441) and Shafi'i law (see *Mohamed Ibrahim v. Ghulam Ahmad* (1864) I Bom HCR 236).

[9] Until the fall of the Mughal Empire, the judicial administration of British India was divided between Supreme Courts, composed of English judges whose jurisdiction did not extend beyond Presidency towns (Calcutta, Madras and Bombay), and 'Company Courts' composed of East India Company administrators assisted by native law officers, who had jurisdiction over *mufaṣṣal* territories (nominally still under the sovereignty of the Mughal Emperor).

[10] Law officers, whose opinions had become only advisory at the beginning of the 19th century, were officially dismissed by Regulation IV of 1832. Following the deposition of the Mughal Emperor, the Indian High Courts Act 1861 was enacted as to fuse both existing Supreme Courts and Company Courts, with the Privy Council in England as the ultimate appellate jurisdiction (see Judicial Committee Act 1833 (3 & 4 Will 4 C 27)).

[11] HC Deb (3rd series), 10 July 1833, vol 19, col 533.

[12] Some compendiums or textbooks date back from the Mughal period and have been subsequently translated either in full, such as *Al-Hidāya* (see Marghinani and Hamilton 2008), or in part, such as *Al-Fatāwā al-'Ālamgīriyya* (see Baillie 1875). Digests incorporating the growing case law have also been published and constantly updated (see Mulla and Hidayatullah 1990; Tyabji and Tayyibji 1968; Fyzee 2005). However, only one legal treatise has had a lasting influence, due largely to the author's position as the first Indian national to sit on the Judicial Committee of the Privy Council: Syed Ameer Ali's *Mahommedan Law* (Ali 1985).

apparatus, although recognised as a mode of alternative dispute resolution and registrar, was stripped of its judicial powers.[13] Following independence, this judicial organisation remained—albeit with the institution of the Indian Supreme Court as the ultimate appellate jurisdiction in place of the Privy Council.[14] Indian Courts have also followed the colonial tradition of relying on well-established sources in regards to Muslim law and only exceptionally on new interpretations or authorities.[15] Parliament has also not ventured into reforming Muslim personal law, unless at the behest of the Muslim community itself, in line with Jawaharlal Nehru's policy regarding minorities.[16] Finally, the legal recognition of non-State actors' opinions (*fatwā*) or rulings through unofficial *fora* such as *dār al-qāḍā'* has been repeatedly denied.[17]

Hence, despite having never undergone a formal codification, Muslim law in India is composed of a relatively fixed set of authoritative sources interpreted through the lens of English jurisprudence, coined as Anglo-Muhammadan law.[18]

---

[13] Kaziz Act 1880. The judicial role of the *qāḍī* was subsequently transferred to civil courts (see *Shama Charan Roy v. Abdul Kabeer* (1899) 3 CWN 158).

[14] Articles 124 to 143 of the Constitution of India 1950.

[15] Some decisions have cited living authors (such as Mahmood 1980 and Engineer 2008) or have relied on more recent compendiums established by Muslim non-governmental organisations (for example the All India Muslim Personal Law Board, *Compendium of Islamic Laws* (AIMPLB 2002)). It is but recently that the Supreme Court and certain High Courts have ventured into new interpretations of Islamic legal sources, most notably in the field of post-divorce maintenance (see *Mohd. Ahmed Khan v. Shah Bano Begum and Ors* 1985 SCR (3) 844, on the interpretation of the term *matā'* in Q 2:241) and on unilateral divorce initiated by the husband (see *Mohammad Naseem Bhat v. Bilquees Akhter and Anr*, 561-A n 158/2009, IA no 336/2009, HC Jammu and Kashmir at Srinagar, 22 October 2009 (on file with author)).

[16] The first Indian Prime Minister had thus declared that whereas Hindu law could be reformed, it would be an abuse of power to do so in regards to minorities: 'The primary responsibility of the majority is to satisfy the minority. The majority by virtue of its being a majority naturally has strength to have its way; it requires no protection. Sometimes it is right to give statutory protection to minorities. It is the duty and responsibility of the majority community to pay particular attention to what the minority there wants, to win it over. I am personally in favour, where such question arises of the minority, whether it is a linguistic minority or a religious minority.' (Lok Sabha Debates, vol. x, pt 2, col 3504 (21 December 1955)). It was then under the Muslim community's pressure that the Mussalman Wakf Validating Act 1913, the Muslim Personal Law (Shariat) Application Act 1937, the Dissolution of Muslim Marriages Act 1939, and the Muslim Women (Protection of Rights on Divorce) Act 1986 were enacted (although the latter with consequences unforeseen by the community). This situation is at odds with the legislative activism pertaining to Hindu law where, acting under Article 25(2)(b) of the Constitution of India 1950, allowing the legislature to circumvent freedom of religion provisions in order to '[provide] for social welfare and reform … to all classes and sections of Hindus', several statutes reforming Hindu personal law were enacted, among which was the Hindu Minority and Guardianship Act 1956.

[17] For a recent example see *Vishwa Lochan Madan v. Union of India & Ors* (2014) 7 SCC 707.

[18] It is thus hardly surprising that the Shariat Act's 'Statement of Object' states that MPL 'exists in the form of a veritable code and is too well known to admit of any doubt or to entail any great labour in the shape of research'.

As such, some authors have advanced its rather fossilised state as 'something it had never been: a fixed body of immutable rules beyond the realm of interpretation and judicial discretion'.[19] This strict observance of what one may qualify as *taqlīd* is illustrated by Justice Shahmiri's reprimand of a local magistrate who endeavoured to expound Islamic law on his own:

> However learned the Tehsildar Magistrate may be in theology, he should have known that he was acting as a Judicial Officer, and it was not for him as such Officer to give his own interpretations of the verse of the holy Quran. Times without number the highest Judicial Courts in India including the Privy Council have sounded a note of warning against entertaining new and novel interpretations of the texts of the Quran and Hadis.[20]

The Justice's reference to the Privy Council only emphasises the influence of English law principles and colonial statutory legacy on the standing of MPL within the Indian constitutional framework, as well as MPL's potential conflicts with otherwise 'secular' legislation which explicitly puts forward the notion of the 'best interests of the child'.

2.1.2 Internal Conflict of Laws Between Muslim Personal Law and Indian Legislative and Constitutional Provisions in Relation to BIC

Given MPL's reliance on a set of fixed rules, the relative reticence on the part of Indian judges to expound novel Islamic legal concepts, and the extreme cautiousness of Parliament regarding unilateral legislation on minority issues, the application of the notion of the 'best interests of the child' to legal disputes involving Muslims has for the most part been framed within the logic of conflict of laws, or whether Muslims could be subject to 'secular' legislation within the ambit of personal legal matters.

2.1.2.1 Legislative Exceptions in Relation to Muslim Personal Law

British colonial legislation has for the most part provided explicit exceptions to its application within subject matters falling within the fields of personal law. As such, the Majority Act 1875, which sets the majority age at 18 years old, states that its provisions shall not affect 'the capacity of any person to act in the following matters (namely), marriage, dower, divorce and adoption' under their

[19] Anderson 1993, p. 172.

[20] *Amad Giri v. Mst Begha* 1955 Cri LJ 1067.

personal law.[21] Similarly, the Transfer of Property Act 1882 removes the obligation of a registered document in order complete a gift of immoveable property in the case of Muslim transactions[22]; whilst the Code of Criminal Procedure 1973 also provides that post-divorce maintenance can be altered or cancelled if 'the woman ... has received ... the whole sum which, under any customary or personal law applicable to the parties, was payable on such divorce'.[23] Finally, whereas 'secular' legislation provides for the maintenance of illegitimate children,[24] it does not provide for a legitimation procedure, which does not exist in Islamic law.[25] The only legislative—although in large part unforeseen—intervention in MPL was that of sections 112 and 114 of the Indian Evidence Act 1872 relating to the

[21] Section 2(a) of the Act. As such it allowed for Muslims to marry after attaining puberty, which in India is set at 15 years old (see Mulla and Hidayatullah 1990; Tyabji and Tayyibji 1968). The recent Prohibition of Child Marriage Act 2006 (PCMA), which sets the capacity to marry at eighteen for a woman and twenty-one for a man—thus circumventing the exception of the Majority Act 1875 by distinguishing between the terms 'child' and 'minor'—has had conflicting applications in regards to Muslims. Whereas the Delhi High Court has deemed it supersedes personal legal provisions in rendering any marriage voidable at the request of the minor party (section 3(1) of the PCMA, see *Jitender Kumar v. State*, WP (Crl) 1003/2010 HC Delhi 10 August 2010 (on file with author)), the Gujarat High Court has held that save for forced marriages (void as per section 12), the resulting marriage is nevertheless valid as per MPL's provisions read in conjunction with the Majority Act 1875 if both parties agreed to it (see *Yusuf Ibrahim Mohammed Lokhat v. State*, Crl Misc App no 13658/2014 HC Gurajat 2 December 2014 (on file with author)).

[22] Section 129 of the Act, thus in line with Muslim contract law which does not require a written deed for such gift to be effective (see also *Hafeeza Bibi and Ors v. Shaikh Farid (dead) by LR and Ors*, (2011) 5 SCC 654).

[23] Section 127(3)(b) of the Code, this provision was used to deny maintenance to a Muslim divorced wife beyond the *'idda* period until the *Shah Bano* decision (see *supra* n 15) which interpreted Islamic law as internally allowing such provisions to be made, later entrenched through the Muslim Women (Protection of Rights upon Divorce) Act 1986, as construed by the Supreme Court in *Danial Latifi and Anr v. Union of India* (2001) 7 SCC 740.

[24] Section 125(1)(b) and (c) of the Code of Criminal Procedure 1973 (formerly section 488 of the Code of Criminal Procedure 1898), see *Sukha v. Ninni* AIR 1966 Raj 163; also *Noor Saba Khatoon v. Mohammed Qasim* AIR 1997 SC 3280 on the application of section 3(1)(b) of the Muslim Women (Protection of Rights on Divorce) Act 1986). It is worth mentioning that the personal law of the illegitimate child is that of his/her mother, whereas it will be that of his/her father if legitimate (as per the father being the natural guardian of the child, see section 19 read in conjunction with section 25 of the Guardians and Wards Act 1890). Hence the illegitimate child of a Muslim father and a Hindu mother can claim maintenance from his father under the Hindu Adoption and Maintenance Act 1956 (see *K.M. Adam v. Gopala Krishnan* AIR 1974 Mad 232).

[25] Although Muslim personal law recognises the acknowledgment of a child under certain conditions (see Mulla and Hidayatullah 1990), this is different from a legitimation procedure: 'while legitimacy is a status which results from certain facts, legitimation is a proceeding which creates a status which did not exist before' (Fyzee 2005, p. 189). It is worth noting however that acknowledgment has been made easier through the presumption of marriage after a prolonged cohabitation, provided by section 114 of the Indian Evidence Act 1872 (see *Mohammed Amin v. Vakil Ahmed* AIR 1952 SC 358).

presumption of legitimacy,[26] which remains contested as to its application in regards to Muslims.[27]

2.1.2.2 Constitutional Exceptions in Relation to Muslim Personal Law

Save for the Muslim Women (Protection of Rights upon Divorce) Act 1986, there has been no direct legislative intervention in MPL following independence. However, inspired by the Universal Declaration of Human Rights, whereby 'motherhood and childhood are entitled to special care and assistance',[28] the Constitution of India incorporates in several of its articles the notion of the 'best interests of the child'. As such, Article 14 proclaims the right to equality, Article 21 the right to life, and Article 15 prohibits discrimination whilst allowing the State to make 'special provisions for women and children' (Article 15(3)). In that regard, Article 23 prohibits human trafficking and forced labour, and Article 24 proscribes the hazardous employment of children below 14 years, notably in factories and mines. In pursuance of these fundamental rights, the Constitution also includes 'Directive Principles of State Policy' which, although non-enforceable, have been considered as the 'book of interpretation' upon which the former must be construed and implemented.[29] Henceforth, Article 39(e) enjoins the State to ensure that 'the tender age of children [is] not abused'; Article 39(f) requires that

[26] This conclusive presumption of section 112 can only be rebutted by proving non-access, and thus even a DNA test proving non-paternity of the child would be disregarded by the Courts (see *Shaik Fakruddin v. Shaik Mohammed Hasan* AIR 2006 AP 48). section 114 provides for a presumption of 'any fact which [the Court] thinks likely to have happened, regard being had to the common course of natural events', which *a contrario* dismisses Islamic law's own presumption of legitimacy for child born several years after the dissolution of marriage (doctrine of the 'dormant foetus').

[27] As a statute of general application without explicit exceptions provided for personal law, it was held to apply to all Indians irrespective of their communal affiliation (see *Sibt Muhammad v. Muhammad Hameed and others* AIR 1926 All 526). However, in making the time of birth—rather than the time of conception as per traditional Islamic law—the determinant factor of legitimacy, whilst not defining the term 'valid marriage', it was questioned whether if, as a rule of substantive law, it would be superseded by the Shariat Act, especially in regards to its effects on many of the subjects included in the latter, such as *li'ān* and inheritance. If the overriding nature of section 112 seem to have been settled in *Dukhar Jahan v. Mohammed Farooq* AIR 1987 SC 1049, Islamic legal provisions regarding the validity of marriage could still be taken into account in relation to the facts of a particular case involving such presumption, as in *Abdul Rehman Kutty v. Aisha Beevi* AIR 1960 Ker 101.

[28] Universal Declaration of Human Rights (adopted 10 December 1948 UNGA Res 217 A(III) (UDHR) Article 25(2); it was preceded by the Geneva Declaration of the Rights of the Child (adopted 26 September 1924 (1924) 21 LoN Official Journal 43), and followed by the Declaration of the Rights of the Child (adopted 20 November 1959 UNGA Res 1386(XIV)).

[29] See *Ashoka Kumar Thakur v. Union of India and Ors* (2008) 6 SCC 1.

'children are given opportunities and facilities to develop in a healthy manner' assuring their freedom, dignity and protection against both exploitation as well as 'moral and material abandonment'; and Article 45 enjoins the State to provide for early childhood care in addition to free and compulsory education for children under the age of 6 years old. Moreover, the Constitution has empowered the Supreme Court with extensive powers as to the review of existing laws vis-à-vis fundamental rights provisions.[30]

Although not explicitly mentioning the Convention on the Rights of the Child (hereafter CRC),[31] the Constitution (eighty-sixth Amendment) Act 2002 serves for a part of its transposition into the Indian internal legal order by not only adding a new fundamental right to education for children up to 14 years old (Article 21A), but also by adding a new directive principle (Article 51A(k)) that declares a fundamental duty requiring the 'parent or guardian to provide opportunities for the education of his child or, as the case may be, ward between the age of 6 and 14 years'. Since independence, several policies and statutes have also incorporated the notion of the 'best interests of the child', whether in terms of procedure[32] or substantive norms.[33] Muslim personal law has nonetheless stayed away from this fundamental rights revolution, mainly due to the conjunction of its status as a minority law and its uncodified nature.

As aforementioned the Muslims' minority position in society made it politically tricky for parliament to unilaterally amend MPL without seeming to distort it following secular or Hindu principles. Notwithstanding, it is its un-codified character

30 Article 32(A) provides that 'the Supreme Court shall have power to issue directions or orders or writs, including writs in the nature of *habeas corpus*, *mandamus*, prohibition, *quo warranto* and *certiorari*, whichever may be appropriate, for the enforcement of the rights conferred by this Part'. The judiciary has grandly extended its prerogatives in such matters notably through Public Interest Litigation (see Deva 2009).

31 Adopted 20 November 1989, entered into force 2 September 1990, 1577 UNTS 3 (CRC). It is worth mentioning that the Indian legal order is a dualist system, whereby international treaties are not directly actionable in a municipal Court, despite their ratification, unless transposed by statute (the CRC was ratified by India on 12 November 1992).

32 As a transposition of the CRC, one could point to the Family Courts Act 1984 creating Family Courts which have exclusive jurisdiction over family matters (including guardianship and custody, see section 7(1)(a)) and whose composition shall be 'committed to the need to protect and preserve the institution of marriage and to promote the welfare of children' (section 3(4)(a)); to the Juvenile Justice (Care and Protection of Children) Act 2000 (amended by the Juvenile Justice (Care and Protection of Children) Amendment Act 2006); and to the institution of 'Child Welfare Committees' (section 29).

33 The most striking inclusion of this notion is in the Hindu Minority and Guardianship Act 1956: Article 13(1) providing that in the appointment of a guardian 'the welfare of the minor shall be the paramount consideration'. Save for MPL, other personal laws have either recognised the legitimacy of a child whose parents' marriage was void or voidable or have been amended accordingly (section 16(3) of the Hindu Marriage Act 1955; section 26(3) of the Special Marriage Act 1954; section 3(2) of the Parsi Marriage and Divorce Act 1936); however, children of a void Christian marriage would only be legitimate in regards to a party who entered the union in good faith or in full capacity (section 21 of the Indian Divorce Act 1869).

that has rendered it immune from judicial scrutiny. Indeed, the Constitution had provided for the 'laws in force' before its commencement to be adapted in order to be consistent with its provisions[34]; moreover 'laws in force' which subsequently derogated from fundamental rights were considered void.[35] Whereas Christians and Parsis had codified most of their personal laws,[36] and Hindus theirs soon thereafter,[37] MPL remained substantively uncodified, the Shariat Act being but a conflict-of-law rule. As such, MPL did not fit in the category of 'laws in force' as defined by the Constitution so as to become amenable to judicial review.[38] Although Article 13 left the possibility for 'laws in force' to be characterised 'as the context otherwise requires', this context never seems to have arisen, with the Supreme Court considering personal laws in general and Muslim law in particular as not falling within the ambit of Article 13 and the judiciary thus passing on the responsibility of their reform to the legislature.[39] However, subsequent statutes substantively amending or codifying parts of Muslim law would be subject to scrutiny and would if need be interpreted in accordance with fundamental rights provisions, as was the case with the Muslim (Protection of Women upon Divorce) Act 1986.[40] The will not to exercise undue influence, on one hand, and the fear of altering religious norms deemed to preserve a minority's social and cultural identity, on the other, have thus left Islamic law with but little opportunity to evolve past its Anglo-Muhammadan inception.

The progressive integration of the notion of the 'best interests of the child' in the Indian legal order has hence been largely done both outside and contrary to Muslim personal law. Outside, as the 'best interests of the child' has but multiplied

---

34 Articles 372 and 372A of the Constitution.

35 Article 13(1).

36 Parsi and Marriage Divorce Act 1936; Christian Marriage Act 1872; Indian Divorce Act 1869.

37 Reference is made here to the Hindu Code Bills which regrouped the Hindu Marriage Act 1955, the Hindu Succession Act 1956, the Hindu Minority and Guardianship Act 1956, and the Hindu Adoption and Maintenance Act 1956.

38 Article 13(2)(b) defines 'laws in force' as including 'laws passed or made by a Legislature or other competent authority ...', whereas 'law' would include 'ordinance, order, bye-law, rule, regulation, notification, custom or usage having in the territory of India the force of law' (Article 13(3)(a)). MPL's substantive provisions do not fit in any of the above categories, neither procedurally nor formally.

39 Justice Gagendragadkar in *State of Bombay v. Narasu Appa Mali* AIR 1952 Bom 84 thus states: 'The Constitution of India itself recognises the existence of these personal laws in terms which it deals with the topic falling under personal law in item 5 in the Concurrent List-List III. ... Thus it is competent either to the State or Union Legislature to legislate on topics falling within the purview of the personal law. ... [The framers of the Constitution] must have been aware that these personal laws needed to be reformed ... yet they did not wish that the provisions of the personal laws should be challenged by reason of the fundamental rights guaranteed in Part III of the Constitution and so they did not intend to include these personal laws within the definition of the expression laws in force.' See also in regards to MPL, *AWAG* [Ahmedabad Women Action Group] *and Ors v. Union of India* AIR 1997 SC 3614.

40 See *Danial Latifi v. Union of India* (*supra* n 23), not to the great satisfaction of the Muslim community.

the legislative and judicial 'opt-out' mechanisms for Muslims, in favour of a 'secular' legal status; and contrary to, as even the interpretation of the legislative framework—which had originally been enacted in accordance with Islamic legal principles—has evolved to seemingly set aside MPL. On a more general level, the example of MPL in India illustrates the difficulty in reconciling Article 2 (i.e. prohibition of discrimination) and Article 3 (i.e. primary consideration to be given to the best interest of the child) of the CRC in its transposition into a pluralist legal system where the protection of minority rights often involve derogations from the full implementation of the 'best interests of the child' principle.[41] The issues of custody and guardianship are at the forefront of such tensions, both for historical reasons as well as because of their inherently encroaching on the field of family law, traditionally regulated by personal law.[42]

2.2 Guardianship and Custody Under Muslim Personal Law and the Guardians and Wards Act 1890

Throughout the nineteenth and beginning of the twentieth centuries, Islamic law was considered as having pioneered the incorporation of the notion of the 'best interests of the child' within the Indian legal order, especially if compared to the then British colonial legal system (subsequently influencing Christian personal law) and Hindu personal law. Indeed, the 'best interests of the child' was largely a primary consideration in the application of MPL, whereas British and Hindu legal frameworks were still largely under the influence of *patria potestas*. This can be shown in regards to the curtailment of the powers conferred to the guardian in relation to the marriage and property of a minor, as well as in the issues surrounding the latter's custody.[43]

---

[41] The most recent example is the judicial review of the Right of Children to Free and Compulsory Education Act 2009, enacted in pursuance of Articles 21A and 15(5) of the Constitution and which provided for a compulsory reservation quota in favour of disadvantaged children, including within private un-aided institutions (section 12(1)(c) of the Act). The Supreme Court ruled that this section could not apply to minority institutions as it contravened Article 30(1) of the Constitution (i.e. the right of minorities to establish educational institutions), characterised as an absolute right (*Pramati Educational & Cultural Trust and Ors v. Union of India* WP (C) no 416 of 2012, SC 6 May 2014 (on file with author)). For a critical review of the argument leading to the ruling, see Kumar 2013.

[42] The other major fields of law in which the 'best interests of the child' have been incorporated are criminal law (see the Juvenile Justice (Care and Protection of Children) Act 2000 and the Commission for Protection of Child Rights Act (CPCRA) Act 2005), labour law (see the Child Labour (Prohibition and Regulation) Act 1986), and education (see the Right of Children to Free and Compulsory Education Act 2009).

[43] Unless otherwise stated, MPL's regulations in regards to guardianship (*wilāya*) and custody (*ḥaḍāna*) will be those of the Hanafi school, which is followed by the vast majority of Muslims in India.

2.2.1 *Powers of the Guardian in Relation to the Marriage of a Minor*

Within the South Asian social context, the issue of guardianship in marriage is deeply linked to the practice of child marriages. During colonial times, this question was left for the most part un-touched by British colonial authorities, their only influence being on the very lax characterisation of marital rape, which only applied if the wife was under the age of consent.[44] The Child Marriage Restraint Act 1929 had also but little influence in curbing the power of a guardian to marry off his ward.[45]

MPL was, however, deemed at the time to be more inclined than other personal laws to incorporate the 'best interests of the child' within its legal framework, especially in an era when Anglo-Muhammadan law was more fluctuant in relations to sources and interpretation. Hence, while child marriages were permitted under Islamic law, they were curtailed in that they would be void *ab initio* if the child was under the age of discretion[46] and voidable in the case of a minor who, although possessing understanding, had not attained puberty. This was notably the case when a minor's guardian had exercised his power of *jabr* in consenting to his/

---

[44] This threshold was originally set at 10 years old (section 375 (Exception) of the Indian Penal Code 1860); the age was then elevated to 12 years (Age of Consent Act 1891) and finally to sixteen (Criminal Law (Amendment) Act 1983). The notion of the 'best interests of the child' seem to have been foreign to British criminal law at the time, as illustrated by the lack of criminalisation of incest—merely an ecclesiastical sin to be dealt with according to personal law—which only entered English criminal law (but not Indian law) through the Punishment of Incest Act 1908 (8 Edw 7 C 45), whose purpose was to protect 'children from the vice', in pursuance of the Prevention of Cruelty to Children Act 1904 (4 Edw 7 C 15).

[45] Under the original Act, a female child was defined as being below fourteen (section 2(a)), and offences under the Act were not cognizable save for a complaint to be filed within 1 year of their alleged committal (section 9). Although a presumption of negligence was provided against guardians of the minor party of a child marriage (section 6(2)), the procedural requirements (such as the obligation of a preliminary inquiry (section 10)) made it almost unenforceable, whilst the marriages could still be recognised as valid under personal law (see *Munshi Ram v. Emperor* AIR 1936 All 111, where Justice Ganga Nath states: 'the question of validity and invalidity of the marriage is beyond the scope of the Child Marriage Restraint Act 1929'; see also *supra* n 21). The addition of the power of injunction (section 12 added by the Child Marriage Restraint (Amendment) Act 1938), the elevation of the minimum age of the bride to 15 years (Child Marriage Restraint (Amendment) Act 1949) and then to 18 years (Child Marriage Restraint (Amendment) Act 1978), and its total overhaul through the Prohibition of Child Marriage Act 2006, which has established the voidability of such marriage (section 3(1)) and rendered the offence cognizable and non-bailable (section 15), had little effect on the statute's already poor implementation (see Law Commission of India (2008) Proposal to Amend the Prohibition of Child Marriage Act, 2006 and Other Allied Laws, Report No. 205, pp. 33–34. http://lawcommissionofindia.nic.in/reports/report205.pdf. Accessed 31 January 2015).

[46] Ali 1880, p. 218.

her marriage, which the minor could then cancel upon attaining puberty by exercising the 'option of puberty' (*khiyār al-bulūgh*). Even though this option was only available against a marriage consented to by guardians other than the father and the grandfather, and immediately upon puberty, the judiciary progressively extended this period so as to start only when the bride or groom had been made aware of their legal right,[47] whilst also allowing it to be exercised against the father or grandfather if the resulting marriage was prejudicial to the interest of the child.[48] This paved the way to the enactment of the Dissolution of Muslim Marriages Act 1939, which opened the 'option of puberty' to all minors, irrespective of the person of their guardian, from the age of fifteen up to 18 years old.[49]

2.2.2 Powers of the Guardian in Relation to the Property and Person of the Minor

2.2.2.1 Characterisation of the 'Natural'/*de jure* Guardian vis-à-vis the *de facto* Guardian

According to traditional Islamic law in India, the 'natural' or *de jure* guardian of a minor is the father, and in his absence the grandfather.[50] Both can name a testamentary guardian (who may well be the mother) in the event of their passing; otherwise the role will fall unto their executor. However, the Muslim *de jure* guardian is not necessarily the 'factual' guardian of the minor, who might have the custody of the latter and/or have possession of his/her property. This right of 'factual' guardianship of the person in Muslim law constitutes *ḥaḍāna* and is separate from the 'factual' guardianship of the minor's estate, which has been coined as *de facto*

47 See *Bismilla Begum v. Nur Mahommad* AIR 1922 All 155.

48 See *Aziz Bano v. Mohammad Ibrahim Husain* AIR 1925 All 720. Justice Sulaiman in his judgment moved beyond the restrictive conditions whereby fraud or negligence on the part of the father or grandfather was required to exercise the 'option of puberty' and included, more widely, the sentiment of the bride (she was Shi'i and considered her marriage to a Sunni as being invalid): 'I hold that the marriage of Shiah woman with a Sunni husband … is valid and legal … [but] I also hold that such marriage, if performed by her guardian, no matter whether he is the father or the grandfather, is capable of being repudiated by her attaining puberty because it may affect her religious sentiment and may, therefore, be made to be to her manifest disadvantage. This is a liberal view to take and is obviously in accordance with justice, equity and good conscience as well as the requirements of the time.'

49 Section 2(vii) of the Act—provided the marriage had not been consummated.

50 One may also add the husband of his minor wife (section 19(a) of the Guardians and Wards Act 1890). Although in the presence of the father, he will not have a preferential right of guardianship under section 12 or 25. He may however sue for the restitution of conjugal rights.

guardianship (albeit sometimes exercised by the same person). Whereas the right of *ḥaḍāna* does not confer any power over the ward, a *de facto* guardian's actions on behalf of the minor may be given legal recognition.[51]

It was the Guardians and Wards Act 1890 (hereafter GAWA) which unified the previous laws pertaining to each Presidency and which is still of general application today. The drafting of the Act shows the will of British colonial authorities to both reflect on English law's own evolution in the matter[52] whilst at the same time granting sufficient leeway for each of India's communities to enforce their own notion of guardianship. As such, whereas the minor's welfare is to be taken in consideration in the appointment of a guardian[53] or in the issuance of orders in relation to his/her custody,[54] it shall however not be construed as 'to take away or derogate from any power to appoint a guardian … which is valid by the law to which the minor is subject' (i.e. personal law).[55] The only duties imposed on a 'natural'/*de jure* guardian in relation to the minor's property is to manage it as a 'man of ordinary prudence' acting reasonably for the

---

[51] There was no consensus on the issue, but in *Hasan Ali and Anr v. Mehdi Hussain and Ors* (1877) IRL 1 All 533 the sale of two minors' estate by a *de facto* guardian in order to satisfy an ancestral debt on the grounds of necessity was upheld (it is worth noting however that the minors had no *de jure* guardians alive). See also *Hurbai v. Hiraji Byramji Shanja* (1896) ILR 20 Bom 116; *Mafazzal Hosain v. Basid Sheikh* (1907) ILR 34 Cal 36; *Ram Charan Sanyal v. Anukul Chandra Acharjya* (1907) ILR 34 Cal 65, and *Ayderman Kutti v. Syed Ali* (1914) ILR 37 Mad 514. According to these decisions, a *de facto* guardian can act upon a minor's immoveable property if it complies with the requirement of necessity. In parallel, a question also arose as to whether a *de facto* guardian could take possession of a gift to a minor in order to render it effective. This practice seems to have been widespread among Indian Muslims, whose social set-up followed the joint family structure, where it was not uncommon for the head of the family (and thus *de facto* guardian) to make a gift of property to minors who would otherwise be excluded by Islamic inheritance rules (such as the maternal grandfather for instance). Indian Courts seem to have accepted this usage at first within the realm of MPL (*Nawab Jan v. Safiur Rahman* AIR 1918 Cal 786, for a general overview see Carroll 1994).

[52] At the time the British legal system was torn between two competing doctrines: on one hand the almost unfettered power of the father over his children within the Common Law, and on the other a greater consideration for the welfare of the child in the care of his/her mother through Equity. The latter progressively held sway following the fusion of the Court of Chancery and the Common Law Courts (Supreme Court of Judicature Act 1873 (Vic 36 & 37 C 66)). Through a series of legislative enactments the mother gained a preferential right of custody for minors of a tender age (up to 7 years through the Custody of Infant Act 1839 (2 & 3 Vic C 54), extended to 16 years in application of the Custody of Infant Act 1873 (36 & 37 Vic C 12)), whilst being allowed to apply for the child's guardianship in the event of the father's death in pursuance of the child's welfare (Guardianship of Infants Act 1886 (49 & 50 Vic C 27)). The subsequent presumption in favour of the mother's custodial privilege was dubbed the 'tender years doctrine'.

[53] Sections 7 and 17 of the Act.

[54] Sections 12 and 25.

[55] Section 6.

protection and benefit of the property.[56] Only if the guardian has been appointed or declared by the Court are his actions circumscribed in regards to the minor's immoveable property[57] and under judicial oversight,[58] consequently facing the risk of being voidable.[59]

The inherent tension between respecting personal legal provisions and the notion of the 'best interests of the child' is pronounced in the interaction between sections 7 and 17—whereby the appointment of a guardian must be guided by the welfare of child—and section 19, which forbids the Court from appointing or declaring a guardian of the minor's person if the latter's husband or father is alive.[60] Furthermore, section 19 provides for the removal of a 'natural'/*de jure* guardian under the sole condition of being unfit; the lack of a reference to the 'welfare of the child' thus renders sections 7 and 17 inoperative in that regard.[61] This apparent contradiction has served nonetheless a purpose, namely the legal empowerment of the *de facto* guardian within a socio-economical context dominated by the joint family structure, whilst at the same time precluding women from gaining full guardianship of their child.

As aforementioned, the paternalistic bias of English jurisprudence at the time, albeit recognising the nurturing role of mothers through the 'tender years' doctrine, was not ready to put the mother on par with the father in regards to guardianship. But perhaps more importantly, within a coparcenary structure whereby the

---

[56] Section 27.

[57] Section 29 runs thus: 'Where a person other than a Collector, or than a guardian appointed by will or other instruments, has been appointed or declared by the Court to be guardian of the property of the ward, he shall not, without the previous permission of the Court,—(a) Mortgage, or charge or transfer by sale, gift, exchange or otherwise, any part of the immoveable property, or—(b) lease any part of that property for a term exceeding 5 years or for any term extending more than 1 year beyond the date on which the ward will cease to be a minor.'

[58] Section 31 provides that the Court's permission for disposing immoveable property will be considered only 'in case of necessity or for an evident advantage to the ward'.

[59] Section 30.

[60] As a result, the paternal control over guardianship appears to override considerations of the welfare of the child, which only resurfaces if the 'natural' guardian applies for custody under section 25 of the Act. Despite some dissenting decisions (see *Kamini Mayi Debi v. Bhusan Chandra Ghose* AIR 1926 Cal 1193), the majority view was indeed that as a 'natural' guardian, the father (or be it the husband) cannot ask to be appointed or declared as such under section 19 (see *Annie Beasant v. Narayaniah* AIR 1914 PC 41; *Mt. Siddiquinissa v. Nizamuddin* AIR 1932 All 215; *Mst Teja Begum v. Gulam Rashul* AIR 1925 Lah 250). For a review of case law and the interaction of section 19 with sections 7 and 17, see Diwan 1978, pp. 151–166.

[61] At least until the 1940s, Courts had—in regards to the place of section 19 within the scheme of the Act and its plain wording—consistently upheld its overriding effect on sections 7 and 17, and concluded that if the welfare of the child was a primary consideration, it would be presumed to rest with the father unless he was proven unfit (see *Harbans Rai v. Mst Biro* AIR 1926 Lah 393; *Sheikh Moideen v. Kunha Devi* AIR 1929 Mad 81; *Mt. Siddiquinissa v. Nizamuddin* (n 60)).

'natural'/*de jure* guardian is not necessarily the manager of the joint property—and as such has *de facto* delegated the guardianship of the property of the minor to another[62]—allowing this other person's action or status as *de facto* guardian to be unrestrictedly challenged would put in peril the existence of the coparcenary as a whole. The protection the *de facto* guardian acquires from section 19 is thus dual in nature: first, he cannot be removed save by the *de jure* guardian; secondly, in acting as the *de jure* guardian's delegate, he does not have to be appointed or declared by the Court and hence is not circumscribed by the limitations imposed by section 29 relating to the transfer, mortgage or lease of the minor's immoveable property.[63] Although not mentioned in any textual source, the existence of the *de facto* guardian was soon recognised by Courts, the leading case being that of *Hunooman Pershad Pandey v. Mussamut Babooee Munraj Koonweree*,[64] where the Privy Council stated that:

> … under Hindu law, the right of a *bona fide* incumbrancer, who has taken as *de facto* guardian a charge of land, created honestly, for the purpose of saving the estate, or the benefit of the estate, is not affected by the want of union of the *de facto* with the *De jure* title.[65]

The powers conferred to the unappointed and undeclared *de facto* guardian are thus far greater under personal law than the ones otherwise provided by the secular legislation, which leaves in large part to the *de facto* guardian the extent to which the notion of the 'best interests of the child' ought to be exercised. In this regard, Muslim personal law was deemed far more protective of the *de facto* guardian's rights.

---

62 Within a coparcenary structure (typically the one of a Hindu Undivided Family), the child has a right to the ancestral property by birth (system of survivorship). The power of delegation from the *de jure* guardian to a *de facto* guardian (in most instances the manager of the coparcenary) is thus presumed.

63 Which in reality is but a share of a larger coparcenary estate otherwise managed by him. The scheme of the 1890 Act is hence very close to the one already put in place through Act XL of 1858 whereby a certificate of administration granted by the Court was not compulsory (section 3) and restrictions on actions taken in relation to immoveable property only applicable to guardians holding such certificate (section 18), despite contradicting interpretations as to the last point (see Ali 1880, p. 424).

64 (1856) 6 MIA 393. For a discussion of the case in light of its historic setting, see Trevelyan 1878, pp. 330–341.

65 The conditions of *bona fide* and 'benefit of the estate' bear a resemblance to the duties set forth in the 1890 Act in relation to the duties of the guardian of property (section 27), which runs thus: 'A guardian of the property of a ward is bound to deal as carefully as a man of ordinary prudence would deal with it, if it were his own and subject to the provisions of this Chapter, he may do all acts which are reasonable and proper for the realization, protection or benefit of the property.'

2.2.2.2 The Exclusive Powers of the 'Natural'/*de jure* Guardian under MPL vis-à-vis the *de facto* Guardian in Relation to Property

Muslims in India are not foreign to the notion of a *de facto* guardian. Most of them live under a joint family structure, which could be enforced up until the Shariat Act through custom and is otherwise statutorily established for certain sub-communities, notably in matters pertaining to inheritance, through integration of the survivorship system.[66] Nonetheless, in the beginning of the twentieth century, in the wake of both a growing divide between Hindu and Muslim political elites and the progressive fixation of MPL's sources within a set of authoritative texts, the use of custom was increasingly criticised by Muslim jurists as leading to legal uncertainty, perverting the due course of justice by incurring multiple delays through endless continuances, and, moreover, being least favourable to the 'best interests of the child'.[67]

Even before the Shariat Act, judges—of whom Ameer Ali[68] was at the forefront—had started to curb the influence of custom in the application of Muslim law in regards to guardianship. The leading case is that of *Imambandi v. Sheikh Haji Mutsaddi*,[69] where a wealthy man had died and left considerable immoveable property to three widows and several children. One of the widows—Zohra—had conveyed shares belonging to her and her two minor children to purchasers, who subsequently had asked for the mutation of names within administrative registers. The other widows and children opposed the sale, notably on the ground that Zohra was not the *de jure* guardian of her children and thus could not act on their behalf in regards to immoveable property. The purchasers argued that Zohra was acting as a *de facto* guardian and as such could alienate the property of the minors. Giving the judgment, Ameer Ali cancelled the sale and went to great length in his exposition of Islamic law in regards to guardianship.

---

[66] See *supra* n 5.

[67] The same arguments were used in Jammu and Kashmir when the judiciary clearly advocated for the instauration of a Muslim Personal Law Act superseding customary law (which was eventually enacted in 2007). Hence, Justice Hussain in an *obiter* urged the State to enact a clear rule of decision in regards to customary law, which 'resulted in chaos and often gives rise to endless litigation and causes delay … [whilst] some of the customs recorded are, on the face it, unreasonable' (*Yaqoob Laway and Ors v. Gulla and Anr* 2005 (3) JKJ 122).

[68] Syed Ameer Ali (d. 1928) was a prominent scholar, jurist and political activist. He was instrumental in advancing Indian Muslims' political agency, notably as a founding member of the All India Muslim League in 1906, whilst as a scholar he championed the modern development of Islam and Islamic law. In 1890, he was made a judge at the Calcutta High Court, before becoming the first Indian to be appointed member of the Judicial Committee of the Privy Council in 1909.

[69] (1918) 20 Bom LR 1022.

Relying on *Mata Din v. Ahmad Ali*, where a deed executed by the *de facto* guardian of an infant was annulled following a claim from the latter once he had attained his majority,[70] Ameer Ali set out to complete the decision by detailing both the character and duties of the guardian according to Muslim law, almost exclusively in reference to the *Al-Hidāya* and *Al-Fatāwā al-ʿĀlamgīriyya*,[71] whilst confirming their consistency with the framework of the GAWA. As such, he acknowledged that in the want of a 'natural'/*de jure* guardian, it is the responsibility of the sovereign (i.e. the Court) to appoint one, which might very well be the mother, who is not barred from being the executrix of the father and as such becoming a legal guardian. Notwithstanding, he does note a distinction between the guardian so appointed and the 'natural'/*de jure* guardian (i.e. father or grandfather). In the first case, the appointed guardian may not sell immoveable property which the minor inherited from his father; in the second, such power is granted, albeit restricted to cases of extreme necessity.[72] In the instance of a fatherless child (*yatīm*) and when no guardian has been appointed (either by the Court or through a will), the existence of a *de facto* guardian may be acknowledged, but with his actions being strictly limited and depending 'on the emergency which gives rise to the imperative necessity for incurring liabilities without which the life of the child or his perishable goods and chattels may run the risk of destruction'.[73] As such, even more so than an appointed guardian, the *de facto* guardian cannot under any circumstances dispose of the immoveable property of the minor. In fact, Justice Ali considers any action on the part of the *de facto* guardian to amount to a *faḍūlī* sale—i.e. a dependent or unauthorised sale which, although complete according to Hanafi doctrine, may be confirmed or dissolved by the proprietor. Although in the case of moveable property such sale is merely voidable, the sale becomes void *ab initio* at the request of the minor child if its object is immoveable property.[74]

---

70 (1911) 39 IA 1. Lord Robson in this instance stated that 'it is difficult to see how the situation of an unauthorised guardian is bettered by describing him as '*de facto*' guardian. He may, by his *de facto* guardianship, assume important responsibilities in relation to the minor's property, but he cannot thereby cloth himself with legal power to sell it'. However, his lordship shied away from answering the general question whether the acts of the Muslim *de facto* guardian were void or merely voidable, leaving the door open for their ratification by the ward upon attaining majority.

71 See *supra* n 12.

72 In the same manner, the purchase of property on behalf of the minor would only be available to the 'natural'/*de jure* guardian, in as much as it is for the benefit of the minor (see *Amir Ahmad v. Meer Nizam Ali* AIR 1952 Hyd 120).

73 *Supra* n 69. Ameer Ali also authorises a *de facto* guardian to accept gifts on behalf of his fatherless ward if it is purely advantageous.

74 In normal circumstance all *faḍūlī* sales are merely voidable, for they are based on the analogy with the notion of agency, but Justice Ali remarks that this concept cannot be applied to an infant.

> For the foregoing considerations their Lordships are of opinion that under the Mahomedan law a person who has charge of the person or property of a minor without being his legal guardian, and who may, therefore, be conveniently called a '*de facto* guardian', has no power to convey to another any right or interest in immoveable property which the transferee can enforce against the infant; nor can such transferee, if let into possession of the property under such unauthorised transfer, resist an action in ejectment on behalf of the infant as a trespasser. *It follows that, being himself without title, he cannot seek to recover property in the possession of another equally without title.*[75] [emphasis added]

Following this decision, Courts were increasingly restrictive in their characterisation of the actions of the *de facto* guardian of a Muslim minor. In *Vekama v. SV Chisty*[76] the sale of the minor's property by the mother acting as *de facto* guardian was deemed void; it was however held that the minor had to seek a declaration from the Court to recover the property and, moreover, that compensation under section 41 of the Specific Relief Act 1877 was available to the *bona fide* purchasers as an equitable remedy. In *Kharag Narain v. Hamida Khatoon*[77] however, such compensation was denied as the sale was considered void *ab initio*.

In *Imambandi v. Sheikh Haji Mutsaddi*, the 'best interests of the child' is not a determinant factor and is for the most part absent. Ameer Ali solely presumes that Islamic legal norms in relation to guardianship are inherently for the child's welfare[78] and thus finds it superfluous to ground his interpretation of Islamic law on the 'best interests of the child' principle. Rather—and in line with the historical context—he considers that it is by a precise and binding formulation (falling short of codification) of the law that such welfare will be achieved. As a consequence, the respected jurist in his taxonomical endeavour renders the issue of guardianship a question of law rather than of fact, supported by the drafting of the GAWA under which the 'welfare of the child' is a primary but not a 'paramount' consideration. In light of the legal framework of the day, Ameer Ali was certainly not wrong in his approach, and indeed Muslim wards were considered more protected than Hindu or even British and European ones. However, the reason underlying this preferential treatment was because Islamic legal norms *happened to be* more protective and not as a direct application of the notion of the 'best interests of child', which was merely incidental in the Justice's reasoning. As such, Ameer Ali did not foresee how this notion would soon be incorporated within the Indian legal

[75] *Supra* n 69.

[76] AIR 1951 Mad 399.

[77] AIR 1955 Pat 475.

[78] He had already stated in one of his earlier works that the numerous instances of misappropriation and embezzlement by family members under pre-Islamic customary law had '[necessitated] the introduction of most stringent rules for the protection of minors in Islamic legislation … [which are] extremely solicitous for the interests of minors' (Ali 1880, pp. 408–424).

system[79] nor how his stringent definition of guardianship in Islamic law would have adverse effects upon its interaction with the provisions of the GAWA. The same logic was nonetheless applied to the question of custody.

2.2.2.3 The Right of *Ḥaḍāna* vis-à-vis the Definition of the Guardian of the Minor's Person

The right of custody of a minor child by his/her mother[80] is a well-established principle in Islamic law, which in accordance with the 'tender years' doctrine rests on the presumption that a minor child would be best nurtured for by the mother during his/her young age[81] and thus grants her a preferential right of custody.[82] This right is inalienable,[83] and a mother can only be deprived of its exercise if she disqualifies herself, either by having contracted another marriage which is not

---

[79] The Justice did not envisage how Hindu law would so radically change its approach of guardianship in favour of the welfare principle, as imported from English law's own evolution on the subject. In fact, solicitous of the preservation of indigenous legal systems in India, he would add as an *obiter* to his judgment in *Imambandi v. Sheikh Haji Mutsaddi* (*supra* n 29) that: 'Their Lordships cannot help deprecating the practice which seems to be growing in some of the Indian Courts of referring to largely foreign decisions. However useful in the scientific study of comparative jurisprudence, foreign judgments … based often on considerations and conditions totally differing from those applicable to or prevailing in India, are only likely to confuse the administration of justice.'

[80] Which is transferable upon death or unfitness to the maternal grandparents and then to other maternal or uterine relatives.

[81] Hanafi law has set these ages at seven for a boy and until a girl attains puberty. On this last point, historically Muslim law was in apparent conflict with section 21 of Regulation X of 1793, re-iterated in section 27 of Act XL of 1858, under which the guardian of the person of a female minor should be entrusted with no one other than a female. In *Kajo and Ors v. Fuseehun* (1884) IRL 10 Cal 15, Justice Mitter, in reference to Ameer Ali, decided however to use *istiḥsān* (i.e. juristic preference) to favour Shafi'i law, which allows the mother's custody of a minor girl until marriage. The Act of 1890 has repealed these previous statutes and thus has reinstated the Hanafi doctrine.

[82] It is worth noting that despite the growing importance of the 'welfare of the child' principle in recent decades, the 'tender years' doctrine is still prevalent in India (see *Kurshid Gauhar v. Siddiqunnissa* AIR 1986 All 314; *Mahdu Baia v. Arun Khana* AIR 1987 Delhi 81).

[83] A divorce settlement, such as in the case of a *khul*' divorce, cannot supersede a mother's right of *ḥaḍāna* (*Hasmat Ali v. Smt Suraya Begum* AIR 1971 All 260), nor can a 'natural'/*de jure* guardian's will deprive her of this right (*In re Isso* AIR 1942 Sind 113).

within the prohibiting degrees of the minor,[84] by living an immoral life,[85] or by residing far away from the minor's 'natural'/*de jure* guardian.[86]

In order for these restrictions to apply however, the right of custody should not have been confused with the guardianship of the person. Indeed, following *Imambandi v. Sheikh Haji Mutsaddi*, it was now settled that 'the mother is entitled only to the custody of the one person of her minor child up to a certain age according to the sex of the child. But she is not the natural guardian: the father alone, or be he dead his executor (under Sunni Law) is the legal guardian'.[87] Notwithstanding, the question arose as to how to know if the custodian could be defined as the guardian of a person characterised as someone 'having the care' of a minor under section 4(2) of the GAWA. There could clearly be an inconsistency between the Act and MPL if the mother in virtue of her right of *ḥaḍāna* could claim the benefits of guardianship under the Act, on par with that of the father as the 'natural'/*de jure* guardian. To resolve this issue and in order for MPL to be consistent with the Act, it was first considered that a differentiation could be made between the 'actual' custodian and the 'legal' custodian.[88] Only the latter would be able to fit within the definition of guardian of a person as per the GAWA, whereby the word 'care' was construed as not relating to the nurturing or physical custody of the minor, but rather care for his/her material and

---

84 In *Ulfat Bibi v. Bafati* AIR 1927 All 581, the Court thus considered in a very patriarchal fashion that: 'A woman who has been divorced … and has married a second husband is not a person herself better suited than the father, however unsuitable the father may be, and not a person who ought to be heard to say that the father is unsuitable. She has abandoned her home and husband either by her own free will, or as the result of her conduct and in the eyes of the law she has lost the right to assert a claim against the father of the child.' Certain decisions have extended this disqualification as to be absolute even in the absence of the father as 'natural'/*de jure* guardian (*Mt Kundan Begam v. Mt Aisha Begam* AIR 1939 All 15). However, in *Tumina Khatun v. Gaharajan Bibi* AIR 1942 Cal 281, it was held that whereas a mother's remarriage with a stranger could deprive her of the *preferential* right of custody; it did not automatically bar her from claiming such right in the absence of a 'natural'/*de jure* guardian (i.e. father or grandfather).

85 Such was the case of prostitutes or 'courtisanes' (see *Mt Kundan Begam v. Mt Aisha Begam* (*supra* n 84)); however the Supreme Court held that in the case of an illegitimate child, a mother cannot be deprived of the minor's custody despite being a 'singing woman' and the mistress of the child's father (*Gohar Begum v. Suggi alias Nazma Begum* 1960 SCR (1) 597).

86 However, the appreciation of the suitable distance is a question of fact and 'it all depends on the circumstances. It the stay is only temporary or is forced or is due to circumstances beyond her control, it is difficult to hold that [the mother] should even then be deprived of the custody of her own children' (*Mt. Sakina Begam v. Malka Ara Begum* AIR 1948 Mad All 198).

87 *Supra* n 69.

88 *Mushaf Husain v. Mohammad Jawad* AIR 1918 Oudh 376.

educational needs, all vested in the 'natural'/*de jure* guardian and coined as 'constructive' custody.[89]

As such, and similarly to issues relating to the guardianship of property, the 'best interests of the child' is an almost irrelevant factor within the legal reasoning pertaining to custody. The aim is rather to fix stringent rules and definitions as to preserve Islamic law from any conflict it might have with custom and secular legislation. Within this endeavour, if the right of *ḥaḍāna* is cemented, it is however at the expense of any acknowledgment of the *legal* guardianship of the mother, being quarantined to a role of rearing in line with the 'tender years' doctrine. The notion of the 'best interests of the child'—although not completely absent—remained for the most part presumed and considered as the logical outcome of this process. However, both the adverse effects created by the aforementioned internal evolution of MPL in relation to the GAWA, as well as the influence of the external and growing recognition of this notion within the broader Indian legal system have ultimately led to its 'paramountcy'.

2.3 The Integration of the Notion of the 'Best Interests of the Child' Within Litigation Amongst Indian Muslims

In the middle of the twentieth century the Muslim personal law of custody and guardianship began to come into conflict with the 'best interests of the child'. The independence of India, coupled with the instauration of its constitutional system incorporating numerous fundamental rights, as well as the rapid transformation of other personal legal systems in line with English law's own evolution in the matter, have all but progressively isolated the application of Muslim law. Whilst the latter had been deemed ahead of its time in its integration of the notion of the 'best interests of the child' within its legal philosophy, it was soon considered adverse to its mechanical application under the newly interpreted GAWA provisions.

[89] In *Mt Siddiqunnissa Bibi v. Nizamuddin* (*supra* n 60), Justice Sen stated: '[the grandmother] has the right of hizanat till the girl attains puberty, but hizanat is not the same thing as guardianship of the person. The guardianship of the person rests in the father'. In *Mt Ghuran v. Syed Biaz Ahmad* AIR 1935 Oudh 492, Justice Srivastava would explain the rights and duties attached to the 'constructive' custody of the father as the guardian of the person: 'In my opinion hizanat is only custody for the rearing up of the child. Although the maternal grandmother has the right of hizanat under the Mahomedan Law, yet the father is responsible for providing funds for the maintenance of the minor and is her natural guardian. Thus he must be deemed to have the care of the person of the minor within the meaning of the definition of "guardian" in section 4(2) … even though the minor is not in his actual physical custody.' The elaboration of 'constructive' custody vested in the 'natural'/*de jure* guardian also definitely allows the latter to claim the restitution of his ward under section 25 of the 1890 Act, which is only open to guardians of the person as defined in section 4(2). Arguably however, this action was already open to them following *Mohideen Ibrahim Nachi v. Mahomed Ibrahim* AIR 1917 Mad 612, which had construed the section to refer to both actual and legal guardians, but not mere custodians.

2.3.1 Adverse Effects of MPL Under the GAWA Relating to the 'Best Interests of the Child'

The progressive 'fossilisation' of MPL's sources and reasoning, which arguably are definitely settled through the enactment of the Shariat Act, have rendered its application immune to juristic evolution or legislative reform. As such, in its application through the provisions of the GAWA, MPL appeared ill-prepared to cope with the consequences of the 'best interests of the child' principle and the substantive norms imposed on the minor's property and most importantly custody.

2.3.1.1 Adverse Effects on the Minor's Property

While the curtailment of the powers of the *de facto* guardian was aimed at protecting the child's interests from embezzlement by unscrupulous members of the family, it also had the effect of 'freezing' the assets of other relatives, especially if the property could not be divided.[90] This posed a problem in the event of an inheritance of immoveable property, whereby the co-heirs could not dispose of it until the ward's majority at the risk of a subsequent contract being void *ab initio*.[91] Directly in conflict with the minor's interest was the impossibility for the *de facto* guardian to take possession of a gift to the minor if the father was still alive, which would have had the result of the gift being declared void,[92] as a direct consequence of *Imambandi v. Sheikh Haji Mutsaddi*.[93] The voidability of such gifts through the *de facto* guardian had a direct impact on the minor's inheritance and thus financial well-being. Indeed, such gifts were often made in order to circumvent Islamic inheritance rules which could otherwise exclude certain classes of heirs or limit their shares, rules which were emphasised by the passing of the Shariat Act repealing all customary provisions in that regard. In order to

---

[90] See for instance *Kharag Narain v. Hamida Khatoon* (supra n 77).

[91] Certain High Courts were thus forced to be creative. *Maimunissa Bibi v. Abudul Jabbar* AIR 1966 Mad 470 thus held that the alienation of property by the mother in concurrence with the majority of the other heirs would be valid as far as the shares of the latter are concerned. In another instance, the mother acting as *de facto* guardian was allowed to transfer the property of the minor without the approval of the Court under section 29 of the 1890 Act in her capacity as guardian *ad litem* during a legal procedure (*Babu Gyanu v. Mohammed Sardar* AIR 1955 Nag 192).

[92] *Musa Miya Muhammad Shaffi v. Kadar Bax Khaj Bax* (1928) 30 Bom LR 766. See also *supra* n 49.

[93] *Supra* n 69.

circumvent this new legal framework, the Madhya Pradesh High Court[94] upheld a gift from a mother (and *de facto* guardian) to her 'adoptive' child by simply ignoring the most recent precedent in favour of an older one.[95] Given the inconsistency of the rulings however, the Supreme Court, whilst not directly tackling the issue, started to reinstate exceptions relating to the succession law of certain Muslim sub-communities.[96]

2.3.1.2 The Non-enforceability of *Ḥaḍāna*

Notwithstanding, the notion of the 'best interests of the child' was even more directly challenged by the non-enforceability of the right of *ḥaḍāna*, when –paradoxically—claimed under section 12[97] or more commonly section 25 of the GAWA, despite the latter's wording conditioning an order from the Court to return a minor to his or her guardian precisely on the former's welfare. However, read in conjunction with section 17(1) enjoining the Court to name a guardian consistent with the law the minor is subject to, section 7(3) [under which a guardian cannot be named unless the previous guardian has been removed (to be read in connection with section 39(j) conditioning the removal of a guardian—save for ill-treatment or being unfit—to personal law)] and section 19 [prohibiting the Court from appointing or declaring a guardian of the person if either the husband or the father of the minor is alive] have—when coupled with the interpretation of MPL in *Imambandi v. Sheikh Haji Mutsaddi*[98]—made it almost impossible for a mother to ask the Court for the return of a child which has been removed from her.

Indeed, while the possibility for the 'natural'/*de jure* guardian to act under section 25 had been allowed from a very early stage,[99] a mother in the presence of the father had virtually no *locus standi* under the 'constructive' custody doctrine. As such, if the father happened to have forcefully taken away the child from her custody, she could not exercise her right of *ḥaḍāna* under section 25 as she was deemed not to have been the guardian of the person of the minor (as defined in section 4(2)) but a mere 'actual' custodian, and thus she could not pursue legal

---

94 *Muni Bai v. Abdul Gani* AIR 1959 MP 225.

95 *Ameeroonissa Khatoon v. Abedoonissa Khatoon* (1875) LR 2 IA 87, which stressed only the *bona fide* nature of the gift for it to be complete, irrespective of its delivery. However, this solution was not upheld by other High Courts, which followed the more recent Privy Council decision and thus voided the gift (see *Abdul Raheman Mahamud v. Mishrimal Shrimal Picha* AIR 1960 Bom 210).

96 Notably in regards to Khojas and Kutchi Memons (see *Controller of Estate Duty Mysore, Bangalore v. Haji Abdul Sattar Sait and Ors.* AIR 1972 SC 2229).

97 Empowering the Court to make an interlocutory order for the production of the child in order to place him under temporary custody of an appointed person.

98 *Supra* n 69.

99 See *Mohideen Ibrahim Nachi v. Mahomed Ibrahim* (*supra* n 89).

action under the 1890 Act.[100] The overall guiding principle upheld by High Courts was to construe the Act in accordance with MPL regulations if the welfare of the child was not prejudiced; the child's welfare, however, was one concern among others and in any case was deemed not to take precedence over personal law. As such, 'where the [personal] law definitely lays down that an appointment of a certain guardian cannot be made, the [secular, i.e. 1890 Act] law cannot disregard the [personal law] law even in the interest of the minor'.[101]

2.3.2 *The Changing Nature of the Notion of the 'Best Interests of the Child' Within Muslim Disputes*

The mechanical application of Muslim personal law under the GAWA was rendered even more problematic after it appeared that the former's norms, applied under *habeas corpus* proceedings, were more favourable to the child's interest, which incurred a change in the interpretation of the GAWA provisions, notably in favour of the mother or maternal relative. However, the notion of the 'best interests of the child' was still viewed through a strong paternalistic bias. Its changing nature from a 'primary' to a 'paramount' consideration within other personal laws did however change its role within guardianship and custody disputes amongst Muslims, but at the expense of MPL's traditional jurisdiction.

2.3.2.1 The Influence of the Notion of the 'Best Interests of the Child' Under *Habeas Corpus* Proceedings

In light of the impossibility to claim the right of *ḥaḍāna* under the procedural provisions of the GAWA, mothers began to use the procedure of *habeas corpus* instead in order to retrieve the custody of minor children.[102] In this regard, their claim was not only rendered admissible but also more likely to succeed. The High

[100] The legal logic at play would even counter the 'tender years' doctrine as even a child of 4 years could not be retrieved by his mother, as in *Hasmat Ali v. Smt Suraya Begum* (*supra* n 83). The same reasoning applied to section 12, whereby it was considered that being inserted in the chapter dealing with the appointment of guardians, the mother—not being qualified to be a guardian in the presence of the father—also lacked *locus standi* (see *Ruzmaniben Tribhovandas Jethabhai v. Minor Narmada* AIR 1962 Guj 227).

[101] *Ansar Ahmad v. Samidan* AIR 1928 Oudh 120.

[102] This procedure was available under the Letter Patents of the different High Courts, then under section 491 of the Code of Criminal Procedure 1898, and finally pursuant to Article 226 of the Constitution of India. Acting as *parents patria*, the High Courts are free from the 1890 Act, in line with the procedure's English origins whereby 'in the jurisdiction *Parents Patria* there are unquestionably some principles of judicial inquiry which are not observed' (per Lord Devlin in *In re K.* [1965] AC at 239).

Courts were not bound by the GAWA (lacking jurisdiction to determine guardianship)[103] but only by personal law, and interestingly they did not follow the 'constructive' custody doctrine.[104] Subsequently, they tended to be considerably more favourable to the mother or maternal relatives, even in the presence of the father, whilst putting greater emphasis on the welfare of the child, albeit influenced by the 'tender years' principle.[105]

The growing discrepancy in the formulation of MPL between the two procedures forced the High Courts to react. They did so by slowly incorporating the notion of the 'best interests of the child' within custody disputes under the GAWA. Clumsily at first,[106] they nevertheless tended to abolish the differentiation between 'actual' and 'constructive' custody in order to bestow on the mother (or maternal relative) the guardianship of the person of the minor in her own right.[107] However, although the 'welfare of the child' was to be of 'paramount' concern, it was interpreted as being consistent with MPL, so that the newly based right of *ḥaḍāna* could not exceed its prescribed duration[108] unless achieved by declaring the father unfit.[109] Moreover, in their appreciation of the facts, the Courts still held a some-

[103] Which, since 1984 is under the exclusive jurisdiction of Family Courts (*supra* n 32). It was however recently held that custody could be determined through a *habeas corpus* proceeding, albeit in application of the substantive provisions of the 1890 Act (*M Kuthbunisha v. SA Jabar*, OP no 777/2008 and A no 5738/2008, HC Madras, 2 February 2009 (on file with author)).

[104] Hence, it could be submitted that the restrictive notion of 'constructive' custody is but an invention of Anglo-Muhammadan law in light of the 1890 Act, rather than being something taking its sources directly from Islamic legal precepts.

[105] See *Mt Haidri Begum v. Jawwad Ali Shah* AIR 1934 All 722.

[106] Often cited, *Mt Samiunnissa v. Mt Saida Khatun* AIR 1944 All 202 declared the mother guardian of her minor daughter's person under section 17 of the 1890 Act, arguing that if 'the personal law of the minor concerned is to be taken into consideration, … that law is not necessarily binding upon the Court which must look to the welfare of the minor consistently with that law'. However, in not addressing the interaction between sections 17 and 19 of the Act, even though the father was still alive, one could submit that the Court decided this case *per incuriam*.

[107] In *Zynab Bi Alias Bibijan v. Mohammad Ghouse Mohideen* AIR 1952 Mad 284, the mother's claim under section 25 of the 1890 Act was declared admissible upon the grounds she could be qualified as a *de facto* guardian of the person of her minor children per section 4(2). This is one of the first instances where the term 'care' was not construed as to refer exclusively to the 'natural'/*de jure* guardian of the child. The notion of the welfare of the child under the guise of the 'tender years' doctrine was also put forward: 'in a petition of this nature, the paramount consideration to be taken into account is the welfare of the minors. The boy being less than 2 years, it is ordinarily necessary that he should have the benefit of the mother's milk'. Notwithstanding, this position was resisted by other High Courts (see *Hasmat Ali v. Smt Suraya Begum* (n 83)).

[108] See *Shama Beg v. Khawaja Mohiuddin Ahmed* ILR 1972 Delhi 73.

[109] See *Mohammad Saddiq and Anr v. Wafati* AIR 1948 Oudh 51.

times very strong patriarchal bias in favour of the father's right of custody.[110] Therefore, although in practice the judicial decisions often led to the same result in favour of the father's right of custody, their legal basis was fundamentally transformed, moving from the mother's legal incapacity to a factual or social basis.

As such, although the Courts were prospectively freed to reflect societal change,[111] their judgments did not make clear whether the notion of the 'best interests of the child' superseded personal law as a 'secular' innovation contained in the GAWA or if it were in fact the application of the 'spirit' of Muslim personal law, which had otherwise been legally restrained by the same Act.[112]

2.3.2.2 The Paramountcy of the 'Best Interests of the Child' in Relation to Muslim Personal Law

It is worth noticing that from the 1940s onwards; the welfare of the child has increasingly been qualified as 'paramount', although this term is nowhere to be found in the GAWA. Here, one cannot deny the influence of English law which, despite Ameer Ali's warning,[113] has consistently been referred to by Indian Courts.[114] Indeed, the term's first inception is in section 1 of the Guardianship of Infants Act 1925,[115] stating that the welfare of the child should be of 'first and par-

[110] Hence, in *Mir Mohamed Bahauddin v. Mujee Bunnisa Begum Sahiba* AIR 1952 Mad 280, the Court granted the father's petition to remove his minor daughter from the custody of her mother on the grounds the latter had re-married for 'it is unlikely that a woman who has married a second husband would be in a position to pay much attention to the upkeep and well-being of the child as she would, if she had not taken to a second husband'; the father, who also had re-married was however deemed a 'fit and proper person to take charge of the custody of the minor … [so as the child] could very well live with the father and it is stated that the father's mother is in the family to look after the child'.

[111] For instance, in favour of women's growing social independence movement, Courts no longer considered their social capacity in light of their economic capabilities (which at the time was more often than not in the hands of the father/husband) and thus disregarded any financial argument usually advocated as being conducive to the child's welfare (*Mohd Yunus v. Smt Shamsad Bano* AIR 1985 All 217).

[112] It was thus decided in principle that in case of a conflict between the 1890 Act and personal law, the former would prevail (*Rafiq v. Bashiran* AIR 1963 Raj 289), but left open the question of the interaction between section 17 (child welfare) and section 19 (guardianship of the person as the right of the father). Hence, was the child's welfare truly limited by MPL, or rather by the Act—precisely contrary to the MPL 'guiding principle'? Mr Latifi (counsel for the appellant, the maternal grandmother) argued in *Shama Beg v. Khawaja Mohiuddin Ahmed* (*supra* n 108) for the latter—although unsuccessfully in this case—interestingly referring to Ameer Ali as an authority.

[113] See *supra* n 79.

[114] Paras Diwan remarks that 'there is hardly any argument before a [Indian] court where a counsel would not try to cite and a judge would not try to rely on an English authority' (Diwan 1978, p. 152).

[115] 15 & 16 Geo 5 C 45.

amount' consideration, and although the statute was not applicable to India, the notion would travel. The implication of this semantic innovation was not perceived at first and was rather used as a synonym for 'primary'—with the 'best interests of the child' being one concern among others, such as the application of personal law. However, a set of legislative reforms pertaining to personal laws, the adoption of public policies revolving around children rights and the emergence of judicial activism in the 1970s contributed in making this notion central to custody and guardianship litigation.

Indeed, sections 12 and 13 of the Hindu Minority and Guardianship Act 1956 provide that in any appointment or declaration of a guardian, the 'welfare of the minor shall be *the* paramount consideration' [emphasis added]. With it subsequently being the *sole* criterion upon which guardianship must be decided within Hindu personal law, the 'best interests of the child' has forced a re-interpretation of the interaction between sections 17 and 19 of the GAWA within litigation amongst Hindus, and has thus entrenched section 17's superseding nature.[116] Irrespective, section 2 of the 1956 Act clearly states that the provisions of the statute shall be 'in addition to' and not 'in derogation of' the GAWA and thus left the interaction between section 17 and section 19 unresolved in regards to other personal laws.

Notwithstanding, the reform of Hindu law naturally had ripple effects and led to the State adopting a number of policies in regards to children, reiterating the 'paramount' nature of their welfare but falling short of making it the sole criterion.[117] Nevertheless, under the influence of English judicial interpretation,[118] the term 'paramount' soon implied the overriding nature of the notion of the 'best

[116] Hence in *Rattan Amol Singh v. Kamaljeet Kaur* AIR 1961 Punj 51, Justice Dua stated: 'By virtue of section 2 of the Hindu Minority and Guardianship Act, 1956, we are obliged to read together and harmonize the provisions of section 19 of the Guardians and Wards Act and section 13 of the Hindu Minority and Guardianship Act; construing them together, the rigour and prohibition contained in clause (b) of section 19 of the Guardians and Wards Act must be considered to have been relaxed to a great extent in the interest of the minor's welfare.'

[117] Department of Social Welfare, National Policy for Children (no. 1-14/74-CDD, 22 August 1974) 3(xiv) states: 'existing laws should be amended so that in all legal disputes whether between parents or institutions, the interest of children are given paramount consideration'. It is worth noting, however, that in line with the wording of Article 3 of the CCR, the new policy of 2013 uses the term 'primary' instead of 'paramount', although formally including Court decisions in its realm (Ministry of Women and Child Development, The National Policy for Children, 2013 (no. 16-1/2012-CW-I, 26 April 2013) 3(vii)).

[118] Per Lord MacDermott in *J v. C* [1970] AC at 710: '[Paramount consideration] must mean more than that the child's welfare is to be treated as the top item in a list of items relevant to the matter in question. I think they connote a process whereby, when all the relevant facts, relationships, claims and wishes of the parents, risks, choices and other circumstances are taken into account and weighted, the course to be followed will be that which is most in the interests of the child's welfare ... because [paramountcy] rules upon or determines the course to be followed.'

interests of the child', at least in regards to custody disputes. In regards to the ones involving Muslims, a series of decisions illustrates this trend, albeit under specific legal and factual circumstances. In *Hassan Bhatt v. Ghulam Mohamad*, the welfare of the child was deemed to override his personal law[119]; and in *Smt Ainunnissa v. Mukhtar Ahmad*,[120] in consideration of the best interests of the child, the father's claim for the custody of his 10-year-old son was dismissed and the minor's own preference to remain with his mother acknowledged.[121] There remained however many discrepancies both within and between High Courts. Moreover, given the nature of the proceedings relating to guardianship and the delays incurred by litigation in India, there are but very few cases which were pursued in front of the Supreme Court in order to unify the law.

However, in 2006 the apex Court in *Nil Ratan Kundu and Anr v. Abhijit Kundu* seemed to be handed the opportunity to settle the issue of the interaction between sections 17 and 19 of the GAWA in favour of the former, stating that:

> In our opinion, in such cases, it is not the 'negative test' that the father is not 'unfit' or disqualified to have custody of his son/daughter which is relevant but the 'positive' test that such custody would be in the welfare of the minor which is material and it is on that basis that the Court should exercise the power to grant or refuse custody of a minor in favour of father, mother or any other guardian.[122]

Moreover, the Court adds that custody cases 'cannot be decided solely by interpreting legal provisions', that in selecting a guardian the welfare of the minor should be the 'paramount' consideration and that for this purpose jurisdictions are bound by neither 'statutes, strict rules of evidence or procedure nor … precedents'. It thus seemed that the notion of the 'best interests of the child' is to be considered as superseding both personal law and the GAWA, falling short of being a constitutional right. However, for the above reasons and also because the case involved a dispute among Hindus, it was still in doubt if it applied in a Muslim context.

In *Athar Hussain v. Syed Siraj Ahmed* such context arose,[123] and the Supreme Court was directly confronted with a conflict between MPL and the provisions of the GAWA as previously interpreted. The maternal grandfather was awarded interim custody of two minors, which the father successfully contested as their 'natural'/*de jure* guardian; the grandfather appealed the decision in front of the High Court of Karnataka, which decided in his favour per MPL as previously

---

[119] AIR 1961 J&K 5; however, the state of Jammu and Kashmir was not at the time subject to a Shariat Act.

[120] AIR 1975 All 67.

[121] Nonetheless, in this particular case the paternity of the child was put in question. Furthermore, while section 17(3) of the 1890 Act provides for the minor's opinion to be taken into account, it is left to the discretion of the Court to assess if he/she can formulate an 'intelligent' preference. There has thus been conflicting views on the admissibility of a minor's testimony: for instance, in *S Rama Iyer v. K V Natraja* (AIR 1948 Mad 294) a girl as old as fourteen was deemed not to be able to formulate such a preference.

[122] 2008 9 SCC 413.

[123] AIR 2010 SC 1417.

interpreted.[124] The father appealed that judgment in front of the Supreme Court. Whilst upholding the High Court's decision, the apex Court based its reasoning on different grounds. While it did find the High Court's statement relating to the superseding nature of personal law over the Act's provision 'doubtful', it interestingly did not explicitly strike personal law down completely. However, it reiterated that the 'welfare of the child' was a paramount consideration which trumped personal law—but only as custody is concerned:

> As far as the matter of guardianship is concerned, the prima facie case lies in favour of the father as under section 19 of the [1890 Act], unless the father is not fit to be a guardian, the Court has no jurisdiction to appoint another guardian. ... However, the question of custody is different from the question of guardianship. The father can continue to be the natural guardian of the children; however, the considerations pertaining to the welfare of the child may indicate lawful custody with another friend or relative as serving his/her interest better.[125]

As such, the Supreme Court—in an effort to articulate in a consistent manner the 'best interests of the child' principle, the provisions of the GAWA, and personal law—seem to have resurrected the 'constructive' custody doctrine. However, 'constructive' custody is no longer used to assert the father's 'natural'/*de jure* right of physical custody, but rather is a 'natural' duty of maintenance. Similarly, if the right of *ḥaḍāna* is considered to qualify as a right of guardianship of the person as per section 4(2) of the GAWA, *prima facie* lying in favour of the mother or maternal relatives, it is similarly not absolute and its duration may be shortened or extended in consideration of the child's welfare.

2.4 Concluding Remarks: The 'Best Interests of the Child', a Foreign Notion to Muslim Personal Law in India?

Despite assertions by the High Courts and the Supreme Court, the law of guardianship in regards to litigation amongst Muslims is not well settled in India. Furthermore, as per the apex Court's own rulings, Family Courts are not bound by strict procedural or substantive rules when it comes to determining custody, a freedom emphasised, moreover, by the fact the parties are not represented by legal counsel in this specialised jurisdiction other than in the capacity of *amicus curiae*.[126] Coupled with its obligation to first settle a dispute through mediation,[127] and given that guardianship is more often than not an incidental question

124 On the basis that his right of *ḥaḍāna* amounted to the 'legal' guardianship of the person of the children (see *supra* n 107). Being an interim order, the conflict was between the interaction of sections 12 and 19 of the Act, the former not explicitly mentioning his/her 'welfare' but his/her 'protection'.

125 *Supra* n 123.

126 Family Courts Act 1984, section 13.

127 Ibid section 9.

accompanying divorce proceedings, empirical studies tend to show that in practice the 'welfare of the child' is far from the primary concern of the Courts, which—despite not being bound by the principle—tend to uphold parental agreements and confirm interim custody injunctions based on the individual judge's own subjective criteria.[128] Moreover, regardless of the *suo moto* jurisdiction of the Court in matters pertaining to guardianship,[129] it is rarely exercised save in extreme circumstances, and family unity remains a constant within Indian legislation.[130] Hence, judges tend not to intervene within agreed-upon familial relations, especially when invoking personal law.

The notion of the 'best interests of the child' as a foreign or 'secular' concept superseding Muslim personal law remains debatable within the Indian legal context. Indeed, although Courts may have grounded its application on MPL's own legal categories, history shows the latter were formed precisely to evade its paramount character. Whether these Anglo-Muhammadan provisions were themselves in contradiction to Islamic law's original *ethos* is equally questionable, and it can—paradoxically—be argued either way in reference to the same overarching authority (i.e. Syed Ameer Ali) who influenced Muslim guardianship law in India perhaps more than anyone else. Notwithstanding, there has never been an attempt by Courts to internally incorporate the notion of the 'best interests of the child' within MPL solely on its own sources or through notions such as *maqāṣid al-sharīʿa* as was done in the case of unilateral divorce.[131] Additionally, Courts have been precluded from elevating the 'best interests of the child' into an enforceable constitutional principle superseding Muslim personal law by guardianship's status as one of the subject matters listed within the Shariat Act as well as by the Act's relative immunity to fundamental rights provisions of the Constitution. As such, as the law stands it is only applicable to custody—or 'actual'/'physical' guardianship of the person—and not to the guardianship of the property of the minor, despite it being sometimes adverse to the latter's interest.

---

[128] Unlike criminal proceedings (most notably under the Prohibition of Child Marriage Act 2006), there are no official statistics pertaining to litigation under the 1890 Act. Some empirical studies have been conducted within specific Family Courts (see for instance in regards to Mumbai, Bajpai 2005), but inferring generalisations within a jurisdiction as wide and diverse as India is a hypothetical effort at best.

[129] Sections 12 and 39 of the 1890 Act. However, while section 12 gives unfettered powers to the Court in matters of custody, section 39 circumscribes the Court's jurisdiction over individuals declared to be or appointed as guardians.

[130] As aforementioned (*supra* n 32), Family Courts Act 1984, section 3(4)(a) requires that Family Court appointments be made so as to ensure a judiciary committed to protecting the welfare of the child *on par* with the institution of marriage, whilst The Juvenile Justice (Care and Protection of Children) Act 2000, section 41(1), states that 'the primary responsibility for providing care and protection to children shall be that of his family'.

[131] See *supra* n 15.

References

Ali SA (1880) The Personal Law of the Mahommedans. W H Allen & Co, London
Ali SA (1985) Mahommedan Law: Compiled from Authorities in the Original Arabic, 4th and 5th edn., 2 vol. Himalayan Books, New Delhi
Anderson A (1993) Islamic Law and the Colonial Encounter in British India. In: Arnold D, Robb P (eds) Institutions and Ideologies, a SOAS South Asia Reader. Curzon Press, London, pp 165–185
Baillie N (ed) (1875) Digest of Moohummudan Law on the Subjects to Which It Is Usually Applied by British Courts of Justice in India, 2 vol. Smith, Elder & Co, London
Bajpai A (2005) Custody and Guardianship of Children in India. Fam Law Q 39:441–457
Carroll L (1994) Definition and Interpretation of Muslim Law in South Asia: The Case of Gift to Minors. Islamic Law Soc 1:83–115
Deva S (2009) Public Interest Litigation in India: A Critical Review. Civ Justice Q 28:19–40
Diwan P (1978) Law of Parental Control, Guardianship and Custody of Minor Children. Eastern Book Company, Lucknow
Engineer AA (2008) Rights of Women in Islam. Sterling, New Delhi
Fyzee AAA (2005) Outlines of Muhammadan Law, 5th edn. Oxford University Press, New Delhi
Ghose R (2014) Islamic Law and Imperial Space: British India as "domain of Islam" circa 1803–1870. J of Colonialism and Colonial Hist 15(1)
Giunchi E (2010) The Reinvention of the Shari'a under the British Raj: In Search of Authenticity and Certainty. J Asian Stud 69:1119–1142
Guenther AM (1999) Dar Al-Harb or Dar Al-Islam: The Controversy Regarding British Presence in India 1870–72. American Oriental Society annual meeting, Baltimore, MD, March 1999
Kumar V (2013) The Right of Children to Free and Compulsory Education Act, 2009: A Juridical Critique of Its Constitutional Perspective. J Indian Law Inst 55:21–44
Mahmood T (1980) The Muslim Law of India. Law Book Co, Allahabad
Marghinani A, Hamilton C (tr) (2008) The Hedaya: Commentary on the Islamic Laws, 2nd edn. Kitab Bhavan, New Delhi
Monckton Jones ME (1918) Warren Hastings in Bengal, 1772–1774. Clarendon Press, Oxford
Mulla DF, Hidayatullah M, Hidayatullah A (eds) (1990) Principles of Mahomedan Law, 19th edn, Tripathi, Bombay
Sinha BS (1976) Custom and Customary Law in Indian Jurisprudence. Indian Socio-Legal J 2:83–97
Trevelyan EJ (1878) The Law Relating to Minors in the Presidency of Bengal. Thacker, Spink & Co, Calcutta
Tyabji FB, Tayyibji M (eds) (1968) Muslim Law: the Personal Law of Muslims in India and Pakistan, 4th edn. Tripathi, Bombay

Chapter 3
Indonesia

Euis Nurlaelawati

Abstract This chapter discusses the legal rules and practices of custody and guardianship in Indonesia. It explores the introduction of the rules in both the law of marriage and the *Kompilasi Hukum Islam* and looks at the details and dynamics of the rules. It also investigates the introduction and the implementation of the notion of the best interests of children in this regard by scrutinizing the relevant articles as well as by studying, in particular, legal decisions issued by religious courts and the discretion afforded their judges. Deploying the socio-historical legal approach, it argues that the introduction of the notion is evident and clear in the Indonesian legal system, even if the notion is vague and implemented according to the subjective preference of the judges. It discloses that although the Indonesian government has developed the procedural rules of both custody and guardianship and that a few judges have tackled custody and guardianship cases in ways to realize the protection of the child's welfare, it is mainly traditionalism and the conservative Islamic social frame of the parents that shape the concept of the best interests of the child in Indonesia.

Keywords Custody · Guardianship · Islamic law · The best interests of the child · Legal practices · Judges · Islamic court · State law · Indonesia

Much of the data in this article has been used in earlier article of the author entitled 'The Legal Fate of Indonesian Muslim Women at Court: Divorce and Child Custody', in Tim Lindsey and Helen Paushacker, Religion, Law and Intolerance in Indonesia, Routledge, 2016.

The author is a senior lecturer at the Faculty of Sharia and Law, State Islamic University, Yogyakarta, Indonesia.

E. Nurlaelawati (✉)
Universitas Islam Negeri Sunan Kalijaga, Jl. Adisucipto, Yogyakarta 55281, Indonesia
e-mail: enurlaelawati@hotmail.com

N. Yassari et al. (eds.), *Parental Care and the Best Interests of the Child in Muslim Countries*, DOI 10.1007/978-94-6265-174-6_3

Contents

3.1 Introduction

This chapter explores the legal rules on custody and guardianship in Indonesian law. It investigates the rules on parental care in the Marriage Law of 1974 (Law No. 1/1974) and in the *Kompilasi Hukum Islam* (Presidential Instruction No. 1/1991, henceforth KHI) and looks at the details and dynamics of the rules on both custody and guardianship. Further, it looks into the introduction and implementation of the notion of the best interests of the child by scrutinizing its legal basis and its implementation by the courts. Looking at the judicial discretion of religious court judges in particular, it explores how the notion of the best interests of the child has been introduced and maintained in the Indonesian legal system.

Custody and guardianship are two of several rights of children to be borne by their parents or in their absence by their representatives. Detailed regulations were introduced into Indonesian law to govern the implementation of these rights, with the main concern of the regulations being the best interests of the child. Classical Islamic legal books discuss both custody and guardianship in a comprehensive way, and legal codifications in Muslim countries include regulations devoted to these issues. Indonesia is not an exception as we shall see.

As a national law, the Marriage Law applies to all Indonesian citizens regardless of their religious affiliation. Conversely, the KHI was issued to provide legal references for Muslim judges in religious courts and is therefore specifically addressed to Indonesian Muslims. With regard to custody and guardianship the KHI deals with the topic more comprehensively than the Marriage Law.

Custody refers to the physical care and upbringing of a minor, including its physical presence with the custodian. It encompasses the right to make day-to-day decisions regarding the child's education, medical treatment and general activities. Article 1(g) KHI defines 'custody' as 'an act of bringing up, taking care of, and educating a child until it reaches majority or is able to care for itself.' Therefore, custody can only be exercised over the minor's person, not over his or her property. The custodian's duties are narrower than those of a 'guardian', who according to Article 1(h) is defined as the person in charge of the care and control of a minor's person or property in its best interests.[1] Guardianship includes the right to make decisions about the minor's upbringing and the disposal of his/her property. The KHI states that 'guardianship is a right that is awarded to a person to act as legal actor representing a child for the child's interest.'

The word 'care' in Article 1(h) KHI indicates 'looking after' in a wider sense than 'custody,' which implies only the 'physical keeping' of the child. Article 107(1) KHI states that guardianship is a right of a child aged under twenty-one or of unmarried children (without a gender perspective), and it encompasses the personal care *and* the protection of the child's property (Article 107(2) KHI). If a guardian fails to perform his task or ignores his task, the court can appoint one of the child's relatives to act as his or her guardian (Article 107(3) KHI). Further, the article advises that it is best to appoint the guardian from within the family of the child.

Guardianship, in particular the duty to financially support the child, falls on the father and his relatives. While the law does not explicitly prescribe the priority of male relatives in guardianship (in the absence of the father), practice suggests this to be the case as this fact is based on the classical Islamic legal opinions on guardianship, as will be discussed below. Thus, decision making about the person and property of minor children is consistently regarded as being vested in the father and in his absence in his (male) relatives.

3.2 Parental Care and the Introduction of the Notion of the Best Interests of the Child

3.2.1 Overview of the Rules on Parental Care in the Marriage Law and the Kompilasi Hukum Islam

Family law is a field of law that has received significant attention from the government. Since Muslims form the majority of the population in Indonesia, family law rests on traditional Islamic family law.[2] Further, the Indonesian government also

[1] Bajpai 2005, pp. 441–457.

[2] Hooker 1998, pp. 107–108.

incorporated a number of local practices and customs as well as statutory law that together with Islamic law build the three sources of family law in today's Indonesia. To understand Indonesian family law applied to Muslims, due attention must be given to the KHI, as well as to the Marriage Law of 1974. The KHI is a compilation of Islamic, mainly Shafi'i rules applied by the judges of the Islamic courts (and Muslims in general), while the Marriage Law applies to all citizens of Indonesia and is therefore to be referred to by judges of both Islamic and civil courts. It must be noted that there are two courts that have jurisdiction over familial issues in Indonesia,[3] namely civil and Islamic courts. While civil courts also hear criminal cases brought by both Muslim and non-Muslims, the Islamic court only hears familial cases where the parties are Muslims. Since 2006, Islamic court have had broader jurisdiction as they are also entitled to hear commercial cases related to Muslim parties.

The Marriage Law provides judges of both courts with a legal basis when dealing with family law issues. It has introduced, among other elements, the necessity to obtain court permission for a polygamous marriage or for the conclusion of underage marriages (under twenty-one) when the parents or guardians or pertinent relatives differ on the permissibility of the marriage. Further, the judges are competent to handle cases related to: the marriageable age; marriage dispensation; marriage prevention; marriage cancellation; divorce by repudiation; a divorce suit; settlement of common property; child custody and alimony in general; child custody and alimony when the father fails to perform his responsibilities; maintenance for the ex-wife and determination of the responsibilities of the ex-wife; the legal status of children; termination of parental custody; determination of guardianship; appointment of a guardian when a minor is abandoned by its parents; and determination of the filiation of a child.

However, while the Marriage Law covers marriage and divorce, it leaves inheritance law untouched. Consequently, the judges of the Islamic courts did not have sufficient positive law to handle inheritance cases. This was a significant problem for Muslims in particular because judges referred to uncodified Islamic law and therefore divergent legal doctrines covered in the traditional legal books; as a result, judgments having diverse legal outcomes were rendered.[4] In 1985, President Soeharto approved the proposal to draft a substantive law that would cover all issues of family and inheritance law, this resulting in a joint decision of the Minister of Religious Affairs and the Supreme Court announcing the project of making the KHI. Within 3 years the project was realized, involving the examination of classical legal texts, comparative studies with three other Muslim jurisdictions (Turkey, Morocco and Saudi Arabia), interviews with a number of religious authorities (*ulama*) and a consideration of court cases.[5]

---

[3] On the history of these two courts, see Lev 1972. See also Hisyam 2001; Noeh and Adnan 1983.

[4] Harahap 1999. See also Nurlaelawati 2010.

[5] Lubis 1995, pp. 1–51; Mawardi 2003, pp. 125–147.

The draft of the KHI was completed with the approval of the *ulama* (Muslim scholars). The *ulama* as well as Muslim judges, and officials of the Ministry of Religious Affairs had convened in 1988, but it was only in 1991 that a consensus was reached and the text issued. The KHI consists of three chapters, namely marriage,[6] inheritance,[7] and endowment,[8] presented in 229 articles. The KHI generally adopts the traditional Islamic legal doctrines, especially those of the Shafi'i *fiqh* texts. However, it also introduced a number of reforms. For example, it established the priority of the mother to care for underage children. Accordingly, although the physical caretaking of the children is the responsibility of both parents, mothers will be granted priority in custody matters when the children are under the age of puberty (*ghayr mumayyiz*).[9] Although this does not firmly follow one of the opinions of the schools of Islamic law, the KHI (as well as the Marriage Law) concurs with the tender age principle whereby minor children are in need of their mothers more than their fathers.

Also, the way in which custody issues are treated in the event of the dissolution of the marriage has been altered. Although custody is a general issue in marriage, it becomes more pressing in the event of the dissolution of the marital bond. According to the Marriage Law, after divorce both parents have principally equal rights to custody and they must care for their child with due regard for its best interests.[10] In case of disagreement, however, the court must settle the case. The solution opted for in the KHI relies on the general principles of Islamic *fiqh* but does not fully adhere to just one Islamic school. Rather, the KHI selected and combined the various opinions. As a consequence, Articles 105 and 156 KHI state that in the event of divorce, children that have not yet reached the age of discernment (*ghayr mumayyiz*) as well as children under 12 years of age shall remain in the custody of their mothers. Children that are *mumayyiz* or over the age of twelve, however, have the option to choose the parent who will be their custodian. If the mother dies, the right to custody is transferred to the mother's female relatives, i.e. the grandmother and the relatives following in hierarchy (Article 156(a) KHI). The financial support of the child, on the other hand, must be provided for by the father according to his financial capacity. This is regulated both in the Marriage Law (Article 41(b)) and in the KHI (Article 156 (d)). This support continues until the children reach majority and are able to support themselves or until they reach the age of twenty-one.

---

[6] The chapter on marriage includes nineteen issues (including the foundation of marriage, engagement, requirements and conditions for a marriage, dower, marriage prohibitions, marriage agreements, marriage during pregnancy, polygamy, the cancellation of a marriage, the annulment of a marriage, rights and duties of spouses, property in marriage, child care, guardianship, dissolution of a marriage, consequences of dissolution of a marriage, reconciliation, and the waiting period).

[7] The chapter on inheritance deals with five issues (including legal heirs, the portions of the heirs, problems raised by *awl* and *rad* (means of calculation), last wills and bequest, and gifts).

[8] The chapter on endowment includes functions, elements, conditions, procedures and registration of *waqf*, and settlement and supervision of property.

[9] Zuhayli 1984, pp. 597–598. See also Al-Jaziri 1990.

[10] Articles 106(1) and 156(c) KHI.

3.2.2 The Introduction of the Notion of the Best Interests of the Child

In 1990 Indonesia ratified the UN Convention on the Rights of the Child (CRC),[11] where the notion of the best interests of children is stressed.[12] This creates the obligation for the courts to take the best interests of the child into consideration when deliberating on the measures related to children in order to protect them financially, physically and psychologically.[13] However, in the regulations on parental care, the notion of the best interests of the child is not stated explicitly as a principle. In fact, the KHI solely stipulates that the right to custody of children under the age of twelve belongs to the mother. Conversely, the right to custody is not awarded automatically to one of the parents when the child is above twelve, but is given to one of them on the basis of the child's preference. Mention is however made of the best interests of the child. Under Article 156 KHI, the right to custody can be transferred from one to another party when it is necessary for the achievement of the best interests of the child.

Further, the notion of the best interests of the child as regards custody is confirmed in Article 2 of Law No. 23/2002 on Child Protection. The law was issued to protect children against discrimination and neglect by their parents (and third parties). It was also a consequence of Indonesia's ratification of the CRC. It is worth noting that Indonesia has ratified a number of international covenants, including the Convention on the Elimination of all Forms of Discrimination against Women (CEDAW) and the International Covenant on Civil and Political Rights (ICCPR).[14] CEDAW requires all state signatories to eliminate discrimination on the basis of gender in public and private spheres.[15] ICCPR stresses that men and women should enjoy equal access to all civil and political rights,[16] and it requires the guarantee of legal certainty for any legal action.[17] The CRC is a specific international treaty that affirms the basic rights of children. To ensure the implementation of the protection of the children, the CRC has laid down four principles,

---

[11] Article 18(1) CRC: 'States Parties shall use their best efforts to ensure recognition of the principle that both parents have common responsibilities for the upbringing and development of the child. Parents or, as the case may be, legal guardians, have the primary responsibility for the upbringing and development of the child. The best interests of the child will be their basic concern.'

[12] Indonesia ratified the CRC on 5 September 1990 through Presidential Decree No. 36/1990.

[13] CWIG 2010.

[14] CEDAW was adopted on 18 December 1979, entered into force on 3 September 1981, and ratified by Indonesia in 1984. Subsequently, ICCPR was adopted on 16 December 1966, entered into force on 23 March 1976, and ratified by Indonesia in 2006.

[15] Article 2 CEDAW.

[16] Article 3 ICCPR.

[17] Article 15 ICCPR.

including non-discrimination, the best interests of the child, the right to survival and development, and respect for the views of the child. Article 2 of the Indonesian Law on Child Protection states that the awarding of the right to custody to parents should strongly consider the four principles specified in the Convention, including the notion of the best interests of the child.[18]

3.3 The Best Interests of the Child in Custody Rulings: Judicial Discretion and Procedural Reforms

The introduction of the notion of the best interests of the child is generally accepted by judges and legal scholars. They fully support the concept and urge that it be appropriately implemented. Nonetheless, clear standards on which the best interests of the child is to be determined and on which conditions the concept of the best interests needs to be implemented are missing. This has led to a variety of legal decisions and practices, demonstrating the many different interpretations of that principle. Additionally, procedural reforms have been introduced by the state to support the implementation of the principle of the best interests of the child.

3.3.1 Custody Regulations: Which Parent 'Deserves' Custody?

According to the Marriage Law and the KHI, mothers have priority in custody for children under the age of twelve. However, courts have not automatically adhered to this principle as in some cases they considered that some mothers were not to be awarded custody, notwithstanding the clear statement of the law. In the following sections, I will draw from my experience and field research to discuss how judges have their own preferences and process of evaluation in custody cases; the analysis will correspondingly consider what the frame of references were within which they operated. Traditionally there is an inclination of the court to give preference to traditional Islamic concepts. This has equally affected men and women, but women have been rather disadvantaged in this regard, as the default rule is the award of custody to the mother, whereas fathers will only have custody if their children that have attained the age of twelve choose so.

The arguments to withdraw custody from the mother that have been put forward by the courts revolve around the idea that the mother also has to meet certain requirements to be a custodian, these requirements being generally taken from

[18] See Article 2 Law No. 23/2002 on Child Protection.

Islamic law. Amongst these conditions are: the marital status of the mother, her social behavior, whether or not she is working and her religious affiliation. While the notion of the best interests of the child is always referred to by judges when resolving custody cases,[19] judges are also of the view that they should be very careful and strict when deciding on the award of custody.[20] When judges appraise that the mother has a 'bad' character and/or lives in conditions that may harm the child, they feel the necessity to rethink awarding her custody. This jurisprudence is founded on the best interests of the child as a justification for transferring custody from one holder to the other. There is, however, ample room for interpretation of what actually constitutes the best interests of the child. Therefore, as this concept remains highly abstract, judges have sometimes based their judgements on their perception of the character of the mother, including their estimation of her religious piety, or her having opted out of Islam (apostasy), or the fact that she is on the labor market, i.e. working outside home.

In Indonesian religious courts, custody cases can be either resolved in a separated action or integrated into a divorce proceeding. Custody cases can be brought by either women or men. Women encounter two difficulties: they might, contrary to the wording of the law, lose their right to custody or, in cases where they are awarded custody, the enforcement of courts' decisions may cause problems (on this issue see below Sect. 3.4). In the context of the first issue, the problem arises particularly when the man argues that the divorce is motivated by the wife's misbehavior.[21] For example, the fact that a wife is working or is not a pious person is raised by husbands to claim that their wives are not psychologically capable of bringing up their children.

3.3.2 Loss of the Right to Custody

Even where the judges generally accept the legal rule that custody of an underaged child attaches to the mother, they also frequently argue that the award of custody for divorced parents must ensure the welfare of the child and that it is not always reasonable to place this responsibility on the mother without due consideration of the interests of the child; as such, mothers of 'immoral' or 'wicked' character, e.g. mothers addicted to drugs or those planning to remarry, have been considered inappropriate to take care of their children. Against the background that neither the Marriage Law nor the KHI specify the conditions under which a parent is to be qualified or disqualified as custodian, other than in relation to the age of the child, the judges of the Islamic courts have a large margin of

[19] Nurlaelawati 2016. See also Sukarti and Hotnida 2010.

[20] Interviews with judges of the courts of Tangerang, Serang and Cianjur.

[21] Based on content analysis of decisions issued by the court and interviews with a number of litigants, females in particular, in Cianjur, Tangerang and Serang.

appreciation. For my recent research on the legal position of women in Indonesia, I collected more than 100 decisions issued by judges of the Islamic courts, including custody cases. Of the thirteen cases on custody from the courts of Tangerang, Serang and Cianjur, the courts refused to award custody to the mother—against the clear wording of the law—in five cases.[22] Although the number is rather small (and less than the cases where custody was awarded), these cases demonstrated an imbalance and a gender bias in the judges' approach to the issue.

In three cases the decisions of the courts (courts of first instances of Serang and Tangerang) to disqualify the mother from custody were mainly based on the fact that she worked outside her home. The court of Serang had to consider a divorce case where the wife was also the mother of a four-year-old boy. Although in some cases working mothers had been awarded custody, arguably because they were able to negotiate their case, in others mothers were often intensively questioned about their capability of bringing up their children. The court of Serang dismissed the mother's petition and custody was awarded to the father, who worked too.[23] The court considered that the mother was disqualified since she was expected as a mother to dedicate her time primarily to her child. The judges seemed to hold on strongly to the traditional Islamic legal doctrine that the wife has no duty to earn a living and must stay home to manage the household. They also, however, seemed to have disregarded the important fact that working provides a ground for the financial survival of divorced women.

The Commission on Child Protection of Indonesia (*Komisi Perlindungan Anak Indonesia*) launched a report about the complaints they had received from a number of mothers who had lost their right to custody. These cases illustrate how the perceived 'bad' or 'immoral' behavior was used as a ground to disqualify mothers from custody. One case involved a mother who was accused of having cheated on her husband. The mother denied these allegations.[24] The husband argued that the misbehavior of his wife would also harm the mental state of their child if the right to custody over their child was awarded to her. Although this may be a reasonable ground to exclude her from her right to custody, the judges' tendency to approve the husband's argument seemed to be motivated less by the welfare of the child and rather by their assumption that the wife might consequently marry the man with whom she had allegedly had an affair. This shows the court's inclination to follow the Islamic rule whereby a mother loses her right to custody when she marries a man who is not related to the child.

Opting out of Islam is regarded by judges as yet another reason to disqualify parents from their right to custody. As opposed to the cases raised above, where the mothers could have still raised their own arguments and views, religious deviance and/or conversion to another religion seems to be an unquestionable reason

22 Nurlaelawati 2013b.

23 Nurlaelawati 2013b, p. 37.

24 Susanto 2012.

for loss of custody. This is shown by a Supreme Court decision of 1996,[25] where the court affirmed that religion, i.e. Islam, is an absolute requirement for custody. The majority of the cases reflect the opinion of the Supreme Court. In one case, referring to the classical legal doctrine, the religious court of Serang gave the right to custody of children younger than twelve to their father, arguing that the mother was not pious and that all the members of her family were non-Muslims.[26] Also a recent case, known as the Freederika Case (No. 382/K.AG/2012),[27] very clearly shows the importance of religion in the award of custody, affecting in particular women. In this case the mother was divorced in 2009, with custody issues over the common daughter not being discussed at the time the divorce was settled. In 2011 the ex-husband petitioned for the custody of his daughter at the religious court of Jakarta Selatan, and his petition was approved. The husband founded his petition on the allegation that his ex-wife was not qualified to care for their daughter as she had committed apostasy. In fact, the mother had begun to observe Christian religious doctrines since she met a Christian man in 2010, who then became a close friend whom she wanted to marry.[28] The mother appealed against the decision and took the case to the Appellate Court of Jakarta, where the ruling was confirmed. The mother filed the case with the Supreme Court, where she expressed her objection to the rulings issued by both the court of Jakarta Selatan and the appellate court of Jakarta.[29] She based her case on Article 2 of Law No. 23/2002 on Child Protection, stating that the award of custody to one parent must be based on two principles, i.e. non-discrimination and the best interests of the child.[30] The Supreme Court, however, upheld the decisions of both courts. It argued that the judges had not distorted any legal rule and had applied them properly.[31]

The main concern of the judges of the religious court and the Supreme Court is the preservation of the religion of the children, as they consider that the award of custody over Muslim children to a non-Muslim parent would endanger and threaten Islam and this must be hindered. Hence, although state law has strived to move away from religious bias in the administration of custody in order to avoid discrimination, it remains difficult for judges to give up the position of alert that a Muslim has to protect his religion from any potential hazard.

These decisions must also be seen as an illustration of the interpretation of the concept of the best interests of the (Muslim) child: it is in this child's interest that he/she is brought up by the parent with whom he/she shares his/her religion. This

---

[25] See decision No. 210/K/AG/1996.

[26] See Nurlaelawati 2010.

[27] See decision of the lower courts No. 0936/Pdt.G/2011/PA.JS and No. 135/Pdt.G/2011/PTA.JK.

[28] See decision No. 0936/Pdt.G/2011/PA.JS.

[29] See decision No. 135/Pdt.G/2011/PTA.JK.

[30] See note 25. In this case the judges also asserted that religion is one of the absolute qualifications for becoming custodian, and someone observing a religion other than Islam is disqualified from it.

[31] See decision No. 382/K.AG/2012.

view is however not held unanimously. Some authors, such as *Sugiri Permana* for example, offer a promising alternative while criticizing the majority's opinion.[32] Relying on comparative studies within Islamic countries, *Permana* considers that the concretization of the concept of the best interests of the child can be based on clear rules. Looking in particular to Sudan, he emphasizes that the child may remain with its mother until the child reaches a certain age even if the mother has a different religion. Under Sudanese law non-Muslim mothers have the right to custody of their child until the child turns five.[33] In his view, it is not appropriate and advantageous for the minor to be suddenly taken from the mother's care and to be passed over to the father.

3.3.3 Parental Agreements on Custody and the Best Interests of the Child

In practice, parents also have recourse to contractual agreements with regard to custody and guardianship. The courts have however the possibility to challenge such agreements if they consider that the agreement endangers the children's welfare. In a case from 1991 (No. 746/1991), the court of Medan had to decide on the custody of two children aged above twelve. The children wanted to stay with their father and the mother had agreed to that arrangement, so that the judges ruled accordingly. Several months later, it was determined that the father had converted to Christianity before the case of custody was settled. Conservative Muslim scholars reacted to the matter and criticized that the judges had not acted in the best interests of the children. The judges responded by stating that had they known about the father's conversion to Christianity, they would not have granted him custody.[34]

The discretion of the court to annul a parental agreement is illustrated by the following case involving an educated father (a doctor), his ex-wife and their two children, aged five and seven.[35] Both parents had petitioned for the award of custody. The judges disregarded the default legal rules and also the demands of both parents. Instead, considering what they perceived as the best interests of the children, they awarded the parents the joint right of custody. The court split custody: the husband was to take care of the children 4 days a week and the mother 3 days.[36] In other cases, the courts interpreted the criteria of *mumayyiz* (i.e. a child that has reached the age of discernment) so as to extend the custody term of the

[32] Permana 2007.

[33] See Welchman 2007, p. 222.

[34] Decision No. 746/Pdt.G/1991/PA.Medan.

[35] Decision No.2113/pdt.G/2010/PA.JS dated 26 May 2010.

[36] Decision No.2113/pdt.G/2010/PA.JS.

mother for her children aged above twelve.[37] Whereas legally the children had the right to choose their custodian and had actually opted for their father with the mother agreeing to it, the court awarded the right to custody to their mother.[38] The decision does not clearly state the basis of the judgement or the reason for disregarding the children's choice and the parent's opinions. It could be argued that the court based its ruling on its assumption of what constituted the welfare of the children in this specific context. Finally, mention can be made of yet another case[39] where the court explicitly based its decision on *ijtihad* (i.e. Islamic juristic endeavor) to deviate from the parents' agreement. Also in this case the court awarded the right of custody to the mother whereas both parents had agreed that the children should stay with the father.[40]

3.4 Enforcement of Custody Decisions

3.4.1 General Aspects

As mentioned above, women face two kinds of difficulties as regards the award of custody. The first is that they can lose custody for reasons that have no legal ground, as discussed above. The second is that even if the mother is awarded custody by the court, the decision is often not executed because of, among other reasons, the rejection of men or fathers of greater financial or persuasive power to hand over the child under their care to mothers. So even though the mothers were awarded custody more often than they were denied this right, this did not mean that they would have the children with them in practice. Of the five female litigants who were awarded custody that I interviewed, only two were able to have the decision executed in practice. Thus, the actual execution of the decisions is the main problem faced by custodian mothers.[41]

In one of the three cases, a mother who had been divorced by her husband spent 2 years attempting by legal means to implement the decision of the appellate Religious Court of Banten, which awarded her custody over her two sons who were still under her ex-husband's supervision. The judges of the first instance court had given the husband custody over the children. The husband took the children to his new house, while the decision was being appealed by the wife. After the appellate court ruled in her favor, the wife asked the father to return the

[37] Decision No. 17/Pdt.G/2004/PAJT, decision No. 652/Pdt.G/2007/PAJT, and decision No. 959/Pdt.G/2005/PAJT.

[38] Decisions No.17/Pdt.G/2004/PAJT, No. 652/Pdt.G/2007/PAJT, and No. 959/Pdt.G/2005/PAJT.

[39] Decision No. 1242/Pdt.G/2007/PAJT.

[40] See Sukarti and Hotnida 2010.

[41] Nurlaelawati 2013b.

children to her, but he refused to do so.[42] The mother went to a number of Centers for Women's Studies and Women's Aid to seek advice. She had not succeeded in bringing the children to her house when I interviewed her, and she was concerned about the future of her sons, as her ex-husband had remarried.[43] She was frustrated and could find no way to have the ruling executed. She went to court to seek advice. The judge of the court, she told me, recommended that she file for the enforcement of the judgement but conceded that it was hard to implement it, as a child is not like a good or chattel that can be reclaimed by force.

As a matter of fact, judges are not unanimous about the execution of custody decisions. Whereas some maintain that such decisions can (and must) be executed, others state that they cannot be executed, because only goods and chattels—but not children—may be taken by force.[44]

3.4.2 Financial Support for Children Under Mothers' Custody

In all divorce judgments, judges must also address the question of financial support for children. Generally the courts decide on the amount based on their evaluation of the financial capability of the husband.[45] More recently, the courts have attempted to improve the actual execution of the decision by asking the husbands to deposit the necessary amount of money at the court. This amount encompasses generally the financial support for children for 1–3 months, together with the amount of money to be paid for spousal alimony within the waiting period. However, in practice there are still problems, as maintenance is often paid irregularly or not at all. In cases where the mothers are awarded the right to custody, the fathers, as it is regulated, are obliged to provide alimony for their children. In fact, all thirty-seven decisions collected from the courts in Tangerang, Serang and Cianjur included the obligation for the father to contribute financially to the upbringing of the children in the mother's custody.[46] Nonetheless, while some fathers abide by their obligations, many others (twelve out of the twelve interviewed fathers) were in fact not paying alimony according to the ruling of the court. Four of the twelve had paid maintenance only during the first few months, and two of the remaining eight made regular payments for a few years but pay it now only irregularly. The other six, however, had not paid any maintenance at all.

[42] Personal interview, Tangerang, 2010.

[43] Personal interview, Tangerang, 2010.

[44] Manan 2006. See also Wahyudi 2014.

[45] See also decision No. 154/Pdt.G/2009/PA Srg (Gugat) 98/Pdt.G/2008/PA Tng.

[46] See also van Huis 2011, pp. 233–253.

3.5 Guardianship: Can Women Be Guardians?

An unmarried child under the age of twenty-one needs a guardian, i.e. someone to take care of the child's person and property. It is only if the legal guardian (generally the father) fails to perform his duty that the Islamic court may appoint one of the relatives to act as the guardian. The reasons for loss of guardianship are addiction to drugs, waste of wealth and property, and failure to perform guardianship in an appropriate manner (Article 109 KHI). While it is recommended by law that the guardian be appointed from within the relatives of the child, a person outside of the family circle may also be chosen as guardian, as well as an institution or a legal entity. Appointed guardians must be mature, sane and honest (Article 107(4) KHI). Equally, parents may bequest guardianship to a person or a legal entity in their last will (Article 108 KHI). Article 109 KHI contains the general rule that the right to guardianship can be transferred from one person to another in the best interests of the child.

Regarding eligibility to be a legal guardian of children who have lost one parent, the KHI does not clearly mention which parent has the right to guardianship. Therefore, both the surviving mother and the surviving father may become the guardian of their child. However, Islamic jurists and traditional religious teachers in Indonesia have considered that the rule of guardianship for the person of the child and for the management of the property is comparable to the rights and duties of marital guardianship. From this they conclude that in the event the father or any other direct male family member dies or goes missing, guardianship must be transferred to the *male* relatives of the child, even if they are distant kin or live far away from the child. The cases of guardianship in Aceh after the Tsunami disaster, as *Salim* observed, confirmed this view as the prevailing one.[47] Most of the judges of the Islamic court of Aceh followed the view that guardianship is a male prerogative.

There are, however, dissenting voices too. These voices stems mostly from female judges. These judges were of the opinion that, from a cultural perspective, children in Aceh usually feel more comfortable living with their female relatives or their mother's relatives.[48] Although Aceh in principle is a patriarchal community, it has a system of matri-local residence, and therefore newly married couples more often than not stay at the bride's parent home or in a house provided for by the parents of the bride. As a result, children become more closely attached to their mother's family. It was within these cultural terms that judges of the Sharia courts in Banda Aceh and Jantho used their margin of appreciation to appoint 100 female relatives (out of 243 appointed guardians) to act as legal guardians for orphaned children 2 years after the Tsunami hit Aceh. Also, they resorted to the appointment of a group of female relatives as guardians, including elder sisters, aunts or

[47] Salim 2006.

[48] Salim et al. 2009, p. 54.

grandmothers from the child's mother's family.[49] In doing so, the female judges in Aceh showed an awareness of the cultural norms of that region. In addition, this tendency demonstrates the rise of gender sensitivity within the court practice and can be seen as an attempt to initiate reforms in the field of guardianship.

3.6 Procedural Aspects in Parental Care Cases

3.6.1 The Engagement of Children in Court Hearings

The best interests of the child are supposed to be strongly considered by judges as the basis of their decisions in resolving cases of custody and guardianship. This has a clear legal basis as regards the award of parental care, in particular as regards custody in cases of divorce. As mentioned above, if there is a dispute in a custody case, judges must decide pursuant to Article 105 KHI. In particular it is the child himself that choses his/her custodian where he/she is above the age of twelve. So the question arises whether children are actually heard in court. Do judges base their decisions on the child's opinion heard in court? Most of the cases in my collection and under my observation do not demonstrate children's involvement in court hearings. This is more evident for cases involving children under the age of twelve.[50] One case shows the involvement of a (male) child aged eight. He was not summoned to court, but under his father's initiation he wrote a letter to the court asking to be left in the custody of his father, with whom he had lived since the separation of his parents 2 years earlier. He succeeded in influencing the judges to award his custody to his father.

The cases of custody involving children aged above twelve often required children's involvement in the court proceeding, as they have the option to choose their custodian. In their research, *Sukarti* and *Hotnida* recorded two cases, one of which involved two children aged nineteen and thirteen, who were summoned to and appeared at court. The children were heard by the panel of judges, who agreed that both of them would go with their father. The judges accepted the children's decision as the children had been living under their father's custody since their parents' separation. However, although some cases demonstrated that children above the age of twelve are summoned to appear before court, cases involving children above seventeen were rarely observed. *Faisal Lukman Hakim*, a practicing lawyer, mentioned that those children are considered to be mature enough to be aware of their interests.[51] Also, it seems that the parents of older children rarely argue about custody as the children themselves mostly follow what their parents agree on, and they mostly determine that the children should live with their mothers.

49 Salim 2006, p. 47. See also Nurlaelawati and Salim 2013.

50 Research done by Sukarti and Hotnida yielded the same results, see Sukarti and Hotnida 2010.

51 Personal interview with Faisal Lukman Hakim, September 2014.

3.6.2 Settlement of Custody Through Mediation

Mediation is a necessary procedure in Indonesian's procedural law. In every case courts must endeavor to reconcile the litigants, in particular in divorce proceedings, as encouraged by the Supreme Court. In 2007, the Supreme Court issued a circular letter which urges judges to make all attempts to reconcile the parties. Notwithstanding, most litigants are not open to reconciliation and are seldom ready to withdraw their divorce petitions as the divorce cases brought to court are usually serious ones and divorce is felt to be inevitable. However, reconciliation mechanisms remain useful for both parties. Even if the reconciliation attempts do not lead to the withdrawal of the divorce petition, it can be observed that those meetings are often used both by judges and the litigants to discuss agreements relating to the distribution of property and the determination of child custody.[52] My field research confirmed that in a number of divorce cases custody was settled within the reconciliation meeting and the case was handled quite peacefully. However in some cases, notwithstanding the settlement reached on the custody issues, the parties later reconsidered the arrangement reached by mediation. In particular, parties would argue that the chosen custodian had not properly performed his or her duties. The parent who was not chosen as custodian therefore often petitioned the court to have the right of custody transferred to him/her and presented reasons why he/she was better suited as the custodian.

3.6.3 Lawyers and Appeals in Guardianship and Custody Cases

Although there is no obligation to be represented by a lawyer in family law cases, cases brought by middle-class litigants often involved lawyers.[53] In fact, with the presence of lawyers, cases were more likely to be appealed against and brought before the Supreme Court.

3.7 Conclusion

From the discussions above, a number of concluding remarks can be drawn. First, the principle of the best interests of the child has been introduced in statutory law in Indonesia and is being considered in judicial practice. Second, the implementation of the best interests of the child has required procedural reforms that have

---

[52] Nurlaelawati 2013a.

[53] See for example decision No. 666/Pdt.G/2012/PA.JB.

been tackled, as is illustrated by the judges' attempts to have rulings enforced by, for instance, requiring husbands to deposit money for the financial support of children whose custody is awarded to their mothers. Third, the principle of the best interests of children introduced in the KHI and the Marriage Law is not clearly defined and gives ample room for judicial discretion. The judges' own personal and cultural terms are therefore the frames of reference within which the notion of the child's welfare is interpreted. In cases where a mother works, for an instance, some judges withdrew custody from her as in their view mothers should spend their time with their children. This does not however apply to men; although fathers work too, the courts prefer to award custody to the father without considering whether he would find enough time to take care of his child. This suggests that patriarchal patterns strengthened by classical legal doctrines inform the judges' legal perspective. Additionally, the rule that women have no financial duties under traditional Islamic law not only contradicts the realities of economic constraints faced by divorced mothers but also adversely affects their relationships with their children. The adherence to conservative religious rules is also illustrated by case law related to a change of religion. Basing their rulings on the (gender- and religion-neutral) rule of Article 156 KHI, whereby for the sake of the child's physically and spiritually safety the court can transfer the right of custody from one nominee to another, courts have withdrawn custody from the non-Muslim custodian on the assumption that the 'spiritual' aspects to be guaranteed also include adherence to Islam. Being raised as a Muslim informs therefore the concept of the best interests of the child.[54] On the other side, the concept of the best interests also allows for the consideration of regional culture, as is shown by the cases awarding guardianship to female relatives of children who lost their parents in the 2004 Tsunami. Therefore, although judges have to some extent been sensitive toward the protection of children and procedural steps were taken to better the financial support for children, it is mainly traditionalism and the conservative Islamic social frame of the parents that shapes the concept of the best interests of the child in Indonesia.

References

Al-Jaziri A (1990) Al-Fiqh ‘ala al-Madhahib al-Arba‘a. Dar al-Fikr, Beirut

Bajpai A (2005) Custody and Guardianship of Children in India. Fam Law Q 39:441–457

CWIG (2010) Determining the Best Interest of the Child, State Statutes. www.childwelfare.gov/pubPDFs/best_interest.pdf. Accessed 12 Nov 2014

[54] The same holds true in the case of *mumayyiz* children (those who have reached maturity or those, according to the KHI, aged twelve or older). For further discussion on this issue, see Nurlaelawati 2010, pp. 145–146.

Harahap MY (1999) Informasi Materi Kompilasi Hukum Islam: Mempositifkan Abstraksi Hukum Islam. In: Bisri CH (ed) Kompilasi Hukum Islam dan Peradilan Agama dalam Sistem Hukum Nasional. Logos Wacana Ilmu, Jakarta, pp 21–80

Hisyam M (2001) Caught between Three Fires: The Javanese Penghulu Under the Dutch Colonial Administration 1882–1942. INIS, Jakarta

Hooker MB (1998) The State and Syari'ah in Indonesia 1945–1995. In: Lindsey T (ed) Indonesia, Law, and Society. The Federation Press, Melbourne, pp 107–108

van Huis S (2011) Akses terhadap Hak-hak Pascaperceraian bagi Perempuan Bercerai di Cianjur. In: Berenschot W (ed) Akses terhadap Keadilan: Perjuangan Masyarakat Miskin dan Kurang Beruntung untuk Menuntut Hak di Indonesia. HuMA, Jakarta, pp 233–253

Lev DS (1972) Islamic Courts in Indonesia: A Study in the Political Bases of Legal Institutions. University of California Press, Berkeley

Lubis MF (1995) The Unification and the Institutionalization of the Islamic Courts in the New Order Era. Studia Islamika 2:1–51

Manan A (2006) Aneka Masalah Hukum Perdata Islam di Indonesia. Kencana, Jakarta

Mawardi AI (2003) The Political Backdrop of the Enactment of the Compilation of Islamic Laws in Indonesia. In: Salim A, Azra A (eds) Shari'a and Politics in Modern Indonesia. ISEAS, Singapore, pp 125–147

Noeh ZA, Adnan AB (1983) Sejarah Singkat Pengadilan Agama Islam di Indonesia. Bina Ilmu, Surabaya

Nurlaelawati E (2010) Modernization, Tradition and Identity: The Kompilasi Hukum Islam and Legal Practice in the Indonesian Religious Courts. Amsterdam University Press, Amsterdam

Nurlaelawati E (2013a) Indonesian Muslim Women at Court: Reform, Strategies and Pronouncement of Divorce. Islamic Law Society 20:242–271

Nurlaelawati E (2013b) Shari'a-based Laws in Indonesia: Position of Women and Children in Legal Practices. In: van Dijk K, Kaptein N (eds) Regime, Change, and Democracy: The Case of Indonesia. Leiden University Press, Leiden, pp 137–165

Nurlaelawati E (2016) The Legal Fate of Indonesian Muslim Women at Court: Divorce and Child Custody. In: Lindsey T (ed) Religion, Intolerance and Democratic Institutions in Indonesia. Routledge, Indonesia

Nurlaelawati E, Salim A (2013) Gendering the Islamic Judiciary: Female Judges in the Religious Courts of Indonesia. Al Jamiah, J Islamic Stud 51(2):247–278

Permana S (2007) Paradigma Baru dalam Penyelesaian Sengketa Hak Asuh Anak pada Peradilan Agama. www.badilag.net/data/ARTIKEL/varia.pdf. Accessed 12 Nov 2014

Salim A (2006) Praktek Penyelesaian Formal dan Informal Masalah Pertanahan. Kewarisan dan Perwalian Pasca Tsunami di Banda Aceh dan Aceh Besar, IDLO, Banda Aceh

Salim A et al (2009) Demi Keadilan dan Kesetaraan: Dokumentasi dan Evaluasi Program Sensitivitas Gender bagi Para Hakim Agama. Puskumham, Jakarta

Sukarti D and Hotnida (2010) Law in Action: Analisis Implementasi UU No. 23 Tahun 2002 pada Putusan Hakim dalam Perkara Hadhanah di Pengadilan Agama, Jurnal al Qalam: Jurnal Keagamaan dan Kemasyarakatan 27:305–330

Susanto CE (2012) Kak Seto Adukan Masalah Hak Asuh Anak ke KY, MICOM, 13 October 2012. http://article.wn.com/view/2012/10/31. Accessed 17 Dec 2014

Wahyudi I (2014) Pembaharuan Hukum Perdata Islam: Pendekatan dan Penerapan. Mandar Maju, Bandung

Welchman L (2007) Women and Muslim Family Laws in Arab States: A Comparative Overview of Textual Development and Advocacy. Amsterdam University Press, Amsterdam

Zuhayli W (1984) Al-Fiqh al-Islamiyy wa Adillatuhu. Dar al-Fikr, Damascus

Chapter 4
Iraq

Harith Al-Dabbagh

Abstract This chapter traces the trajectory of the principle of the best interests of the child in the Iraqi legal order, analyses its implementation and shows how it is perceived and interpreted in jurisprudence. Generally, the principle of the best interests of the child is not expressly recognised as a general principle in the national legal order. However, it is the foundation of the entire children's protection policy in Iraq and operates as an underlying consideration. Also, Iraqi Personal Status law makes explicit reference to the child's best interests as regards custody. This has given courts ample room to interpret and consider the award, loss and revocation of custody on a specific case-by-case basis. The Iraqi Personal Status law regulates custody in one article with nine paragraphs. The principle of the best interests of the child is mentioned on three occasions. Most notably, in 1986, the Iraqi legislature abolished the automatic loss of custody for a mother who remarries and ordered that each case be considered on its own merits. The right to custody is thus not an absolute and discretionary right of any given parent. By putting the child and its best interests in the centre of focus, the judge may noticeably change the order of devolution of custody established by the legislature, awarding custody as is justified by the child's best interests.

Keywords Best interests of the child · Iraq · Custody (*ḥaḍāna*) · Guardianship (*wilāya*) · Visitation rights · Personal status law · CRC

The author is Professor of Comparative Law at the University of Montreal, CERIUM Research Fellow.
The editors of this book wish to thank Global Affairs Canada for providing a first translation of this originally French text and Tess Chemnitzer and Jocasta Godlieb who have revised and edited this translation.

H. Al-Dabbagh (✉)
University of Montreal, P.O. Box 6128, Downtown Station, Montreal, QC H3C 3J7, Canada
e-mail: harith.al-dabbagh@umontreal.ca
URL: http://www.aldabbagh.openum.ca

N. Yassari et al. (eds.), *Parental Care and the Best Interests of the Child in Muslim Countries*, DOI 10.1007/978-94-6265-174-6_4

Contents

4.1 Introduction

Over the last decades, many Muslim countries have introduced the notion of the child's best interests into their national legal order as the guiding principle governing the various aspects of the rights of the child. This concept is promoted and emphasised by the International Convention on the Rights of the Child of 1989 (hereinafter CRC), whose Article 3(1) proclaims that 'in all actions concerning children, whether undertaken by public or private social welfare institutions, courts of law, administrative authorities or legislative bodies, the best interests of the child shall be a primary consideration'.[1] It has thus become a guiding principle, which must clarify, permeate and be embodied in all domestic standards, policies and decisions as well as budget allocation decisions related to children.[2]

Iraq has been a party to the said Convention since 1994, and therefore bound to respect its provisions, notably regarding the best interests of the child. However, the protection of children and the consideration of their interests were already a major concern of the national legislature long before the ratification of the UN Convention, as demonstrated by the significant number of laws relating to children enacted since the country gained independence in 1932.[3] This contribution intends

[1] Several articles mention these interests, namely those concerning: the separation of the child from his family (Article 9), parental responsibility (Article 18), adoption (Article 20), deprivation of liberty (Article 37) and juvenile justice (Article 40). It should be emphasised that the CRC was not the first international text consolidating the notion of the 'best interests of the child,' which had already appeared in the Declaration of the Rights of the Child of 1959, a non-binding legal text in contrast with the CRC.

[2] See Committee on the Rights of the Children 2013.

[3] For an overview, see al-Hadithi 2014, p. 109.

to trace the trajectory of this notion in the Iraqi legal order, analyse its implementation through the rules in effect and to understand the way in which jurisprudence perceives and interprets this notion in disputes brought before the courts. Particularly for Iraq, this issue cannot be overstated. In a quarter of a century, the country has experienced three major wars and 12 years of economic embargo which have had profound consequences. With half of Iraq's population under the age of 18 years, it is the children who have been the most severely affected by the violence, precariousness and the ravage of the country's economic and social infrastructure,[4] with an estimated 4.5 million orphaned or abandoned children.[5] Moreover, in the context of the exacerbated religious sectarianism that has reigned in the country since 2003, it is essential to also consider the impact of the traditional teachings of the Hanafi and Ja'fari schools of law on the state laws regarding children.[6]

In the necessarily limited framework of this contribution, this review will focus in particular on child custody and guardianship, and assess how the child's best interests are considered in litigation. The overarching objective is to measure the impact of the introduction of this notion in the Iraqi legal order, to compare results and draw appropriate conclusions regarding the dynamics of the legal evolution in the country.

To do this, the applicable rules shall be described and critically reviewed in order to reveal their strengths and weaknesses. First the origin and historical evolution of the principle of the best interests of the child in Iraqi law shall be traced (Sect. 4.2), and second the legislative framework in force in custody and guardianship matters will be specified (Sect. 4.3) in order to better understand the procedural aspects and judicial practice which constitutes the living law in this matter (Sect. 4.4).

4.2 Historical Perspectives

In the following sections, light shall be shed on the origin and evolution of the principle of the best interests of the child in Iraq. As an idea, the best interests of the child was initially intimately linked to the evolution of personal law and family law in general (Sect. 4.2.1) before asserting itself as a legal concept in various

[4] Combined second to fourth periodic reports of States parties due in 2011, Iraq, doc. CRC/C/IRQ/2-4 of 2 December 2013, para 58.

[5] According to the statistics of the Ministry of Planning and Cooperation, reported by Almada Newspaper, 4 April 2014, http://almadapaper.net/ar/printnews.aspx?NewsID=462653 (Accessed 24 August 2016).

[6] For the Hanafi *fiqh* I have referred to the compilation by Qadri Pacha in Egypt of 1879 titled *Al-Ahkam al-Shar'iyya fi-l-Ahwal al-Shakhsiyya* (hereinafter Qadri Pasha Code) and for the Ja'fari *fiqh* to the Ja'fari Draft Code of Personal Status prepared by the Iraqi Ministry of Justice in 2013.

aspects of public law and private law in the late 1970s (Sect. 4.2.2) until finally being established as a guiding principle under the CRC and as such integrated in national law (Sect. 4.2.3).

4.2.1 Family Law in Iraq

The child as a weak and vulnerable being needs to be protected, maintained and educated. This need for special protection is not new. One can already find traces of that in the Mesopotamian laws, notably the Code of Hammurabi. Article 191 of the Babylonian code (approx. 1750 B.C.) provides that

> if a man, who adopted a child and raised it, founds a household and has children and then wishes to put the adopted child out, then this child shall not simply go his way empty-handed; the adoptive father shall give him of his wealth one-third of a child's portion, and then he may go. He shall not give him of the field, garden, and house.[7]

At the formation of modern Iraq in 1921, following the collapse of the Ottoman Empire, the status and condition of Iraqi children was very confusing and ill-defined. The child's status, like all matters of family law was governed by the Sharia. However, the Sharia encompasses the different interpretations of *fiqh* and incorporates habits and customs in all their variety. Iraqi Sunnis generally turned to the Hanafi *fiqh* while Twelver Shiites followed the teachings of the Ja'fari *fiqh*. Despite some similarities, the two schools differ considerably when it comes to concrete solutions.[8] Judges therefore had to rule according to the religious provisions specific to the school (*madhhab*) to which the litigants belonged. In addition, non-Muslims Iraqis were permitted the application of their own religious laws in matters of personal status. This statutory pluralism is the legacy of the tradition of the personality of laws which goes back to the foundation of the Islamic City.[9]

Following independence in 1932 (end of the British mandate), the need for a unified legal order became sorely felt in Iraq. This unification was necessary to offset the legal insecurity generated by the absence of an official codification and the recourse to medieval treatises of *fiqh* and fatwas. The multitude of sources to which a judge could refer generated divergent judgments on similar cases, creating chaos and instability in family life whose first victims were women and children.[10]

The initial forays in this direction, however, were quickly aborted, after meeting opposition from conservative forces, notably the Shiite clergy.[11] It was not

---

[7] See Scheil 1904, p. 40.

[8] As for example in the field of marriage conclusion, its dissolution and inheritance.

[9] See Al Dabbagh 2008, pp. 3–34.

[10] See Explanatory Memorandum (*al-asbāb al-mūjiba*) annexed to the Personal Status Code No. 188-1959.

[11] For more details, see Al Dabbagh 2007, pp. 1510–1511.

until the fall of the monarchy and the proclamation of the Iraqi Republic on 14 July 1958, that the controversy was resolved: 'The unification of laws and the establishment of a stable society in its rights and duties being one of the goals of the Revolution',[12] the country could no longer remain split regarding family law and inheritance. The Personal Status Code was finally promulgated and published in the Official Gazette on 30 December 1959.[13] This composite work drew its sources from the entire *fiqh* without confining itself to a particular school, as well as from established Iraqi jurisprudence and the codifications of Muslim countries. Its first article reveals its normative eclecticism, providing that in the case of a legislative gap, the judge shall decide 'according to the principles of the Islamic Sharia that align best with the provisions of this Code'.

In this spirit of synthesis, the 1959 Personal Status Code applies to all Muslim Iraqis without distinction between Sunnis and Shiites. The courts have, for the first time, a corpus juris at their disposal to unify and harmonise legal practice in a domain that had given rise to significantly divergent interpretations. It is true that this unification is only partial as non-Muslim communities are excluded from its scope of application and thus remain subject to their own religious laws. Nevertheless, the Personal Status Code No. 188 of 1959 has now become common law and was therefore also referred to in order to remedy gaps or conflicts between non-Muslim statutes.[14]

It is important to note that the codification was also an opportunity for the legislature to introduce many innovations into classical Islamic law, notably promoting the condition of women and children. The Code has been revised many times, and has introduced many noteworthy changes, particularly: setting the marriage age to eighteen, outlawing forced, customary (unregistered) and unauthorised polygamous marriages, as well as marriages under duress (*jabr*), restricting polygamy and repudiation, establishing the right of the wife to divorce on grounds of discord and disagreement, and recognizing the right to housing for divorced women, as well as strengthening the mother's right to custody.[15]

The Code is still in force, but its effectiveness is now being challenged by Article 41 of the new Iraqi Constitution of 2005 proclaiming the freedom of all Iraqis to observe the legal provisions of their confession or rite in matters of personal status. In March 2014, a new draft law designed for the Shiite community (Ja'fari Personal Status Code) was announced by the Minister of Justice and approved by the Council of Ministers. This code may substantially alter the regulations that have been in force until now and constitutes a major setback for

[12] Explanatory Memorandum to the Personal Status Code, para I.

[13] The Code entered into force on the very day of its publication.

[14] There are seventeen officially recognised non-Muslim religious communities in Iraq and thus theoretically seventeen community statutes to be applied in the domain of personal status. For more details, see Al-Dabbagh 2013–2014, p. 319f.

[15] See Al Dabbagh 2007, p. 1514f.

children's and women's rights by allowing marriage for girls from the age of nine,[16] restoring matrimonial guardianship and the duty of obedience for the wife, and favouring the father in the award of custody.[17]

4.2.2 *The Emergence of the Concept of the Child's Best Interests*

The notion of the best interests of the child is not expressly recognised as a general principle in the national legal order. However, it is the foundation of the entire children's protection policy in Iraq.[18] Indeed, many provisions protecting the child are found in various pieces of social, economic, and criminal legislation such as the Law on Social Welfare, the Juvenile Welfare Act, the Labour Code, and the Education Code.[19]

Thus we see the child's interest as a legal concept is not entirely unknown to the domestic law. It has appeared since the late 1970s in various texts, such as those relating to, for example, parental authority or youth protection.[20] Thus, the Protection of Minors Law (guardianship of property) No. 78 of 1980 and the Juvenile Welfare Act (juvenile delinquency) No. 76-1983 contain numerous references to the notions 'interest of the minor' (*maṣlaḥat al-qāṣir*)[21] and 'interest of the youth' (*maṣlaḥat al-ḥadath*).[22] It is generally a directive to the judge to consider the child's best interests in certain cases, such as the implementation of educative or rehabilitation measures or the management of the child's assets.[23]

In matters regarding custody, however, the concept of the 'interests of the child under custody' (*maṣlaḥat al-maḥḍūn*) was expressly introduced in 1978 under the second amendment of the Personal Status Code No. 188-1959.[24] According to the explanatory memorandum of the reform, Article 57 of the Personal Status Code

---

[16] Bourgoin 2014.

[17] The draft law can be consulted on the information website Al-Masalah, http://almasalah.com/ar/news/ar/NewsDetails.aspx?NewsID=18949 (Accessed 20 July 2016).

[18] Khadim 2010, p. 239f.

[19] For example, Article 1 of the Law on Compulsory Education No. 188-1976 imposes free and compulsory education for every child having reached the age of six. The Labour Code No. 71-1987 prohibits employment of any person under the age of 15, whatever the type of job.

[20] It should be noted however that the legislative provisions refer to the interest of the child (*maṣlaḥat al-ṭifl*), without the adjective 'superior' or 'best'.

[21] See for example the Articles 2(4), 23, 34, 35(3), 37, 43, 54, 68(4) of the Protection of Minors Law No. 78-1980.

[22] See for example the Articles 2(3), 27, 28, 37, 42, 89, 95(1) of the Juvenile Welfare Act No. 76-1983.

[23] On the best interests of the child in the field of guardianship over property, see Sect. 4.3.3.

[24] Law No. 21-1978 on the Second Reform of the Personal Status Code, Official Gazette no. 2639 of 20 February 1978.

regulating custody 'has been entirely revised and its formulation has been simplified so that its provisions now stipulate that the basis of custody is the consideration of the interest of the minor before any other consideration…'.[25]

In its current wording, Article 57 Personal Status Code consists of nine paragraphs at least three of which make explicit reference to the best interests of the child.[26] Paragraph 2 requires the court to determine custody on remarriage of the mother according to the best interests of the child. Paragraph 4 enables the judge to extend custody in favour of the mother until the age of 15 when it is established as being in the best interests of the child. Paragraph 7 makes the best interests of the child a condition for the transfer of custody to the father or a third person, in case of death or failure of the mother to appropriately care for her child. Moreover, the order to avoid any harm to the child is also found in paras 1, 6, and 9b. This makes it possible to terminate custody, regardless of who holds it (father, mother, third party), where the existing custody arrangement proves prejudicial to the child (*taḍarrur al-maḥḍūn*).[27] Finally, para 5 allows the wishes of a child aged 15 years or over to be taken into account.

The legislature did not explain the reasons for the introduction of such a reform, and the Explanatory Memorandum to the 1978 Law does not provide much further assistance. It merely mentions that the old regulation on the matter was deficient and did not cover all the issues brought before the courts. Indeed, this major reform, which extended also to other legal issues than custody,[28] was formulated as 'the aspiration of the Revolution to make the family an important link in the chain of the revolutionary March as being the smallest unit on which rests the solidity, the prosperity and the well-being of the whole society. In order to strengthen the unity of the family and its cohesion in a significant manner, it was essential to review and reformulate some old texts and to add new ones…'.[29] According to its drafters, the 1978 reform was guided by the principles of the Islamic Sharia best suited to the spirit of that time, case law, particularly the jurisprudence of the Court of Cassation, and the principles of equity.[30]

These statements clearly illustrate that the introduction of the principle of the best interests of the child was part of a global reform movement initiated by the Baath party in 1977 to modernize the socioeconomic structures and establish a socialist regime.[31]

---

[25] See Explanatory Memorandum to Law No. 21-1978 on the Second Reform of the Personal Status Code No. 188-1959, para 4.

[26] However, no explicit definition of this notion has been given by the legislature.

[27] Paras 1, 6, 9b of Article 57 Personal Status Code.

[28] The amendment of 1978 also concerned the capacity to marry, forced marriage, divorce and inheritance.

[29] Explanatory Memorandum to Law No. 21-1978 on the Second Reform of the Personal Status Code.

[30] Ibid.

[31] See the Law on the Reform of the Legal System No. 35-1977, Official Gazette no. 2576 of 14 March 1977.

4.2.3 The Consolidation of the Child's Best Interests as a Principle Derived from the CRC

Although the principle of the best interests of the child had its origins in domestic law, it was reaffirmed as a principle following the ratification of the CRC in Iraq in 1994.[32] The Explanatory Memorandum of the Ratification Law No. 3-1994 emphasises the importance of children in the life of nations to guarantee a bright future and Iraq's place as a member of the United Nations. However, this accession was accompanied by a reservation pertaining to Article 14(1) which guarantees the child's freedom of religion, as according to the legislature the child's 'change of religion is contrary to the precepts of the Islamic Sharia'.[33]

It must be made clear from the outset that no special procedure exists in Iraqi law allowing the incorporation of an international convention into the national legal order. A convention is an integral part of domestic legislation, therefore they are routinely approved and ratified. Theoretically, the provisions of such a treaty ratified in the usual way and published in the Official Gazette could directly be invoked before the courts.[34] However, treaties are not accorded superiority over domestic law, with the result that a judge may apply the treaty as part of the law, unless the provision in question does not lend itself to immediate application because of ambiguity or the need to enact a law to facilitate its application.[35]

Indeed, close scrutiny of Iraqi jurisprudence reveals the low priority of the CRC. Court decisions rarely refer either to the Convention or to the principle of 'the child's best interest' that ensues from it.[36] In legal circles, the ratification of the CRC went almost unnoticed, receiving only scarce attention in legal literature. The few texts dealing with it point out that the principle was known in Iraqi law well before the ratification of the CRC. Thus, the best interests of the child had formed the philosophy underlying the legislative policy regarding children for quite some time. After briefly touching on a number of provisions relating to children,[37] Dhari Khalil Mahmud claims that the protection granted by Iraqi law goes well beyond the standards recognized by international instruments.[38] These instruments only reinforce the solutions already adopted in domestic law without

[32] Law No. 3-1994 on the Ratification of the Convention on the Rights of the Child, Official Gazette no. 3500 of 3 July 1994, p. 94. Iraq also adhered to the two optional protocols to the Convention by Law No. 23-2007, Official Gazette no. 4042 of 7 March 2007, p. 1.

[33] Article 1 Law No. 3-1994.

[34] The full text of the CRC has been published in the Official Gazette no. 3500 of 3 July 1994, p. 94, together with the ratification law.

[35] Ajil (n.d.).

[36] Among approximately 200 decisions analysed in the framework of the present study, only one first instance decision referred to the Convention on the issue of custody see Sect. 4.4.1.

[37] Notably in labour law, criminal law and family law.

[38] Mahmud 2002, pp. 38–39.

contradicting them in any way. Because of this alleged conformity, Mahmud seems to dismiss any questioning of domestic law in the light of Iraq's international commitments. Even where the need for harmonisation is recognised, it has also been argued that it is not necessary to review and consolidate the disparate texts relating to children into one single code.[39]

Nevertheless, the respect for the child's best interests is far from being fully integrated into Iraqi law. In its concluding observations on the first periodic report of the Republic of Iraq in 1998, the Committee on the Rights of the Child, which is charged with monitoring the implementation of the CRC by the States Parties, concluded that efforts made to translate the principles proclaimed by the CRC into the national framework remain insufficient.[40] In this respect, the Committee noted with regret that the general principle of the best interests of the child, set out in Article 3 of the Convention, has not yet been taken up as a consideration in any measure or decision relating to children, including in the field of family law. According to the Committee, efforts need to be intensified to integrate the general principles of the Convention into judicial and administrative decisions as well as into the elaboration and implementation of all projects and programs related to children.[41] It expresses particular regret that the provisions and principles of the Convention have not been fully taken into account in legislation and recommends the State Party 'take all appropriate measures to set in motion, if necessary, a process of reform of the legislation and to adopt, for example, a Child Code to guarantee that the Convention is fully implemented'.[42]

In its second to fourth reports submitted in one document in 2013, Iraq emphasised that the whole child protection policy in the country is based on the four principles proclaimed by the CRC, and notably that of the best interests of the child.[43] In order to reunite all the disparate texts relating to the child, the Government prepared a draft law—the Law on the Protection of the Iraqi Child—in 2011, but it is yet to see the light of day.

4.3 The Legislative Framework in Force

In order to see the extent to which the child's best interests are taken into account by the legislature, the applicable rules on custody and guardianship must first be examined. Hereby, the issue of visitation rights, often associated with the rights

---

39 RK al-Juburi 1994, p. 32.

40 Concluding observations of the Committee on the Rights of the Child: Iraq, doc. CRC/C/15/Add.94 of 26 October 1998.

41 Ibid., para 16.

42 Ibid., para 7.

43 Combined second to fourth periodic reports of States parties due in 2011, Iraq, doc. CRC/C/IRQ/2-4 of 2 December 2013, para 64.

of custody, deserves to be examined separately insofar as it also calls into question the best interests of the child. In what follows, first custody (Sect. 4.3.1), second visitation rights (Sect. 4.3.2), and third guardianship rules (Sect. 4.3.3) will be scrutinized in more detail.

4.3.1 Child Custody (Ḥaḍāna)

Etymologically, *ḥaḍāna* is the act of carrying, taking in one's arms, and embracing. The Iraqi legislature provides no definition of this term. The Explanatory Memorandum of the second amendment of the Personal Status Code defines it as raising a minor, ensuring his needs are met, and protecting him from harm. This obviously includes the duty to keep the child under one's roof and to look after his health, safety, moral development, and education and ensure the child's protection.[44]

Custody is covered by a single text in Iraqi legislation, Article 57 Personal Status Code, which consists of nine paragraphs organizing the various aspects of custody. Strangely, this article remains silent on many points likely to pose difficulties in practice. Jurisprudence has endeavoured to fill the gaps in the law by referring to the 'principles of the Sharia that align best with the text of the Code' in accordance with Article 1 para 2 Personal Status Code.[45] The application of these provisions has been extended to non-Muslims for two reasons, firstly, the provisions do not question the religious beliefs of the parties concerned (*ᶜaqīda*), and secondly due to the lack of specific provisions in community statutes.[46]

Against this background we will successively examine the award of custody (Sect. 4.3.1.1), its loss (Sect. 4.3.1.2), and the important question of the remarriage of the custodial mother (Sect. 4.3.1.3), the latter having twice been the subject of legislative intervention.

4.3.1.1 The Award of Custody

Under Article 57(1) Personal Status Code, 'the mother has a preferential right concerning custody during the marriage or after its dissolution, unless this is

[44] It should be noted however that the protection of the financial interests of the child is an attribute of guardianship to which the father is entitled during the marriage and in the case of divorce, as we will see.

[45] The drafters of the Code acknowledged that it was impossible for them to codify all the global and specific questions and contented themselves with regrouping the general principles governing personal status, leaving it to the courts to refer to the *fiqh* treatises to derive from them the specific solutions (*aḥkām al-juz'iyya*) that are best adapted to the provisions of the present code. See Explanatory Memorandum to the Personal Status Code, para J.

[46] BA al-Juburi 2009, pp. 72–73.

detrimental to the child.' Therefore, the right to custody is automatically awarded to the mother and this priority is accorded regardless of whether she is still married to the father or not. For the legislature, the priority given to the mother in custody matters is explained by the fact that 'the mother is closer to the child than the father and has a better understanding of his feelings and emotions than anybody else.'[47] She is therefore the person best able to exercise *ḥaḍāna* at least during the first part of the child's life given the affection and care she provides to the child.[48]

Muslim scholars are unanimous in acknowledging the need to keep the child close to its mother in the first phase of his life, but they are divided on the duration of this custody. The law certainly reinforces the priority of the mother concerning custody, but brings some attenuation to her exercise of this right. Indeed, the award of custody to one or the other parent operates according to the child's age. One can infer from Article 57 paras 4, 5, 7 and 8 Personal Status Code the following order of custody: (i) The mother has the priority in keeping the child until the age of ten; (ii) after that age, custody devolves to the father until the age of 15; (iii) maternal custody may, however, be prolonged until 15 years at the latest, if it is in the best interests of the child; (iv) after the age of 15, the child may choose his custodian (father, mother or one of his relatives) until his majority (18 years); and finally (v) at any time, the court may grant custody to a third person in case of incapacity of the parents.

In other words, the mother enjoys priority, second is the father, followed by a third person chosen by the court (without preference for the maternal line). It is clear that custody goes *de plano* to the mother until the age of ten. Beyond this age, the ex-husband can claim the child unless the mother is able to establish that prolongation is in the child's best interests, then it will be extended until the child is 15 years old. The judge may award custody of one child or the children to a third person when the situation so warrants. In the absence of a qualified person, the child will be placed in a children's home run by the state.

It is important to note that such a regulation deviates from classical Islamic law on at least three points: first, the legislature has considerably reduced the order of devolution of custody: mother, father, third person chosen by the court.[49] Second, no preference is given to the mother's or father's side when custody is awarded to a third person.[50] Third, the legislature gave up the traditional distinction between

[47] Explanatory Memorandum to the Second Amendment of the Personal Status Code, para 4.

[48] Al-Zaydi 2011, p. 146.

[49] The *fuqahā'* set up a quite long hierarchy for the devolution of custody: the mother, the father, the maternal grandmother, the maternal foremother, the full sister, the uterine sister, the half-sister, the full niece ... etc. See for example Article 384 Qadri Pasha Code.

[50] In Hanafi law, the right to *ḥaḍāna* is acquired through the maternal line rather than the paternal line (Article 384 Qadri Pasha Code). In Ja'fari law, the paternal line is preferred (Article 120 Ja'fari Draft Code of Personal Status).

boys and girls regarding the termination of maternal custody.[51] This position has been criticised by certain authors who have denounced it as an Western-inspired reform, foreign to Islamic teachings and the concept of the family prevalent among the Arabs as it weakens the role of the father in the education of his children.[52] For Ahmad al-Kubaysi, the legislature has brought about a disastrous remodelling of the Iraqi family, who, from a legal point of view, is henceforth reduced to the father, mother, and children, excluding ascendants and descendants and relatives in the collateral line.[53] Furthermore, he deems it inopportune to give the adolescent child the choice to remain with one of his parents or relatives because the child, who is not yet mature, in all likelihood will choose the party of greatest laxity who may fail to provide adequate supervision or instil good values.[54] However this last point does not appear very convincing, as even though the law requires the court to consider the wishes of a child who has reached the age of 15, the judge is not bound by them. Indeed, the court will assess if the child has the necessary maturity to make this decision. Moreover, urbanisation and changes in society have led to a weakening of ties with the extended family that prevailed in the past under a tribal society in favour of the nuclear family prevalent in contemporary Iraq.

In any event, the statutory provisions on the allocation of custody based on the age of the child displays an appreciation *in abstracto* of the best interests of the child, namely that of being cared for in early childhood by his mother and later educated and supervised by his father. Although, in principle, the child needs both parents, at some stage in his evolution and development the child may need one parent more than the other. The Muslim tradition indeed apprehends the child as part of a group, a family community whose design determines in large measure the extent and nature of the rights granted to its members.[55] However, as we shall see, the appreciation *in concreto* is not completely absent from the judge's approach when deciding on the custody.

4.3.1.2 The Loss of Custody

We have seen that the right to custody is automatically awarded to the mother until the age of ten, and may be extended until 15 years if it is in the best interests of the child. However, in order to exercise custody of the child, the mother must meet the

[51] The classical *fiqh* distinguishes between girls and boys to decide on the end of the *ḥaḍāna* period ensured by the mother. In Hanafi law, maternal custody lasts until the age of seven for boys and nine for girls (Article 391 Qadri Pasha Code). At the Ja‘faris, the children may be entrusted to the custody of their father or the paternal family from the age of 2 years on, for boys as well as girls (see Article 117 Ja‘fari Draft Code of Personal Status).

[52] See al-Kubaysi 2010, p. 219.

[53] Ibid., pp. 226–227.

[54] Ibid., pp. 220–221.

[55] Gannagé 2008, pp. 420–421.

requirements provided in Article 57(2) Personal Status Code, i.e. be of full age and sound mind, honest (trustworthy, *amīna*), and capable of educating and protecting the child. The mother who does not meet these conditions will lose her right to custody. The priority of the mother thus gives way in the face of physical or mental incapacity, as in the case where the mother suffers from dementia or a contagious disease such as leprosy, scabies, etc.,[56] or when the mother suffers from a condition that may be detrimental to the child, such as schizophrenia.[57] Where the father alleges the mother suffers from an illness that prevents her from taking care of the children under her custody, his claim must be substantiated by submitting the mother to a medical examination.[58]

Thus, maternal custody of the child may be revoked in many possible situations, such as infringement of the child's physical or moral integrity, neglect of the child's education, or misconduct or immoral behaviour of the mother. However, the allegations against the mother must be proven as fact to result in the loss of custody. Fathers seeking custody often challenge the honesty and integrity (*amāna*) of the mother in order to justify a review of the award of custody.[59] *Amāna* usually refers generally to anything that is likely to harm the child or is contrary to his interests. In this respect, the courts must be vigilant.[60] The integrity of the mother (*amāna*) being presumed, anyone who alleges misconduct of the mother must prove it by legally admissible evidence.[61]

A mother who no longer fulfils one of the conditions required by law loses her right. Custody will then be passed on to the father, unless the best interests of the child require otherwise, in which case custody will be awarded to a third person chosen by the court with due consideration of the child's interests.[62] Often, when the mother loses custody, the maternal grandmother intervenes as a third party requesting to be entrusted with the child. The judge may grant this request and grant her custody hereby bypassing the father if it is in the best interests of the child.

Despite the silence of the text, the conditions that must be fulfilled by the mother have been extended to the custodial father and all entitled parties. The Court of Cassation rightly held that the conditions laid down in para 2 of Article 57 Personal Status Code must be fulfilled by all applicants for custody, whether man or woman. Consequently, in the case of a father who was unable to educate and protect the child, custody was instead awarded to the maternal grandmother

---

56 Karim 2004, p. 265.

57 Cass.perso. 25 October 1982, no. 5560/perso./82, cited in al-Mashahadi 1999, p. 140.

58 Cass.perso. 9 March 2002, no. 26/perso/2001, Al-Nashra al-Qada'iyya, no. 1, 2007, p. 5.

59 For judicial applications, see Sect. 4.4.2.7.

60 In this sense, al-Zaydi 2011 p. 149.

61 Cass.extended 27 February 1985, no. 1718/1st extended/1984, cited in al-Mashahadi 1999, p. 99.

62 Cass.perso 6 October 1984, no. 777/perso/1984, cited in al-Karbasi 1989, p. 120.

who fulfilled the legal requirements.[63] In that particular case, the father was a physician in Basra, while the two children lived in Baghdad until the death of their mother. Likewise, a father's action against his ex-wife to claim custody of their daughter, who was over the age of ten, was dismissed after it was established that the father suffered from epilepsy and was an alcoholic.[64]

It should also be noted that the loss of custody does not happen automatically. Rather the person claiming custody must do so in court, by invoking a change in the situation of the person having custody that is likely to harm the child. For example, a mother who suffered from epileptic seizures was deemed to have lost one of the conditions for the exercise of custody; the allocation of custody to the father was therefore deemed in the best interests of the children in accordance with Article 57(7) Personal Status Code, particularly given their maternal grandmother lived with her sick daughter (the mother in question) in the same house.[65] Likewise, where a father was incapable of exercising custody of his young daughter, placing the daughter in the custody of the maternal grandmother who fulfilled the legal conditions of aptitude was found consistent with the interest of the child, as it allowed her to stay close to her grandmother.[66]

Finally, it must be pointed out that a father's claim to custody of a child aged over 10 years is subject to this being in the child's best interests.[67] Otherwise, the court may extend maternal custody until the child is 15. This will be the case in particular where the father is deemed unfit to assume his custodial obligations. Thus, custody was returned to the mother in a case where the girl under the custody of her father was subject to heavy housework and could not devote herself to her studies full time.[68]

4.3.1.3 Remarriage of the Mother

The majority of the *fuqahā'*[69] believe that the custody of the mother expires once she marries a person foreign to the child, i.e. a person not related to the child in a degree prohibiting marriage (*maḥram*). In Ja'fari law, remarriage in all

63 Cass.civ. 15 November 1995, no. 8/1st civ./1995, Al-Mawsu'a al-'Adliyya, no. 30, 1996, p. 2.

64 Cass.shar'i 15 April 1964, no. 258/shar./64, cited in al-Miyahi 2009, p. 53.

65 Cass.perso. 4 July 1979, no. 814/perso/79, Majmu'at al-Ahkam al-'Adliyya, no. 3, 1979, p. 23.

66 Cass.extended 30 October 1984, no. 581/extended/1982 cited in al-Karbasi 1989, p. 120.

67 Article 57-7 Personal Status Code.

68 Cass.perso. 13 January 2009, no. 14/perso1/2009, cited in Khadim 2010, p. 243.

69 In Hanafi law, the mother loses the right to custody if she remarries with a spouse who is not related to the child in a prohibited degree (Article 383 Qadri Pasha Code). In Ja'fari law, a woman who remarries forfeits the right to custody, whether the new husband is related to the child or not. See Mughaniyya 1998, p. 379. On the justification of the two currents, see Linant De Bellefonds 1973, pp. 167–168.

circumstances is grounds for loss of custody.[70] The Zahirites, on the other hand, claim that the remarriage of the mother has no effect on custody.[71]

Iraqi law has undergone an evolution on this point. Until 1986, the Personal Status Code sided with the opinion of the majority (*ra'y al-jumhūr*) by depriving the mother of custody once she remarried a stranger to the child. Thus, it was found that a mother who married her cousin had forfeited her custody since she married a stranger to the child.[72] This condition was particularly severe for the mother. With remarriage constituting a cause for automatic loss, the divorced or widowed mother had to make a difficult choice between remarrying or keeping her child. The judge had no discretionary powers and had to withdraw custody from her. With a view to guaranteeing the mother's 'right to have a happy marital life',[73] the legislator intervened twice in 1986[74] and 1987[75] to redraft paras 9b and 2 of Article 57 Personal Status Code. The first text deals with the remarriage of the mother after the death of her husband, while the second relates to the remarriage after divorce.

These reforms meant that the remarriage of the divorced mother no longer entailed *ipso facto* the loss of custody. The judge was instead required to rule according to the best interests of the child,[76] and could allow the mother to retain custody where it was in the best interests of the child. Where a marriage is dissolved by death, the mother may keep custody despite a remarriage, if she fulfils the other conditions of aptitude. Also, her new husband must commit himself at the marriage to take care of the child and not to harm him. The judge may then order the maintenance of custody.[77] Thus, he now has the discretionary power to rule based on the best interests of the child in case of the mother's remarriage.

In practice, the same criteria seem to be applied without distinguishing between divorce and death of the ex-husband. Thus, in a case where the father contested the custody of his divorced ex-wife because of her remarriage, it was found that 'the custody of children is maintained in favour of the mother, notwithstanding her

---

70 See Article 118 Ja'fari Draft Code of Personal Status.

71 Al-Sa'di and Kashkul 1994, p. 247.

72 Cass.perso 1 April 1980, no. 2951/perso/1979, Majmu'at al-Ahkam al-'Adliyya, no. 2, 1980, p. 56.

73 Explanatory Memorandum to the Decree-Law of the RCC No. 560 of 28 June 1986, published in the Official Gazette no. 3105 of 7 July 1986. The drafters declared the reform to be in conformity with the opinions of the *fiqh* that are most suited to the spirit of the time. It must also be recognised that the tragic circumstances of the war have promoted these measures to a great extent.

74 Law No. 65-1986 promulgated by the Decree-Law of the RCC No. 560 of 28 June 1986, Official Gazette no. 3105 of 7 July 1986.

75 Law No. 106-1987 promulgated by the Decree-Law of the RCC No. 834 of 31 October 1987, Official Gazette no. 3176 of 16 November 1987.

76 Article 57(2) *in fine*.

77 Article 57(9)(b).

remarriage to a stranger, as long as she fulfils the conditions of article 57(9)(b) Personal Status Code'.[78] Likewise, in a case where the father requested the withdrawal of custody from his remarried ex-wife, the Court of Cassation approved of the trial judge's having maintained custody on the grounds that the mother had continued to fulfil the conditions of aptitude, that maternal custody did not harm the child and that the new husband had committed himself to caring for him.[79] On this last point, the courts introduce the new spouse as a third person to ensure his commitment towards the child. Moreover, the law considers the new husband's failure to keep this commitment as a legitimate grounds for divorce for the wife (*tafrīq*).[80] Finally, it goes without saying that the remarriage has no impact whatsoever on custody where the child who is over the age of 15 wants to live with his mother.

Opponents of these reforms criticised in particular that the legislature had placed the new husband of the mother above the blood relatives of the child, insinuating that he would be more attentive towards the child than his uncle and aunt for example, ignoring the fact, that 'the husband of the mother is the most detestable person to the child and the most hated in his heart'.[81] However, this criticism is hardly convincing, insofar as the maintenance of custody is not at all automatic: the reforms merely reflect the confidence the legislature grants a judge to assess the situation and to decide according to the best interests of the child. Conversely this approach should be welcomed, as the criticism seems to be founded on a dubious presumption. In many cases, a stranger may show the same or more compassion and attention to the child than a close relative, evincing the same affection towards the child that normally exists between human beings united by close family ties.

4.3.2 *Visitation Rights (*Mushāhada*)*

The award of custody to the mother does not affect the legal guardianship (*wilāya*) the father exercises over the child. The father may request and receive information regarding the health, education, and well-being of the child. The dividing line between *ḥaḍāna* (custody) and *wilāya* (guardianship) is not always easy to draw. Indeed, the custodial mother may exercise certain tasks linked to paternal authority to defend the best interests of the child and to manage his day-to-day affairs. A closer look at the jurisprudence on this point reveals that the mother actually

[78] Cass.perso 25 February 2014, no. 597, www.iraqld.iq/VerdictsTextResults.aspx?VSC=020620141838973 (Accessed 24 August 2016).

[79] Cass.perso. 14 June 2009, no. 2134/perso1/2009 (unpublished).

[80] Article 57(9)(c).

[81] Al-Kubaysi 2010, p. 228.

enjoys some prerogatives of guardianship, except as regards the child's travels.[82] Even where the mother who has custody is autonomous in her decisions relating to the daily life of the child, she must do so under the supervision of the father. The father in his capacity as the legal guardian, enjoys, according to Article 57(4) Personal Status Code, a right to supervise the affairs of the child, his education and schooling. The father has this right for the entire period of custody, whether initial or extended. Through this right, he can track the performance of duties by the custodial mother.

In order to do so, the father has the right to regularly see the child entrusted to the mother. These visitation rights, called *mushāhada* (seeing the child), are not regulated by the Personal Status Code. Article 57(4) only sets in stone that 'the child shall spend the nights at the home of the mother who has custody'. This issue gave rise to an important dispute in which the legislature ultimately intervened. Under the Decree-Law of the Revolutionary Command Council (RCC) No. 211-1984,[83] the duration and location of the visit is set by agreement of the parties, failing which the court will decide, taking into account what is convenient for the parties and the child. Consequently, the parents may agree upon the organisation of visits and forward this agreement to the court for approval. The custodial mother will not be able to prevent the father from having regular contact with the child under the terms of the agreement. Thus, in a case in 2009 a mother was bound to abide by an agreement which stipulated that the father must be allowed to see the child on the 1st and 15th of every month, on working days for 3 h each time (from 9 a.m. to noon), in the head office of the Women's and Children's Committee situated in the locality A.[84]

In case of disagreement, the court determines the visiting hours, sets its duration and specifies the date and place while respecting the circumstances of each party as well as the best interests of the child. In general, visitation rights are exercised in the place of residence of the custodian according to the Decree-Law No. 6-1992 of the RCC, while respecting that the frequency of contact does not cause an abnormal inconvenience for the custodian and the child.[85] If not agreed otherwise, the father may see his child in the premises of a feminist organisation, or failing that, in the premises of a government authority; the latter only in the absence of a feminist organisation within civil society organisations in the locality

[82] This position seems to be influenced by the Shiite doctrine which considers *ḥaḍāna* as a kind of guardianship over the child and the demented person. The holder will be attributed the prerogatives of the *walī* concerning the education and supervision of the child and the observation of his behaviour see Hussayn 2011, pp. 386–387.

[83] Amended by Decree-Law No. 6-1992.

[84] Cass.perso. 20 July 2009, no. 2982/perso1/2009, cited in 'Alwan 2011, p. 55.

[85] Cass.perso 2 September 2008, no. 2627, http://qanoun.iraqja.iq/view.984 (Accessed 24 August 2016).

where the custodian is resident.[86] Thus, a visit may not take place in an unsuitable place such as the seat of the municipal council[87] or a police station.[88]

Preventing the father from visiting his child is however in itself not an automatic reason for loss of custody. The withdrawal of custody can only be pronounced after formal notification to the custodian mother has been unsuccessful. In one case, the court determined that custody did not need to be withdrawn from the custodian for not allowing the father to have access to the child, as it was possible to send a formal notification reminding the mother of the necessity to respect this obligation and granting her a reasonable grace period.[89] The court may only terminate custody when it can be verified that the mother is recalcitrant or has repeatedly failed to fulfil her commitment. Accordingly, where the mother had failed to comply for more than four months after being notified, custody was withdrawn.[90]

Visitation rights for grandparents are not enshrined in the Code but established case law seems to admit them after the death of one of the parents. Therefore, there seems to be no right of access for ascendants during the lifetime of the child's parents. However, visitation rights may transfer after the death of the person entitled to visitation rights: for example, visitation rights are transferred upon death of the father to the paternal grandmother.[91] Likewise, the paternal grandfather may request to oblige the wife of his deceased son (daughter-in-law) to allow him to see the grandchildren.[92] It is regrettable that the legislature has not thought about regulating this issue to enable the child to maintain emotional ties with the extended family.

It should finally be noted that visitation rights include taking the child out of the agreed location (*iṣṭihāb*) during the scheduled hours, as long as the child spends the night at the custodian's home. Thus, a minor girl was permitted to accompany her father outside of the agreed location during the scheduled contact hours.[93] Should the mother relocate inside Iraq, this will not result in the loss of custody. The father is instead entitled to exercise his visitation rights in the new locality where the mother resides. However, a custodian is not permitted to travel abroad with the child without the father's consent, in order to protect that father's

[86] Cass.perso. 21 September 2008, no. 2890, http://qanoun.iraqja.iq/view.711 (Accessed 24 August 2016).

[87] Cass.perso. 6 July 2009, no. 2425/perso1/2009, Al-Nashra al-Qada'iyya, no. 11, 2010, p. 9.

[88] Karim 2004, p. 271.

[89] Cass.perso. 11 December 2013, no. 9459/perso./2013, Majallat al-Tashri' wa-l-Qada', no. 2, 2014, p. 201.

[90] Cass.perso. 26 June 2012, no. 2099, www.iraqld.iq/VerdictsTextResults.aspx?VSC=221120125331740 (Accessed 24 August 2016).

[91] Cass.perso. 17 December 2008, no. 3711/perso1/08 cited in al-Miyahi 2009, p. 143.

[92] Cass.perso. 16 September 1979, no. 2005/perso/79, Majmu'at al-Ahkam al-'Adliyya, no. 3, 1979, p. 27.

[93] CA Dhi-Qar, 15 July 2013, no. 248/exec./2013, www.iraqld.iq/VerdictsTextResults.aspx?VSC=181120135436938 (Accessed 24 August 2016).

right to supervise the living-conditions, education, and training of the child. The courts have upheld this, approving the loss of the mother's custodial right for travelling outside of the country with the child without the consent of the father as this hampered his right to see to the affairs of the child.[94] However, loss of custody cannot be based on a mere suspicion that the custodian intends to leave the country with the child.[95]

*4.3.3 Guardianship (*Wilāya*)*

Guardianship can be defined as the set of rights and duties exercised by the legal representative of the minor regarding his person and property. Any person who has not reached the age of legal majority (18 years) does not have capacity to act. As such, the minor may not perform legal acts on his or her own. These acts are exercised by his/her legal guardian (*walī*) or testamentary guardian (*waṣī*) within the limits laid down by law.[96] Guardianship is an exclusive prerogative of the father whether during the marriage or after its dissolution. Under Article 102 Civil Code of 1951, the father is the legal guardian of the minor child. In case of the death of the father, this right devolves to the *waṣī* designated by the father, failing this, to the paternal grandfather or the *waṣī* designated by the latter, failing this to the person appointed by the court from among the close male relatives (*ᶜaṣaba*). This pattern corresponds to the classical Hanafi law.[97]

Law No. 78-1980 on the Protection of Minors (LPM) reformed the Civil Code provisions substantially by establishing a comprehensive regime for the protection of incapable persons. This legislation, which mainly regulates the management of the minor's property,[98] applies to all Iraqis regardless of their denomination.[99] It has set up an institution called 'Directorate for the Protection of Minors' (DPM), which goes beyond financial considerations to exercise increased control over the acts performed by the representative in order to protect the minor's best interests. Since the law entered into force, a guardian may now only dispose of the child's property with the authorisation of the DPM.[100]

---

94 Cass.perso. 23 April 2007, no. 1675/perso1/07, Al-Nashra al-Qada'iyya, no. 4, 2007, p. 7.

95 Cass.perso. 21 December 2007, no. 3627/perso1/07, Al-Nashra al-Qada'iyya, no. 4, 2007, p. 10.

96 Al-Hakim et al. 1980, pp. 65–66.

97 Linant De Bellefonds 1973, p. 184f.

98 Incapacitated adults, absent and missing persons are equated to minors within the meaning of the law.

99 BA al-Juburi 2009, p. 100.

100 Article 43(1) LPM.

The law has introduced significant restrictions on the powers of guardians and has imposed a supervisory regime to preserve the rights of protected persons. Thus, the *walī* of a minor is the father and then the court.[101] In case of the death or incapacity of the father, representation is exercised by the testamentary guardian (*waṣī*). This is the person designated by the father to manage the affairs of his ward[102] or failing that, the person chosen by the court and, in that case, the mother has priority over third persons according to the best interests of the child. If no person exists, guardianship devolves to the DPM until a guardian is appointed by the court.[103]

The guardian must be of full age, sane, and with full legal capacity. It is not possible to designate as a guardian a person who has been convicted of a crime affecting honour or integrity, or a person known for his/her bad behaviour, or who has no legitimate means of subsistence. The court may order the dismissal of the guardian in case of failure or inability to properly conduct the minor's affairs or a conviction carrying a prison sentence of more than 1 year.[104] The person exercising guardianship, legal or testamentary, operates under the supervision of the DPM. The court may withdraw guardianship in case of bad behaviour of the *walī*. Guardianship ends at the majority of the child, unless the court decides otherwise.[105]

The DPM henceforth directly assumes the protection of the minor with due consideration of his best interests and closely monitors the management of his property. This means that the guardian can only perform day-to-day administrative acts[106] when dealing with the minor's property, while acting as a good family father[107] in accordance with the powers of the guardian set out in Articles 43 to 56. Any act beyond mere administration, such as disposing of said property requires the authorisation of the DPM. It follows that no act of disposal can be performed, except in case of immediate necessity or utility for the minor and then only by auction following a specific procedure assessed by the judge at various phases in the process.

Among the 106 articles of the 1983 Law, some expressly refer to the 'best interests of the minor' as a criterion for consideration. Article 23 gives the DPM the right to have recourse to the courts to withdraw custody and entrust it to another person in the best interests of the child, in accordance with Article 57 Personal Status Code. Under Article 68(4) LPM, the DPM may request the court to dismiss the guardian where this is justified by the best interests of the child.

---

[101] Article 27 LPM.

[102] Often by means of a will or a document left by the deceased.

[103] Article 34 LPM.

[104] Article 32 and 38 LPM.

[105] Article 27–33 LPM.

[106] Administrative acts are normal management operations usually encompassing the dispatching of day-to-day affairs and getting the best return out of a property.

[107] Article 41 LPM.

Article 34 provides that in the absence of a testamentary disposition by the father, the court will designate a *waṣī,* while according the mother priority over third persons according to the best interests of the child. This is an innovation that allows the mother to assume the prerogatives linked to both custody and guardianship in the case of the death of the father.

Article 43 subjects a significant number of legal acts to the authorisation by the DPM, which must consider said acts in view of the child's best interests. Such acts include all disposal of real estate, furniture, transactions (*ṣulḥ*) over a sum exceeding 100 dinars, property rental for a period over 1 year. The authorisation of the DPM is also necessary for the guardian to purchase on behalf of the minor, to mortgage its property, to collect and invest payments due to the child, and to build on the minor's behalf. After authorisation by the DPM, Article 54 allows the guardian to erect buildings on land belonging to the minor if this proves to be in the minor's best interests. Likewise, the DPM may authorise the sale of a building belonging to the minor if it turns out to be in his interest and financially advantageous.[108] Finally, the acquisition of real property on behalf of the minor may also be authorised by the DPM, with the possibility of erecting buildings, if this proves to be in the interest of the child.[109]

DPM decisions to grant or deny authorisation may be challenged by way of cassation proceedings before the competent Court of Appeal, whose decisions are then final. This right of appeal is given to the legal or testamentary guardian as well as to the Attorney General.[110] The few judgments issued in these matters reveal the underlying perceptions of the best interests of the child. These judgements include a case where a testamentary guardian was authorised to sell a building in which the minors possessed undivided shares, because the income derived was minimal and the sale price once deposited with the DPM[111] would bring a higher return, the more so since the minors possessed another building where they lived with their mother.[112] Similarly, authorisation was granted to sell a house belonging to minors in order to buy another, after having established that this was in their interest, given that the new house was bigger and of a better quality construction than the old one.[113] On the other hand, the decision of the DPM refusing the request of a mother, as testamentary guardian, to dispose of the sum of 500 dinars as expenditure for the medical treatment of her daughter, was quashed. In that judgment, the judges referred to the medical report, which confirmed the daughter had suffered a double fracture that required surgery. According to the

108 Article 55(2) LPM.

109 Article 56(2) LPM.

110 Article 58 LPM.

111 The DPM has an investment fund destined to safely invest the property of minors and make it yield a profit. See Articles 60–64 of the Law.

112 CA Baghdad 13 February 1989, no. 10, cited in RK al-Juburi 1994, p. 47.

113 CA Baghdad 1 February 1989, no. 6, cited in RK al-Juburi, p. 46.

appeal judges, the DPM needed recourse to expertise (consulting with a specialist surgeon) to estimate the expenditure to be incurred and take the necessary steps in the child's best interests.[114]

In the same vein, the testamentary guardian can only bring an action for sharing joint ownership after obtaining authorisation from the DPM. Indeed, joint ownership entailing the sale of the shares belonging to minors requires the authorisation of the DPM under Article 43(1) LPM.[115] Authorisation from the DPM was also required for the acquisition of a building on behalf of minors. Arguing for the children's interest, the court held that the new building was to be registered exclusively in their names and that its value needed to be equivalent to property held in co-ownership that was sold.[116]

4.4 Court Practice

In this final part we will have a look at how the concept of the child's best interests is interpreted and implemented by the courts and the criteria the judges applied to assess what constitutes the best interests of the child. This review will focus primarily on custody rights and visitation rights, taking into account the substantial body of case law issued in this field by the Court of Cassation.

Three points should be addressed here. First of all, it is important to know what the legal nature of custody is according to case law, and whether is it a right of the child or a right of the parents (Sect. 4.4.1). Then, it is necessary to identify the criteria on which the courts rely to assess the child's best interests (Sect. 4.4.2). Finally, it is important to give a general outline of the course of legal proceedings and the procedural aspects (Sect. 4.4.3).

4.4.1 The Legal Nature of Custody

The *fuqahā'* are divided on the question of whether custody is an exclusive right belonging to the child or to one of the parents or jointly to the child and the custodial parent.[117] The majority *fiqh* maintains, however, that *ḥaḍāna* is a right of the mother who cannot be compelled to ensure the exercise of it, while the Hanafis

[114] CA Baghdad 13 February 1989, no. 9, ibid.

[115] CA Dyiala 4 January 2009, no. 3/civ/09, http://qanoun.iraqja.iq/view.1022 (Accessed 24 August 2016).

[116] CA Dhi-Qar 23 June 2010, no. 141/civ/10, http://qanoun.iraqja.iq/view.1532 (Accessed 24 August 2016).

[117] See Mughaniyya 1998, p. 382–383; Salih 2009, p 120f.

consider it to be a right of the child and, thus, an obligation of the mother.[118] Finally, for certain others it is a joint right held by both the mother and the child himself.[119]

A review of Iraqi jurisprudence reveals that it perceives custody as a 'right of the child' himself which the mother cannot cede or renounce since it does not belong to her. Thus, it has been found that the mother cannot renounce custody as part of a transaction[120] concluded with the father, because it is a right of the child and not the mother: it cannot in this case be the subject of a transaction.[121] Similarly, when a '*khulᶜ*' is given in return for the renunciation of the mother's custody right of her daughter, this renunciation is void for being contrary to public policy. In fact, according to Article 130(2) of the Civil Code 'particularly deemed to be of public policy [are] the provisions concerning personal status…'. Based on the nature of the agreement, the action of the father requesting the return of the daughter to him was therefore dismissed.[122] Similarly, a judgment approving the transfer of custody following a mother's renunciation was subject to appeal, as the provisions relating to custody are deemed public policy. The mother's renunciation had no effect, the more so as it was not in the interests of the children.[123]

It its noteworthy that though the mother may not refuse to exercise custody, she may renounce other rights. For example the expenses linked to the maintenance of the child are primarily the responsibility of the father. He must pay the divorced mother for breastfeeding and for taking care of the child once the waiting period is over.[124] Thus, the father has to pay the mother who has been entrusted with the child's custody the so-called *ujrat al-ḥaḍāna* until the child reaches the age of ten.[125] The mother may however forgo this right, as she may do with any other right she has. This does however not apply to *ḥaḍāna* because the latter is a right of the child.[126] An agreement between the parents to manage custody thus seems to have no effect, even if it is accepted for the organisation of visitation rights, as discussed above.[127]

---

118 Linant De Bellefonds 1973, pp. 152–153.

119 Karim 2004, p. 264.

120 Article 698 CC defines the transaction as 'a contract by which the parties end an actual or prevent a pending dispute and this by means of mutual concessions'.

121 Cass.civ. 6 March 1960, no. 134, cited in al-Karbasi 1989, p. 121.

122 Cass. shar'i 20 February 1970, no. 3238/shar./70, Al-Nashra al-Qada'iyya, no. 1, 1970, p. 106. The *khulᶜ* will be deemed valid and the clause deemed unwritten.

123 Cass.perso 14 January 2001, no. 5181/perso/2000, Al-Mawsu'a al-'Adliyya, no. 94, 2002, p. 16.

124 The mother has no right to remuneration (*ajr*) for custody of her children during the marital relationship. The same applies during the waiting period (*ᶜidda*) in case of a revocable divorce (*ṭalāq rajᶜī*). See Article 57(3) Personal Status Code.

125 Cass.perso. 20 January 2014, no. 10050, www.iraqld.iq/VerdictsTextResults.aspx?VSC=100320148738969 (Accessed 24 August 2016).

126 Al-Miyahi 2009, p. 31.

127 See Sect. 4.3.2.

As a consequence, custody being a right of the child implies that the mother is bound to ensure its exercise and should be judicially compelled to fulfil this function. But older case law seems to allow the mother to refrain from caring for the child, as long as there is another custodian who agrees to do so. It follows that a mother cannot refuse to assume custody of her child, unless there is another custodian related in a prohibited degree (*maḥārim*) who agrees to fulfil this task.[128] This interpretation appears to comply with Ja'fari law which considers *ḥaḍāna* as a right of the mother.[129] The remuneration that the repudiated mother receives while being the custodian also clashes with the qualification 'legal obligation'.

That being said, custody has been found to be a right jointly belonging to the custodial parent and the child. The Court of Cassation in the past concluded that 'concerning custody the court must take into consideration the best interests of the child before the interests of the parties'.[130] It follows that custody is more or less a joint right with, however, priority given to the child where his interests are challenged. Generally, three different rights may come into conflict: those being the child's right to custody, the right of the custodial mother, and the right of the father in his capacity of legal guardian. There are several court decisions that illustrate this complex balance between the various opposed interests. They show that the custodial mother cannot elect domicile in a foreign country when it 'prevents the father from exercising his supervisory rights in accordance with Article 57(4) Personal Status Code and the principles of the Islamic Sharia the most consistent with the text of the law'.[131] In a similar vein, the jurisprudence seems to make a distinction between guardianship and custody, even when these two qualities are united in the person of the mother. Thus, the mother who has been deprived of the testamentary guardianship of her daughter due to mismanagement does not lose her right to custody. Article 57(8)(b) Personal Status Code in fact provides for the child to remain with his mother in case of the death of the father as long as she fulfils the legal requirements.[132]

Finally, one case provides a good illustration of the evaluation the judge engages in between the opposing interests of a father and a maternal grandmother through recourse, for the first time, to the provisions of the CRC. In this case, the father brought an action to claim custody of his child who, following the death of the divorced mother, had stayed with his maternal grandparents. The court verified that both parties satisfied the material and physical requirements for custody and followed the request of the father. To justify his decision, the judge expressly cited Article 9 CRC ratified by Law No. 3-1994, ensuring that the child shall not be separated from his parents against his will, unless the competent authorities decide

---

[128] Cass.shar'i 4 November 1973, no. 35/shar./73, Al-Nashra al-Qada'iyya, no. 4, 1973, p. 176.

[129] Al-Kubaysī 2010, p. 214.

[130] Cass.plen. 7 May 1977, no. 77/plen.ass./1977, Majmu'at al-Ahkam al-'Adliyya, no. 2, 1977, p. 63.

[131] Cass.perso. 29 September 1980, no. 2026/perso/80, Majmu'at al-Ahkam al-'Adliyya, no. 3, 1980, p. 27.

[132] Cass.perso. 30 July 2009, no. 3193/perso1/2009, cited in 'Alwan 2011, pp. 73–74.

that such separation is necessary in the best interests of the child. He also relied on para 7 of Article 57 Personal Status Code providing that, if the mother dies or fails to satisfy one of the conditions for custody, the child shall be entrusted to the father or to others, according to the best interests of the child. The judge came to the conclusion that *ḥaḍāna* is a right of the child and not of his parents or relatives. The child's interest in this case was best served when the child was raised by his immediate family, able to benefit from the benevolence and supervision provided by a father who united all the legal requirements.[133]

4.4.2 The Assessment of the Child's Best Interests

As we have seen above, the child's best interests are, *prima facie*, an abstract consideration. The child is entrusted to his mother for as long as it is assumed that the child needs maternal assistance in his development and education, from birth until the age of ten. After this period, the child will be entrusted again to the father, the sole holder of legal guardianship (*wilāya*). This scheme complies with the requirements of Islamic law. However, this does not mean the absence of any concrete approach to the best interests of the child. The law allows a departure from this rather formal distribution of roles whenever it is in the child's best interests. This is explicitly stated in paras 2, 4, 7 of Article 57 Personal Status Code.[134] The interests are determined on the basis of the circumstances of each case.

In practice, jurisprudence is bolder. In many recent judgments, the Court of Cassation held the child's best interests as the prevailing criterion concerning custody. Thus, according to the court 'custody is based on the consideration of the child's best interests before any other consideration'.[135] More specifically, the Court held that

> custody, in its allocation and extinction, revolves around the best interests of the child under custody according to Article 57(2) Personal Status Code… (*al-ḥaḍānata tadūru wujūdan wa-ʿadaman maʿa maṣlaḥati al-maḥḍūni istinādan li-l-māddati 57(2) min qānūni al-aḥwāli al-shakhṣiyyati …*).[136]

The consideration of these interests seems to have precedence over the presumptions in the provisions of the Personal Status Code organising custody

[133] PSC Hay Al-Shab, 13 May 2008, www.f-law.net/law/archive/index.php/t-15940.html (Accessed 24 August 2016).

[134] It should be borne in mind that these exceptions include the remarriage of the mother, the extension of custody for the benefit of the mother and the transfer of custody to the father or a third person.

[135] Cass.perso. 28 May 2006, no. 1720/perso1/06, Al-Nashra al-Qada'iyya, no. 7, 2007, p. 9.

[136] Cass.perso. 29 May 2014, no. 3268/perso, www.iraqld.iq/VerdictsTextResults.aspx?VSC=250820149032669 (Accessed 24 August 2016).

according to the age of the child. At the instigation of the Court of Cassation, the courts have started to focus on this notion, without however recognising its quality as a principle of international law or attempting to define it. Thus, Iraqi law contains no definition of the term 'best interests of the child under custody' (*maṣlaḥat al-maḥḍūn*). Only a jurisprudential analysis will allow us to determine precisely what the courts mean by this notion. In this analysis, judgments delivered by personal status courts of first instance (hereinafter PSC) are most illustrative of this approach.

In the following, the criteria developed by the courts in assessing what is considered in determining the child's best interests will be examined. In general, the analysis of case law reveals the following elements as being instrumental: the child's age, the family environment, his moral, emotional and physical needs, as well as his state of health.

4.4.2.1 Age of the Child

In many decisions the age of the child under custody is taken into account by the courts. The Court of Cassation pointed out, for example, that a child aged 3 years had a pressing need for his mother.[137] In another judgment, the court concluded that the award of custody to the mother was in the interest of the child, notably because the latter was a young child and in need of affection and assistance from his mother.[138] The age is also taken into consideration in the arrangement of visitation rights. The place and frequency of contact should take account of the condition of the child and, particularly, his age. Thus, a judgment which set the number of visits to three times a month, when the child was still an infant and has an increased need for maternal assistance, was disregarded.[139] In another judgment, the Court of Cassation held that the father could not see his infant son more than once a month as this may have caused harm. The duration of the visit was not permitted to exceed 2 h in this case.[140]

4.4.2.2 Separation of Siblings

The desire to keep siblings together seems to impact on the allocation of custody. Thus, in one case, the grandmother asked the court to grant her custody of her two granddaughters instead of the father. The court dismissed her action. On appeal

---

[137] Cass.perso. 11 December 2013, no. 9459/perso1/2013, Majallat al-Tashri'wa-l-Qada', no. 2, 2014, p. 201.

[138] PSC Dyoaniah 22 February 2012, no. 4298/perso/2012, www.iraqld.iq/VerdictsTextResults.aspx?VSC=080120133944499# (Accessed 24 August 2016).

[139] Cass.perso. 15 April 2009, no. 130/perso1/2009, Al-Nashra al-Qada'iyya, no. 8, 2009, p. 8.

[140] Cass.perso. 6 July 2009, no. 2425/perso1/2009, Al-Nashra al-Qada'iyya, no. 11, 2010, p. 9.

she claimed that the fact that one of the girls lived with her aunt while the other stayed with her father was likely to cause them harm. The Court of Cassation quashed the first judgment and criticised the trial judge for not having investigated the reasons why the two sisters lived apart and for not having measured the impact of this situation against the best interests of the children. This latter point was emphasised by a letter from the primary school of one of the girls reporting that she suffered from 'family problems'.[141] However, the court specified that it is not essential that custody of all children be entrusted to only one custodian, with the crucial point on which the court must rule being the consideration of the best interests of each child.[142]

4.4.2.3 Rupture with the Usual Social Environment

Some decisions of trial judges demonstrate a concern to not cut the child off from the environment he is used to. Thus, in one case, the father requested custody, arguing that the custodial maternal grandfather and his wife were frequently absent for work reasons. While recognising this fact, the judge dismissed the request considering that the child's best interests would be affected if custody vacillated and changed hands periodically between the parties, finding that the transfer of custody could disturb the child and cause psychological disorders.[143] In another case, a husband requested the withdrawal of custody claiming that his wife had left the marital home without legitimate reason to move in with her parents in another location, accompanied by their minor children. He invoked the protection of the best interests of the children and the harm caused by the rupture with their usual environment. The Court of Cassation criticised the trial judge for not having investigated whether the best interests of the children, aged over 10 years, justified the extension of custody for the benefit of the mother, in accordance with Article 57(4) Personal Status Code.[144] Correspondingly, the court had to consider a mother's request for extension, where the father was a shepherd circulating in the desert without fixed abode, and issued its decision in accordance with the best interests of the child.[145]

141 Cass.perso. 24 August 2009, no. 105, http://qanoun.iraqja.iq/view.1359 (Accessed 24 August 2016).

142 Cass.perso. 13 August 2002, no. 1292/perso./2002, Majallat al-Qada', no. 3 and 4, 2002, p. 261.

143 PSC Mishkhab, 27 October 2010, no. 45/perso/2010, www.iraqld.iq/VerdictsTextResults.aspx?VSC=290820139875688 (Accessed 24 August 2016).

144 Cass.perso. 24 June 2012, no. 2014, www.iraqld.iq/VerdictsTextResults.aspx?VSC=280120132532337 (Accessed 24 August 2016).

145 Cass.shar'i 20 November 1974, no. 428/shar./74 cited in al-Miyahi 2009, p. 23.

4.4.2.4 Financial Capacity of the Parents

It would appear that the ability to meet the child's needs financially is not a determining criterion, at least when custody is entrusted to the mother. Thus, a judgment by the trial judge, which based the preference given to the father solely on his financial capacity and not on any harm suffered by the child in the care of its mother, was overturned. The initial decision had been based on an expert report that favoured the father, a dentist, on the grounds that his financial situation enabled him to provide the child with better living conditions.[146] The Court of Cassation found that the father must maintain the child (maintenance obligation), even where the child remains under the mother's custody, the latter having a priority right until the age of ten. Better financial circumstances alone cannot lead to the loss of custody.

4.4.2.5 Living Conditions of the Parents

The living conditions of the parents may be taken into account when awarding custody, given that they may affect the child. The jurisprudence on this issue is well established. For example, a mother was awarded custody despite her remarriage as the father was bigamous and had seven other children, and the mother's new husband had committed himself to taking care of the child and ensuring his well-being.[147] Similarly, a maternal grandmother was awarded custody when an assessment showed that she was a mature, upright, healthy woman with a very high standard of living, while the father, who was a physician working in a rural area, lived under unstable and precarious conditions.[148] In yet another case, the judge justified the award of custody to the mother, *inter alia*, by the fact that her house was spacious and well appointed, and thus better suited than that of the father with regard to size and the number of inhabitants (the father shared his house with his parents).[149] In another judgment, the court concluded that the mother's house met all the requirements and offered a favourable environment and that the mother was better qualified to raise her daughter and take care of her particularly in light of the child's age, who being only 2 years old, needed her mother.[150]

---

146 Cass.perso. 7 February 1980, no. 2777/perso/1979, Majmu'at al-Ahkam al-'Adliyya, no. 1, 1980, p. 32.

147 Cass.perso. 4 September 2012, no. 6840, www.iraqld.iq/VerdictsTextResults.aspx?VSC=200120133635506 (Accessed 24 August 2016).

148 Cass.civ. 15 November 1995, no. 8/1st civ./1995, Al-Mawsu'a al-'Adliyya, no. 30, 1996, p. 2.

149 PSC of Souk Al-Shioukh, 30 September 2013, no. 1071/perso/2013, www.iraqld.iq/VerdictsTextResults.aspx?VSC=030620145734382 (Accessed 24 August 2016).

150 PSC Dhat al-Salasel 04 November 2012, no. 2368/perso/2012, www.iraqld.iq/VerdictsTextResults.aspx?VSC=030420131440661 (Accessed 24 August 2016).

4.4.2.6 Professional Situation of the Custodian

Many decisions address the issue of the employment of the custodian, notably the mother, when it is likely to affect her ability to take care of the child. In this, it is the actual availability of the parents which seems to be taken into consideration. Thus, custody was awarded to a nurse whose work did not affect her ability to take care of the child when it was established that she did not perform any night duty and that her sister, who lived with her, took care of the child during her absence.[151] Similarly, is was decided that the work of the custodian as a manager of a hairdressing salon would not harm the children as it did not prevent her from taking care of them.[152] In the same vein, custody of the mother was extended because the father, a truck driver, was often away for work and incapable of providing for the daily needs of the child.[153] Clearly, begging in the streets and using the children to attract the sympathy of passers-by made a defendant unfit to exercise custody.[154]

4.4.2.7 Aptitude and Integrity of the Custodian

It should be remembered that Article 57(2) Personal Status Code requires that the custodian be an upright person able to raise and protect the child. The integrity (*amāna*) of the guardian has been the subject of many decisions. Judges take into account the mother's keeping bad company or misconduct. For example, a divorced mother who engaged in a sexual relationship with another man was deprived of custody, because she was not considered trustworthy (*amīna*) to take care of her children. According to the judge, the phone calls and text messages (SMS) exchanged with a third person left no doubt about the mother's misconduct.[155] However, such an interpretation seems erroneous because, according to the Court of Cassation, a mere accusation of adultery which has not been established by a criminal conviction judgment does not lead to the loss of custody.[156] In the same vein, the mere allegation by the father that the mother had stolen money from him did not undermine her integrity and did not lead to her losing custody.[157]

---

151 Cass.perso. 5 July 1969, no. 352/perso/69, Qada' Mahkamat al-Tamyiz, vol. 6, 1969, p. 38.

152 Cass.perso.kurd. 7 June 2000, no. 67/perso/2000, cited in Ahmad 2010, p. 121.

153 PSC Dyoaniah 29 September 2011, no. 2012/perso/2011, www.iraqld.iq/VerdictsTextResults.aspx?VSC=090120138437883 (Accessed 24 August 2016).

154 Cass.perso. 28 November 2007, no. 3427/perso1/07, cited in al-Miyahi 2009, p. 89.

155 PSC Nassyriah 31 March 2013, no. 262/perso/2013, www.iraqld.iq/VerdictsTextResults.aspx?VSC=300520132677658 (Accessed 24 August 2016).

156 Cass.perso. 5 February 1985, no. 2295/perso/1983, cited in al-Mashahadi 1999, p. 142.

157 PSC Dhat Al-Salasel 23 October 2012, no. 2620/perso/2012, www.iraqld.iq/VerdictsTextResults.aspx?VSC=040420132333924 (Accessed 24 August 2016).

However, custody was withdrawn after a criminal conviction carrying a prison sentence.[158] In the same spirit, the custody of a child aged 5 years was transferred to his father because of the mother's remarriage with a repeat offender convicted of homicide, since the best interests of the child have to be taken into account.[159] Correspondingly, a mother who presumably assaulted her child was deemed to have lost the confidence (*amāna*) required, making her unfit to exercise custody.[160] However, custody was maintained when it was established that the perpetrator of the assault (cigarette burns) was the grandmother and not the mother who immediately denounced this act.[161] Finally, it should be noted that a judgment declaring the wife disobedient (*nāshiz*) has no effect on her right to custody, as long as she fulfils the conditions required by law. It should be remembered that in this case, the mother had left the marital home and refused to return to her husband.[162]

4.4.2.8 Emotional Ties Between the Child and the Custodian

Some trial judgments take into account the absence or presence of the parent after the rupture in the life of the child. A father was declared more suited as custodian of the three children, as the plaintiff (mother) was considered negligent towards her children for leaving them with the father for a longer period of time without inquiring about their health or asking after them and without providing them with any care. Additionally, as the mother had renounced custody in return for a divorce, she had made them 'a bargaining chip' to further her own ends.[163] Correspondingly, custody was maintained despite the custodian's new husband breaching his commitment to care for the child, when the mother refused to abandon her child who was living with her after moving into the house of his grandfather.[164] In another case, custody was also maintained when it was established that the mother, desirous to keep custody, had moved herself and her daughter to live in a house independent of her new husband, who was visiting her from time to time.[165]

---

158 Cass.perso. 27 March 1988, no. 465/perso/1987, Majmu'at al-Ahkam al-'Adliyya, 1998, p. 97.

159 Cass.perso. 15 January 2001, no. 152/perso/2001, Majallat al-'Adala, no. 3, 2001, p. 46.

160 Cass.perso. 8 May 1979, no. 419/perso/79, Majmu'at al-Ahkam al-'Adliyya, no. 3, 1979, p. 23.

161 PSC Dyoaniah 29 September 2011, no. 2012/perso/2011, www.iraqld.iq/VerdictsTextResults.aspx?VSC=090120138437883 (Accessed 24 August 2016).

162 PSC Baayyia 20 October 2011, no. 6288/perso/2011, www.iraqld.iq/VerdictsTextResults.aspx?VSC=290820138774095 (Accessed 24 August 2016).

163 PSC Dyoaniah 31 October 2011, no. 3394/perso/2011, www.iraqld.iq/VerdictsTextResults.aspx?VSC=090120135235241 (Accessed 24 August 2016).

164 PSC Dhat Assalasel 16 October 2011, no. 1674/perso/2011, www.iraqld.iq/VerdictsTextResults.aspx?VSC=291120126243524 (Accessed 24 August 2016).

165 PSC Annasr, 29 October 2009, no. 113/perso/2009, www.iraqld.iq/VerdictsTextResults.aspx?VSC=100920123937876 (Accessed 24 August 2016).

4.4.2.9 Religious Disparity

The law does not explicitly state that the child and the custodian must share the same religion. The Personal Status Code is silent on the issue. The Hanafis permit a Christian or Jewish mother to exercise custody where there is no concern that she might influence the religious convictions of the child.[166] For the Ja'faris, on the other hand, the holder of custody must necessarily be Muslim when the child is Muslim,[167] because for them, custody amounts to a kind of guardianship (*wilāya*) and guardianship of a non-Muslim over a Muslim is not permitted. The jurisprudence seems to support this position by withdrawing custody when the religion of the custodian is not the same as the child. It should be noted that in Iraqi law only the union of a Muslim man with a Jewish or Christian woman (*kitābiyya*) is allowed and that minor children obligatorily follow the religion of their father.[168] Thus, in one appeal, the Court of Cassation held that 'when the religion of the custodian differs from the one of the child, she cannot be worthy of watching over his faith and maintaining the dictates of the Muslim religion of the father, thus losing one of the conditions laid down in para 2 of Article 57 Personal Status Code'.[169] It is this provision which most likely explains Iraq's reservation on Article 14 of the CRC, which recognises the child's right to freedom of conscience and religion. The Committee on the Rights of the Child, in its observations, has expressed its concerns over this reservation and invited the State party to consider its withdrawal.[170]

4.4.3 Course of Proceedings and Procedural Aspects

In what follows first the action for claiming custody will be considered (Sect. 4.4.3.1), then the extent of the judge's investigative and discretionary powers (Sect. 4.4.3.2) and finally the means of appeal (Sect. 4.4.3.3).

[166] Article 384 Qadri Pasha Code provides in this regard that 'the mother or any other Christian or Jewish *ḥāḍina* has also the right to custody for the child until he is capable of discernment regarding religion if the father has no concerns that she might inspire the child to a different belief than the Muslim belief'.

[167] Article 121 Ja'fari Draft Code of Personal Status of 2013.

[168] See Al-Dabbagh 2013–2014, pp. 362–365.

[169] Cass.plen. 16 February 1980, no. 635/plen.ass./1979, Majmu'at al-Ahkam al-'Adliyya, no. 1, 1980, p. 32.

[170] Concluding observations of the Committee on the Rights of the Child: Iraq, doc. CRC/C/15/Add.94 of 1998, para 6.

4.4.3.1 Legal Action

It has already been stated that custody goes automatically to the mother from the child's birth until the age of ten, both during the marriage and after its dissolution. Whoever challenges the right of the mother must bring a legal action to claim custody by invoking the lack of one of the conditions required by Article 57(2) Personal Status Code or harm inflicted upon the child in the proximity of his mother. The case law is constant on the fact that the mother is the principle custodian, anyone who claims the contrary must establish that custody is vitiated by one of the legal grounds for loss of custody.[171] Thus, in order to be transferred custody, the father must go to court, even during the marriage.[172] In case of dissolution of the marriage, the father is obliged to return the children to his ex-wife, the latter having a priority right regarding custody, unless the child would suffer harm.[173]

Moreover, the mother does not have to bring a legal action in order to be awarded custody for a child under 10 years. It is therefore logical that where this right is not contested, there will be no legal action. However, Iraqi jurisprudence recognises the mother's right to bring an action even in the absence of any contestation also during the marriage. According to the Court of Cassation, the custodian may request a declaratory judgment confirming her right to custody.[174] However, as such judgments have often served to allow the mother to leave the country in order to settle abroad with the child, the most recent case law subordinates the admission of the petition to the existence of a legitimate interest. Moreover, the judgments often tend to an explicit statement that they do not constitute authorisation to travel. According to the Court of Cassation, when the mother requests a declaratory judgment of her status as a custodian, the court must ascertain the mother's intent and include this in the judgment, clearly indicating that the award of custody excludes the right to travel with the children out of Iraq, in order to protect the 'visitation' rights of the father recognised under Article 57(4) Personal Status Code.[175] Thus, the request may be granted when the wife wishes to perform administrative steps regarding the children—enrolment in school, medical care, obtaining food rations, production or replacement of identity cards, obtaining

---

[171] PSC Najaf 4 December 2007, no. 3586/perso3/2007, www.iraqld.iq/VerdictsTextResults.aspx?VSC=251020125732733 (Accessed 24 August 2016).

[172] PSC Kadhimyia 5 January 1984, no. 1323/perso/83, www.iraqld.iq/VerdictsTextResults.aspx?VSC=161220121335031 (Accessed 24 August 2016).

[173] Cass.perso. 18 February 2014, no. 234, www.iraqld.iq/VerdictsTextResults.aspx?VSC=120520149030029# (Accessed 24 August 2016).

[174] Cass.perso. 14 December 2008, no. 3557/perso1/08 cited in Al-Miyahi 2009, p. 19.

[175] Cass.perso. 13 March 2012, no. 900, www.iraqld.iq/VerdictsTextResults.aspx?VSC=010820128240315 (Accessed 24 August 2016).

family allowances—provided she does not take the children out of Iraq without the authorisation of their father.[176]

The father has the right to custody from the age of ten. However, the father cannot forcibly take the child who is older than 10 years from his mother, but will have to apply to the court who decides in the light of the child's best interests.[177] So when the father requests the child to be handed over to him, the mother may respond with a request for an extension of custody, which the judge will decide according to the best interests of the child. For example, a trial court's judgment pronouncing the loss of the defendant's right and giving custody to the plaintiff (the father) was affirmed as there was no justification for the extension of custody of his two daughters beyond the legal age.[178]

Procedurally, these actions are brought before the Personnel Status Court (PSC). No time limit is imposed to bring an action. The father may for example request to take back the child long after it has reached the age of ten. Furthermore, the loss of custody is not permanent and the action may be reintroduced whenever circumstances change. For example, in one case, custody was initially entrusted to the Muslim father over the non-Muslim mother, her later conversion justified her reintegration into custody, notwithstanding the withdrawal pronounced previously, because actions for custody may be filed according to the best interests of the child and changes in circumstances.[179] Similarly, it was found that 'upon the death of the father, the mother is favoured to regain custody of her children even aged over 10 years. The close relatives of the paternal line cannot challenge her right.'[180] Finally, when withdrawal was pronounced due to remarriage, the mother may have her custody restored following a subsequent divorce and after the expiry of the legal waiting period (*ᶜiddat al-ṭalāq*).[181] An action claiming custody may therefore be introduced several times in the event of a change in circumstances.

4.4.3.2 The Discretionary and Investigative Powers of the Judge

The trial judge must investigate the circumstances of the case to reach a reasoned decision based on the best interests of the child. In order to assess what constitutes the best interests of the child, the judge has in fact four means consolidated by practice: the report of the social study (*taqrīr al-baḥth al-ijtimāᶜī*), the official

176 Cass.perso. 20 January 2014, no. 10153, www.iraqld.iq/VerdictsTextResults.aspx?VSC=100320144938902# (Accessed 24 August 2016).

177 Cass.perso. 28 July 1975, no. 1005/perso/75, Majmu'at al-Ahkam al-'Adliyya, no. 3, 1975, p. 79.

178 Cass.perso. 18 December 2013, no. 9718, www.iraqld.iq/VerdictsTextResults.aspx?VSC=030620149846964 (Accessed 24 August 2016).

179 Cass.extended 29 May 1982, no. 294/ch.extended/82, cited in al-Mashahadi 1999, p. 139.

180 Cass.perso. 21 July 2009, no. 2981/perso1/2009, cited in 'Alwan 2011, p. 84.

181 Al-Karbasi 1989, p. 118. This is contrary to the Malikis who take the judicially pronounced forfeiture as definitive. Linant De Bellefonds 1973, p. 168.

report on the local findings (*maḥḍar al-muᶜāyana*), the medical psychological examination report (*taqrīr al-lajna al-ṭibbiyya*) and the testimonies by the parties. Among the elements considered, the judge may not give priority to one element to the exclusion of others, but must conduct a comprehensive analysis to determine what constitutes the best interests of the child.

Regarding medical expertise, psychology committees have been instituted in the Ministry of Health, composed of three members who are doctors specialised in psychiatric and mental illnesses. The court must refer the child and the parties to the litigation to an examination by the medical committee to ascertain the best interests of the child.[182] The powers devolved to the committees include in particular 'recommending that the child be entrusted to a custodian (male or female) according to their psychological state, provided the best interests of the child are observed'.[183] In the face of the practical difficulties involved in this decision, the reports usually contain the following phrase: 'Considering that the parties concerned are healthy and sane, the committee leaves it to the court to decide what is best for the child'.

As to the social study, a social research office has been instituted near the personal status courts to undertake sociological research for all the issues referred by the judge, including matters of divorce and custody. The social worker—a graduate in sociology or social work—must submit to the judge a detailed report containing his/her recommendation, if necessary after having conducted a field study.[184] Although the judge is not bound by the results of this medical and social expertise, he often tends to abide by it. For example in one case the judge held that 'the father must return the child aged 5 years to the mother because she has a priority right during the marriage and after its dissolution in accordance with Article 57(1) Personal Status Code, unless this is detrimental to the child. The survey conducted by the social worker recommends entrusting the child to his mother. The findings of the court reveal that the house inhabited by the latter is in a better condition…'.[185]

Testimonial evidence is often used when one of the parties alleges harm to the child or seeks to undermine the integrity of the custodian. The judge has a sovereign discretionary power to assess the probative force of such allegations. Should a father produce testimonies to support his claim of dishonesty by the custodian, the court has the discretionary power to assess the evidentiary value of the testimony and give priority to counter-testimonies produced by the mother.[186] Likewise, the

182 Cass.perso. 25 August 2009, no. 2515/perso1/2009, cited in 'Alwan 2011, p. 71.

183 Article 2(a) Instructions no. 1-1995 Concerning the Medical Committees Issued by the Minister of Health.

184 See Rules Governing the Social Study no. 1-2008 Issued by the Supreme Judicial Council.

185 Cass.perso. 28 juillet 2009, no. 3142/perso1/2009, cited in 'Alwan 2011, pp. 79–80.

186 Cass.perso. 25 June 2012, no. 1896, www.iraqld.iq/VerdictsTextResults.aspx?VSC=221120128729134 (Accessed 24 August 2016).

court may give priority to the evidence produced by the defendant to assess that the award of custody to the father is in the best interests of the children, while maintaining it in favour of the mother may disadvantage them.[187]

The following recent judgment provides a good illustration of the steps usually taken by the trial judge in a custody case. In the case, the mother requested the return of the child into her custody, while the father with whom the child was living claimed to hold custody on the grounds that the mother resided in a rural area devoid of essential needs. After having heard both parties and the witnesses, the judge took note of the medical and psychiatric examination certifying that the parties concerned (father, mother, child) were all sane and healthy. He then examined the report of the social worker outlining the findings on site. It was found that the plaintiff lived in a two-storey house in a sub-district with her parents and her two other children while the father inhabited one floor in his brother's house with his second wife and his children of this union. The judge ordered the return of the child to the mother for the following reasons: First, the child was very young and needed the care and affection of his mother, particularly given the mother was a housewife and fully dedicated to this task. Secondly, the child's best interests required that he live with his two other brothers whose custody had been awarded to the mother. Finally, the social study report attested the personal and material ability of the plaintiff to exercise custody and that the dwelling inhabited by her offered adequate living conditions. The judge concluded that the father had not proved the lack of one of the conditions laid down in Article 57(2) Personal Status Code.[188]

4.4.3.3 The Control of the Court of Cassation

The decisions of the Personal Status Court are delivered in first and last instance and thus, only an appeal in cassation can be lodged against them. Moreover, when a minor is involved, referral to the Court of Cassation is mandatory. The trial judge must immediately forward the decision to the Court of Cassation that it may exercise its supervisory function even if no appeal has been brought by the parties concerned.[189] An appeal in cassation does not suspend the enforcement of the judgment entrusting custody to the mother which was issued in the best interests of the children.[190]

187 Court of First Instance Ali Al-Gharbi, 20 March 2014, no. 162/perso/2014, www.iraqld.iq/VerdictsTextResults.aspx?VSC=050520141439882 (Accessed 24 August 2016).

188 PSC Dyoaniah 3 November 2011, no. 3129/perso/2011, www.iraqld.iq/VerdictsTextResults.aspx?VSC=090120131370817 (Accessed 24 August 2016).

189 See Article 309 Code of Civil Procedure. The aim is to ensure through the high courts the legality of judgments concerning the interest or challenging protected persons.

190 CA Ninive, ch. civ. 15 September 2010, no. 129, http://qanoun.iraqja.iq/view.1657 (Accessed 24 August 2016).

The trial judge has, as observed above, a broad discretion in awarding or withdrawing custody, but he is subject to the oversight of the regulating court regarding the measures of investigation to be taken before issuing his judgment. The Court of Cassation emphasises the need for the judge to order the appropriate measures of investigation in order to assess the best interests of the child. Thus, 'when the divorced mother claims the return of children over 10 years of age taken by the father, the court shall proceed to the necessary verifications to establish if the children's best interests require the extension of maternal custody and pronounce its judgment in the light of the results obtained'.[191] Similarly, when a plaintiff (father) claimed his ex-wife had deserted the child and left him with her mother (maternal grandmother) in order to move to join her new husband in another city, the court had to require him to prove this fact and proceed to the necessary verifications to assess the best interests of the child.[192] Similarly, in another case, a father claimed that the mother had entrusted her child to a third person (her aunt) following her remarriage, and that the aunt was likely to harm the child. The court was required to inquire whether the best interests of the child recommend leaving him with his mother despite her remarriage, which included summoning the new husband to the trial as a third person to establish whether he would commit himself to protecting and taking care of the child.[193] Similarly, the judge must listen to the wishes of the child aged 15 to assure himself of his choice to stay with his father or his mother.[194]

Any judgment pronounced without having undertaken the necessary verifications may be censured by the Court of Cassation. Thus, 'the judgment of the trial judge who had found that the child might suffer deplorable repercussions at his father's home' was subsequently appealed. 'The court cannot on its own authority conclude that a prejudice exists without ordering an expert psychiatric and social report. The court may, once the verifications have been made, deliver its decision in the light of the medical report and the social study'.[195] A decision delivered before the measures of investigation were carried out (medical examination, social study) was revoked.[196] In this case involving a little girl whose mother was deceased, the court had to go as far as possible in its investigations in order to determine who was best suited to keep the little girl, including ordering a medical examination to ascertain what is in her best interests. After that, the court could entrust the child to a third person over the father, in accordance with Article 57(7) Personal Status Code.[197]

---

[191] Cass.perso. 18 July 2012, no. 3870, www.iraqld.com/VerdictsTextResults.aspx?VSC=230120135431537 (Accessed 24 August 2016).

[192] Cass.perso. 15 November 2001, no. 152/perso/2001, Majallat al-'Adala, no. 3, 2001, p. 26.

[193] Cass.perso. 6 June 2012, no. 1778, www.iraqld.com/VerdictsTextResults.aspx?VSC=130920127837281 (Accessed 24 August 2016).

[194] Cass.perso. 24 August 1980, no. 2885/perso/1979, Majmu'at al-Ahkam al-'Adliyya, no. 3, 1980, p. 47.

[195] Cass.perso. 13 May 2009, no. 1742/perso1/2009, Al-Nashra al-Qada'iyya, no. 9, 2009, p. 6.

[196] Cass.perso. 30 July 2009, no. 2941/perso1/2009, cited in 'Alwan 2011, p. 76.

[197] Cass.perso. 6 October 1984, no. 777/perso/1984, cited in Al-Karbasi 1989, p. 120.

In contrast, when the measures of investigation are completed, the Court of Cassation may content itself with confirming the assessment of the trial judge. The reasons given by the court are generally quite concise. On occasion however the judgment may tend to loquacity in order to indicate the approach it intends to favour, as in the following judgment: 'the judgment which is challenged is well founded and complies with the provisions of the Sharia and the law, because under Article 57(1) Personal Status Code the mother has a priority right to custody of her children aged under 10 years, as long as she fulfils the legal conditions. The investigations conducted by the court attest to the aptitude of the mother. First, in her report, the social worker recommended leaving the child under maternal custody. Then, the local findings on the socio-economic conditions of the parties have revealed that the father is married to another woman. Finally, the medical report indicates that the mother is the most suitable to have custody of the two children. On these grounds, the appeal will be dismissed…'.[198]

4.5 Conclusion

To conclude, in spite of a certain automatism in the initial award of custody, the judge enjoys wide discretionary powers. He can assess the best interests of the child in the light of the circumstances and the evidence presented. The right to custody is not an absolute and discretionary right of the parents. By using the concept of the best interests of the child, the judge may noticeably change the order of devolution of custody established by the legislature, awarding custody as is justified by the child's best interests. The judge may thus readjust the whole custody regime around the fundamental idea of the child's best interests.

References

Ahmad GhS (2010) Al-Mabadi' al-Qanuniyya fi Qada' Mahkamat Tamyiz Iqlim Kurdistan 1999–2009 [Legal Principles in the Jurisprudence of the Court of Cassation of the Region of Kurdistan 1999–2009]. Matba'a Manara, Irbil

Ajil TK (n.d.) Idmaj al-Nusus al-Dawliyya fi-l-Qawanin al-Dakhiliyya [The Integration of International Texts in Domestic Laws], Majallat al-Tashri 'wa-l-Qada'. www.tqmag.net/body.asp?field=news_arabic&id=1299&page_namper=p3. Accessed 20 July 2016

Al Dabbagh H (2007) Droit de la famille et nouvelle Constitution irakienne, Revue de la recherche juridique – Droit prospectif 3:1507–1542

Al Dabbagh H (2008) Principe de la personnalité des lois et droit de la famille en Iraq: Approche comparative des droits iraquien et égyptien. Arab Law Quarterly 22(1):3–34

198 Cass.perso. 8 November 2004, no. 9889/perso/2004, Majallat al-Qada', no. 1, 2005, p. 207.

Al-Dabbagh H (2013–2014) Le statut juridique des minorités non-musulmanes en Irak: Heurs et malheurs du pluralisme juridique, Annuaire Droit et Religions 7:319–376

Al-Hadithi HS (2014) Nadzra ila Waqi' al-Tufula fi-l-'Iraq: Mu'alaja Qanuniyya [A Look at the Situation of Children in Irak—A Legal Study]. Majalla al-'Arabiyya li-l-Fiqh wa-l-Qada' 42:109–133

Al-Hakim 'AM, al-Bakri 'AB and al-Bashir MT (1980) Al-Wajiz fi Nazariyyat al-Iltizam fi-l-Qanun al-Madani al-'Iraqi [Short Theory of Obligations in the Iraqi Civil Code], vol 1, Matabi' Jami'at al-Mawsil, Mosul

Al-Juburi BA (2009) Al-Wajiz fi Sharh Mawadd al-Ahwal al-Shakhsiyya li-Ghayr al-Muslimin fi-l-Qanun al-'Iraqi [Short Commentary on the Provisions Regarding the Personal Status of Non-Muslims in Iraqi Law]. Maktabat al-Jil al-'Arabi, Mosul

Al-Juburi RK (1994) Al-Himaya al-Qanuniyya li-l-Tifl [The Legal Protection of the Child], thesis submitted to the Judicial Council, Baghdad

Al-Karbasi 'AM (1989) Sharh Qanun al-Ahwal al-Shakhsiyya Raqm 188–1959 [Commentaries on the Personal Status Code No. 188–1959], Dar al-Hurriyya, Baghdad

Al-Kubaysi A (2010) Al-Wajiz fi Sharh Qanun al-Ahwal al-Shakhsiyya wa-Ta'dilatuhu [Short Commentary on the Personal Status Code and its Amendments], vol 1, 3rd edn. Al-Maktaba al-Qanuniyya, Baghdad

Al-Mashahadi I (1999) Al-Mukhtar min Qada' Mahkamat al-Tamyiz: al-Ahwal al-Shakhsiyya [Selected Decisions of the Court of Cassation on Personal Status]. Matba'at al-Zaman, Baghdad

Al-Miyahi FK (2009) Da'wa al-Hadana wa-Tatbiqatuha al-Qada'iyya: Dirasa fi Daw' al-Fiqh wa-l-Qanun [The Action for Custody and Its Judicial Application]. Al-Maktaba al-Qanuniyya, Baghdad

Al-Sa'di 'AZ and Kashkul MH (1994) Sharh Qanun al-Ahwal al-Shakhsiyya [Treatise on the Personal Status Code], Wizarat al-Ta'lim al-'Ali wa-l-Bahth al-'Ilmi, Baghdad

Alwan RJ (2011) Al-Mukhtar min Qada' Mahkmat al-Tamyiz al-Ittihadiyya: Qism al-Ahwal al-Shakhsiyya [Selected Decisions of the Federal Court of Cassation: Personal Status Part], vol 1. Maktaba Sabah, Baghdad

Al-Zaydi HM (2011) Al-Hadana fi Qanun al-Ahwal al-Shakhsiyya al-'Iraqi: Dirasa Muqarana [Custody in the Iraqi Personal Status Code: Comparative Study]. Majallat al-Tiqani 10:143–163

Bourgoin A (2014) Mariage des enfants en Irak – La loi qui transforme les fillettes en esclaves, Paris Match, 19 March 2014. www.parismatch.com/Actu/International/Irak-la-loi-qui-transforme-les-fillettes-en-esclaves-554734. Accessed 20 July 2016

Gannagé L (2008) Synthèse. In: Khaïat L, Marchal C (eds) L'enfant en droit musulman (Afrique, Moyen-Orient), Société de législation comparée, Paris, pp 418–433

Hussayn ShM (2011) Hadanat al-Umm fi-l-Fiqh al-Islami wa-l-Qanun al-'Iraqi [The Custody of the Mother in Islamic Law and Iraqi Law]. Majallat al-Qadissiyya li-l-Qanun wa-l-'Ulum al-Siyasiyya 1:382–406

Karim FA (2004) Al-Wasit fi Sharh Qanun al-Ahwal al-Shakhsiyya al-'Iraqi [Treatise on the Iraqi Personal Status Code]. Wizarat al-Ta'lim al-'Ali wa-l-Bahth al-'Ilmi, Jami'at al-Sulaymaniyya, Sulaymaniyah

Khadim FK (2010) Mazahir al-Himaya al-Madaniyya li-Huquq al-Tifl fi-l-Tashri'at al-'Iraqiyya al-Nafidha [Aspects of the Legal Protection of the Child in Iraqi Legislations]. Majallat al-Huquq al-Jami'a al-Mustansiriyya 6–7:230–256

Linant De Bellefonds Y (1973) Traité de droit musulman comparé, vol 3. Mouton & Co., Paris/The Hague

Mahmud DhK (2002) Mabda' Masalih al-Tifl al-Fudla fi-l-Qanun al-Dawli wa-l-Qanun al-'Iraqi [The Principle of the Best Interests of the Child in International and Iraqi Law]. Majallat al-'Adala 1:19–44

Mughaniyya MJ (1998) Al-Fiqh ‘ala al-Madhahib al-Khamsa [The *Fiqh* According to the Five Schools], 4th edn. Mu’assasa al-Sadiq li-l-Tiba‘a wa-l-Nashr, Tehran

Salih NH (2009) Hadanat al-Tifl wa-Himayatahu fi-l-Fiqh al-Islami [Custody and Protection of the Child in Islamic Law]. Majallat Kulliyat al-‘Ulum al-Islamiyya 20:120–149

Scheil V (1904) La loi de Hammourabi (vers 2000 av. J.-C.), 2nd edn. Ernest Leroux, Paris

Chapter 5
Jordan

Dörthe Engelcke

Abstract The concept of the best interests of the child was introduced for the first time in Jordanian statutory law in 1951. Since then references to the best interests of the child have increased, which was partly the result of the impact of the Convention on the Rights of the Child, which Jordan ratified in 1991. The Convention pressured governments to adopt the concept of the best interests of the child as the defining principle of legislation and the judicial process. However, the concept of the best interests of the child has not been fully incorporated into Jordanian statutory law and remains absent in the relevant procedural laws. Legal practice further demonstrates that the concept has been applied selectively. Children's rights are usually not considered in isolation from the rights of parents, and courts try to balance the rights of the various parties (mother, father, and child). It is unlikely that this will change in the near future since none of the relevant state as well as non-state actors have yet fully embraced the concept of the best interests of the child.

Keywords Best interests of the child · Custody · Guardianship · Visiting right · Convention on the Rights of the Child · Jordan

The author is an early career fellow at the Lichtenberg-Kolleg, the Göttingen Institute for Advanced Study, University of Göttingen. She would like to thank the Islamic Legal Studies Program at Harvard Law School for hosting her as a visiting fellow in the academic year 2014/2015 during which this manuscript was researched and written. She would also like to thank Stephen Wiles from Harvard Law School library who helped gathering and compiling source material, and the volume's editors for their useful comments and feedback.

D. Engelcke (✉)
Lichtenberg-Kolleg, Geismar Landstr. 11, 37083 Göttingen, Germany
e-mail: d.engelcke@gmail.com

N. Yassari et al. (eds.), *Parental Care and the Best Interests of the Child in Muslim Countries*, DOI 10.1007/978-94-6265-174-6_5

Contents

5.1 Introduction

This chapter traces the concept of the best interests of the child in the Jordanian legal system. It finds that despite increasing references being made to the best interests of the child in Jordanian personal status law, the concept remains absent in the relevant procedural laws. Similar to statutory law, legal practice demonstrates that the concept has been applied selectively. Overall, the concept of the best interests of the child has not yet been fully incorporated into the Jordanian legal system. A lack of advocacy for a full adoption of the principle makes it unlikely that this will change in the near future.

5.2 Historical Setting of the Jurisdiction

Jordan was integrated into the Ottoman Empire in 1516 and remained part of the Ottoman Empire until the latter's formal dissolution after World War I. The British mandate of Transjordan, installed in 1922, formally achieved independence in 1946 as the Hashemite Kingdom of Jordan. Transjordan largely inherited the legal system of the Ottoman Empire.[1] Article 58 of the Trans-Jordanian Basic Law of 1928 stipulated that the laws that existed prior to 1914 when the area of what later became known as Jordan was still officially part of the Ottoman Empire would remain in

[1] Welchman 1988, pp. 868–886.

force until amended or repealed.[2] This law provided for a degree of continuity between the Ottoman Empire, the mandate of Transjordan, and independent Jordan.

This was equally true for family law. In 1917 the Ottomans had issued the first codified family law, the Ottoman Law of Family Rights (OLFR).[3] Since the Ottoman Empire was dismantled shortly after the law was issued, the Ottomans were unable to implement it. However, the British mandate authorities decided to apply the OLFR to all Muslim citizens and to cancel the provisions of the OLFR that applied to non-Muslims, who were allowed to continue to apply their own personal status laws.[4]

During the Ottoman Empire the various non-Muslim religious communities had been organized as *millets*, political and social organizations, which allowed these communities to administer their own affairs. The *millets* enjoyed a certain degree of legal autonomy. Among other things they were allowed to operate their own courts.[5] This autonomy was largely preserved throughout the mandate period and on into the present. As a result the Jordanian legal system continues to be divided into religious, regular, and special courts (Article 99 Jordanian Constitution). Regular courts have jurisdiction over all people in regular and criminal matters (Article 102) while family law is adjudicated by religious courts which are divided into sharia courts and courts of other religious communities (Article 104). The sharia courts hear all cases that concern disputes over parental care if the parties are Muslim. In cases of mixed marriages between a Christian and a Muslim, the civil courts have jurisdiction except if all of the concerned parties accept the jurisdiction of the sharia courts. [6] Christian courts have jurisdiction to adjudicate cases that arise between members of their community with respect to all issues relating to personal status law. [7] In practice this division means that Christian children are subjected to different laws outside the jurisdiction of the state—i.e. the legal rights of children and what is seen in their best interests might vary considerably based on their religious affiliation.

5.2.1 The Introduction of the Concept of the Best Interests of the Child

After independence the Jordanian government continued to apply the 1917 OLFR. The OLFR did not contain any custody (*ḥaḍāna*) provisions. It was not before 1951 that the Jordanian government issued a new family law, the Jordanian Law of

[2] Abu Nowar 2006, pp. 287–288.

[3] I refer to the Arabic translation of the 1917 OLFR. The law was translated from Ottoman Turkish into Arabic by Yusuf Ibrahim Sadr. See Sadr 1924 vol. 1; 1929 vol. 2, pp. 353–373.

[4] Ibid., p. 43.

[5] Millet is the Turkish form of the Arabic term *milla*, which signifies national as well as religious community. See Tsimhoni 1993, p. xv.

[6] See Article 4 of Law No. 28 of 2014 [*qānūn majālis al-ṭawā'if al-masīḥiyya*], Official Gazette of 1 September 2014, pp. 5140–5151.

[7] The jurisdiction of the Christian courts is regulated by Law No. 28 of 2014.

Family Rights (JLFR), which was still heavily influenced by the OLFR. The JLFR for the first time made a limited attempt to codify provisions relating to custody.

The 1951 law introduced some limited provisions regarding the age of custody. It was the first time that the concept of the best interests (*maṣlaḥa*) of the child was introduced in Jordanian personal status law. Article 123 declared that custody for boys ends at the age of seven and custody for a girl at the age of nine. The judge is allowed to extend the custody period of women to the age of nine for boys and to the age of eleven for girls if he finds that this is in their interest (*maṣlaḥathumā*). No provisions relating to guardianship of children were codified.[8]

It is not entirely clear why this provision was introduced. Apart from a general trend of legal reform that saw legal provisions and thereby regulations increase over time, no secondary literature looks at the process of reform to explain why this step was taken. The only article that focuses on the 1951 law remarks that the law adopted the custody provisions of the 1929 Egyptian law but does not clarify the context in which this happened.[9] At the time there were no women's groups who were engaged in legal reform, and it is therefore unlikely that the move can be attributed to legal advocacy. The number of women's groups began to increase starting in the 1990s. At that time women's groups began to formulate concrete demands regarding overall personal status law reform including provisions relating to child law.

These demands were encouraged and supported by international law. The Convention on the Rights of the Child (CRC), which entered into force in 1990, considerably increased the debate over children's rights on the international as well as the national level. Its emphasis on the best interests of the child increased, at least in theory, the pressure on local legislators to adopt this principle, and it gave international backing to national advocacy for children's rights.

5.2.2 The Impact of the Convention on the Rights of the Child (CRC)

Jordan ratified the Convention on the Rights of the Child (CRC) on 24 May 1991. The CRC was published in the Official Gazette in 2006.[10] Like other MENA states, Jordan has stipulated reservations against certain articles of the convention (Articles 14, 20, and 21). The articles in question concern the right to freedom of religion (Article 14) and questions regarding adoptions (Articles 20, 21). The Jordanian government justified its reservations with reference to Islamic law that

---

8 Law No. 92 of 1951, Law of Family Rights, Official Gazette of 16 August 1951.

9 Anderson 1952, p. 206.

10 Law No. 50 of 2006 [*qānūn al-taṣdīq ʿala ittifāqiyyat ḥuqūq al-ṭifl*], Official Gazette of 16 October 2006, pp. 3991–4024.

does not permit the practice of adoption.[11] Up to now, these reservations have not been lifted, which is surprising at least with respect to Article 20 of the Convention since the CRC explicitly recognizes in Article 20 the system of *kafāla* as one of the legitimate systems of adoption. By doing so the CRC automatically recognizes the existence and validity of sources of law other than international law.[12]

To date, Jordan has submitted four national reports in 1993, 1998, 2005, and 2011. The National Council of Family Affairs (NCFA) is the state agency that coordinates these reports. The following analysis is based on all published CRC documents, including national reports, minutes of meetings, and concluding observations of the CRC Committee. Special attention is paid to how the Jordanian government has responded to questions relating to the concept of the best interests of the child, which the CRC promotes. Article 3 of the Convention stipulates that: 'In all actions concerning children, whether undertaken by public or private social welfare institutions, courts of law, administrative authorities or legislative bodies, the best interests of the child shall be a primary consideration.' This obliges state parties to comment on how they have addressed this provision. The Jordanian government was careful to emphasize that it has adopted the concept of the best interests of the child. However, a closer look at the position taking of the government and the relevant statutory laws makes it obvious that Jordan has not fully incorporated this principle. Moreover, the government has justified its reservations to the Convention with reference to the best interests of the child. This indicates that different definitions of what is in the best interests of the child continue to coexist on the national and international levels.

With respect to Article 14, which concerns the right to freedom of belief, the Jordanian government's report states that 'every child has the right to receive religious instruction in accordance with the wishes of the parents.'[13] It is clear that the government does not see freedom of belief as a right of the child. The choice of religious instruction is perceived as a right of the parents. The positioning of the Jordanian government thereby makes it obvious that religious freedom has been interpreted as the right to practice one's faith freely, not to change it.[14] The government declared that allowing children to change their religion would jeopardize social cohesion and that a child, moreover, was not fit to make such a decision.[15] This attitude is clearly reflected in the current custody laws that allocate custody rights differently according to the religion of the mother (see more below). The right to receive an Islamic upbringing is presented as being in the best interests of the child.

[11] Jordanian government, Committee on the Rights of the Child: Initial report of state parties, 25 May 1993, p. 23.

[12] Paradelle 1999, p. 109.

[13] Jordanian government, Committee on the Rights of the Child, p. 14.

[14] Committee on the Rights of the Child, Summary Record of the 622nd Meeting: Geneva, 3 pm, chairperson: Ms. Ouedraogo, 18 May 2000, p. 3.

[15] Jordanian government, Third periodic report of states parties: Jordan, 11 July 2005, p. 9.

Under the umbrella of the National Task Force for Children (NTFFC), which had been set up in 1995 and which was presided over by Queen Noor, non-governmental and governmental organizations working in the area of children's rights, submitted a parallel report in 1998. However, the coalition was careful to emphasize that this was not a move to oppose the government.[16] The report of the NTFFC was published as an annex to the Jordanian government's 1998 report. It agreed with some of the reservations the government had stipulated, most notably regarding Article 14 of the Convention. The report declared that freedom of belief does not mean that individuals are allowed to choose or abandon their religion.[17] There was thus consensus over how religious rights should be interpreted. This makes it unlikely that sufficient pressure will be generated to amend custody regulations that differentiate between the custody rights of Muslim and non-Muslim mothers since these provisions aim to guarantee that the Muslim child of a Christian mother receives a Muslim upbringing.

The impact of the CRC on helping establish the concept of the best interests of the child in Jordan is difficult to assess. This is partly the case because the legal status of the Convention remains unclear. This necessarily limits the impact it can have. In order to be legally binding, laws have to be published in the Official Gazette. Despite the CRC being published in the Official Gazette, the legal status remains in limbo because the Jordanian Constitution does not define the place of international law. During the constitutional reform process in 2011, women's groups lobbied for the inclusion of a clause in the Constitution that places international law over national legislation. The demand was not answered.[18] The Jordanian Court of Cassation had issued a decision in 2003 stating that international law takes precedence over national law.[19] However, since there is no specification about the place of international law in the Constitution, the sharia court administration, the Chief Islamic Justice Department (CIJD), tends to refer to Article 105 of the Constitution giving the sharia courts exclusive jurisdiction over family law, blood money and *waqf* property, as well as to Article 106 which stipulates that sharia courts apply the provisions of the sharia. In interviews, sharia judges have typically argued that the sharia is above international law and that this is the reason why sharia judges do not have to be trained in international law, as international law is regarded as invalid in sharia courts.[20] This limits the possibility of actually applying the Convention in the sharia courts. When asked whether the concept of the best interests of the child was derived from international law,

---

[16] National Task Force for Children (June 1998), Periodic report by the non-governmental organizations in Jordan on the Implementation of the Convention on the Rights of the Child during the period 1993–1998, p. 49.

[17] Ibid., p. 57.

[18] Confirmed by personal interviews with various women's rights activists in Jordan.

[19] Jordanian government, Fifth periodic report submitted by Jordan, p. 4.

[20] Personal interview with Mansour Tawalbe, sharia judge at the CIJD, 20 September 2012, Amman.

the president of the sharia court in Zarqa rejected that assertion. Instead he emphasized the rights given to children in Islam.[21]

Despite its unclear legal status, women's groups have used the CRC as an advocacy tool to call for family law reform. The Convention has encouraged these groups to mobilize, which is one of its main effects. In 1998 the independent Jordanian Women's Union (JWU) launched a national and regional campaign calling for an amendment to family law regarding the legal marriage age. It was the first time a campaign was organized around a proposed amendment to family law.[22] The campaign was motivated by the submission of Jordan's second periodic report on the implementation of the CRC, which the Jordanian government submitted in 1998. The timing therefore seemed favorable to launch the campaign. In September 1998, at the end of the campaign, the JWU submitted its suggestions to the Jordanian National Commission for Women (JNCW), a semi-official entity, which then transmitted the proposal to the government.[23]

Since then women's groups have used the concept of the best interests of the child, albeit selectively, to push for reform. In the 2000s the JWU proposed to reform the visiting rights so as to allow the party who is not the custodian, either the father or the mother, to see the child once a week for 2 h in a place that would be determined by the court. The grandparents should be allowed to see the child once a month and the uncles once a year. The JWU justified these demands with reference to realizing the best interests of the child, who should be able to construct health relationships with the various members of the family.[24]

In 2007, when the comprehensive review of the 1976 Personal Status Law (hereafter 'the 1976 law') began, the JNCW, which coordinated the advocacy efforts of women's groups, issued a list of demands. These demands built on as well as expanded the demands articulated during the 1990s. Most of the demands are not justified with reference to the best interests of the child, which is probably the case because women's groups have approached personal status law reform from an angle of women's rights and not children's rights. They seek to expand women's rights within the family. Expanding the custody rights of mothers has been one of their main focus areas. They thereby approach custody rights as a right of the mother rather than adopting the concept of the best interests of the child.

Owing to the unclear place of international law in the legal system of Jordan and because of the way advocacy for family law has been conducted, the impact of the CRC is difficult to assess. It has likely increased debate over children's rights and the concept of the best interests of the child. It has also encouraged women's groups to mobilize for personal status law reform. These calls sometimes explicitly mentioned the best interests of the child, but in most cases they did not.

---

21 Personal interview with the president of the sharia court of Zarqa, 1 October 2012, Zarqa. This view was repeated in other interviews with practitioners working in the sharia courts.

22 Personal interview with Amneh Zou'bi, president of the JWU, 22 June 2011, Amman.

23 Husseini 1998.

24 JWU (undated), p. 2.

5.3 Regulations on Parental Care

5.3.1 Custody Provisions

The 1976 Personal Status Law (PSL) considerably expanded the provisions relating to custody (Articles 154–166) in comparison to the 1951 JLFR.[25] An analysis of the provisions introduced makes it clear that the concept of the best interests of the child is not the principal consideration when determining custody and visiting rights; rather, the interests and rights of the parents are paramount. The 2010 Personal Status Law (hereafter 'the 2010 law') introduced more detailed provisions relating to custody and guardianship of children. Like in other areas of law, the court also gained considerably more oversight over family relations and children's rights. The concept of the best interests of the child features much more prominently in the 2010 law than in the 1976 law. However, like in the 1976 law the provisions introduced have not made the best interests of the child the dominant consideration for the determination of custody rights. The following discussion analyses what role the concept of the best interests of the child plays with respect to the chain of custody, the duration of custody, its conditions, and its revocation. A comparison between the provisions of the 1976 and the 2010 law allows an assessment of the developments with respect to the concept of the best interests of the child.

Article 154 of the 1976 law declares that the biological mother (*al-umm al-nisbiyya*) deserves the *ḥaḍāna* of her child if she is married (in the event of a breakdown of the marriage). After the mother, the right to custody is transferred to whoever is next in line according to the Hanafi school. The article does not mention the best interests of the child. Custody is therefore primarily seen as the right of the biological mother.

Article 157 of the 1976 law stipulates that if there are several potential custodians who are on the same level of eligibility, then the judge chooses the fittest for custody. Again, choosing a custodian does not explicitly depend on realizing the best interests of the child. However, Lynn Welchman remarks that '[i]n the presentation of the traditional rules, the right of the child to the best (most appropriate) custodian is an underlying theme; the 'right' of the parent is either a duty or a right shared with the ward.'[26] One may thus argue that the article can be seen as an implicit protection of the best interests of the child.

The 2010 law preserved the right of the mother to custody but amended the chain of custody that had previously followed the provisions of the Hanafi school. The amended Article 170 stipulates that after the mother, the custody right is transferred to the maternal grandmother, then the mother of the father, and then to the father. This moves the father up the custody chain. After the father, it is for the court to decide who is most appropriate to care for the child. The article does not

[25] Personal Status Law No. 61 of 1976, Official Gazette of 12 January 1976, p. 2756ff.

[26] Welchman 2007, p. 134.

mention the best interests of the child, but as mentioned above the consideration to choose the most appropriate custodian could be read as reflecting the legislature's intention to protect children's rights.

With respect to the duration of custody, Article 162 of the 1976 law stipulates that a mother who fully dedicates herself to child custody, who literally 'imprisons' herself (*ḥabasat nafshā*), is granted custody until the child reaches puberty. The article does not specify an age when puberty starts and does not mention the best interests of the child as a justification for the extension of the duration of the custody period, unlike Article 123 of the 1951 law had done. Article 161 stipulates that a female custodian who is not the mother loses custody of a boy who turns 9 years old and of a girl who turns 11 years old. These provisions are not justified with reference to the best interests of the child either.

Article 173 of the 2010 law stipulates that if the child is ill and unless the best interests of the child require otherwise, the custody period of the woman is extended so that the woman can care for the child. It is accepted by default that women are better equipped to care for the child because of their distinct female qualities. Custody rights therefore remain connected to the gender of the parent. Article 173 also stipulates that the custody of the mother continues until the child turns 15 years old, and for any other custodian until the child turns 10 years old. After turning fifteen, the 2010 law—for the first time—gives children the right to choose to stay with their mother or their father until they reach legal majority (18 years of age), at which time the custody period for boys and girls automatically ends. This demonstrates that custody is still largely seen as a right of the mother, but it also shows that the children's views should be taken into consideration at a certain age. The article does not mention the best interests of the child. However, in interviews legal practitioners often state that the change is 'in the best interests of the child.'[27] The change therefore seems to be primarily one of interpreting how the best interests of the child are to be understood in practice. The amendment indicates that the autonomy of the child has increased. Children are seen as capable of determining what is in their interest starting from the age of fifteen whereas previously, at least in theory, this capability was not recognized by lawmakers. Changing understandings of the best interests of the child are therefore closely linked to changing understandings of mental capacity and self-determination.

During a meeting in August 2012, representatives of various women's associations led by the JNCW discussed the next steps of family law reform. Hamdi Murad, a prominent religious scholar who attended the meeting, explained that there was no specific age mentioned in the Islamic legal sources regarding custody rights and that custody can therefore only be regulated by taking into account the best interests of the child.[28] This could mean that in the future the best interests of the child will slowly replace biological predispositions of parents as the

---

[27] Conversations with various lawyers and women's rights activists in Jordan.

[28] The meeting, attended by the author, took place at the Sisterhood is Global Institute (SIGI) in Amman, 30 August 2012.

determining factor in allocating custody. It could do so because Islamic law seems to be favorable or at least not opposed to this development.

The 2010 law stipulated for the first time that non-Muslim women lose custody when a child turns 7 years (Article 172), even though this had already been established in legal practice as demonstrated below.[29] Mansour Tawalbe, a sharia judge at the CIJD, explained that this article was introduced in the 2010 law because Christian women can be married to Muslim men and any resulting children—who are consequently Muslim—should receive a Muslim upbringing. This could only be guaranteed by withdrawing the mother's custody rights and having the children growing up in the household of the Muslim father. For that reason they should not stay with the Christian mother until the age of fifteen.[30] A religious upbringing is thereby given priority over the mother's 'natural' capacity as a caretaker or the best interests of the child. Moreover, the article implicitly assumes that providing the child with an Islamic education is ultimately in the child's best interest. This position explains the existence and nature of the reservations to Article 14 of the CRC.

The only two articles of the 1976 law that explicitly mentioned the best interests of the child relate to travelling with a minor child. Article 164 stipulated that the fact that the *walī* or the female custodian (depending on who has custody rights) travels with the child inside the country does not impact on their right to custody as long as it does not negatively affect the best interests of the child. If it does, the minor is handed over to the other party.

Similarly, Article 166 stipulates that it is not allowed for the female custodian to travel with the child outside of the country except with the agreement of the *walī* and after it is ensured that the best interests of the child are guaranteed. The law does not mention the opposite case—the father travelling with the child—but in its 1998 report to the Committee of the Rights of the Child, the Jordanian government stated that a man who had custody did not require the permission of the mother if he wanted to take the child out of the country.[31]

The 2010 law assigned greater responsibility to the judge to supervise the travels of the child. Article 177 stipulates that, where the *walī* has not agreed to the travel in advance, a custodian needs to obtain permission from a judge before undertaking travel with the child outside of the country for a temporary purpose; the permission of the judge is conditioned on the child's best interests being guaranteed. The judge is also in charge of putting in place sufficient guarantees that ensure the return of the child to the country.

Being eligible to serve as a custodian is subject to certain conditions. According to Article 171 of the 2010 law, custody may be granted to an adult of sound mind

[29] The JWU had demanded that non-Muslim mothers should have the same custody rights as Muslim mothers. Personal interview with Hala Deeb, member of the Jordanian Women's Union, 11 September 2012, Amman.

[30] Personal interview with Mansour Tawalbe, sharia judge at the CIJD, 20 September 2012, Amman.

[31] Committee on the Rights of the Child, Concluding observations of the Committee on the Rights of the Child: Jordan, 25 April 1994, p. 7.

who does not have a dangerous contagious disease. The custodian needs to be caring and capable of bringing up the child and guaranteeing their religious and moral maintenance as well as their health. The custodian cannot be an apostate. The female custodian cannot be married to a man who is a stranger (*ghayr maḥram*) to the child.

According to Article 172 of the 2010 law, the right to custody is to be revoked if one of the above conditions is no longer met. If the child turns 7 years old and the custodian is a non-Muslim woman, the custody period ends. The right to custody is also withdrawn if the custodian lives with somebody whose right to custody was previously withdrawn because of his or her behavior or because the person is an apostate or has a dangerous disease.

The 2010 law further expands the discretionary power of the judge. Article 183 stipulates that if the custodian refrains from allowing the enforcement of a judgment in relation to the seeing, visiting, or accompanying of the child—such that the custodian does not allow the other party to see the child without good excuse—the judge can temporarily revoke custody rights for a period not exceeding six months and transfer the custody rights to whoever comes next in line. Paragraph (b) of the same article stipulates that a person who has temporary custody needs to allow for the enforcement of a judgment relating to the seeing, visiting, etc. of the child.

The loss of custody is not a permanent but a revocable decision. According to Article 174 of the 2010 law, the right to custody is to be reinstated if the reason why it was withdrawn is no longer applicable.

5.3.2 Visiting Rights

As was the case earlier, the 2001-amended Article 163 stipulates that the mother and the *walī* have equal rights with respect to *mushāhada* (visiting rights) of the child if someone else has custody. If there are differences of opinion with respect to the *mushāhada* of the child, it will be determined that the mother and the *walī* can see the child once a week, the grandparents once a month, and everyone else once a year. The new article introduces the concept of the best interests of the child with respect to visiting rights. This 'best interest' is determined by the judge. The judge determines the duration of *mushāhada* and the place while considering the best interests of the child in the event the parties cannot agree on that.

The 2001 amendments caused great controversy mainly because of the divorce provisions they introduced. The lower house of parliament voted against them twice in 2003 and 2004.[32] The women's right organization Mizan therefore asked sharia judge Wasif al-Bakri to analyze the 2001 amendments and to determine whether they were in accordance with sharia. With respect to the new visiting

---

32 For a short overview of this process see Clark and Young 2008, pp. 333–353.

rights, Al-Bakri explained that to a certain extent the amendments simply confirmed an already established reality that had been confirmed in various decisions by the sharia court of appeal—i.e. that the right of the mother and the father were indeed equal.

The new and important aspect of the amendment according to al-Bakri was the fact that it gives the judge the right to determine the place and time of the visiting rights (*mushāhada*) if the two parties cannot agree on those issues. Al-Bakri explained that previously the judge often entrusted the bailiff to determine where and when the parent who did not have custody could see his child. These meetings mostly took place in police stations or security centers or in the corridors of the court. Al-Bakri concluded that those places were inappropriate for visiting purposes and could negatively impact on the psychology and state of mind of the child. He added that 'for this reason the judge is given the right to determine the place and time of visiting in order to meet the best interests of the child.'[33] Despite references to the best interests of the child, the law attempts to realize the rights of all three parties and does not approach the matter only from the perspective of the child.

The 2010 law introduced more detailed provisions and determined who had the right to see the child and when. As a result the sharia courts gained greater oversight over children's matters. Article 181, para (a) stipulates that the mother and the father, and if the father is not present the paternal grandfather, have the right to see (*ru'ya*), visit (*istizāra*) and accompany (*iṣṭiḥāb*) the child once a week and to communicate by modern communication means with the child where the other party has custody rights. The grandparents have the right to see the child once a month, and this applies if the place of residence of child is inside the country.

Article 181, para (b) stipulates that if the place of residence of the *walī* who has the custody rights and the child is outside of the kingdom, then it is for the court to determine the place and the time of visitation, which should take place at least once a year. The court does so while taking into account the age of the child and his or her conditions in order to achieve his or her best interests and the best interests of the party who is demanding visitation. The article also stipulates that people who have the right to see, visit, and accompany the child should not be prevented from doing so. This makes it obvious that the concept of the best interests of the child has become more prominent but that the primary objective of the court is to vindicate everyone's right in a balanced way rather than putting the best interests of the child above the rights of the parents.

Similarly, Article 181, para (c) stipulates that if the place of residence of the child is inside the kingdom and the person who has the right to see, visit, and accompany him lives outside the kingdom, then it is for the court to determine the place and time of the seeing, visiting, and accompanying. The court does so by taking into account the age of the child and his conditions and seeks to meet his best interests and the best interests of the party who is demanding to see the child.

Article 181, para (d) stipulates that in the cases mentioned in paras (b) and (c) of this article, it is for the court to give permission for the child to stay overnight

[33] Al-Bakri (undated), p. 29.

(*mabīt*) with the person who has the right see him. Article 182 stipulates that it is for the judge to change the time and place of visitation when requested and it does so in accordance with what is in the child's best interest.

Article 181, para (e) stipulates that a demand to see, visit, accompany, and communicate with the child, requires agreement with the custodian so as to identify the time and place for this as well as to determine what is feasible. If the custodian does not agree, then it is for the judge to determine the time, place, and feasibility. Again, the judge takes into account the best interests of the child and the best interests of the party who is demanding to see the child. The primary function of the judge in these cases seems to be to balance the interests of all the parties involved.

5.3.3 The **wilāya** *and* **wiṣāya** *Provisions*

The 2010 law distinguishes between two forms of guardianship: the *wilāya*, a natural relationship that implies guardianship over a person, and the *wiṣāya*, which is a form of assigned guardianship in the event the *walī* is absent. The provisions of the 2010 law make it clear that the concept of the best interests of the child is not the principal consideration when assigning either form of guardianship. Guardianship is still perceived as a natural right of the father rather than the child or the mother. However, the father's guardianship can be restricted or even withdrawn if he violates the rules of what is considered *good* guardianship. However, these demands were not met. The JNCW had asked to make the *wilāya* shared between the father and the mother and to make the mother the default *waṣī* of her children.[34]

Article 223 of the 2010 personal status law stipulates that the *walī* of a minor is his father. Next in line is any *waṣī* the father may have appointed, then the grandfather, then any *waṣī* the grandfather may have appointed, and then the court or the person the court sees fit to act as *waṣī*.

The *walī* needs to fulfil certain requirements. The 2010 law stipulates that the *walī* needs to be sane, an adult, and capable of carrying out the *wilāya*. Furthermore, a non-Muslim is not permitted to act as the *walī* of a Muslim.[35]

The *wilāya* can be revoked in certain cases: if the *walī* becomes insane or if there is a judgment that withdraws his guardianship. These judgments are revocable and, upon submission of a demand to the court, the *wilāya* can be reinstated if the reasons for its withdrawal no longer exist (Articles 225, 2010 law). The *walī* has authority over the financial affairs of the child, but if the *walī* spends the money in an inappropriate way, the court can restrict the *wilāya* or withdraw it completely (Article 226).

In her study on law and gender in urban areas in seventeenth and eighteenth century Syria and Palestine, Judith Tucker observed that a father's right to guardianship

---

[34] Khader 2010, p. 23.

[35] See Article 224 of the 2010 law.

was not an absolute right. 'If the interests of minor children were not being well served by their father, it was up to the court to protect those interests; the welfare of minor children could take precedence over the authority of the father.'[36] The provisions of the 2010 law should subsequently not be understood as a legal innovation but, at least partially, as the official blessing being given to a long-established practice.

The 2010 law for the first time codified provisions relating to the *wiṣāya*.[37] Pursuant to Article 231 the *waṣī* needs to be adult. He needs to be able to carry out the affairs of the minor. He cannot have been convicted of a crime. He cannot be bankrupt or insolvent. He cannot have lost the *wilāya* or the *wiṣāya* over another minor. He cannot be a party in a legal dispute with the minor.

A woman's right to act as the *waṣī* of her children was codified for the first time by the 2010 law. Article 232 stipulates that the *waṣī* can be male or female. This may again indicate that the law merely codified an already existing legal practice. Cases handled by the sharia court of appeal, as demonstrated below, show that women did serve as *waṣī* of their children even prior to 2010. Moreover, Margaret L. Meriwether finds that women in eighteenth and nineteenth century Damascus were appointed as *waṣī* more frequently than men. Out of the 492 cases Meriwether examined, women served as *waṣī* in 268 of them. In 205 cases those women were the mother, and they were otherwise women on the father's side of the family.[38] Nevertheless, even in 2010 it is only the father, grandfather or a male judge who can appoint a woman a *waṣī*. A woman's right to act as the *waṣī* of her children thereby continues to be subject to voluntary male concession rather than its being perceived as a 'natural' right (Article 230).

Like the *wilāya*, the *wiṣāya* is subject to judicial control (Article 235). The *waṣī* can manage the financial affairs of the minor with respect to daily activities (paying for housing). However, if he wants to sell the minor's property, put a mortgage on it, or invest parts of it, then he needs the permission of the court (Article 237). Every six months the *waṣī* needs to prepare a report which is submitted to the court (Article 239).

Rather than presenting a case of legal innovation, the law appears to have simply officially embraced an already established practice. Cases of the sharia court of appeal in Amman demonstrate that the court carried out strong financial oversight even before the enactment of the 2010 law. Furthermore, Meriwether remarks with respect to eighteenth and nineteenth century Damascus that 'courts were quick to support the rights of minors to recover money properly due to them. Islamic law and the courts took the legal rights of children seriously.'[39] Courts during that time, for example, had to approve the sale of property by the *waṣī*.[40]

---

36 Tucker 1998, p. 138.

37 The term is sometimes translated as executor or simply legal guardian. In contrast to the *wilāya* this form of guardianship is generally understood as oversight over the child's financial matters.

38 Meriwether 1996, p. 228.

39 Ibid., p. 227.

40 Ibid., p. 232.

The *wiṣāya* ends when the child turns 18 years old except if it has been decided otherwise. The *wiṣāya* is also terminated if *walī* returns, if the *waṣī* loses his mental capacity, if there is evidence that he is absent, if he dies, if the minor dies, if the time period of a temporary *wiṣāya* ends, or if the *waṣī* submits his resignation (Article 241). The *wiṣāya* can also be revoked if the *waṣī* offends or ignores the administrative authorities, a court order, or if a child staying with the *waṣī* is seen as endangering the best interests of the child (Article 242). There are no provisions that stipulate that the *walī* can resign from his guardianship. This demonstrates the difference between these two forms of guardianship. The *wiṣāya* is primarily a duty which is often temporary whereas the *wilāya* is primarily perceived as a natural right that carries certain obligations but that cannot be abandoned.

The court can revoke the *wilāya* based on a demand by a third party or its own assessment.[41] The state itself can also become the *waṣī* of the child, and the court can assign the *wiṣāya* to a representative of an official organization.[42] This type of judicial interference by the court is justified as a means of preserving the best interests of the minor. The interest of the minor is put above the rights of the *walī* or the *waṣī*, which can be withdrawn by the court if the interest of the minor is endangered. This puts children's rights above male prerogatives normally understood as naturally granted by sharia. These new provisions demonstrate the increasing judicial oversight which subordinates religious prerogatives to increasing state control and state norms. The *wilāya*, a religiously legitimized natural right of male family members (normally the father), can be taken away by the state if it is not carried out 'appropriately'. The natural right of the guardian is thereby made at least partially subject to the protection of the minor.

5.3.4 Parental Agreements on Parental Care

The court only intervenes when there is a dispute over parental care and/or when harm is inflicted upon the child. Entitlement to custody, the period of custody, visiting rights, etc. are not considered an issue of public order. Parents are therefore free to conclude among themselves a parental agreement over all matters relating to custody. The Sharia Enforcement Law (*qānūn al-tanfīdh al-sharʿī*) allows the couple to amend any provision of the visitation agreement in front of the enforcement judge (*qāḍī al-tanfīdh*). It is also possible for the couple to annul a previous agreement and conclude a new agreement in front of the family reconciliation office (*maktab al-iṣlāḥ wa-l-tawfīq al-usrī*).[43]

[41] See Article 228 of the 2010 law.

[42] See Article 232, para (c) of the 2010 law.

[43] Personal interview with Ashraf Omari, sharia judge at the CIJD, 12 July 2015, per e-mail.

5.4 Judicial Practice

5.4.1 The Court System

In accordance with Article 99 of the Constitution, religious courts (sharia courts and the courts of other religious communities) are competent to hear cases relating to personal status law, including matters of parental care. The sharia courts are courts of first instance. Their decisions can be appealed in front of the sharia court of appeal within a period of 30 days pursuant to Article 136 of the Sharia Court Procedures Law.[44] Until 2015, decisions issued by the sharia court of appeal were final and not subject to appeal.

However, the amended Sharia Court Formation Law No. 20 of 2015 (*qānūn muʿaddal li-qānūn tashkīl al-maḥākim al-sharʿiyya*) creates a sharia supreme court (*al-maḥkama al-ʿulyā*). It divides the sharia court system into courts of first instance, courts of appeal, and the sharia supreme court.[45] The law entered into force 16 August 2015.[46] Since then decisions that are issued by the court of appeal are subject to appeal in front of the supreme court which is based in Amman.[47]

All parties who are allowed to claim custody under the personal status law can bring cases in front of the court. The Sharia Court Procedures Law does not prescribe explicit time periods to regulate the length of custody trials. However, according to sharia judge Ashraf Omari, custody judgments are normally issued quickly after three or four sessions. In cases where there is severe disagreement between the two parties, the proceedings can take longer. In these cases the court can issue a temporary custody determination which will have effect until the end of the proceedings. This temporary decision is subject to appeal in front of the sharia court of appeal.[48] Muslim mothers automatically keep their children after the age of fifteen if no alternative party has filed a claim in front of the court. Similarly, non-Muslim mothers can keep their children after the age of seven if the father does not object. Sharia judge Omari explains that this happens when the father is able to guarantee the religious upbringing of his children.[49]

Article 97 of the Sharia Court Procedures Law No. 31 of 1959 was amended in 2001 by Law No. 84. An additional para (d) was added that stipulated that in cases of custody and visitation rights, the judge can issue an order for the immediate implementation of a judgment where the final decision is pending. The Jordanian government explained that this would allow expediting the procedures if this was

---

[44] Articles 135–152 of the 1959 Sharia Court Procedures Law outline the conditions and procedures of appeal cases.

[45] See Article 3 of the 2015 amended Sharia Court Formation Law.

[46] Personal interview with Ashraf Omari, sharia judge at the CIJD, 2 June 2015, per e-mail.

[47] See Article 21 of the 2015 amended Sharia Court Formation Law.

[48] Personal interview with Ashraf Omari, sharia judge at the CIJD, 2 June 2015, per e-mail.

[49] Personal interview with Ashraf Omari, sharia judge at the CIJD, 12 July 2015, per e-mail.

deemed necessary, for example in cases in which this is seen as beneficial for the child.[50] Similarly, the Sharia Enforcement Law stipulates that the judge can expedite a final court decision relating to custody in cases in which there is a fear of serious harm or perdition (*al-ḍarar al-jasīm aw al-halāk*) or the possibility that the child might be taken out of the country.[51]

The use of social assistants or mediators in these cases is not the norm according to sharia judge Omari. Article 11 of the 1959 Sharia Court Procedures Law stipulates that the sharia court administration can set up reconciliation offices in sharia courts to address family disputes if it deems it necessary to do so. In 2013, order number 17 was issued in accordance with Article 11 of the 1959 Sharia Court Procedures Law that organizes these family reconciliation offices. However, Article 4 of the 2013 order once again stipulates that the sharia court administration sets up these offices in all sharia courts 'as needed' (*ḥasab al-ḥāja*). So far 14 reconciliation offices have been set up.[52]

Whereas the concept of the best interests of the child has been introduced in personal status laws, this concept is absent in the relevant procedural law. None of the 160 articles of the 1959 Sharia Court Procedures Law (*qānūn uṣūl al-muḥākamāt al-shar'iyya*) mention the best interests of the child. Similarly, the 2006 Sharia Enforcement Law (*qānūn al-tanfīdh al-shar'ī*) and the new 2013 Enforcement Law do not refer to the concept of the best interests of the child.

The following analysis of judicial practice is based on a collection of custody, *wilāya*, and *wiṣāya* cases adjudicated by the sharia court of appeal between 1951 and 1999.[53]

5.4.2 An Evaluation of the Concept of the Best Interests of the Child in Custody Cases

An analysis of custody cases adjudicated by the sharia court of appeal makes it obvious that custody was supposed to be for the benefit of the child and that it could be taken away when the rights of children or their best interests were endangered, which was often the case when the court feared that the moral integrity of

---

50 Jordanian government, Third periodic report of states parties: Jordan, p. 37.

51 Article 7, para (c) of the 2013 Sharia Enforcement Law.

52 www.sjd.gov.jo/Pages/viewpage.aspx?pageID=200.

53 This collection of judgments was put together in two volumes and published by Ahmad Muhammad 'Ali Dawud, a judge at the sharia court of appeal in Amman. See Dawud 1999a, b. Obtaining access to Jordanian court decisions is considerably more difficult than in the case of other MENA countries like Egypt or the Gulf States since Jordan has so far refrained from publishing court decisions. I obtained the one judgment from a lawyer friend in Amman, but I was not able to access any other decisions. This custody judgment from 2012 does not mention the best interests of the child. It only refers to Articles 170, 171, and 172 of the PSL in justifying the decision.

the minor (girl) could be compromised. However, this did not mean that the best interests of the child were the paramount considerations in all cases, and overall the court tried to balance the rights of various parties.

Without referring to the best interests of the child, the court ruled that the party who is not the custodian should not be prevented from seeing the child. And if the child lives with the mother, she should not be allowed to travel to a faraway town that would prevent the father from seeing the child. The court also considered the opposite case and ruled that the father could travel with the child if it was assured that the mother would be able to see her child daily, and this would only apply to cases in which she does not have custody. If the mother is the custodian, the father could not take the child away from her. The court reaffirmed again that neither party could be denied opportunities to see the child. The court does not justify this position with respect to the best interests of the child. After this general statement the court described the specific circumstances at hand. A man who lived in Kuwait had asked through his father (who was present in Jordan) that the mother who had custody rights send the child to live with him in Kuwait. The case specifies that he was remarried to a foreigner. The court explained that it could not be imposed on the mother to give up her child since the travel (between Jordan and Kuwait) would present an obstacle to her legal right. Furthermore, the court also referred to the best interests of the child and declared that it was obvious that it was in the best interests of the child to stay with his mother for the moment, and the court reaffirmed that custody was for the benefit of the child. Interestingly, the court specified that the fact that the husband was remarried was contrary to the best interests of the child. The court therefore dismissed the claim of the father and ruled that the child would stay with the mother until the father was able to live in his country (Jordan) or close by.[54]

Basing itself on the rules of *fiqh*, the court ruled that where several claimants have an equal right to custody, then the court will favor the fittest, most pious, and most senior.[55] This was an implicit commitment to the best interests of the child. Similarly, the court ruled that the stipulation of a man to keep his child after a *khulʿ* divorce was void (*bāṭil*), but the *khulʿ* divorce itself was valid. The mother would keep the child during the custody period as usual. The court justified the decision by stating that the right of the child (to female care) cannot be revoked even when the mother was divorced through *khulʿ*, in the course of which she had stipulated that she would leave the child with the father. In this case the court ruled that the *khulʿ* was valid but that the condition (giving up the child) was not.[56]

A mother could lose her right to custody in cases involving neglect (*ihmāl*). The court ruled that if neglect was established based on the testimony of witnesses, the mother's right to custody would be withdrawn. If none of the other women entitled

---

[54] Sharia court of appeal Amman, 18 March 1965, case no. 9096, cited in Dawud 1999a, p. 497.

[55] Sharia court of appeal Amman, 18 August 1953, case no. 8130, cited in Dawud 1999a, p. 495.

[56] Sharia court of appeal Amman, 24 June 1957, case no. 9527, cited in Dawud 1999a, pp. 498–499.

to custody filed a custody claim, then the court of first instant's judgment giving the child to the father had been correct.[57]

Despite legal provisions stipulated by the Family Law, legal practice demonstrates that a mother will not always lose custody even if she marries a stranger. In a case handled by the sharia court of appeal, an aunt had filed a claim against the mother to have her custody rights revoked because the mother had married a stranger. The court ruled that in this case the judge gets to appoint as custodian whomever he pleases, but that the preference is for the mother, 'because she is most caring.'[58]

The courts were also concerned about protecting the moral integrity of children and ensuring their religious upbringing. In one case the court ruled that a mother who worked in an establishment of 'debauchery' as a singer or prostitute would lose her right to custody.[59] The court rulings declare that the *ḥaḍāna* is for the benefit of the child. If the judge learns that the father has other children living in his home and the judge is afraid that the girls in question might be seduced by them, then the court does not separate the girls from their mother.[60]

The court also ruled that a difference of religion between the female custodian and the child does not affect her right to custody except if there is fear that the child would be familiarized with a religion other than Islam, and this only applies if the child has reached the age of seven.[61] In one case a woman's right to custody was revoked because she had enrolled the child in a missionary school in Bethlehem. The claimant, the uncle of the child, was able to prove that the child suffered great harm as a result of enrolment in this school teaching subjects that are contrary to an Islamic education.[62]

5.4.3 *An Evaluation of the Concept of the Best Interests of the Child in* wilāya *and* wiṣāya *Cases*

An analysis of forty-three *wilāya* and *wiṣāya* cases handled by the sharia court of appeal between 1951 and 1999 makes it clear that neither the *wilāya* nor the *wiṣāya* are assigned with regard to what is considered to be in the best interests of the child. Rather, both institutions are seen as natural tasks carried out either by the father or, in his absence, by the paternal grandfather. In August 1955 the court ruled that the *wilāya* of the paternal grandfather was the 'natural *wilāya*' and did not have to be installed (by the court).[63] Similarly, the biological grandfather

57 Sharia court of appeal Amman, 16 September 1957, case no. 9586, cited in Dawud 1999a, p. 499.

58 Sharia court of appeal Amman, 28 January 1959, case no. 10175, cited in Dawud 1999a, p. 500.

59 Sharia court of appeal Amman, 26 December 1959, case no. 10672, cited in Dawud 1999a.

60 Sharia court of appeal Amman, 23 January 1951, case no. 5689, cited in Dawud 1999a, p. 495.

61 Sharia court of appeal Amman, 20 March 1951, case no. 5835, cited in Dawud 1999a.

62 Sharia court of appeal Amman, 9 April 1961, case no. 11411, cited in Dawud 1999a, p. 500.

63 Sharia court of appeal Amman, 8 August 1955, case no. 8848, cited in Dawud 1999b, p. 1405.

cannot become a party to a lawsuit over the children of his deceased son because he automatically assumes the *wilāya* without a court having to confirm that.[64]

Most of the cases adjudicated by the court between 1951 and 1999 were related to financial matters such as the selling and managing of property of the minor. Like Ottoman judges, Jordanian judges took the protection of the financial rights of the minor seriously. The judge had financial oversight over how the *waṣī* handled the financial affairs of the minor. Most of these cases, however, do not refer to the best interests of the child. Yet, in one case the sharia court of appeal ruled that if the *waṣī* harmed the 'best interests of the minors and does not do right by them', then it is for the judge to appoint a different *waṣī* to protect 'children's rights'.[65]

Many of these cases refer to the minor as an orphan. The term orphan was commonly used when the child had lost his father regardless of whether the mother was still alive, emphasizing the patrilineal family.[66] In one of the cases the mother of the 'orphan' had asked to gain financial oversight over how the *waṣī* handled the financial affairs of her child. The claim was denied, and the judge ruled that it is the judge who carries out this type of financial oversight. The judgment is justified with reference to the rules of *fiqh* and not with reference to the best interests of the child.[67]

The above-mentioned judgment makes it clear that even when the mother was still alive, she would rarely act as the *waṣī* of her children. The right of the mother to assume the *wiṣāya* was only formally introduced into statutory law in the 2010 Family Law. However, this did not mean a woman could not act as the *waṣī* of her children prior to the enactment of the law. In July 1978 the sharia court of appeal ruled that the annulment of the *wiṣāya* of the mother, which had been registered in Saudi Arabia, would enter into force when the father was reinstalled as the *walī* of his children. The mother would consequently remain the *waṣī* of her children until the father was reinstated as their *walī*. The court justified its decision by stating that the absence of the father was likely the reason why the mother had been assigned the *wiṣāya* in the first place. In the father's absence somebody had to handle the children's affairs. The main objective of the court was to avoid a situation in which children would be left without a caretaker. The judgment does not mention the best interests of the child.[68] In another case the mother had appealed the ruling of a sharia judge in East Amman who had taken away her *wiṣāya* over her children. The court of appeal rejected her appeal because the decision was of an administrative nature (*idārī*) in order to 'protect the rights of the minors' and was therefore not subject to appeal.[69]

---

[64] Sharia court of appeal Amman, 19 April 1972, case no. 17041, cited in Dawud 1999b, p. 1411.

[65] Sharia court of appeal Amman, 22 October 1957, case no. 9644, cited in Dawud 1999b, p. 1406.

[66] Agmon 2006, p. 147.

[67] Sharia court of appeal Amman, 28 March 1962, case no. 12025, cited in Dawud 1999b, pp. 1409–1410.

[68] Sharia court of appeal Amman, 29 July 1978, case no. 20238, cited in Dawud 1999b, p. 1414.

[69] Sharia court of appeal Amman, 3 August 1983, case no. 23908, cited in Dawud 1999b.

5.4.4 *An Evaluation of the Concept of the Best Interests of the Child in Relation to Visiting Rights Since the Enactment of the 2010 Law*

Women's groups have criticized the application of the visiting rights provisions of the 2010 law. The JWU carried out a study on visiting rights cases.[70] The study criticized that the terms seeing, visiting, accompanying, and sleepover were not clearly defined and that there was no legal consistency in how judges understood and applied these terms. The study also found that women who had remarried (*ghayr maḥram*) were given the right to see their children for several hours but that no visiting rights were granted in the new marital home. By contrast, the study found that visiting rights were given to fathers who were remarried. The study also found that the courts did not consider visiting and seeing rights as rights of the child that help fulfil the best interests of the child, but that they consider visiting rights as interests of the person who is asking for them.

According to the study, courts did not base their decisions on objective legal reasons when ruling for or against visitation rights. If mothers who were remarried were allowed to see their children in their marital home, then this was an indication that the ex-husband, the father of the child, had agreed to that; but if there was a conflict between him and her or between his and her family, then the court would deny this right. The relationship of the parents was thereby crucial for the decision of the court rather than the best interests of the child.[71]

The Enforcement Law allows for the imprisonment of an individual who has been found guilty of not complying with a judgment that requires him to deliver the child or for non-compliance with a ruling on visitation rights.[72]

5.5 Conclusion

The concept of the best interests of the child was introduced for the first time in Jordanian statutory law in 1951 to allow judges to extend the custody period by 2 years for boys and girls in cases in which it was considered in the best interests of the child. However, this did not mean that courts previously had never taken the

---

[70] The study specified that 204 cases based on the 2010 law were examined. It explained that the judgments concerned cases that were received by the Children's Home (literally hostelry for children (*dār ḍiyāfat al-ṭifl*)), which was set up in 1996 to offer an alternative to the security centres where visitation usually took place. The study also specified that the cases studied concerned children between 2 months and 18 years of age. The study does not specify in which period the judgments were issued or by which court.

[71] JWU (undated).

[72] See Article 15 of the 2013 Sharia Enforcement Law.

best interests of the child into consideration or that they were only doing so with respect to this specific area of the law. With respect to urban areas in seventeenth and eighteenth century Syria and Palestine, Judith Tucker observes that '[w]ithout surrendering in any way the net distinction between mothers and fathers, the muftis and courts allowed for a certain shading of the boundaries of parental roles when it appeared to be in the best interests of the child to do so.'[73] The increasing references to the best interests of the child in statutory law should therefore not necessarily be understood as a legal innovation, but rather as in many cases confirming an already established practice.

A closer look at Jordanian legislation and judicial practice, however, reveals that the concept of the best interests of the child has not been fully incorporated into the Jordanian legal system. It can at best be described as an implicit guiding principle. It has neither been incorporated into the sharia court's procedural rules nor in the provisions that govern the enforcement of custody awards. Children's rights therefore continue to be group-based rather than universal. They depend on the religious affiliation of the parents and the gender of the child. Children's rights are never considered in isolation from the rights of parents, and, generally speaking, the courts try to balance the rights of the various parties (mother, father, and child). Overall, protecting children from material and social harm was the primary lens through which children's rights were approached.

In 1992 Jordan ratified the Convention for the Rights of the Child (CRC). As a result, pressure increased to adopt the concept of the best interests of the child as the defining principle of legislation and the judicial process. Through the reporting process, Jordan is obviously keen to portray its laws as reflecting the best interests of the child. Nevertheless, Jordan has maintained its reservations to Articles 14, 20, and 21 of the Convention. The way in which these reservations are justified demonstrates the limits of the application of the concept of the best interests of the child. Freedom of consciousness (Article 14) is not seen as a right that should be given to children. Rather, giving the child a religious upbringing is primarily seen as a right of the parents, and in marriages between a Muslim man and a Christian woman it is seen as a right of the father in order to ensure that his children receive an Islamic upbringing. This approach is reflected in the relevant custody laws and their application.

Overall, it is unlikely that the best interests of the child will become the principal lens through which children's rights are addressed in Jordan in the foreseeable future since none of the actors (state as well as non-state) have yet fully embraced this concept. State actors have primarily tried to balance the interests of various parties, and women's rights groups have primarily approached family law reform from a women's rights perspective. They have sought to expand women's rights within the family, often compromising the best interests of the child along the way.

---

[73] Tucker 1998, p. 115.

References

Abu Nowar M (2006) The History of the Hashemite Kingdom of Jordan. Ithaca Press, Reading

Agmon I (2006) Family & court: Legal culture and modernity in late Ottoman Palestine. Syracuse University Press, Syracuse

Al-Bakri W (undated) Dirasa hawla Ta'dilat Qanun al-Ahwal al-Shakhsiyya allati Tammat bi-Mujib al-Qanun al-Mu'aqqat Raqam 2001/86 [Study about the amendments to the Personal Status Law which were issued in accordance with the Temporary Law 2001/86], Mizan, Amman

Anderson JND (1952) Recent developments in shari'a law: the Jordanian Law of Family Rights 1951. Muslim World 42:190–206

Clark JA, Young AE (2008) Islamism and Family Law Reform in Morocco and Jordan. Mediterranean Politics 13(3):333–353

Dawud AM'A (1999a) Al-Qarrarat al-Isti'nafiyya fi-l-Ahwal al-Shakhsiyya [The decisions of the Court of Appeal regarding Personal Status Law], part 1, Maktabat Dar al-Thaqafa li-l-Nashr wa-l-Tawzi', Amman

Dawud AM'A (1999b) Al-Qarrarat al-Isti'nafiyya fi-l-Ahwal al-Shakhsiyya [The decisions of the Court of Appeal regarding Personal Status Law], part 2, Maktabat Dar al-Thaqafa li-l-Nashr wa-l-Tawzi', Amman

Husseini R (1998) Women activists examine changing marriage laws. Jordan Times (4 September 1998)

JWU (undated) Dirasa Tahliliyya li-l-Ahkam al-Qada'iyya fi Da'awa al-Ru'ya wa-l-Mabit wa-l-Istizara wa-l-Istihab al-Sadira bi-Mujib Qanun al-Ahwal al-Shakhsiyya al-Mu'aqqat Raqam 36 li-Sanat 2010 [Analytical study of the legal provisions regarding claims for seeing, sleepovers, visiting, and accompanying issued in accordance with the temporary personal status law No. 36 of 2010]

Khader A (2010) Bayan al-Matalib fi Majal al-Islah al-Qanuni [Statement of demands in the field of legal reform], JNCW

Meriwether ML (1996) The Rights of Children and the Responsibilities of Women: Women as Wasis in Ottoman Aleppo 1770–1840. In: El Azhary Sonbol A (ed) Women, the Family, and Divorce Laws in Islamic History, 1st edn. Syracuse University Press, Syracuse, pp 219–235

Paradelle M (1999) Legal Pluralism and Public International Law: An Analysis Based on the International Convention on the Rights of the Child. In: Dupret B et al (eds) Legal Pluralism in the Arab World. Kluwer Law International, Boston, pp 97–113

Sadr YI (1924) Majmu'at al-Qawanin [Collection of Laws], vol 1. Matba'at Sadr, Beirut

Sadr YI (1929) Majmu'at al-Qawanin [Collection of Laws], vol 2. Matba'at Sadr, Beirut

Tsimhoni D (1993) Christian Communities in Jerusalem and the West Bank Since 1948: An Historical, Social, and Political Study. Conn Praeger, Westport

Tucker JE (1998) In the House of the Law: Gender and Islamic law in Ottoman Syria and Palestine. University of California Press, Berkeley

Welchman L (1988) The Development of Islamic Family Law in the Legal System of Jordan. Int Comp Law Q 37(4):868–886

Welchman L (2007) Women and Muslim Family Laws in Arab States: a Comparative Overview of Textual Development and Advocacy. Amsterdam University Press, Amsterdam

Chapter 6
Lebanon

Marie-Claude Najm

Abstract Lebanon does not adopt any State religion and, specifically, is not a Muslim State. However, the Lebanese Constitution grants the religious communities judicial and legislative prerogatives in personal status matters. As part of personal status through the marriage, custody and guardianship fall within the jurisdiction of religious courts and are governed by religious laws. Yet there are some situations where civil courts enjoy jurisdiction over such issues and rule on the basis of civil law. For example, civil courts may hear personal status matters in cases involving children in danger, or in cases related to the protection of the child's assets and supervision of the guardian's acts. Such interference has sometimes caused a conflict with religious authorities, namely *sharhi* courts, which enjoy the general jurisdiction over custody and guardianship matters. Lebanon's ratification of the CRC in 1991 reflects the on-going trend towards universal values, amongst which is the concept of the best interests of the child. During the two last decades, a growing number of civil and religious statutory laws and court rulings have introduced express reference to the best interests of the child as a paramount rule in various matters relating to child law. Specifically, where the traditional Islamic law regulations do not explicitly, or only rarely, refer to the notion of the best interests of the child, the new codifications introduced it in many of their provisions, and court practice indicates an increasing reference to this standard. However, the concept of the best interests of the child is far from being fully implemented in the Lebanese legal system. It is indeed to a large extent dependent on religious courts, which do not consider themselves bound by the international treaties ratified by the State or by the interpretation given to such norms. Decisions related to child welfare are still mostly based on

The author is Professor at the Faculty of Law and Political Science of Saint-Joseph University (Beirut) and Director of the Centre of Legal Studies and Research for the Arab World (Centre d'études des droits du monde arabe (CEDROMA)).

M.-C. Najm (✉)
Faculty of Law and Political Science, Saint-Joseph University,
B.P. 17-5208, Mar Mikhael, Beirut, 1104-2020, Lebanon
e-mail: marieclaude.najm@usj.edu.lb

N. Yassari et al. (eds.), *Parental Care and the Best Interests of the Child in Muslim Countries*, DOI 10.1007/978-94-6265-174-6_6

religious rules, customs and practices and thus on elements such as the marital status or the religious affiliation of the parents. The path is yet to be followed.

Keywords Lebanon · Islamic law · Minor children · Custody (*ḥaḍāna*) · Guardianship (*wilāya*) · CRC · Best interests of the child · Juvenile protection

Contents

6.1 Introduction

6.1.1 Specific Features of the Lebanese State as Compared to Muslim Countries

Unlike most States in the Middle East, Lebanon does not adopt any State religion and, specifically, is not a Muslim State. Article 9 of the Lebanese Constitution recognizes the 'absolute' freedom of conscience and declares: 'The State, in rendering homage to the Almighty, respects all creeds and guarantees under its protection the free exercise of all religious rites provided that public order is not disturbed'. The Lebanese State is therefore equidistant from all religions and does not embrace any of them as its own.

However, under the same Article 9, the State 'guarantees that the personal status and religious interests of the population, to whatever religious sect they belong, are respected'. This subtly drafted provision is the fundamental basis for the judicial and legislative prerogatives of the religious communities in personal status matters. It is through such prerogatives conferred upon the communities that religious laws are made applicable in a non-religious State such as Lebanon.

The eighteen religious sects that enjoy such jurisdiction in Lebanon are the 'historically recognized communities' designated in the law,[1] i.e. the twelve

[1] Annex I of Legislative Decree No. 60/1936 of 13 March 1936 Regarding the Status of the Religious Communities, amended by Legislative Decree No. 146/1938 of 11 November 1938, and Article 1 of the Law of 2 April 1951 Regarding Jurisdiction of Religious Courts for Christian and Israelite Communities.

Christian communities,[2] the four Muslim communities,[3] the Druze community (also referred to as *'al-muwaḥḥidīn'*) and the Israelite (Jewish) community.

As part of personal status (and marriage in particular), matters related to custody and guardianship fall within the jurisdiction of religious courts and are governed by religious laws.[4] Consequently, the applicable rules differ across sectarian institutions. In the absence of a regular and permanent publication of the case law emanating from religious courts, the researcher is often left to conduct a door-to-door enquiry at the various religious courts.[5]

6.1.2 Islamic Law in Lebanese Positive Law

Islamic law in Lebanese positive law can be defined as the set of rules in force that are based on the *fiqh* and that vary depending on the Muslim sect concerned.[6] Pursuant to Article 242 Law of 16 July 1962 on the Regulation of the Sharia Sunni and Ja'fari courts, the personal status of the Sunni community is governed by the Law of 25 October 1917 (Ottoman Family Code), still in force, and, in the absence

---

[2] The Christian religious communities are the Maronite, Greek-Orthodox, Greek-Catholic (Melkite), Armenian-Orthodox (Gregorian), Armenian-Catholic, Syriac-Orthodox (Jacobite), Syriac-Catholic, Assyrian (Nestorian), Chaldean, Latin (Roman Catholic) and Evangelical communities as well as the Coptic community, which has more recently been recognized and included in the list of historical communities by virtue of Law No. 553/1996 of 24 July 1996.

[3] The two main Islamic sects are the Sunni and the Shia (Ja'fari-Twelver or Imami Shia). The Alawite and the Ismaili (Sevener Shia) are the smallest Muslim Shia communities. The Alawite community has only recently been organized in Lebanon, by virtue of Law No. 448/1995 of 17 August 1995; Alawite courts have therefore been established and they shall apply Ja'fari law and customs (Article 32 of the above-cited law). The Ismaili community does not yet enjoy any legal organization.

[4] Marriage and all of its effects fall under the jurisdiction of the religious authority that has celebrated the marriage (Article 14 Law of 2 April 1951; Article 23(1) Legislative Decree No. 60/1936), which can be the religious authority of either the husband or the wife (Article 15 Law of 2 April 1951).

[5] The author wishes to express her sincere gratitude and thanks to Nayla Geagea, who enabled her to consult a set of recent and unpublished religious court decisions on matters of custody that were cited in Human Rights Watch 2015. Unless otherwise specified, all such unpublished religious court decisions on matters of custody that are cited in the present chapter have been previously cited in the said report. To avoid repetition, the report will therefore not be repeatedly cited hereafter. The author also wishes to express her thanks to Sheikh Mohamed Nokkari, *sharhi* judge, lecturer at Saint-Joseph University and Notre Dame University, and former Director General of Dar Al-Fatwa, who provided her with recent unpublished court decisions on custody and guardianship.

[6] Bilani 1963. The laws applicable in matters of personal status in Lebanon can be consulted in the Arabic version of the code featuring a French translation by Mahmassani and Messarra 1970. The reforms or amendments made to these laws during the past decades are only available in the official Arabic version.

of any other provision, by the rules of the *fiqh* in the Hanafi school.[7] In 2011, Article 242 Law of 16 July 1962 was amended in order to make the resolutions of the Supreme Islamic Council—headed by the Mufti of the Republic—the main source of reference for Sunni courts,[8] which raised legitimate criticism on the Parliament's renouncement of its right to legislate in the field of personal status law. This amendment enabled the Supreme Islamic Council to issue a new Family Law in 2011.[9] The new law, which addresses cases related to the care of children, visitation and spousal maintenance, is applicable to all ongoing proceedings before *sharhi* Sunni courts in Lebanon (Article 36 of the Law) and abrogates all previous conflicting provisions (Article 38 of the Law).

The Shia community is governed by the rules of the Ja'fari school (that are enforced in the Lebanese legal system although not formally codified) as well as by the 1917 Ottoman Family Code when the latter is not contrary to the Ja'fari rules.[10] The lack of codification of Ja'fari rules led the president of the Supreme Ja'fari Court in 1994 to draft a *Guide to Ja'fari Justice*, reedited in 2010, which collects and explains rules related to personal status matters in Ja'fari law.[11] The Guide however is not binding on judges.

As to personal status in the Druze community, it is governed by the Law of 24 February 1948, which has codified the customs and traditions of the Druze in personal status matters.

All such laws—even those whose provisions have been formally and organically enacted by the Lebanese State and thus are part of the Lebanese legislation[12]—are not characterized as State civil laws. Their content has indeed been determined (and can only be amended) by the religious authorities. Further, the Lebanese civil courts do not exercise any control on the way religious law is made applicable before the religious courts, even for those courts whose organization and function are set by the Lebanese State.[13] However, decisions issued by the religious courts can be challenged before the Plenary Assembly of the Court of

[7] In 1875, the traditional rules of the Hanafi doctrine on personal status and inheritance were drafted by Qadri Pacha in Egypt in a book titled *Al-Ahkam al-Shar'iyya fi al-Ahwal al-Shakhsiyya 'ala Madhhab al-Imam Abi Hanifa* in order to facilitate the tasks of the courts. This book has not been promulgated as a law; it is, however, still taken in consideration by the courts in the absence of any other provision.

[8] Law No. 177/2011 of 29 August 2011 amending Article 242 of the Law of 16 July 1962.

[9] Decree No. 46/2011 of 1 October 2011.

[10] Article 242 Law of 16 July 1962.

[11] Guide to Ja'fari Justice, by Sheikh Abdallah Nehmé, Dar-el-Balagha editions, Ghubairi, Lebanon, 2010.

[12] Such is the case, for instance, for the above-mentioned Druze Law of 24 February 1948.

[13] Due to historical reasons, the organization and functioning of the Muslim and Druze courts are determined by the Lebanese State. This is not the case for other non-Muslim religious courts, which are not part of the State apparatus. The non-Muslim religious authorities in Lebanon directly establish their own laws as well as the organization and functioning of their courts.

Cassation—which is the highest civil court in Lebanon—in the following two cases: (1) lack of jurisdiction and (2) violation of a substantial formality pertaining to public order, i.e. a formality that is critical to due process (e.g. when a judgment is issued despite the defendant not having been notified or allowed to present a defense). Such review cannot, therefore, extend to the merits of the case.

6.1.3 Purpose of the Chapter

The purpose of this chapter is to follow the path of the notion of the best interests of the child in Lebanese domestic law and to explore the ways in which courts interpret the notion in the field of custody and guardianship for Muslim children.[14] Emphasis will be put on the specific features of the Lebanese legal system and on court practice in order to answer the most relevant issues.

After briefly describing the international legal framework of Lebanon's child law regime and its impact on Lebanese internal policy agendas, institutions, laws and court practices (Sect. 6.2), the present chapter will focus on the religious laws' frames of reference regarding custody and guardianship for Muslim children in Lebanon and their most recent implementation by religious courts (Sect. 6.3). Finally, the impact of civil laws in such cases will be addressed (Sect. 6.4).

6.2 The Impact of the UN Convention on the Rights of the Child (CRC)

Paragraph B of the Preamble of the Lebanese Constitution states: 'Lebanon is … a founding and active member of the United Nations Organization and abides by its covenants and by the Universal Declaration of Human Rights …'.

Lebanon is indeed a State Party to a certain number of human rights covenants. For instance, Lebanon has ratified the CEDAW (United Nations Convention on the Elimination of all Forms of Discrimination against Women of 18 December 1979), although making and maintaining reservations, notably on its provisions prescribing gender equality in the transmission of nationality to children and in marital and family rights and duties.

More importantly for our purpose, Lebanon ratified the Convention on the Rights of the Child (CRC) on 14 May 1991. Unlike other MENA States, Lebanon has not stipulated any reservation thereto.

---

14 The definition of the child is somehow ambiguous in Sunni and Ja'fari law in Lebanon. By contrast, Druze law clearly sets at eighteen the age at which a child reaches adulthood. This falls in line with Lebanese civil laws (Code of Obligations and Contracts 1932; Law No. 422/2002 on Juvenile protection) and with CRC and ILO Convention norms.

The CRC states that in all matters concerning children 'the best interests of the child shall be a primary consideration' (Article 3), and thus it clearly favors a child-focused approach in family law. The Convention adds that:

> State Parties shall ensure that a child shall not be separated from his or her parents against their will, except when competent authorities subject to judicial review determine, in accordance with applicable law and procedures, that such separation is necessary for the best interests of the child (Article 9).

It further notes that children have a right to maintain direct contact with both parents on a regular basis unless it is not in their best interests (Articles 9 and 10). The CRC also requires that children be given a right to express their views in all matters concerning their welfare (Article 12).

The principle of the best interests of the child is therefore, through the ratification of the CRC, explicitly recognized in the Lebanese legal system. And clearly, the ratification of the CRC has had an impact on the institutional and legal framework pertaining to child issues in Lebanon.

On the institutional level, in 1994 the State created the High Council of Childhood that is in charge of overseeing the proper application of the Convention under the authority of the Ministry of Social Affairs. Further, Lebanese ministries (namely the Ministries of Labour, Social Affairs, Education, Justice, Public Health and Interior) have set up special departments and units dedicated to child-related issues, while national committees and parliamentary working groups were formed to review laws and coordinate strategies. They collaborate with NGOs to offer protective and rehabilitative social services. However, the work of governmental institutions and NGO's remains hampered by limited human resources and funding, and insufficient implementation of the relevant laws.

On the legal level, the ratification of the CRC—combined with societal pressures, lobbying by non-governmental organizations and the efforts of human rights activists—has highly influenced the policies and agendas of Lebanese lawmakers and pushed them to enact a series of laws pertaining to the child's interest and protection in various fields of the law such as child labor,[15] criminal law,[16] access to

[15] For example, consistent with ILO Convention No. 138, Law No. 536/1996 raises the minimum working age.

[16] Law No. 414/2002 authorizes the government to ratify the Optional Protocol of CRC on the sale of children, child prostitution and child pornography. Law No. 164/2011 on human trafficking increases penalties for trafficking and exploitation offences which force children to participate in violations of the law, prostitution, sexual exploitation, begging, slavery, forced labour, implication in armed conflicts, terrorist acts, organ removal and child pornography; it also widens the category of trafficking when a minor is involved, by making unnecessary any proof of force, violence, deception, abduction or material favours.

health,[17] education[18] and social security.[19] More importantly for our purpose, the Lebanese Parliament adopted Law No. 422/2002 of 6 June 2002 on Juvenile Protection. This law, which addresses the situations of children threatened or at risk (i.e. a child in a situation that exposes him/her to exploitation, or threatens his/her health, safety, morals, or upbringing; a child exposed to sexual abuse or physical violence; and a child found begging or vagabonding), grants juvenile judges the mandate to issue protective orders and directs them to base their decisions on the children's best interests; it is, furthermore, seen as one of the most significant improvements in child protection in Lebanon.[20]

Finally, the ratification of the CRC has also pushed the religious authorities to take into consideration in a more explicit manner the notion of the best interests of the child. Specifically, whereas the traditional Islamic law regulations do not explicitly, or only rarely, refer to the notion of the best interests of the child (*maṣlaḥat al-ṭifl, maṣlaḥat al-maḥḍūn*), the new codifications have introduced the notion in many of their provisions, and court practice indicates an increasing reference to the notion in court rulings, as we will show later in the chapter.

The notion of the best interests of the child has therefore become an explicit frame of reference in Lebanese domestic law and court practice, which has influenced the rules on custody and guardianship.

However, that said, the implementation of the concept—and, specifically, the way in which it is perceived and interpreted in the field of parental care—is to a large extent dependent on non-State authorities because personal status matters fall within the authority of religious courts, which do not consider themselves bound by the international conventions ratified by the State or by the interpretation given by the State to such norms. Decisions related to child welfare still depend on elements such as marital status or the religious affiliation of the parents, as will be described in Sect. 6.3 below.

6.3 Religious Laws' Frames of Reference and Their Implementation by Religious Courts

The law applicable to Muslim children in Lebanon draws a clear distinction between child custody (*ḥaḍāna*) and legal guardianship (*wilāya*).[21] *Ḥaḍāna* refers to the material and moral upbringing of the children until they no longer need care; custody is hence, by nature, of limited duration. Conversely, *wilāya* refers to

17 Decree No. 162/1999 and Decree No. 4265/2000 facilitate children's access to medical facilities, particularly at institutions receiving government funding.

18 Law No. 220/2000 decreed the rights of disabled children to a proper education and to be admitted in educational institutions. Law No. 17/2011 raised the age of mandatory access to compulsory free public education to 15 years.

19 Article 80 Law No. 220/2000 amended the Lebanese Social Security Code by providing social security benefits to the sons and daughters of qualified beneficiaries until the age of 25.

20 See the comprehensive field study by UNICEF 2012.

21 El-Husseini Begdache 2008; Moukarzel Hechaime 2008b; Moukarzel Hechaimé 2010.

the supervision of children's upbringing and the making of decisions related to their education, health care and assets until they reach adulthood.

Parental care questions generally arise before the courts in the context of married couples who separate or divorce. However, other situations may occur where parental care is at stake, mainly children born to unmarried parents. The status of illegitimate children in Lebanese law, and specifically in Islamic Lebanese law, is very unfavorable. As an illegitimate child is not allowed under Islamic law to bring a claim against his or her alleged father in order to establish filiation before the court, illegitimate children are thus deprived of all rights of any kind towards their alleged father.

In Islamic law, legitimate filiation (*nasab*) is established by the blood relationship between the child and his/her validly married parents.[22] However, a strict and rigid application of this rule would have left many children without established filiation. Islamic *fuqahā'* have hence creatively developed many legal fictions in order to attenuate the rigidity of the rule in practice and thus bring illegitimate children (children born outside the pregnancy period required for the presumption of legitimate paternity, children born outside a valid marriage, and also non-biologically related children such as children of unknown filiation) within the category of legitimate filiation (*nasab*). One of the most simple mechanisms, as it is based on liberal rules and very low requirements, is the *iqrār* acknowledgment of valid paternity (or maternity), which entails all the consequences of legitimate filiation.[23] Such rules are clearly based on the—although not explicitly mentioned—best interests of the child. *Sharhi* courts very often issue decisions establishing the marriage (*ithbāt al-zawāj*) on the sole basis of the declaration of the father and mother of the child and thereby establish the child's *nasab* (legitimate filiation) to his or her parents.[24] However, under Article 332 of the Guide to Ja'fari Justice, the father cannot establish the legitimate filiation of a child born of adultery, even should he marry the mother while she is pregnant.

The rules on child custody and guardianship that will be described below will therefore only address the situation of legitimate children, which is the only situation falling within the jurisdiction of religious courts.

6.3.1 *Custody* (Ḥaḍāna)

6.3.1.1 Attribution of Custody

Priority Custody Rule Based on Age and Gender

In religious laws applicable to Muslims in Lebanon, custody is a joint right and duty of the parents.[25] In cases of separation, however, custody is awarded follow-

---

[22] Articles 332, 333 and 350 Qadri Pacha Code; Article 334 Guide to Ja'fari Justice.

[23] See, for example, Article 350 Qadri Pacha Code.

[24] Shtaura Sunni Court, 19 October 2015, unpublished, provided by Sheikh Nokkari.

[25] E.g. Article 17 Family Law 2011.

ing a priority rule based on the age and gender of the child.[26] This time-limited rule is actually a common feature of almost all Lebanese religious laws.[27]

In the Shia community, maternal custody ends when the boy reaches 2 and the girl 7 (Article 348 Guide to Ja'fari Justice). In the Sunni community and only until recently, mothers were granted custody over their children until the boy reached the age of 7 and the girl the age of 9, in accordance with the teachings of Hanafi doctrine. The same cut-off age is provided for in Article 64 of the Druze Personal Status Law of 24 February 1948. In response to intense lobbying by women's organizations, the Sunni community increased the cut-off age at which the child's custody reverts to the father. The New Sunni Family Law of 2011 provides that *ḥaḍāna* is vested in the mother until the children reach 12 for both boys and girls,[28] unless provided otherwise by the judge on the basis of the child's interests and by virtue of a ruling under the Sharia rules and procedures.[29] It is to be noted, in this respect, that the feminists' claim—aiming to extend the duration of the mother's *ḥaḍāna* and not to revoke the automatic custody devolution—was made from a women's rights and gender-equality perspective, rather than on grounds specifically related to the child's best interests. The increase of the cut-off age may, however, be linked to the best interests of the child. At age 12 and higher, the child is deemed old enough to give his or her own opinion regarding custody arrangements.

Finally, if the mother cannot, for any event, be the custodian, the duty is passed down the maternal line (to the maternal grandmother, paternal grandmother, full sisters, uterine sisters, consanguine sisters, etc.) in *Sunni* and in Druze law.[30] By contrast, in Ja'fari Law, in the event of the death of the custodian mother (during the *ḥaḍāna* period) or the father (after *ḥaḍāna* has reverted to him), the other parent has priority over all the other paternal or maternal relatives to raise the child.[31]

---

[26] Moukarzel Hechaime 2008a.

[27] In Christian statutes also, cut-off ages are generally set in the laws: 2 for both boys and girls (Articles 123–124 Catholic Personal Status Law; as a matter of fact, this law does not set a specific cut-off age for custody but provides for the right of the mother to feed her child until he/she reaches 2, after which the court rules on custody on the basis of the child's interest); 14 for boys and 15 for girls (Article 57 New Orthodox Personal Status Law of 16 October 2003); 11 for boys and 13 for girls (Article 93 Coptic Orthodox Code of 9 December 2010); 7 for boys and 9 for girls (Articles 128–132 Armenian Orthodox Personal Status Law; Article 61 Syriac Orthodox Personal Status Law; Article 111 Assyrian Personal Status Law). However, all of these Christian personal status laws provide for a custody determination at the judge's discretion based on the best interests of the child.

[28] Article 15 Family Law 2011.

[29] Article 17 Family Law 2011.

[30] Article 57 Druze Law 1948.

[31] Articles 351 and 352 Guide to Ja'fari Justice.

Compliance with the Best Interests of the Child Standard

In any event, such a determination of custody has been severely criticized because it lies upon automatic and rigid criteria of age and gender and thus fails to address the child's best interests as a primary consideration. It is also discriminatory and inequitable towards women. In this respect, child custody rules cannot be correctly assessed without taking into consideration the discrimination against women in accessing divorce and obtaining spousal maintenance and financial compensation, as this discrimination can affect the rights of the child. Indeed, in many cases women give up maternal custody rights in order to obtain a divorce and the judge ratifies the agreement between the ex-spouses without addressing the best interests of the child or the woman's reasons for renouncing her rights.[32]

At the same time, it would be inaccurate to state that the *ḥaḍāna a* rules in Muslim law are indifferent to the interests of the child standard. In fact, whereas the Western conception of the best interests of the child is assessed *in concreto*, on a case-by-case basis, the religious view is to consider the best interests of the child *in abstracto*, even without explicit or formal reference to the notion. The children are perceived as a global abstract category rather than as individual persons with varying and specific situations, needs and environments. The rule is obviously based on the belief that the interests of children are best served when they spend their early childhood years with their mother (or, in her absence, a female family member). In other words, the rationale behind the rule is that it is in the best interests of the child to benefit from the mother's caring, tenderness, love and affection—all qualities that are attributed to women—as long as the child is in need of physical care and emotional fostering and to benefit from the father's authority, guidance, discipline and education—amongst which is religious education—when he/she becomes a maturing child. The rules are seen as an expression of the inherently biological qualities and abilities respectively possessed by parents (as well as their strengths and weaknesses) which relate to the fulfilment a child's needs. The 2011 Family Law applicable before Sunni courts, which contains many explicit references to the child's interests, provides, very significantly, indications on the way the child's interests are perceived in Islamic law, such interests being closely linked to the need to raise the child in accordance with Islamic moral and religious values and teachings. Thus, the law defines custody as the duty to raise the child and take care of him/her during the period determined by the law in accordance with the child's interest in having an Islamic religious and moral upbringing.[33] The custodian has to be able to provide the child with an Islamic religious and moral education.[34] Finally, when assessing the interests of the child whose custody is at issue, the judge is invited to consider, amongst the criteria to be contemplated

[32] Beirut Sunni Court, 13 April 2010, unpublished; Baabda Ja'fari Court, 15 March 2010, unpublished.

[33] Article 11 Family Law 2011.

[34] Article 12 Family Law 2011.

in any event, the need to provide the child with a proper environment for his/her Islamic religious and moral education.[35] More generally, none of the Sunni and Ja'fari jurisdictions perceives or interprets the best interests of the child without the reference to Islam.[36]

Deviating from the Age and Gender Criteria

One question to be addressed is whether the judges deviate from the automatic age and gender criteria. The answer to this question differs significantly from court to court based on the applicable statutes as well as the judge's discretion.

The applicable rules differ along sectarian regulations. For instance, while the Druze court has no discretion to consider special circumstances,[37] the Sunni court can extend the maternal custody period if it deems this extension to be in the best interests of the child.[38] However, in the overwhelming majority of cases reviewed, the judges automatically follow the legal criteria and order the transfer of custody to the father at the end of the maternal custody period without further analysis into the best interests of the child.[39] A few judgments have departed from the general tendency to adhere to the legal custody age. In these decisions, judges ruled for children to remain with their mothers' care past the maternal custody age relying on considerations of the best interests of the child.[40]

In some cases, judges solicited the opinions of the children, either before applying the maternal custody age[41] or at the end of the maternal custody age.[42] In all

---

[35] Article 21 Family Law 2011.

[36] The importance given to religious affiliation in custody determinations is not specific to Muslim jurisdictions, as it can also be observed in non-Muslim jurisdictions. This is but one a sign of the significant role that religion plays in a country such as Lebanon.

[37] Article 64 Druze Law 1948.

[38] Article 17 Family Law 2011.

[39] Baabda Ja'fari Court, 10 May 2012, unpublished; Supreme Sunni Court, 5 December 2011, unpublished; Beirut Sunni Court, 11 January 2011, unpublished (the judge ordered the mother/defendant to hand over her children to their father on the following grounds: 'Custody, when it expires with the child's reaching the legal age, does not revert …, if the moral and financial guardian seeks custody of the child once the *ḥaḍāna* period has expired, the mother must hand him over to him' (as required in Article 20(a) of the New Family Code).

[40] See for example Supreme Sunni Court, 13 January 2011, unpublished, provided by Sheikh Nokkari. It is worth noting that the Christian mother in this case had previously converted to Islam.

[41] Baabda Ja'fari Court, 9 January 2012, unpublished; Beirut Ja'fari Court, 16 February 2009, unpublished.

[42] Beirut Sunni Court, 5 June 2010 and 13 May 2010, unpublished (children who had reached the end of the maternal custody period and chose to live with their father); Higher Sunni Court, 5 December 2011, unpublished; Beirut Ja'fari Court, 10 June 2009, unpublished (the court declared that the children—who were aged 12 and 14 and expressed the wish to remain with their mother—were mature enough to participate in this decision).

such cases, this appeared to be part of an assessment of the best interests of the children, and the judges sometimes clearly indicated that they heard the children in order to make a decision consistent with their best interests.[43] In some cases, mainly before Ja'fari courts, judges deviated from the cut-off ages when the child—having reached the 'age of choice'—expressed a preference for which parent he/she wished to reside with. This is in line with the provisions of Article 355 of the Guide to Ja'fari Justice, allowing the children who have reached the *bulūgh* age (which is 15 years for boys and 9 years for girls)[44] to choose the parent with whom they wish to reside. In other cases though, the judges refused to hear the opinion of the children although they were 13 or 14 years old[45] and even as much as 15 years old.[46]

Parental Agreements and Visitation Rights

It should be noted in this respect that the law recognizes extrajudicial agreements on parental care (Article 26 Family Law 2011; Article 360 Guide to Ja'fari Justice). In theory, the court can decide against a parental agreement on custody if it deems the agreement to be contrary to the interests of the child. However, this is a very rare situation, and we have not found specific rulings in that respect. In any event, no custodian parent can deprive the other parent of visitation rights.[47] Such visitation rights are determined by the parents' agreement and, if not, by the judge.[48]

Impact of Criminal Law

Violations of custody rules, as described above, are punishable under criminal law. Article 495 of the Lebanese Criminal Code provides that any person who kidnaps or removes a minor child in order to take him/her away from his/her custodian or guardian will be sentenced to imprisonment ranging from 6 months to 3 years. Article 496 of the same Code provides that any person who is guilty of failing to relinquish a child in violation of a court order shall be sentenced to imprisonment ranging from 2 months to 2 years.

That said, the Lebanese legislation can be considered as incomplete with regards to the right of a child—of separated parents—to maintain personal and direct contact with each of his/her parents on a regular basis (as provided for in Article 9(3) of the CRC), and especially when parents reside in different States

43 Beirut Sunni Court, 7 November 2009, unpublished.

44 Article 356 Guide to Ja'fari Justice.

45 Saida Ja'fari Court, 2 April 2009, unpublished (ordering the mother at the end of maternal custody period to hand over her children to their father).

46 Baabda Ja'fari Court, 2 July 2012, unpublished (refusing to consider the daughter's wish to remain with her mother).

47 Article 28 Family Law 2011; Article 359 Guide to Ja'fari Justice.

48 Article 29 Family Law 2011.

(Article 10(2) of the CRC). Specifically, Lebanon has failed to sign and ratify important international conventions such as the 1980 Hague Convention on the Civil Aspects of International Child Abduction.

The Lebanese administration tries to prevent cases of illicit transfer and non-return. For instance, under the current administrative practice at the General Security Directorate, no child is delivered a passport without the prior consent of both parents. Further, the applicable laws generally forbid the custodian parent from travelling with the child without the prior approval from the other parent, or a court's decision, in order to keep the family together and keep the child in the same country as the one where his/her parents live.[49] However, in contrast with the general prohibition imposed on the custodian mother against travelling with the child without the father's prior authorization,[50] the prohibition imposed on the father is restricted to the period of the mother's *ḥaḍāna*.[51] Further, the Guide to Ja'fari Justice only considers the case of a custodian mother who is not allowed to travel to a place where the father would be prevented from exercising his guardianship over the child.[52]

In any event, any of the parents can request from the courts a ruling preventing the child from travelling (*qarār man*[c] *safar*).

6.3.1.2 Loss of Custody

While it is necessary for a court, in determining custody, to assess the parents' ability to care for their children, it should be noted that the personal status laws provide for the loss of maternal custody on various grounds which do not all directly relate to the mother's fitness to raise the child. Two grounds for the revocation of custody will be specifically addressed below as they are critical to the 'best interests of the child' test.

Impact of the Mother's Remarriage

One significant example is the remarriage of the mother. In such cases, mothers lose custody in the Shia, Sunni and Druze confessions[53] (although for Sunni and

49 Article 22 Family Law 2011; Articles 65 and 66 Druze Law 1948.

50 Articles 22(a) and 22(b) Family Law 2011; Article 66 Druze Law 1948.

51 Article 22(d) Family Law 2011; Article 65 Druze Law 1948.

52 Article 358 Guide to Ja'fari Justice.

53 Article 349 Guide to Ja'fari Justice (however, the mother can recover *ḥaḍāna* if she divorces from her new husband, Article 350). Under Article 13(2) Family Law 2011 and Article 56 Druze Law 1948, the mother loses custody if she remarries to someone who would not himself be prohibited from marrying the child (on account of kinship). The Family Law 2011 provides however that the court can decide otherwise on the basis of the child's interests.

Druze it can be transferred to the maternal grandmother). This condition does not apply to the father, who may remarry without facing such consequences. In a decision issued on 16 March 2011, the Supreme Sunni Court revoked a remarried woman's custody over children born from a first marriage despite the fact that she divorced her second husband by *khul*ᶜ when she discovered that her new marriage could lead to her losing custody over her children. In a judgment issued by the Beirut Sunni Court on 18 May 2010, the judge also revoked maternal custody 'because the woman's attention is diverted from the child as she is worried about her marriage and its preparations'.

The revocation of maternal custody in cases of remarriage fails to consider the best interests of the child under the specific circumstances of the case, as the decisions reviewed do not address whether the mother's new relationship would actually interfere with her exercise of custody or not.

Here again, this statutory and court position can be viewed in the language of the best interests of the child as abstractly assessed. It is assumed that the new marriage creates a conflict of duties between the new family and the needs of the preceding children; or also that the relationship between the new husband and the children from the first marriage is a conflicting one. In other words, the mother's remarriage is deemed *in abstracto* not to meet the best interests of the child.

Impact of Religious Affiliation and the Child's Religious Education

Another significant example is the loss of maternal custody because of the mother's religious affiliation and neglect of the child's religious education.

In the Lebanese legal system, minor children automatically belong to the religious sect of their father.[54] The law presumes that religious education is a key criterion for the well-being of a child. Thus, religious statutes in Lebanon generally prescribe the loss, or at least the limitation, of maternal custody if the mother's religion differs from that of her child and she fails to show 'due commitment' to the child's religious education. In Ja'fari jurisprudence a non-Muslim mother may not have custody of her Muslim children.[55] As the custodian must be able to raise the child within the Islamic teachings and values, the law applicable to Sunnis limits a non-Muslim woman's custody to the age of 5 (instead of 12) and denies judges' discretion to rule otherwise.[56] The rationale behind this rule is that once children reach an age at which they may be influenced by the non-Muslim parent's behavior, it is not in their best interests to be cared for by the non-Muslim parent. But a non-Muslim mother could also lose her custody of the child earlier than the age of discernment if it becomes clear that she is teaching the child her religion.

---

[54] Article 12 Decree No. 60/1936.

[55] Article 358 Guide to Ja'fari Justice.

[56] Article 14 Family Law 2011.

Court practice reflects these rules. In a decision issued by the Beirut Sunni Court, upheld by the Supreme Sunni Court, the judge rejected the petition of the father to revoke maternal custody because his daughter was residing with 'her mother's Nazarene (Christian) family', but only after the judge ascertained the 'authenticity of the mother's embrace of Islam'.[57] In some cases the judge evaluated the child's belief as well, by questioning her in order 'to find out whether she was memorizing Nazarene prayers in violation of Sharia'.[58] In a similar case, the judge determined that the child 'knew nothing about Christian prayers and their religious hymns' and established her ability to 'recite the opening chapter of the Quran and some short Quranic chapters, and perform ablutions and prayers before upholding maternal custody'.[59]

By focusing on religious affiliation without further analysis, these decisions also fail to meet, *in concreto*, the best interests of the child. Whereas the CRC views freedom of religion as a right that should be given to the children, religious laws and judges see the religious education of the child as a right and duty of the father.

In contrast with Muslim Sunni and Ja'fari rules, the Law of 1948 applicable to the Druze community does not contain any requirement or even reference to the religious affiliation of the custodian.

6.3.2 Guardianship (Wilāya)

In conjunction with the concept of custody, Muslim religious laws applicable in Lebanon recognize the concept of guardianship. Guardianship entails the responsibility to care for the child in two ways: guardianship of the person (*wilāya ᶜalā al-nafs*) and guardianship of property (*wilāya ᶜalā al-māl*). Guardianship of the person refers to taking care of the minor's personal affairs such as education and discipline, whereas guardianship of property refers to the administration of the minor's assets.

6.3.2.1 Attribution of Guardianship Over Minors

Whereas the *ḥaḍāna* is a joint right of both parents, the *wilāya* as a general rule is a right granted to the father of the child, even when the child is in the mother's custody.[60] Thus, unlike custody, guardianship is not influenced by the marital sta-

57 Beirut Sunni Court, 29 August 2009; Supreme Sunni Court, 17 March 2010, both unpublished.

58 Beirut Sunni Court, 29 August 2009, unpublished.

59 Beirut Sunni Court, 11 November 2010, unpublished.

60 For instance, Article 13(2) Family Law 2011 requires that the woman custodian enable the guardian in the fulfillment of his *wilāya* duties as regards mainly the child's Islamic religious and moral education.

tus of the parents. The legal guardian of a legitimate child is the father in Hanafi, Ja'fari and Druze law.[61] As legal guardian, the father is entitled to supervise the child's upbringing and to make all decisions on the child's behalf regarding his or her education, assets, travel and residence as long as he is alive and able to handle such duties. The *wilāya* is therefore a guardianship over both the person of the child and his or her assets, and it ends at the child's reaching the age of majority.

6.3.2.2 Court Supervision

The law restricts the guardian's powers to dispose of the child's assets, requiring the court's authorization for dealings of significant value. Lebanese judges have financial supervision over the way in which the guardian manages the financial interests of the child (Law of 16 July 1962). The law applicable to the Druze community contains more limitations on the powers of the father over the assets of his minor child. For example, in the event the father mismanages the assets of the child, the law orders the judge to designate an ad hoc *waṣī* to request the annulment of such acts on the occurrence of certain events.[62]

The vast majority of the cases adjudicated by the religious courts are related to financial matters such as the managing and selling of the minor's assets. Specific measures in this respect are even imposed by the Code of Obligations and Contracts on all Lebanese, irrespective of their religious affiliation. For instance, the guardian is not allowed to buy the minor's assets for himself without a judge's authorization (Article 378 Code of Obligations and Contracts). Civil judges often supervise the guardian's use of a minor's real property.[63]

6.3.2.3 Guardianship Through Appointment (*Wiṣāya*)

Upon the father's death, guardianship is not automatically transferred to the mother.[64] In such an event, dissociation occurs between the rights and duties conferred regarding the person of the child and those conferred regarding the assets of the child. Those two kinds of prerogatives are not necessarily granted to the same person.[65] Thus, the *wilāya* (protection of the person) becomes distinct from the *wiṣāya* (protection of assets).

---

[61] Article 420 Qadri Pacha Code; Article 81 Druze Law 1948.

[62] Article 84 Druze Law 1948.

[63] First Instance Tribunal of Beirut, judgment no. 582 issued on 23 October 2014, unpublished; judgment no. 3 issued on 20 January 2015, unpublished.

[64] Under Hanafi law, upon the death of the father, guardianship is granted to the male members of the father's family. However, the mother can be granted guardianship by appointment (*wiṣāya*), either by the father himself or by the judge.

[65] Gannagé 2003, fascicule 1: Observations préliminaires, Capacité, no. 18.

Under Hanafi law, the *wiṣāya* (protection of assets) is granted in accord with a specific hierarchy: the *waṣī* will be, first, the person named by the father, then the person named by that person, the paternal grandfather, the person named by the paternal grandfather, the judge or the person named by the judge.[66]

Under Ja'fari law, the testamentary *waṣī* designated by the father will exercise his duties if the paternal grandfather is deceased or unable to perform his duties.[67] The *waṣī* has to be an adult, in good mental health, Muslim if the child is Muslim, honest and of good conduct.[68]

In contrast with the legal *wiṣāya* and the hierarchy of *waṣī* existing under Islamic law, Druze law only establishes two kinds of *waṣī*: the testamentary *waṣī* (designated by the father) and in the absence of such, the *waṣī* designated by the judge.

It should be noted, finally, that the mother can be named *waṣī* either by the father or by the judge.[69]

The powers of the *waṣī* are regulated by law and subject to the court's supervision. The *sharhi* court of first instance is directly in charge of protecting and preserving the minor's interests and closely supervises the management of his/her assets by the *waṣī*. The court's approval is specifically required in order for the *waṣī* to sell any assets, whether movables or real estate, of the minor child.[70] Such sale can only occur through auction and in the event of immediate need on behalf of the child; additionally, all phases of the auction procedure occur under the court's scrutiny.[71] The *waṣī* also needs to petition the court in order, for example, to buy assets for the minor's account, mortgage the minor's assets, receive or place sums that are due to the minor.[72]

Such supervision is reinforced by the relevant provisions of civil law. For instance, Articles 133 and 135 Decree No. 3339 of 12 November 1930 (Code of Real Property) confer upon the minor child a legal mortgage over the real estate of the *waṣī* as a guarantee against a mismanagement on the part of the *waṣī*. The inscription of such mortgage at the Real Estate Registry is made at the request of the *waṣī* or the *sharhi* court.

In Druze law, the powers of the *waṣī* are very limited. The *waṣī* can undertake management acts without authorization. However, acts of alienation require the prior approval of the judge[73] and can only occur under certain circumstances (e.g.

---

66 Article 434 Qadri Pacha Code.

67 Article 652 Guide to Ja'fari Justice.

68 Article 653 Guide to Ja'fari Justice.

69 See Shtaura Sunni Court, ruling no. 105 of 22 April 2015 (unpublished, provided by Sheikh Nokkari), naming the mother legal *waṣī* over her minor daughter with the obligation to manage her interests and preserve her assets.

70 Article 391(2) Law of 16 July 1962.

71 Articles 394–434 Law of 16 July 1962.

72 Article 391 Law of 16 July 1962.

73 Articles 100 and 101 Druze Law 1948.

the need to pay debts left by the minor's parents or the need for funds to raise the child). Finally, the *waṣī* cannot sell his own assets to the minor, buy the minor's assets or borrow sums of money belonging to the minor.[74] However, the father can undertake such acts with the court's approval.[75]

Whether the supervision is exercised over the guardian father or over the *waṣī*, the Islamic and Druze rules have to be implemented alongside and consistent with Lebanese criminal law provisions. Articles 90–94 of the Criminal Code provide for the mandatory loss of *wilāya* or dismissal of *wiṣāya* by the criminal judge under certain circumstances, such as when the father or the *waṣī* is sentenced for a crime and is not able to undertake the duties of *wilāya* or *wiṣāya*.

6.4 The Interference of Civil Laws and Civil Court Practice

Although domestic rules on custody and guardianship are framed within the religious laws in force in Lebanon, there are some situations where civil laws are applicable to such issues. For example, civil courts may hear personal status matters where an international situation is involved and the conflict-of-law rule might designate a civil law. This is the case, in particular, for children born from a civil marriage concluded abroad between Lebanese spouses or between Lebanese and foreign spouses (Sect. 6.4.1).

Moreover, even in domestic situations, civil courts may hear cases involving children. The religious authorities' jurisdiction being limited to personal status matters, conflicts of qualification can often occur regarding jurisdiction as well as the applicable law. The minor's capacity is but one example of this concurrence of attribution. As seen above, whereas religious laws govern matters related to guardianship, the minor's capacity is determined by provisions in the Code of Obligations and Contracts, this Code being applicable to all Lebanese irrespective of their religious affiliation and containing provisions applicable to the child's actions in matters falling outside the scope of jurisdiction of the religious authorities, such as contracts, trade, torts/delicts, etc. Further, the emergency situation resulting from the need to protect a child in danger is governed by civil law and falls under the jurisdiction of the State judge, i.e. the juvenile protection judge (Sect. 6.4.2).

---

[74] Articles 105 and 106 Druze Law 1948.

[75] Article 87 Druze Law 1948; Article 378 Code of Obligations and Contracts.

6.4.1 The Application of Foreign Civil Laws in International Relations

Foreign civil laws are applicable in the case of children born from a civil marriage celebrated abroad between Lebanese spouses or between Lebanese and foreign spouses. This is a consequence of the law applicable to marriage. In Lebanese private international law, the law applicable to the marital relationship governs all consequences of marriage, such as filiation, parental authority over children born from the marriage, alimony issues, and even ultimate effects such as divorce and separation as well as their consequences on child custody and alimony. Therefore, when the marriage is governed by a foreign civil law, such a law also regulates custody and guardianship matters.

A marriage concluded outside Lebanon between Lebanese spouses, or between a Lebanese and a foreigner, is recognized in Lebanon if it has been concluded in any of the forms—civil or religious—authorized by the foreign legal system.[76]

As to the marriage regime, it depends on the mode of celebration of marriage. A civil marriage concluded in a foreign country between two Lebanese, or between a Lebanese and a foreigner, falls within the jurisdiction of civil courts[77] and is governed by the foreign civil law of the country of celebration.[78] Thus, civil marriages concluded by Lebanese abroad are governed by the foreign civil law irrespective of the links between the spouses and such foreign country, notably irrespective of whether the spouses are domiciled in or residents of the country of celebration.[79] Lebanese courts have consistently applied this rule.[80]

Muslim communities, however, are excluded from the above-mentioned regulation. While a marriage concluded in a foreign civil form by two Muslim spouses—at least one of which is Lebanese—will similarly be recognized in Lebanon, it will be governed by the corresponding Muslim marriage rules[81] and fall under the jurisdiction of Muslim courts.[82] This exception has been restrictively applied by Lebanese courts, however. Accordingly, civil marriages concluded between a

[76] Article 25(1) Legislative Decree No. 60/1936 amended by Legislative Decree No. 146/1938.

[77] Article 79 Code of Civil Procedure.

[78] Article 25(2) Legislative Decree No. 60/1936.

[79] This quite unique rule in private international law is actually inevitable in the Lebanese legal system. In the absence of a general civil law rule governing marriage in Lebanon, the only solution is indeed to submit such marriages to the civil law of the country of celebration (Tyan 1974, no. 172).

[80] Cassation Court, Plenary Assembly, 13 November 1986, [1987] Al-Adl 151; First Instance Court of Mount Lebanon, 7 May 2009, [2010] Al-Adl 1296.

[81] Article 1 Legislative Decree No. 53/1939 of 30 March 1939.

[82] Article 79 Code of Civil Procedure.

Muslim and a Christian[83] or between a Muslim and a Druze have been subject to civil jurisdiction and law.[84]

In all such cases where the marriage is governed by the foreign civil law of the country of celebration, that law will also extend to all issues regarding custody and guardianship.

The conflicts on *ḥaḍāna* are exacerbated when a foreign parent (more often the mother) wishes to take the children to his/her country of origin or when the Lebanese parent (often the father) wishes to come back to Lebanon with the children. With the proliferation of mixed marriages, such conflicts have increased. Lebanon is not a State party to any of the international treaties on this issue and is specifically not party to the 1980 Hague Convention on the Civil Aspects of International Child Abduction. However, the Lebanese State has signed some bilateral cooperation agreements, such as the 12 July 1999 agreement with France, but such agreements have a very limited practical impact. The conflict is therefore often brought by the parent that is deprived of his or her child's custody before the criminal courts under Article 496 of the Criminal Code, addressing the non-delivery of a child. The Lebanese Court of Cassation requires the existence of a custody decision in order to convict a parent under Article 496 of the Criminal Code.[85]

6.4.2 The Impact of Lebanese Civil Law on Juvenile Protection

As indicated in Sect. 6.2 above, the ratification of the CRC by Lebanon and the adherence to the standard of the child's best interests have had a serious impact on child protection in the Lebanese legal system. Illustrative here is the Lebanese legislature's adoption of Law No. 422/2002 of 6 June 2002 Regarding the Protection of Juvenile Delinquents or Juveniles in Danger. This child protection law gives the juvenile State court legal grounds to intervene and take protection measures if a child is in a situation of danger.

A child is deemed in danger or at risk under Article 25 of the law if he or she: is exposed to exploitation or is threatened in his/her health, safety, morality or upbringing; is a victim of sexual abuse or physical violence; or is in a situation of begging or vagabonding.

Article 26 of the Law gave the court the right to take the needed measures (protection measures, supervised freedom measures or corrective measures) upon the petition of the minor child or one of his/her parents or guardians or people responsible for him/her, or the social assistant or the public prosecutor, or upon received information. The court can also take such decisions on its own motion in urgent

[83] Cassation Court, 29 March 2005, [2006] Al-Adl 665.

[84] Cassation Court, Plenary Assembly, 9 May 1996, [1996] Al-Adl 11.

[85] Cassation Court, Criminal Chamber, 23 December 2006, no. 361/2006, unpublished.

matters. The public prosecutor or the court can order, save for urgent situations, that a social investigation takes place and that the minor be heard before taking any such measures. Article 26 directs the judge to take into consideration the interests of the child when assessing the need to order any of these measures.

The intervention of the juvenile judge on the basis of Law No. 422/2002 has sometimes triggered a conflict with religious authorities, namely *sharhi* courts, which enjoy general jurisdiction over custody matters. In some cases related to the custody of children of divorced couples, the implementation of this law has indeed caused a confrontation between two different conceptions of the interests of the child. In a case where a Sunni court had issued a decision ordering a mother to hand over her child to the father due to the expiry of the *ḥaḍāna* period, the mother requested that the juvenile protection judge suspend the execution of the Sunni court's decision and produced an expert report on her child's health. In a decision issued on 24 October 2007, the juvenile protection judge accepted the request and based the decision on the interests of the child in the specific case. The decision has been severely criticized by religious authorities for exceeding the jurisdiction of the civil judge under Law No. 422/2002 and for encroaching on the religious courts' jurisdiction over *ḥaḍāna* matters. The civil judge, in any event, overruled the ruling of the religious court.

It should be noted in this regard that the Court of Cassation has refused to enforce decisions issued by religious courts when they conflict with child protection measures. In a decision issued on 7 July 2009, the Court ordered that a child remain in the mother's care for protection reasons as decided by the juvenile court, although a religious court had transferred custody to the father.[86] Hence, the Court of Cassation refused to give civil recognition to a religious judgment that contravenes child welfare and protection, which is a key component of the public order. Whereas the Court of Cassation had always exercised limited control over religious court decisions (on the grounds of Article 95 of the Civil Procedure Code), this decision for the first time reviewed a substantive aspect of a religious court's decision when public order was at stake.

In another case where the Sunni court had ordered a mother to hand over her daughter to the child's father due to the expiry of the *ḥaḍāna* period but the juvenile judge ordered that the young girl remain in her mother's custody, the Plenary Assembly of the Court of Cassation—which has jurisdiction to decide over a conflict of jurisdiction between a civil court and a religious court—issued an important decision on 23 April 2007 whereby it declared that it is up to the juvenile judge to decide whether the child is to remain under the custody of her father, of her mother or even of a specialized institution. The Plenary Assembly added that the measure taken by the juvenile judge cannot be considered as intruding on the Sharia court's jurisdiction in *ḥaḍāna* matters because (i) it constitutes a protective measure aiming to preserve the child from an environment that could become

---

86 Khamis and Al-Aridi 2011.

dangerous for her and (ii) it does not infringe on the legal prerogatives of the *walī* since the father remains in charge over the child's legal interests.[87]

Such a ruling has, undoubtedly, led some religious courts to further consider the best interests of the child in custody cases brought before them (see the decisions cited above in Sect. 6.3 of this chapter).

Finally, with regards to the rights of children deprived of their family environment and put under special State protection and assistance such as placement in suitable institutions for the care of children, the Lebanese law does not contain a specific unified law. However, the Lebanese State has, through the services of the Ministry of Social Affairs, undertaken several steps in order to protect and assist children that are temporarily or permanently deprived of their family environment. Such measures consist, mainly, in placing abused children in one of the institutions approved by the Ministry for the care of children (or for their hospitalization if needed). Additionally, the Ministry has entered into agreements with some institutions of civil society in order to keep children under their family's care with social and psychological follow-up programs.

One other major problem regarding child protection in Lebanon is the vast number of the 'street children', i.e. minor children for whom the streets (in the broad sense of the word) represent their usual place of living and who do not enjoy sufficient protection and assistance. This situation is one of the sad consequences of the Lebanese war and the situation currently prevailing in the region, and the vast majority of these children are non-Lebanese (mainly Syrian and Palestinian). The specific problem lies in the fact that, unlike orphans or children with special needs, the identity of street children cannot be accurately ascertained. These children are also subject to a high level of labor exploitation and/or sexual abuse.

The Lebanese Criminal Code has addressed in some of its provisions the situation of street children. Article 617 punishes the parents of a minor child, or the family members that are in charge of raising him/her, if they do not fulfil their duties if they do not fulfil their duties and leave the child to wander despite having the means to provide for the child. Article 618 punishes any person who, for his or her own personal interest, impels a minor child to beg. Further, such situations can be addressed under Law No. 422/2002.

However, the legal framework is not sufficient as it primarily entails the use of repressive police measures to punish street children in proceedings before competent courts, an approach which does not constitute a solution to the problem.[88]

---

87 Court of Cassation, Plenary Assembly, decision no. 22 of 23 April 2007, cited by Khamis and Al-Aridi 2011.

88 Rabah n.d.. See also the study conducted by the Consultation and Research Institute 2015.

6.5 Conclusion

Lebanon's ratification of the CRC without reservation reflects the on-going trend towards universal values, amongst which is the concept of the best interests of the child. During the two last decades, an increasing number of statutory laws and court rulings have introduced express reference to the best interests of the child as a paramount rule in various matters relating to child law. However, the concept of the best interests of the child is far from being fully implemented in the Lebanese legal system. Decisions related to child welfare are still based on religious rules, customs and practices and thus on elements such as the marital status or the religious affiliation of the parents. More generally, the gap is still huge between family law in Lebanon and the social reality of Lebanese families, where women work and significantly contribute to sustaining the family; further, the content and interpretation of family law is far from meeting the Lebanese people's individual aspirations to justice, liberty and gender equality. Regarding the child's protection and best interests standard, only the adoption of a unified civil law in personal status matters would put an end to the large disparities in the religious laws as to various issues such as the determination of the minimum age of marriage, the rights and obligations of parents towards their children, alimony, custody and guardianship. Such a situation will, however, hardly evolve as long as the religious authorities remain as influential and powerful as they currently are in the Lebanese civil and political society. The path has yet to be followed.

References

Bilani B (1963) Droit musulman. In: Catala P, Gervais A (eds) Le droit libanais, vol 1. LGDJ, Paris, pp 98–126

Consultation and Research Institute (2015) Children Living and Working on the Streets in Lebanon: Profile and Magnitude. https://data.unhcr.org/syrianrefugees/download.php?id=8478. Accessed 22 Mar 2016

El-Husseini Begdache R (2008) L'enfant en droit musulman au Liban. In: Khaïat L, Marchal C (eds) L'enfant en droit musulman (Afrique, Moyen-Orient), Actes du colloque du 14 janvier 2008. SLC, Paris, pp 165–188

Gannagé P (2003) Jurisclasseur de droit comparé, Liban, fascicule 1: observations préliminaires, Capacité. LexisNexis, Paris

Human Rights Watch (ed) (2015) Unequal and Unprotected—Women's Rights under Lebanese Personal Status Laws (report researched by Nayla Geagea and Youmna Makhlouf, written by Nayla Geagea and Lama Fakih with the contribution of Youmna Makhlouf). Human Rights Watch, New York

Khamis F, Al-Aridi F (2011) Protecting children in danger in light of the law and case law in Lebanon, 2nd edn. Friedrich-Ebert-Stiftung, Lebanon (in Arabic)

Mahmassani M, Messarra I (1970) Les Codes de statut personnel en vigueur au Liban. Documents Huvelin, Faculté de droit et des sciences politiques, USJ, Beirut

Moukarzel Hechaime A (2008a) Liban: l'enfant dans une famille brisée. In: Khaïat L, Marchal C (eds) L'enfant en droit musulman (Afrique, Moyen-Orient), Actes du colloque du 14 janvier 2008. SLC, Paris, pp 351–356

Moukarzel Hechaime A (2008b) Liban: la protection de l'enfant. In: Khaïat L, Marchal C (eds) L'enfant en droit musulman (Afrique, Moyen-Orient), Actes du colloque du 14 janvier 2008. SLC, Paris, pp 373–375

Moukarzel Hechaimé A (2010) Actualités du statut personnel des communautés musulmanes au Liban. Droit et cultures 59:121–164

Rabah Judge Ghassan (n.d.) Study on the Legal Aspects of Street Children in Lebanon. High Council for Childhood, Arab Council for Childhood and Development, UNESCO (in Arabic)

Tyan E (1974) Précis de droit international privé, 2nd edn. Librairie Antoine, Beirut

UNICEF (2012) Strengthening the Child Protection System in Lebanon, Challenges and Opportunities. UNICEF, Beirut

Chapter 7
Pakistan

Ayesha Shahid and Isfandyar Ali Khan

Abstract A general view prevalent in Pakistan based on classical Hanafi principles is that in cases of marital breakup the father is to be given custody of a male child at the age of seven and custody of a female child on her attaining puberty. However, the emphasis on the principle of the 'best interests of the child', as introduced in the Guardians and Wards Act 1890, remains a priority of the judges in Pakistan. This chapter traces the evolution and development of the best interests of the child principle in Pakistani child law. By including a review of judicial cases from 1997 to 2014, the chapter evaluates the application of this principle by the superior judiciary in Pakistan.

Keywords Pakistan · Child custody · Best interests of the child · Islamic law · Guardians and Wards Act 1890 · Superior judiciary

Contents

Ayesha Shahid is a lecturer in law in Brunel Law School, Brunel University London.
Isfandyar Ali Khan is a practicing lawyer and a development practitioner in Pakistan with specialization in Alternative and Community Based Dispute Resolution, Access to Justice, Human Rights, Democracy and Governance.

A. Shahid (✉)
Brunel Law School, Brunel University London, London, UK
e-mail: ayesha.shahid@brunel.ac.uk

I.A. Khan
National Centre for Dispute Resolution, London, UK
e-mail: isfandyaralikhan@yahoo.co.uk

N. Yassari et al. (eds.), *Parental Care and the Best Interests of the Child in Muslim Countries*, DOI 10.1007/978-94-6265-174-6_7

7.1 Introduction

The independence of the Indian sub-continent from British colonial rule, and its subsequent partition into two independent states, led to the creation of Pakistan.[1] Pakistan was carved out of the Muslim majority areas of British India in 1947 as a result of the demand of the Muslim population of British India to be given their own separate homeland. The majority of the Pakistanis are Sunni Muslims and are followers of the Hanafi school of thought.[2] A general view prevalent in Pakistan based on classical Hanafi principles is that in cases of marital breakup the father is to be given custody of a male child at the age of seven and custody of a female child on her attaining puberty. However the courts in Pakistan have deviated from this classical Hanafi principle and have based their judgments on the 'Best Interests of the Child' principle. This chapter aims (i) to trace the trajectory of this notion in Pakistan's legislation, (ii) to analyze the reasons for establishing it as a fundamental principle in child law in Pakistan and (iii) to detect the ways in which the superior judiciary in Pakistan perceives and interprets this notion. It addresses the question to what extent the courts in Pakistan have deviated from applying the classical Islamic law of *hadana* (custody) and *wilaya* (guardianship) in custody and guardianship cases by examining the judgments of the superior courts from 1997 to 2014.[3]

---

[1] Under the Constitution, Pakistan is a federal republic comprising five provinces: Baluchistan, Punjab, Sindh, Khyber Pukhtun Khawa and the Gilgit Biltistan province, which are ethnically, linguistically and culturally diverse regions. In addition to the provinces, Pakistan also consists of Federally Administered Tribal Areas, Provincially Administered Tribal Areas, the Federally Administered Northern Area, and the Islamabad Capital Territory. Also, the western part of the former princely state of Kashmir (Azad Jammu) is de facto controlled and administered by Pakistan. There are an estimated 177.1 million people in Pakistan. Of the total, around 91.59 million are male and 85.51 million are female. The population of children and adolescents, ages 0 to 19, is estimated to be around 82.05 million, which is projected to increase to 84 million in 2015 and 86 million in 2020. From 1998 to 2010, an additional 28 million children and adolescents were added to the total existing population (Bureau of Statistics).

[2] Nearly all Pakistanis are Muslims (97%), with Sunnis the clear majority within this group (77%) and Shiites the minority (20%). Religious minority groups (3%) include Christians, Hindus, and Parsees.

[3] For a comprehensive and thorough analysis of case law from 1947 to 1997 see Ali and Azam 1998.

The first section examines the evolution and development of the 'Best Interests of the Child' principle in the Indian sub-continent within the wider frame of British colonial rule in the Indian sub-continent. It analyzes the concept of *hadana* (custody) and *wilaya* (guardianship) in the light of rules laid down in *Hedaya* and *Fatawa-i-Alamgiri*, the two classical commentaries on Islamic law. In the second section, post-colonial constitutional debates and legislative reforms in Pakistan are assessed. Pakistan's international and regional commitments to child rights are examined in this section with a particular focus on the UN Convention on the Rights of the Child, the SAARC Convention on the Promotion of Child Welfare in South Asia, and the UK-Pakistan Protocol. This section also highlights the institutional measures and recent legislative changes at the federal and provincial levels that have taken place in Pakistan under the 18th Constitutional Amendment. Section three provides a detailed analysis of various provisions of the Guardians and Wards Act 1890 (Act VIII of 1890) in relation to the welfare of the child principle. This section also analyzes custody and guardianship cases decided by the superior judiciary from 1997 to 2014 to assess the responses of the judiciary and the frames of reference used by the courts while interpreting the best interests of the child principle.

7.2 Historical Overview of Custody and Guardianship Law in Pakistan

The historical evolution of the custody and guardianship law followed in Pakistan can be traced back to the Anglo-Mohammadan law introduced by the British colonizers in the Indian sub-continent. Prior to the British rule, when the Indian sub-continent was governed by the Muslim Mughal dynasty, Islamic law generally held the field and remained the law of the land in settling civil and criminal disputes.[4] Courts were also established by the Mughal rulers at the central, provincial, district, and *tehsil* (Pargana) levels.[5] These courts had defined jurisdiction in civil, criminal, and revenue matters and operated under the authority of the ruler. Common customs and traditions, however, were also invoked in settling secular matters as these rulers were not particularly keen on applying Islamic law to each and every sphere of life and let the indigenous customs and institutions continue side by side with Islamic law and institutions.[6] *Qadis* and *Muftis* took local custom into consideration when applying the law. While interpreting the law, the *Qadis* primarily relied on using independent reasoning or *Ijtihad*. But when the British

---

[4] Bilimoria n.d.

[5] Hussain 2011, p. 5.

[6] Hussain 2011, p. 6.

came to India they introduced a new system of courts for 'maintain[ing] effective political control with minimal military involvement'.[7]

When the British arrived in India in 1772 they were bewildered by the diversity of customary rules, norms and practices as well as the vastly different views on marriage, succession, contract, severance, property, and inheritance rights that governed a range of ethnic and religious communities. These communities had their own complex system of community-based, informal juridical hearing courts or *panchayats*. The British rulers contemplated that to achieve economic and political stability in India, it was necessary to establish 'Rule of Law with the declared consistency, clarity, certainty, and finality of statutes or black letter law'.[8] To simplify and facilitate this task, the British moulded un-codified Islamic law into a fixed set of Islamic rules for ease of application by the colonial courts and the English judges who were unfamiliar with the customary and religious law. The then Governor-General, Warren Hastings, initiated a legislative reform process through the codification of laws. The result was a series of enactments which included the Code of Civil Procedure (1908), the Penal Code (1860), and the Code of Criminal Procedure (1898). In the area of personal law the British, in consultation with indigenous legal experts, *Hindu Pandits* and the *Ulemas*, devised the so-called Anglo-Hindu law for Hindus and Anglo-Mohammedan law for Muslims, along with separate personal laws for Indian Christians.[9] These laws remained operative even after the independence from British colonial rule. While framing laws for the Muslims in India, the British relied specifically on the commentaries of *Hedaya* and *Fatawa-i-Alamigiri*, which were based on the teachings of the *Hanafi* school of thought.[10] These commentaries were followed as a final and unquestionable authority by the judges and legal scholars of the Indian sub-continent in family matters. The area of child custody largely reflects this position, and even in recent cases courts have cited these two documents as the highest source of authority for *Hanafi* jurisprudence.

Following the principles of classical Islamic law, the two commentaries laid down rules for awarding guardianship and custody. The Arabic term '*hadana*' has been used commonly by South Asian writers for custody of a child, following its use in Hamilton's *Hedaya* and Baillie's Digest.[11] By contrast, the Arabic term

[7] Bilimoria n.d.

[8] Bilimoria n.d.

[9] Bilimoria n.d.

[10] The 12th century Central Asian lawyer Burhanuddin al-Marghinani was the author of *Hedaya*. *Hedaya* was the standard legal text book in Muslim India and it remained the basis of Muslim law for centuries. Commissioned by Warren Hastings, *Hedaya* was translated by Charles Hamilton in 1791. *Fatawa-i-Alamgiri* is a collection of authoritative *fatwas* compiled under the orders of Moghul Emperor Aurangzeb in the seventeenth century by a panel of *ulama* headed by Shaikh Nizam Buhanpuri. This was again translated under the orders of Warren Hastings, by Baillie under the title of *A Digest of Moohummudan Law, Part I* in 1957.

[11] Hamilton 1982 and Baillie 1957.

wilayat is sometimes defined as a right[12] or power[13] and sometimes as a duty[14] 'incumbent on a person on the grounds of kinship, by testament or by court order towards another person of imperfect or no legal capacity',[15] e.g. for 'an infant, an idiot or a lunatic'.[16]

Guardianship was divided into three types. Guardianship for purposes of marriage, guardianship (*wilayah*) for purposes of management and preservation of property, and guardianship (custody or *hadana*) for purposes of bringing up children. It also laid down three ways of appointment (1) by natural right, (2) by testament, and (3) by appointment by a judge. Guardianship for the purpose of marriage is allowed because of the necessity of a proper and suitable match, which may not always be available. It belongs to the father and grandfather or to the paternal uncle or a guardian appointed by the court in their absence. When a minor is given in marriage by a guardian other than the father or the grandfather, the minor may exercise the option of puberty to ask the court to annul the marriage. If it was the father or the grandfather who consented to the marriage, a legal presumption is raised that they acted in the best interests of the minor. The presumption is, however, not conclusive and such a marriage can also be set aside where it is plainly undesirable and injurious to the minor, for instance, where the father is not a man of proper judgment or is of reckless character and has married his minor daughter to an immoral man. Abu Yousuf and Imam Muhammad, the disciples of Imam Abu Hanifa, consider that an evidently unequal or undesirable marriage or a marriage for less than a proper dower of a minor female is not valid, but Imam Abu Hanifa does not share this view. According to the principles laid down in *Hedaya* the guardianship of a minor for the management and preservation of his/her property devolves (1) first on his/her father, (2) then on the father's executor, (3) next on the paternal grandfather, (4) then on his executor, (5) then on the executors of such executors, and (6) finally on the ruling power or his representative—i.e. a *qazi* or judge. Ultimately it rests upon the *qazi* to appoint a guardian for an infant's property when there is no near guardian (i.e. the father, the father's father, and their executors). The other paternal kinsmen, who are termed 'remote kindred', and the mother succeed, according to proximity, to the guardianship of an infant for the purpose of education and marriage. They do not have the right to be guardians of the minor's property unless appointed to do so by the ruling authorities, or unless appointed to be a guardian in the original proprietor's will, which has been duly attested by competent witnesses. The general rule is that a guardian, executor, or anyone who has the care of the person and property of a minor can enter into a contract for the ward which is (or is likely to be) advantageous and not injurious to the ward. A guardian may sell or purchase moveable items on behalf

[12] Rahim 1911, p. 343.

[13] Mahdi and Malek 1998, p. 156.

[14] Nasir 2009, p. 186.

[15] Nasir 2009, p. 186.

[16] Rahim 1911, p. 344.

of his/her ward, either for an equal rate or at such a rate that may leave a slight loss, but not at such a rate which would make the loss great and apparent.[17]

It is interesting to note that there is no clear distinction made between custody and guardianship at all times; as a result their relationship necessarily manifests 'a complex structure of rights and duties distributed between the entitled person(s)'.[18] Custody is often perceived only as a form of 'guardianship of person', as it rests with the mother only during the early years of the child; the natural guardianship being always entrusted with the father. Thus Jamal Nasir had described *hadana* as 'the earliest form of guardianship of person',[19] when the mother is needed to nurse an infant and to care for, bring up or raise a child.

Under classic Hanafi law, as followed in the commentaries mentioned above, custody (*hadana)* belongs to the mother for a girl up to the age of puberty and for a boy up to the age of seven, while *wilayah* belongs to the father. The father's custody continues until puberty for a boy and not just until puberty for a girl, but rather until she can safely be left to herself and trusted to take care of herself. The mother's right to the custody of her infant child is subject to certain other limitations; for example, she loses her right if she has become an apostate, leads an immoral life, is wicked, or is unworthy to be trusted and neglects to take proper care of the child.[20] If a mother is disqualified from exercising custody, then the custody of a female child is awarded to the child's maternal or paternal grandmother how high soever.[21]

Detailed rules were also laid down to determine the place or location where the child could remain in the custody of the mother.[22] A boy or a girl having passed

---

[17] Hamilton 1982, vol. 4, p. 553.

[18] Mahdi and Malek 1998, p. 157.

[19] Nasir 2009, p. 186.

[20] Baillie 1957, p. 728.

[21] If the grandmother has died or is married to a stranger, then the full sister is entitled. If the sister has died or is married to a stranger, then the half-sister of the mother (uterine and consanguine sister) is entitled to custody of the child. In the absence of a sister, the daughter of the full sister and then the daughter of the half-sister (consanguine and uterine) can have the custody of the girl child. In the same way the maternal aunt and then the paternal aunts how high soever can have the custody. In the absence of the mother and other female relations, custody belongs to the father and other male relations in the same order as that of maternal relations. If the mother remarries, she forfeits her right to custody. A mother is disqualified if she marries a man not related to the child within the prohibited degrees. This rule is strictly applied in cases that involve custody of a female child, but if the subsequent marriage is dissolved by death or divorce then the right to custody will revive.

[22] According to the rules laid down in *Hedaya*, before the completion of *iddah* the proper location to exercise *hadana* is the domicile of the parents. None of the parents can take the child out of the custody of the latter. After completion of her *iddah*, a mother may take her child to her own birthplace provided that the marriage had been contracted there, and that it is so close to the husband's residence that the husband can visit the child and return to his residence before nightfall. There is also no objection to her moving with the child from a village to the city or chief town of the district if this is advantageous to the child and in no way injurious to the father. If the child's mother is dead and *hadana* has passed to the maternal grandmother, the child cannot be taken to the grandmother's own city, even though the marriage had taken place there.

the period of *hadana* has no option to be with one parent in preference to the other; instead he or she must necessarily remain in the charge of the father.

Bearing in mind the classical rules as laid down in the various commentaries based on classical Sunni Hanafi jurisprudence, the British enacted the Guardians and Wards Act in 1890. The major part of this Anglo-Muhammadan law was assimilated into Pakistani law through Article 224 of the 1956 Pakistan Constitution, which provided for the incorporation of pre-existing law 'save as is otherwise expressly provided in the Constitution' and 'so far as is applicable and with necessary modifications.'[23]

7.3 Constitutional and Legislative Reform in Pakistan

7.3.1 The Creation of Pakistan: Constitutional Framework and the Quest for Muslim Identity

At the time of its creation, the founder and first Governor-General of Pakistan, Mohammad Ali Jinnah, envisaged Pakistan as a secular state and not a theocratic state. He elaborated on this idea in his presidential address to the Constituent Assembly on 11 August 1947, in which he clearly stated:

> You may belong to any religion or caste or creed that has nothing to do with the business of the state … there is no discrimination, no distinction between one caste or creed and another … [The] fundamental principle [is] that we are all citizens and equal citizens of one state … in course of time Hindus would cease to be Hindus and Muslims would cease to be Muslims, not in the religious sense, because that is the personal faith of each individual, but in the political sense as citizens of the State.

While outlining the contours of a secular state, he also stated that the members of each religious community would be free to go to their respective places of worship. In his presidential address he laid the foundations of a modern and democratic Pakistan where everyone was equal before and afforded the protection of the law. However, soon after his death the advocates of religious nationalism started asserting their position in the Constituent Assembly. Since then major debates have focused on the appropriate role of Islam in the state, the implementation of Islamic law, and the Islamization of society. Thus religion has been manipulated and used for political purposes and imposed in a selective and narrowly defined manner, often serving to bolster insecure regimes since the early days of independence.[24] Both religious and liberal groups have played the 'Islamic card' as soon as they realized that religion was the only binding force to bring together an otherwise multi-ethnic and culturally diverse community.[25] The religious and conserva-

---

[23] Davis 1985, p. 119.

[24] Critelli 2012, p. 676.

[25] Ali 2012, p. 45.

tive forces also demanded a clear manifestation of Islamic identity. This was clearly reflected when in 1949, soon after independence, the First Constituent Assembly of Pakistan passed the Objectives Resolution to maintain its Islamic identity. The Objectives Resolution reiterates that 'sovereignty over the entire universe belongs to Almighty God alone and efforts shall be made to enable Muslims to order their lives in accordance with the teaching and requirements of Islam'. The Objectives Resolution privileged one religion over all others but was still passed, overriding the serious concerns of the minority members of the Constituent Assembly.

Later Pakistan was declared an Islamic Republic under the 1956 Constitution. Article 198 of the Constitution provided that the legislature would bring all laws into conformity with the 'Injunctions of Islam'. It also prohibited the enactment of any law repugnant to Islam. As compared to the 1956 Constitution, any reference to the injunctions of Islam was initially excluded in the 1962 Constitution. Following protests from the National Assembly, however, the Islamic provisions of the 1956 Constitution were reinserted, and the word 'Islamic' was also reinserted into the official name of the state.

The 1973 Constitution of Pakistan, clearly states in its preamble that 'all laws have to be in conformity with the *Qur'an* and *Sunnah*'. Islam was officially declared as the state religion in the 1973 Constitution. The Islamic character of the Constitution was further strengthened when, in 1985, Article 2-A was incorporated into the 1973 Constitution so as to require that all laws be consistent with the injunctions of Islam as laid down in the *Qur'an* and *Sunnah*. The effect of this move was to render Islamic law the constitutional basis of all state law.[26] One can thus argue that religion and Muslim identity have played a dominant role in framing the constitutional history of Pakistan. The constitutional history of Pakistan laid down the ideological parameters of the state and defined its duties and obligations towards Islam.[27]

In addition to Islamic provisions, the protection of marriage, family, mother, and child is an acknowledged policy principle under Article 35 of the 1973 Constitution. Pakistan's commitment to children is enshrined in the Constitution as Article 35 binds the state to 'protect … the mother and the child'. Article 37 of the 1973 Constitution lays down commitments for promoting social justice and eradication of social evils. This includes the state's obligation 'to remove illiteracy and provide free and compulsory secondary education within minimum possible period' and to 'make provision for securing just and humane conditions of work, ensuring that children and women are not employed in vocations unsuited to their age or sex, and for maternity benefits for women in employment'.[28] This is further strengthened by the inviolability of the privacy of the home, which is a fundamental right under Article 14 of the 1973 Constitution. These provisions support

---

[26] Yefet 2009, p. 349.

[27] Ahmad 1993, p. 40.

[28] Articles 37(b) and 37(e) of the Constitution of Islamic Republic of Pakistan.

parental guidance through the institution of marriage and the strengthening of the family as the primary unit of the social system, within the inviolable right of privacy of the home. Respect for the responsibility, rights, and authority of parents flows naturally from these provisions, which are also considerably supported by Islamic traditions and norms. The family system in Pakistan provides a traditional safety net to all the family members in which women and children enjoy emotional, social, and economic security. Joint family systems and extended family systems are prevalent. Even people living in nuclear families have close links with their extended families.

7.3.2 Pakistan's Commitment to International and Regional Human Rights and Child Rights Instruments

Pakistan is a party to several UN human rights instruments that deal with child rights, including the international Bill of Rights and the UN Convention on the Rights of the Child 1990 to name but a few. The Universal Declaration of Human Rights, 1948, stressed that 'motherhood and childhood are entitled to special care and protection' and referred to the family as the natural and fundamental group unit of society. The foundation of the rights and principles in the Universal Declaration of Human Rights provides a legal as well as a moral obligation for countries to respect the human rights of each individual, including children. Pakistan has ratified the International Covenant on Economic, Social and Cultural Rights (ICESCR) and the International Covenant on Civil and Political Rights (ICCPR) in 2008 and 2010 respectively. Ratification of these international treaties imposes further obligations on Pakistan to take measures for providing a conducive environment for the protection of children's rights in the country. The Government of Pakistan ratified the United Nations Convention on the Rights of the Child (UNCRC) on 12 December 1990. At the time of ratification, Pakistan made a general reservation that the provisions of the UNCRC shall be interpreted according to the principles of Islamic principles and values. The reservation was withdrawn on 23 July 1997. The UNCRC has not been incorporated into the national law in Pakistan and is therefore not directly enforceable in national courts. International conventions are not enforceable in Pakistan until there is enabling legislation making them the law of the land. Pakistan has not introduced any such law in regard to the UNCRC, and therefore the Convention cannot be invoked in the courts. In addition, in 2001 the Government of Pakistan signed the Optional Protocol to the UNCRC on the sale of children, child prostitution, and child pornography which was ratified in 2011. The Government of Pakistan has also signed the Optional Protocol to the UNCRC on the involvement of children in armed conflict in 2001, but it has not been ratified.

The provisions of Article 12 of the UNCRC do not have specific comparable provisions in Pakistani law. Pakistan is a federal state in which every province has separate legislation on issues of family law and child welfare. There is no mechanism to unify the legislation, and thus different provisions apply in the different provinces.[29] The UN Committee on the Rights of the Child, in its Concluding Observations to the Pakistan's Country Report, has urged Pakistan to ensure that the principle of the best interests of the child is formally incorporated into the legislative, executive, and judicial branches of power by, inter alia, including reference to the best interests of the child in legislation as well as in other settings such as cases of divorce involving children, *kafalah* of Islamic law, child protection, guardianship, and juvenile justice.[30] The Committee also recommended that the state party must ensure in practice the implementation of this principle in all judicial and administrative decisions and in programmes, projects, and services having an impact on children.

Civil society organizations in Pakistan have been criticizing the pace of implementation of the UNCRC in domestic legislation. They have also emphasized the need for taking capacity building initiatives required for child protection and juvenile justice. At various civil society forums,[31] Pakistan has been urged to undertake measures to the maximum extent of their available resources, including establishing independent monitoring mechanisms; enacting efficient legislation to prohibit and prevent the employment of children as domestic workers; ratifying the Optional Protocol to UNCRC on the involvement of children in armed conflicts; expediting the adoption of the Charter of Child Rights Bill which has been pending for many years at the national level; strengthening measures aimed at providing protection and assistance to vulnerable segments of society, including those children affected by natural disasters to protect them from trafficking and exploitation at work; taking steps to implement laws and policies with a view to eliminating under-age and forced marriage; continuing its efforts for a systematic and sustained training process of children as well as developing the Child Protection Management Information System (CPMIS) and advancement in child immunization; and ensuring and allocating sufficient resources for girls' education in all provinces.

In 2002, during the South Asian Association for Regional Countries' (SAARC) Decade of the Rights of the Child, the Convention on Promotion of Child Welfare in South Asia was adopted. The purpose of the Convention is to solidify the commitments that the South Asian countries have made at the world summit and to other international bodies by encouraging mutual cooperation and assistance. The aim is to protect the rights of the child while realising the full potential of each child and the responsibilities and duties of the signatory states. The Convention

---

29 Ali and Jamil 1994, p. 24.

30 UNCRC Convention on the Rights of the Child, Distr. General, CRC/C/PAK/CO/3-42 October 2009, Advance unedited version, Original: English, Committee on the Rights of the Child, Fifty-second session, Consideration of reports submitted by States parties under Article 44 of the Convention, Concluding observations: Pakistan.

31 www.thenews.com.pk/Todays-News-5-258379-Enforce-child-rights-laws (accessed 1 October 2015).

also provides for setting up regional arrangements to assist Member States. The Convention states that countries should recognize the rights of a child as laid out in the UNCRC, uphold the rights of the family as primary caregivers, and recognize the best interests of the child. To achieve their goals, the states' regional priorities should be recognizing the need for essential services such as education and health, both preventive and curative, and providing appropriate legal and administrative safety nets such as national laws that protect the child from abuse, exploitation, neglect, violence, discrimination, trafficking, and child labor.

7.3.3 The UK/Pakistan Judicial Protocol and Child Abduction

Child abduction is an issue that involves disputes of custody and guardianship and that gives rise to the question of transnational jurisdiction. In such cases, a parent may need to take legal action to secure return of the children. Pakistan has not signed or ratified the Hague Convention on the Civil Aspects of Child Abduction 1980; however, as a party to the UNCRC, Pakistan is under an obligation to 'take measures to combat the illicit transfer and non-return of children abroad' and to that end must 'promote the conclusion of bilateral or multilateral agreement or accession to existing agreements.' Under Article 35, the Contracting States must 'take all appropriate national, bilateral and multilateral measures to prevent the abduction, the sale of or traffic in children for any purpose or in any form.' Other relevant obligations are set forth in Articles 9 and 10, which include the child's 'right to maintain contact with both parents if separated from one or both' and the 'right of children and their parents to leave any country and to enter their own in order to be reunited or to maintain the child-parent relationship'. Article 18 embodies the principle that 'both parents have joint primary responsibility for bringing up their children and the State should support them in this task.'

A recent development in relation to child abduction has been that in January 2003 judges from Pakistan and the UK signed the UK-Pakistan Protocol on Children Matters. This is a judicial understanding which aims to secure the return of abducted children to the country where they normally live, without regard to the nationality, culture, or religion of the parents.[32] The judges agreed that the child's welfare is a priority and that the courts of the country where the child normally lives are usually in the best position to decide on matters of custody and where a child should live. The Protocol asks judges to consider any existing court orders made by the courts in the child's 'home' country.[33] The judge may then order the

[32] The Protocol can also be used when parents are seeking permission to take a child temporarily to Pakistan for a holiday.

[33] For instance, if a child is taken to Pakistan, or does not return from a holiday there, and the parent has an existing residence order or a prohibitive order against the person who has taken the child, the Protocol can be used to help return the child to the UK.

child to be returned to the country where he or she normally lives. Liaison judges have been appointed in both the UK and Pakistan to communicate with each other on individual cases to ensure that each is aware of court orders from the other's country. It is important to note, however, that the Protocol has not been incorporated into the law of both countries, and judges are not legally bound to abide by its provisions. Notwithstanding, as its provisions are in line with the usual practices of the courts, judges can and do make orders referring to the Protocol.

Pursuant to Section 361 of the Pakistan Penal Code it is an offense to remove a male child under the age of fourteen or a female child under the age of sixteen from the lawful guardian. The case law as to whether this provision can be invoked in cases of parental child abduction is conflicting. Although this section has been used against a parent who has removed a child from the other parent, case law is more in favor of the non-applicability of this section in parental child abduction. The term lawful guardian has been interpreted to mean 'any person lawfully entrusted with the care or custody of such minor'. If the removing parent believes themselves to be entitled to lawful custody, then this section would not apply to them unless they removed the child for an unlawful reason. The superior courts of Pakistan have consistently interpreted the relevant provisions as excluding abduction by a parent, particularly when the abducting parent is the father, because in their view the '... father of a child[,] being always a natural guardian along with the mother, can never be ascribed or attributed the offence of kidnapping of his own child ....'. The Lahore High Court in *Muhammad Ashraf v. SHO and others*[34] decided in this judgment that the

> [f]ather of a child is always a natural guardian along with the mother. He can never be ascribed or attributed the offence of kidnapping of his own child ... The only fetter placed upon the right of a father to the custody of the child is that when he takes the child from the custody of his wife for a purpose recognized in law as immoral or unlawful, in such a circumstance removal of the child, would amount to an offence.

While this view may exonerate the father from penal consequences, it cannot protect him from actions for the production and custody of the child.

In Pakistani law, various provisions can be used regarding a case of trans-national parental abduction perpetrated by a foreign parent. For example, the case may be lodged under Section 491 of the Criminal Procedure Code (Cr.PC) for the production of the child (Power to issue directions of the nature of habeas corpus) and under Section 7 or 25 of the Guardians and Wards Act for the custody of the child (respectively, Power of the Court to make an order as to guardianship and Title of guardian to custody of ward). If it is established that the father or the mother removed the child for *mala-fide* intentions, then he/she is a criminal. Still, the parents are expected to produce the child in court and to hand him/her over to the parent to whom the court has temporarily granted custody. Violation of the court's orders would then lead to the detention or punishment of the offending parent, even though that parent may be the primary caregiver, a situation that is arguably not in the child's best interests.

---

[34] *Muhammad Ashraf v. SHO and others*, 2001 P Cr. L J 31.

According to the Pakistan Penal Code (PPC), child abductions by a non-parent are of a criminal nature and are tried before the criminal court. Removal of a child by a parent is not criminal and is dealt with by the family or civil court. Consequently, the trans-national movement of a child without the consent of the foreign parent would not lead to the detention of the alleged abductor, nor would that parent be punished under any section of the PPC for bringing the child to Pakistan. Under Section 361 of the Pakistan Penal Code, it is an offense to remove a male child under the age of fourteen or a female child under the age of sixteen from the lawful guardian. This section lays down that 'whoever takes or induces any minor under 14 years of age, if a male, or under 16 years of age if a female, out of the keeping of the lawful guardian, is said to kidnap such minor from lawful custody'. The offense of abduction has also been defined under Section 362 of the Code, under which 'whoever by force compels or by other deceitful means induces any person to go from any place is said to have abducted that person.'

The matters of custody, wrongful removal, and guardianship of children in Pakistan are normally dealt with under the provisions of the Family Courts Act, 1964, and the Guardians and Wards Act, 1890. Section 9 of the Act of 1890 requires that application in such cases be made to the Family Court having jurisdiction at a place where a minor ordinarily resides. However, one remedy for child abduction that has been used with some success in Pakistan is the writ of habeas corpus.[35] A writ of habeas corpus can also be used in family law, for example a parent who has been denied custody of his other children by a trial court or whose child has been illegally removed may file a habeas corpus petition.

This petition would have previously been made directly to the High Court under Section 491 of the Criminal Procedures Code or Article 199 of the Constitution of Pakistan. However a habeas corpus petition is now normally made to a Court of District or Sessions Judges. A petition could still be heard by a High Court, and this depends on the discretion of the judge. An application for habeas corpus does not determine who should have the ultimate custody of the child, and the application must be attached to a substantive application.

In the last few years, High Courts throughout Pakistan have dealt with cases involving child abduction in connection with mixed marriages between Pakistanis and British, Canadian and French nationals. These cases appear to have been resolved judiciously.

The UK-Pakistan Protocol has been enforced by Pakistani courts, and mothers are allowed to take their children back to the United Kingdom. Recently, the High Court of Azad Kashmir-Pakistan had a child who had been recovered from the custody of the father and handed over to the British mother, Najma Begum, following her application. The Court stated that, in light of the Protocol, the relevant court in the United Kingdom would have to decide about the future and custody of

[35] The Extradition Treaty of 1931 was signed under the British mandate and could be used as a basis of cooperation in child custody cases.

the child. The mother of the child had filed a habeas corpus application with the High Court under Section 491 of the Cr.PC.

7.3.4 Foreign Orders

Although foreign orders are not automatically enforceable, they can be considered by Pakistani courts, and the higher the level of the foreign court that issued the order the more weight it is accorded in Pakistan. The Civil Procedures Code of 1908 contains provisions for the enforcement of certain foreign decrees, but although custody orders can be used as supporting documents, they are not directly enforceable. The case of Misbah Rana—a 12-year-old, Scottish-Pakistani girl—is also quite a significant case. In this case Misbah's mother, Louise Campbell, approached the High Court of Lahore and filed a habeas corpus petition against her ex-husband and Misbah's elder sister, both of whom had illegally taken Misbah to Pakistan. The mother in this case claimed that Misbah should be sent back to Scotland and the custody matter decided by the relevant court in Scotland, as per the Protocol. Louise Rana was worried that Misbah would be forced to marry at her early age, whereas Misbah consistently denied, through a news conference, that her Pakistani family was trying to force her into such a union. After listening to both parties' arguments, the Court ordered that Misbah should be handed over to the British High Commission within seven days so that the case could be decided as per the Protocol and the custody issue heard in Scotland's relevant court. Upon hearing that she would be handed over to her mother, Misbah protested against the Court's decision and expressed the desire not to go back to Scotland. Owing to Misbah's wish to stay with her father, both parties decided to settle the issue outside the court. The court allowed Misbah to stay with her father and granted access to her mother so that she could visit her daughter under certain measures. In this case the High Court violated the UK-Pakistan Protocol, and the child's custody was decided by mutual agreement. However, the court respected Misbah's point of view, which is central in the field of child rights as envisaged in Article 9(2) of the UNCRC: 'In any proceedings ..., all interested parties shall be given an opportunity to participate in the proceedings and make their views known.' Article 12 of the UNCRC also states that the child's point of view should be taken into consideration by the courts.

7.3.5 Institutional and Legislative Measures at Federal and Provincial Levels under the 18th Constitutional Amendment

In December 1980 the Government of Pakistan established the National Commission for Child Welfare and Development (NCCWD) in order to promote child welfare and planning and development. The NCCWD, positioned under the Human Rights Division (erstwhile Ministry of Human Rights of Ministry of Law, Justice and Human Rights), has the mandate to monitor, review, and coordinate the implementation of the UNCRC. The Commission consists of several national expert committees, one of them being for the protection of rights of children (including juvenile justice, family environment, abuse, neglect, exploitation, and child labor).[36] At the provincial level, the Provincial Commission for Child Welfare and Developments as well as the provincial Social Welfare Departments (SWDs) are the main actors which have the mandate to monitor progress on the implementation of the UNCRC and its Optional Protocols.

In the Parliament there are Standing Committees on Human Rights in the National Assembly and the Senate that provide oversight on public policy, monitor the human and child rights situation in the country, receive complaints on child rights violations, conduct inquiries, hold hearings, and make recommendations.

After the 18th Constitutional Amendment, the NCCWD has been consulting with and advocating for the establishment of an independent National Commission on the Rights of the Child (NCRC) for the effective monitoring of all national and provincial programmes. With an independent status, the NCRC will ensure effective monitoring of national programmes which are designed to directly or indirectly benefit children. In this regard, the establishment of the NCRC was announced by the Prime Minister of Pakistan in 2012. Pursuant to this announcement, a series of provincial and national consultations were held, and a draft bill was finalized for legislation.

Some other measures taken by the Government of Pakistan include the adoption of several programmes in the area of basic health and welfare, including the National Hepatitis Control Program (2005–2010), the National Maternal, Newborn and Child Health Program (2006–2012), the National Nutrition Program, and the expansion of the Lady Health Workers Program.[37]

7.3.6 Legislative Measures at Federal and Provincial Levels

The most significant development with respect to law-making has been the passage of the 18th Constitutional Amendment to the Constitution of Pakistan in 2010. Consequent to the 18th Amendment, the subject of the child in terms of legislative and administrative competence as well as financial authority has been devolved to the provinces. The Federal Government, therefore, can now legislate

---

36 Government of Pakistan, Women Development Division, National Commission for Child Welfare and Development. www.pakistan.gov.pk/divisions/ContentListing.jsp?DivID=20&cPath=185_191_399_404 (accessed 1 October 2015).

37 Pakistan's Fifth Periodic Report to the UN Committee on the Rights of the Child on implementation of the Convention on the Rights of the Child, National Commission for Child Welfare and Development, Ministry of Law, Justice and Human Rights Government of Pakistan.

on child related issues only in relation to Federal territories and those areas not forming part of a province. For instance, the Federal government has adopted legislation in the area of education and protection of the child such as the Islamabad Capital Territory (ICT) Free and Compulsory Education Act 2012. Thus child welfare has become a provincial matter. This in turn has brought many challenges for the government, and it has, in particular, taken time for provinces to understand their newly assigned roles and responsibilities. However, provinces soon realized the mechanics and implications of the 18th Amendment, and as a result a number of legislative and administrative measures have been taken by the provincial assemblies and provincial governments. In the Khyber Pakhtunkhwa (KP) province, the Child Protection and Welfare Act (KPCPWA), 2010, has been enacted, which provides mechanisms at local and provincial levels for the welfare and protection of children at risk. It is based on the principle of the best interests of the child. Under the KPCPWA, the Child Protection and Welfare Commission (CPWC) has been established to review provincial laws and regulations affecting the status and rights of children and to propose new laws; to implement policies for the protection, rehabilitation, and reintegration of children at risk; and to monitor the implementation and violation of laws. In KP, CPWC has launched an awareness campaign on child rights through print and electronic media and has arranged a number of seminars, consultations, and workshops.[38] In 2011, the KP Government also promulgated the KP Borstal Institutions Act (BIA), under which separate detention places will be established for juvenile convicts for their basic education and for training regarding their mental, moral, and psychological development. In the province of Sindh, the Sindh Child Protection Authority Act (SCPAA), 2011, has been promulgated, through which an authority has been constituted which will monitor and ensure implementation of the child-protection related provisions under the UNCRC in the province. The law seeks to establish district level child protection institutions. In 2011, the Remand Home Rules were also notified by the Government of Sindh. The Remand Home is a temporary place of custody for child inmates where they are being provided care, protection, and treatment. Under the SCPAA, an eleven member Sindh Child Protection Authority (SCPA) has been set up to coordinate and monitor child protection issues at provincial and district levels. The Authority is working to establish an institutional mechanism for child protection and for the setting of minimum protection and standards for all institutions relating to children, including educational institutions, orphanages, shelter homes, child parks, and hospitals; ensuring implementation is an additional aim.

KPCPWA and the SCPAA are in conformity with the CRC, in which a child is defined as a person below 18 years of age in accordance with the CRC definition given in Article 1. These laws use 'the best interests of child' as a basic principle in taking actions for and against children. In CPWA 2010 the best interests of the

[38] The Commission, through its Child Protection Units (CPUs) located in relevant districts, is raising awareness on child protection issues. By 2012, a total of 459 (235 male and 224 female) awareness sessions were conducted with 335 Child Protection Centres (CPCs).

child is defined as a 'primary consideration, in all actions either by public or private bodies, for protection, survival, development and participation of children'.

The next section discusses in detail the family law in Pakistan and provides an in-depth analysis of the Guardians and Wards Act 1890.

7.4 Parental Care and the Principle of the Best Interests of the Child in Pakistani Law

7.4.1 Features/Characteristics/Duality of the Pakistani Family Law System

The legal system in Pakistan is based on English Common Law and Islamic law. The former is more influential in the area of commercial law while Islamic law principles are followed in family law. The key laws governing marital and family relationships are based on Islamic principles and derive inspiration from the two primary sources of Islamic Law, the *Qur'an* and *Sunnah.* The principle of *Ijtihad* and other accompanying juristic techniques have also been used by the framers of law to formulate family law in Pakistan. At independence, Pakistan inherited four pieces of legislation regarding women's and children's rights: the Child Marriage Restraint Act 1929,[39] the Shariat Application Act 1937,[40] the Dissolution of

[39] The framers of the Act, bearing in mind the societal norms, did not invalidate the child marriage. However, under the Act the father or the guardian may be punished for contracting their children into such marriages. In 2009 a private member bill to amend the CMRA was tabled in the National Assembly, the Child Marriage Restraint (Amendment) Bill, 2009. Among other provisions, it seeks to 'remove the gender disparity in age' of marriage for males and females and to set 18 years as the minimum age of marriage for both. It also proposes to raise the punishment for violations from 1 month to 2 years and the fine from one thousand to one hundred thousand rupees. Once the age of marriage for females is raised to 18 years under the CMR (Amendment) Bill, amendments will be required in the option of puberty provision in the Dissolution of Muslim Marriage Act 1939 to provide effective relief to victims of under-age marriages.

[40] The second piece of legislation that Pakistan inherited from Pre-Partition India was the Shariat Application Act 1937. This act laid down that in family matters regarding Muslims, Muslim personal law had to be applied. A substantial portion of personal law, therefore, remained un-codified and subject to interpretation by the courts. After the creation of Pakistan, the first legislative attempt made by the Punjab Legislative Assembly was the New West Punjab Muslim Personal Law (Shariat) Application Act (IX of 1948) that enlarged the scope of personal law to questions relating to succession, including succession to agricultural land (whereas the previous Act applied only to intestate succession). However these changes were not welcomed in all parts of the country as men were still not willing to give women their share in property. As a result, to deprive women of their inheritance rights, amendments were made to the same Act in the Province of Sindh and the passage 'save questions relating to agricultural land and other than charitable institutions and charitable and religious endowments' was deleted from Section 2 of the Shariat Application Act.

Muslim Marriages Act 1939,[41] and the Guardians and Ward Act 1890.[42] All personal laws enforced in pre-partitioned India are still valid and operative in Pakistan. After independence from the British Colonial rule in 1947, no reforms were made to family law in the first 14 years of Pakistan's history. To review family laws for the first time in 1951, a seven-member Commission on Marriage and Family Laws, also known as the 'Rashid Commission', was setup by the government.[43] The Commission was established with the ostensible aim of identifying areas of reform in family law. The Commission submitted its final report along with a dissenting note by a member of the Commission. The report stated that Islam is a very progressive religion, and not a clergy-dominated religion, and that changes in the law must be brought by exercising the right to *Ijtihad*. The Commission's report recommended wide-ranging reforms in Muslim family law (divorce, inheritance, and marriage) aimed at enhancing the legal status of women. While making its recommendations the Commission gave careful consideration to the opinions of learned, liberal, and enlightened persons that were obtained from the circulation of a questionnaire. The report of the Commission was considered to be a significant document but at the same time a challenge to contemporary Muslim thought. The report received severe criticism from different religious groups and generated heated debate, with members of the religious community denouncing its recommendations as 'distorting the religion of God and [being] the worst type of heresy.' The report and the dissent highlighted the conflicting views that dominate the politics of family law.

The question of custody of the child was also raised in the questionnaire drafted by the Marriage and Family Laws Commission. The question was as follows:

> At present the mother is entitled to the custody of her minor child only up to [a] certain age i.e. the male child up to seven years and [the] female child till she attains puberty. These limits have no authority either in Qur'an or Hadith but have been fixed as a result of

---

[41] The Dissolution of Muslim Marriages Act 1939 came as a relief for Muslim women who were given some protection against the wrongly interpreted and misapplied Islamic divorce laws. Before this Act, Muslim women hardly had a basis to get a divorce, and due to the pressure of customary practices they were also denied access to the right to divorce by *khula*. Only men's right to unilateral divorce was accepted. The Act laid down eight grounds for divorce: where the husband's whereabouts were unknown for 4 years; the failure to provide maintenance for 2 years; the failure to perform marital obligations for 3 years; the husband's impotence, cruelty, and incompatibility of temperament; hatred and adultery; insanity or suffering from leprosy or venereal disease; the husband's interference in the wife's management of her property; and the husband's interference with the performance of the wife's religious beliefs or practice. On these bases a woman could obtain a judicial decree for the dissolution of her marriage (*Tanseekh-i-Nikah*), this dissolution being called *Faskh*. One important aspect of the Act is that dissolution of marriage does not affect a woman's right to dower or the option of puberty. Moreover, the husband's consent to the dissolution is not needed. These grounds were included by adopting the juristic technique of *Talfiq*.

[42] To be discussed in detail in the next section.

[43] The Commission was composed of six Modernists (three men and three women) and one Traditionalist religious scholar, Maulana Ihteshamul Haq.

> opinions of some Muslim Jurists. Do you consider it admissible to propose some modifications?[44]

In answer to this question, the Commission stated in its report as follows:

> In the opinion of the Commission it is admissible to propose changes in [a] matter of custody of minor children as the Qur'an and Sunnah have not fixed any age limit and some of [the] great Mujtahid Imams have expressed the view that the [matter] of age limit in this respect is an open question.[45]

Maulana Maududi (1903–1979), an eminent Pakistani religious scholar, while expressing his views on the issue of custody stated:

> The right thing in this regard is that the interest of the child should be kept above everything else. In every particular case preference should be given either to the father or mother after giving full consideration to the prospects of education and training in their respective custodies … also under [whomsoever's] custody they might be, no restrictions should be placed on children meeting the other party.[46]

Justice Tanzil ur Rehman a senior Supreme Court judge stated:

> In granting the right of upbringing, the child's security and betterment should be kept in mind, and as long as there is no ma'ani (hindrance/hurdle) the mother's custody will be preferred. In certain situations, [the] child has to be given the option to choose between the two. Sometimes such circumstances may arise in which it would be appropriate to give the child to [the] maternal grandmother or maternal uncle even in the presence of the parents. If it is not appropriate to hand over the child to the mother due to her religion or profession then the court will decide by itself to whom the custody may be granted.[47]

However Maulana Amin Ahsan Islahi (1904–1997) commenting on the reply of the Commission responded:

> It is correct that there is no explicit implication of Qur'an and Sunnah which prescribe[s] the age limit. But it does not mean that legists have fixed the limit just out of fancy and had no sound reasons for these deductions … a careful study of the verdicts of Prophet Mohammad (PBUH) in the cases that were brought before him reveal that a very basic consideration has been the welfare and wellbeing, education and training, protection and interests of the minor.[48]

The questionnaire responses reflected the tensions that exist between the Modernists and the Traditionalists particularly in the context of the interpretation

---

44 Report of the Commission on Marriages and Family Laws, The Gazette of Pakistan, Extraordinary, Karachi, 20 June 1956, 1210.

45 Ahmad 1959, p. 218.

46 Ahmad 1959, p. 220.

47 Rehman 1991, pp. 886–887.

48 Pakistani Muslim scholar famous for his Quranic commentary '*Tadabbur ul Qur'an*'. He also served as a member of the Marriage and Family Law Commission set up by the Government of Pakistan in 1956. He was one of the founding members of Jamaat-e-Islami but abandoned the party in 1958.

and application of family law reform in Pakistan.[49] Traditionalists viewed legislation based on the *Qur'anic* precepts of law as the textual and immutable boundaries of Islamic family law jurisprudence. They viewed legislation as divinely ordained and capable of interpretation only by *Mujtahids*, through the process of *Ijtihad.* Modernists on the other hand were of the view that law is something changeable, vibrant, and subject to interpretation.[50] In the process of broadening the scope of *Ijtihad,* the modernists envisioned a separation of legislative and judicial functions.[51] In addition, the Modernists advocated that the judiciary should not be limited to scholars trained in Islamic law who would apply the code mechanically. Instead, the judiciary should include secularly trained judges who could and would interpret and apply the code and Common Law in tandem and on a case-by-case basis.[52] The Modernists' agenda was social justice whereas the Traditionalists' agenda was to protect Islamic law from Western imperialist influences as well as to exert their own positions of power and authority in the community.[53]

The clash between the Modernists and Traditionalists clearly surfaced in the discussions of the members of the Commission who used *Ijtihad* as a vehicle for bringing change and reforming family law in Pakistan. The Commission specifically claimed in its report that independent legal reasoning, or *Ijtihad,* and the subsequent interpretation and application of family laws (both in the *Qur'an* and *Sunnah* and, later, in the Muslim Family Law Ordinance) was not limited to the *Mujtahid*, but that even a secular judge could exercise *Ijtihad.*[54] Coulson has very aptly depicted the difference of opinion between the Modernists and the Traditionalists' approach by stating that the clash between the two was on:

> A single, determinative issue: the judicial power of interpretation versus traditional Islamic law as already interpreted by centuries of jurists... In other words, which was to prevail: the codified Islamic law or the common law function of judges to interpret and modify that law through their decisions?[55]

Despite the fact that the recommendations of the Commission provided a road map for legislative reform, no action was taken on them. It was 5 years later in March 1961 that the Muslim Family Laws Ordinance 1961 (hereafter MFLO) was promulgated which incorporated some of the recommendations of the

---

[49] The Traditionalists and the Modernists stand between the two extreme groups, the *Ulema* and the Secularists. The *Ulema*, or the orthodox religious leaders, hold the extreme right-wing point of view while Secularists advocate a complete separation between religion and state.

[50] Pearl 1969, p. 168.

[51] Haider 2000, p. 292.

[52] Haider 2000, p. 292.

[53] Haider 2000, p. 293.

[54] Report of the Commission on Marriage and Family Laws, Gazette of Pakistan, Extraordinary, 20 June 1956.

[55] Coulson 1957, p. 137.

Commission.[56] Under the MFLO, registration of marriage and divorce was made mandatory, a procedure was laid down for pronouncing divorce, and restrictions were imposed on polygamy. The MFLO was a significant step towards giving women and men equal rights, yet the MFLO failed in the sense that its reforms were weak and watered-down versions of the recommendations of the Commission on Marriage and Family Laws. Specifically, its reforms were prescriptions for procedural safeguards rather than clear prohibitions of certain acts. Additionally, it also remained silent on the issue of custody of minors. In sum, the MFLO reflected a compromise between the Traditionalists and Modernists. This compromise weakened the effect of the reforms. In 2000 the Federal Sharia Court held in *Allah Rakha v. Federation of Pakistan* PLD 2000 FSCI that it had jurisdiction to examine whether the MFLO is consistent with Islam because the codified laws applicable to Muslims do not come under the category of Muslim personal laws as mentioned in Article 203(c) of the Constitution. However, this judgment has been assailed before the Supreme Court, and there has been no alteration of the law to date.[57]

The main law that deals with custody and guardianship cases therefore remains the same, i.e. the Guardians and Wards Act 1890.

7.4.2 The Guardians and Wards Act, 1890 (Act VIII of 1890)

The Guardians and Wards Act (hereafter GWA) is the main piece of legislation that governs custody and guardianship cases in Pakistan. The GWA consolidated the earlier, sketchy legislation on the subject which included Act 40 of 1858, which was for minors in the Presidency of Bengal and Madras, Act 20 of 1864 for the Presidency of Bombay, Act 9 of 1861, and Act 1874 for minors in territories beyond the jurisdiction of chartered High Courts. With the passage of time and after independence from the British colonial rule, some provisions of GWA lost their relevance and became obsolete and redundant; for instance in Section 5 the power of parents to appoint a guardian where one of them is a European British subject has been omitted under the Federal Laws (Revision and Declaration) Ordinance 1981. The other legislative instrument was the West Pakistan Family Court Act, 1964 (hereafter WPFCA). Section 5 WPFCA confers exclusive jurisdiction on the Family

[56] Some of the Commission's recommendations were incorporated in the Muslim Family Law Ordinance (MFLO) promulgated by Pakistan's first military ruler, General Ayub Khan (1958–1969), in 1961.

[57] The Federal Sharia Court established in the Constitution by Article 203B(c) has jurisdiction to examine certain laws to ensure they are not repugnant to Islamic principles. The Court has original and appellate jurisdiction, but it does not have jurisdiction over the Constitution, Muslim personal law, or any laws relating to the procedure of any court or tribunal.

Courts to adjudicate upon matters specified in the Schedule, of which item No. 5 refers to the custody of children. This provision has been made subject to the provisions contained in the MFLO and the Conciliation of Courts Ordinance of 1961. Section 25 WPFCA confers on the Family Court the status of a District Court for the purpose of the GWA and further provides that while dealing with these matters the same procedure as prescribed under the GWA shall be followed. Section 47 GWA catalogues orders made by a Court, which are all appealable to the High Court, of which clause; (c) refers to an order made under Section 25. The Family Court as constituted under the WPFCA, having exclusive jurisdiction to deal, inter alia, with custody of children, is not a District Court in terms of the definition as laid down in Section 4(4) GWA and Section 2(4) Civil Procedure Code 1908. This with the exception that the deeming provision contained in Section 25 WPFCA has conferred that status on it while dealing with cases under the GWA. There is a separate law for Family Courts in Azad Jammu and Kashmir, which is The Azad Jammu and Kashmir Family Courts Act, 1993. These courts have exclusive jurisdiction to hear cases in the region concerning divorce, maintenance, custody, dower, restitution of conjugal rights, and guardianship.

The objectives of the GWA are to promote the interests of children to make sure that a child may not suffer any discrimination or disadvantage because of the marital status of his or her parents.

Recently, the Law and Justice Commission of Pakistan in its meeting in 2007 considered some further sections of the GWA and proposed to amend Section 6 of the Act by deleting the expression 'who is not a European British Subject'.[58] The Commission also considered the discriminatory provisions contained in Section 19(b) of the Act, prescribing that the court is not to appoint a guardian for a minor whose father, in the opinion of the court, is not unfit to be guardian of the person of the minor. This proviso potentially excludes the mother even if she herself has a right to custody of the minor. Two honourable female members of the Commission stated that in the presence of the mother having custody, no guardian of the person of the child may be appointed if the mother is not, in the opinion of the court, unfit to be guardian of the person of the minor. This proposed amendment was approved by the Commission along with consequential amendment in Section 41(e) of the Act with regard to reference to the mother of the minor therein.

Another legislative provision relevant in custody cases is Section 491 of the Criminal Procedure Code 1898, under which if a minor is held forcibly, interim custody is immediately restored to the mother. The WPFCA and the West Pakistan Family Court Rules are also invoked in such cases. Certain constitutional

[58] The Law and Justice Commission of Pakistan is a Federal Government institution, established under an Ordinance (XIV) of 1979. The Commission is headed by the Chief Justice of Pakistan and comprises twelve other members, including the Chief Justice of the Federal Shariat Court, Chief Justices of the High Courts, the Attorney General for Pakistan, the Secretary of the Ministry of Law & Justice, the Chairperson of the National Commission on the Status of Women, and four other members, one from each Province.

provisions may also be invoked in such disputes, such as the writ jurisdiction of the High Courts under Article 199 of the Constitution.

In Pakistan, the GWA is applicable to custody and guardianship cases while keeping in view the personal law to which the minor/ward is subject.[59] Under the Majority Act 1875 (No IX), minority ceases upon the completion of 18 years, unless a guardian of the person, or property, or both, of the minor has been or shall be appointed before the minor has attained the age of 18 years, or the property of the minor is under the superintendence of a court of wards, in which case the age of minority is prolonged until the minor has completed the age of 21 years. Accordingly, notwithstanding classical Islamic law, a child remains a minor until the completion of 18 years. Until then, the court has the power to appoint a guardian for the child and her or his property or both under the provisions of the GWA.

A minor is subject to the same personal law as his/her father. This law applies to Muslim and non-Muslim citizens of Pakistan. The established view is that 'where the provisions of the personal law are in conflict with the provisions of the GWA, the latter will prevail over the former'.[60] Section 25(1) explicitly concerns custody. It states that:

> If a ward leaves or is removed from the custody of a guardian of his person, the Court, if it is of the opinion that it will be for the welfare of the ward to return to the custody of his guardian, may make an order for his return.

This proviso allows the court to intervene and to re-establish the original arrangement of child custody in cases of divorce or separation between the husband and wife. But since both divorced parents may retain a form of custody, the mother exercises actual custody while the father relies on legal custody. The provision has been applied to transfer custody from one parent to the other, bearing in mind the welfare of the ward.[61] In other words, the Act provides room to the courts to disregard classical Hanafi custodial hierarchy and empowers them to decide simple custody disputes between parents according to the minor's welfare. If one of the parents has been declared unfit or has lost custodial rights for some other reason, Section 19(b) enables a court order in the child's welfare. The court shall be guided by the law to which the minor is subject and shall consider the

---

[59] The relevant provision in this respect is Section 3 of the Majority Act 1875, which reads as follows: 'Subject as aforesaid, every minor, of whose person or property or both a guardian, other than for a suit within the meaning of Order XXXII of the First Schedule to the Code of Civil Procedure 1908 (No V), has been or shall be appointed or declared by any Court of Justice before the minor has attained the age of 18 years, and every minor of whose property the superintendence has been or shall be assumed by any Court of Wards before the minor has attained that age shall, notwithstanding anything contained in the Succession Act 1925 (No XXXIX) or in any other enactment, be deemed to have attained his majority when he shall have completed his age of 21 years and not before. Subject as aforesaid, every other person domiciled in Pakistan shall be deemed to have attained his majority when he shall complete his age of 18 years and not before.'

[60] Mulla 1938, p. 45.

[61] Section 25(1) Guardians and Wards Act, 1870.

statutory factors listed above. When the minor's father is living and has not been declared unfit, the court may not appoint a guardian but may apparently give mere custody to another person.

The GWA empowers the court to hear the child's opinion in guardianship and custody cases if the child is capable of articulating his preferences. The court, however, is not obliged to ascertain from the minor his wishes. What is required is to keep the best interests of the child in view and to reconcile the child's opinion and the welfare rule if there is a conflict in these two requirements. The GWA does not state a specific age limit for the age of the child to be capable of expressing his preferences, and there is case law available in custody and guardianship cases where children have been heard in court. Ali, in her review of judicial cases from 1947 to 1997, argues that neither the GWA nor the case law makes a clear distinction between the words 'guardianship' and 'custody'; the terms are often used interchangeably, and no clearly defined parameters have been drawn to determine the nature and extent of the privileges inherent in the persons awarded either custody or guardianship of a minor.[62] Ali is of the view that the only inference that can be drawn from the case law analysis is that the word guardian is mostly used to refer to the legal guardian while custody is taken to refer to the mother or any female relative having physical possession of the minor.[63]

7.4.3 Law of Guardianship in Pakistan

7.4.3.1 Jurisdiction

The application for guardianship should be made under the provisions of the GWA to the court having jurisdiction in the place where the minor ordinarily resides. If the application is with respect to the guardianship over the property of the minor, then it may be made either to the court having jurisdiction in the place where the minor ordinarily resides or to a court having jurisdiction in a place where the minor has property.

7.4.3.2 Who May Be a Guardian?

According to Section 4(2) GWA, a guardian is 'a person having the care of the person of a minor, or of his property, or of both his person and property'. A guardian can be a *de facto* or a *de jure* guardian. Pursuant to the GWA, a father is the natural guardian of a child under the age of 18 years. A *de jure* guardian is

[62] Ali and Azam 1998, p. 151.

[63] Ali and Azam 1998, p. 151.

appointed by the court. A *de facto* guardian is a related person other than the father or grandfather, e.g. the mother, a brother or an uncle. Other persons—such as the mother, other relatives (except the father and father's father), or an institution like an orphanage—may voluntarily choose to take in charge the person or the property of a minor; a mother, however, is the next possible guardian after a father, unless the latter, by his will, has appointed another person as the guardian of the child. While appointing a *de jure* guardian, the character, the capacity, and the fitness of the individual should be taken into consideration.[64]

7.4.3.3 Court Proceedings

A person, including a relative or friend, who is interested in becoming a *de jure* guardian must apply to the court under the provisions of the GWA in order to be appointed as a guardian; he is not bound to wait until his legal title or fitness to act as guardian is disputed by another person. The procedure for such an application is stated in Section 10 of the GWA, and no order should be made unless notice of the application is given to persons interested in the minor.

During the court proceedings, the court exercises parental jurisdiction over the child. The court is also empowered to give temporary custody and order protection of the person and property of the minor during the maintenance of the case.

While appointing a guardian, the court must have regard to the welfare of the minor, which covers factors such as the age, sex, and religion of the child; the character and capacity of the proposed guardian and his nearness to the child; the wishes, if any, of the deceased parents as well as any existing or previous relations of the proposed guardian with regards to the minor or his or her property; and if the child is old enough to form an intelligent preference, then such preference should also be considered.

7.4.3.4 Effects of Being Appointed as de jure Guardian

A guardian is responsible for ensuring that the minor is supported, fed, housed, clothed, and educated in a manner suitable to his or her position in life, and to the fortune which he or she is likely to enjoy upon attaining the age of majority. The *de jure* guardian appointed by the court is entitled to such allowance as the court

---

64 A charitable society is not a person within the meaning of Section 4(2) of the GWA and thus cannot be appointed as the guardian of the person, or property, of the minor. It is due to the fact that anyone having an interest adverse to that of a minor cannot be appointed as a guardian. However, it has been held by courts that a manager of a registered society can be appointed as the guardian of a child. In the latter context, it has also been stated that the meaning of person in the context of being appointed a guardian should not be confined to an individual, despite Section 3(39) of the General Clauses Act as it would then conflict with GWA Sections 43(4) and 45.

thinks fit for the minor's care and for the effort that he or she goes through while undertaking the duties. The allowance can be paid out of the property of the ward.

A guardian appointed by the court without the court's permission cannot remove the ward from the limits of the court's jurisdiction. The permission can be special or general and can be specified in the court order. Illegal removal of a ward from the court's jurisdiction is punishable with a fine not exceeding Rs. 1000[65] or a jail term extending to 6 months.

7.4.3.5 Cessation and Revocation of Guardianship

A court, on the application of any interested person or on its own motion, may remove a guardian appointed or declared by it, or even a guardian appointed by will, for the following reasons (amongst others):

- For abuse of trust;
- For continued failure to perform the duties of his trust;
- For incapacity to perform the duties of his trust;
- For ill-treatment or neglect in taking proper care of the ward;
- For contumacious disregard of any of the GWA's provisions or of any of the court orders;
- For conviction of an offense implying a defect of character;
- For having an interest adverse to the faithful performance of his duties;
- For ceasing to reside within the local limits of the court's jurisdiction;
- For bankruptcy or insolvency in the case of a guardian of property.

A guardian may also apply to the court for discharge from the responsibility of being a guardian. A person also ceases to be a guardian in the case of his or her death, removal; upon the ward ceasing to be a minor; upon the female ward's marriage to a husband who is not unfit to be her guardian; or upon the court itself assuming superintendence of the minor.

7.4.4 Judicial Decisions in Custody and Guardianship Cases in Pakistan

As discussed earlier in this chapter, a general view prevalent in Pakistan based on classical Hanafi principle is that in cases of marital breakup the father is to be given custody of a male child at the age of seven and custody of a female child on her attaining puberty. The courts in Pakistan, however, have deviated from this classical Hanafi principle and have based their judgments on the 'Best Interests of the Child' principle. This section provides a review of cases from 1997 to 2013

[65] Approximately 10–12 Euros.

in which the courts have upheld the principle of the best interests of the child and given custody to the best-suited person. Pakistani courts have demonstrated considerable sensitivity for the child's emotional and financial well-being in interpreting the concept of 'welfare', and while upholding the principle courts have at times granted custody even to a grandparent if such grandparent appears better placed to ensure the child's welfare than, for example, the mother of the child. At the same time, as shall be shown below, parenting agreements have been taken into consideration by the courts when deciding child custody disputes.

7.4.4.1 Case Law

Visitation Rights and Violation of a Parental Agreement

In *Ali Hayat v. Khalid Shafi and 2 others*,[66] the contention of the father/applicant was that the children's mother had moved them to a new house and denied him his visitation rights in violation of the parenting agreement at the time of divorce. The contentions of the mother were that the present application under Section 491 Cr.PC was ineffectual as the children were allowed to remain in her custody in pursuance of the parenting agreement and that according to the this agreement all disputes had to be first referred to a mediator. The High Court directed that both parties should follow the parenting agreement and might sit together to renegotiate the agreement, keeping in view the best interests and welfare of their children; that as an interim measure the mother would allow the father to meet the children three times a week for two hours each, and such interim measure would be valid for up to thirty days; that both parties would not remove the minors from the city without an order of the competent court; that the father would continue to deposit monthly expenses; and that in the event of a failure to reach an amicable settlement outside court within thirty days, the parties would be at liberty to approach the Guardian Judge for redressal of their grievance. The court further held that in matters pertaining to children the courts should not go into legal technicalities and should decide the case keeping in view the facts and circumstances of each case, mainly taking into consideration the welfare of the child.

Failure to Provide Maintenance

In *Iftikhar Ahmad Chisti v. District Judge, Chakwal and others*,[67] the failure to provide maintenance to the children, a second marriage, and children from the second marriage were reasons for not granting custody to the father despite his claims

---

[66] *Ali Hayat v. Khalid Shafi and 2 others*, YLR 2013 954.

[67] *Iftikhar Ahmad Chisti v. District Judge Chakwal and others*, PLD 2012 Lah 670.

that he could provide a better education to the children. In this case a constitutional petition for custody of the minors was filed by the father (as a suit of petitioner (father) for the custody of minors was dismissed concurrently by the Guardian Court and Appellate Court). The petitioner admitted that he had failed to pay the maintenance under the decree of the Family Court and that he had been detained in civil prison. The Court held that if a father failed to make maintenance payments and then litigated against the custody of minors and finally did not pay the maintenance even after the decree of the court and preferred to go to civil prison, it could be safely presumed that he was not interested in the welfare and well-being of the minors. The petitioner was also living with his second wife, and he had children from his second wife. The court further held that the step-mother could not bestow the love and affection which would be given by the real mother. In such circumstances it was not in the welfare of the minors to be given to the petitioner. The court further held that the petitioner's contentions that better education facilities were available at the place where the petitioner was residing and that the petitioner had better financial means than the respondent were not valid grounds for putting the minors in his custody.

Failure to provide maintenance by the father was also a ground for not awarding custody to the father in *Karim Bakhsh v. Muhammad Bakhsh*;[68] instead the custody of the child was given back to the maternal uncle as he and the maternal grandmother were looking after the child, and the minor had also expressed his willingness to live with his maternal relatives.

Although the courts have held that providing maintenance is the responsibility of the father, his wealth and financial status cannot be the grounds for giving him the custody of the child. In *Mst. Iram Shahzad and 2 others v. Additional District Judge, Lahore*,[69] the Court held that the ostensible wealth of father can never be a ground entitling him to custody of his minor whereas age, gender, and the marital status of the parties are factors which are to be taken into consideration for arriving at a conclusion as to how the interests and welfare of the minor can be best protected; moreover, such factors are not to be considered in contradistinction to the welfare of minor. The court held that the welfare of the minor is of paramount importance and the sole determining feature/factor. Referring to Islamic law, the court held that it is the responsibility of the father to provide maintenance to the child, but the court also categorically dismissed the option of sending the child abroad and to be looked after by a maid. The Court further held that '[n]o mother deserves to be put through the agony of permanently parting with her offspring or forced yet again to invoke the jurisdiction of a foreign court'; therefore the custody was awarded to the mother of the minor.

[68] *Karim Bakhsh v. Muhammad Bakhsh*, CLC 1997 316.

[69] *Mst. Iram Shahzad and 2 others v. Additional District Judge Lahore*, PLD 2011 Lah 362.

Custody and Prohibited Degree of Relationship

The courts have also taken into consideration prohibited degrees of relation while awarding custody of the child. In *Mst. Aziza v. SSP, District Tando Muhammad Khan and 3 others*,[70] the court allowed the application for recovery of a minor who was living with grandparents and a cousin who came under a prohibited degree of relationship. The court held that as the relationship between the minor and her cousin fell within the prohibited degree, it was therefore in the best interests of the child that she should live with her real mother instead of her cousin and grandparents, who could hardly walk and hence could not contribute towards the welfare of the minor. The court also held that under Islamic law the mother was most entitled to the custody of the minor girl.

Age of the Child and Recognition of Motherhood

In *Mst. Gulnaz v. Mst. Amina and others*[71] the court held that 'as [the] mother of minors was alive and able to take care of her minors and there could be no better cradle for the minors than their mother's lap, denying such natural right would be utter cruelty and grave injustice'. The Court further held that it would be best and in the interests and welfare of the minors that they were reunited with their mother. In this case, the Court very clearly emphasized the significance of the mother's role and how it is linked to the welfare of the child as there could be no better substitute for the minors than the mother herself.

Second Marriage and Awarding Custody to Grandparents

The second marriage of the mother has in some cases resulted in her not being awarded the custody of the child. In *Mst. Aneeta Tanveer v. Muhammad Younas*,[72] the Family Court refused to give custody of the minor child to the petitioner (mother) who had entered a second marriage after a mutually agreed divorce from her first husband. The facts of the case were that after the mother's second marriage the child was living with the maternal grandfather and was being well looked after by him. The court held that: (i) the petitioner mother of the minor had no source of income; (ii) she had remarried, and she had been blessed with three children after her remarriage; (iii) her second husband was a stranger as far as the minor was concerned; (iv) her second husband had declined to testify about his income and whether he was willing to shoulder responsibilities in connection with

---

[70] *Mst. Aziza v. SSP, District Tando Muhammad Khan and 3 others*, YLR 2012 2881.

[71] *Mst. Gulnaz v. Mst. Amina and others*, CLC 2012 761.

[72] *Mst. Aneeta Tanveer v. Muhammad Younas*, YLR 2010 513.

the minor; (v) the maternal grandfather was a retired servant and was receiving a pension; (vi) the maternal grandfather had his own house, whereas the mother and step-father of the minor lived in a rented house; (vii) the real father of the minor had no objection to the child's remaining with his maternal grandfather; and finally (viii) the child had been receiving education while living with the maternal grandfather. Taking into consideration these grounds, the court decided that it was in the best interests of the child to remain with the maternal grandfather.

Josip Stimac and others v. Melitta Syed Shah and others[73] was a case of an Austrian drug trafficker travelling with her children who was arrested at the airport. A case under Section 9(c) and Section 15, Control of Narcotic Substances Act, 1997 was registered against her, and she was subsequently confined in jail as an under trial prisoner; the minors were also confined with their mother, especially for the reason that at the time of her remand before the magistrate she requested to keep them as she was a foreigner and had no relation or friend in Pakistan to take care of them. The mother of minors wrote a letter to the Austrian embassy seeking to have the minors sent to Austria so that they could live with her parents (the petitioners). The Austrian embassy could not succeed in getting the minors released without the court's order for custody. Making reference to Article 199(1)(b)(i) of the Constitution and Section 491 Cr.PC, the maternal grandparents of the minors (through their counsel) moved the High Court for release of the minors and their transfer to the custody of the grandparents, contending that they were in custody improperly and illegally. The request further alleged that with their mother herself having made a request that the minors be sent to her parents abroad, it was in the welfare of the minors to live with their grandparents and elder brother and to have a proper education as the parents of minors were involved in drug trafficking and had a blatant track record. The grandparents had obtained a custody order from the Austrian courts for the minors. The court held that '*prima facie* it seemed in the welfare of the minors that they should be sent back to their home country, which, undoubtedly, was a welfare state and capable of taking care of even those children whose parents were not there'. The High Court observed that

> there was apprehension that the minors may not be used as a shield or carrier for any sordid business and if it so happened, the life of the minors shall be ruined, therefore, it was in the best interest of the minors that their custody be given to the grandparents as requested, particularly when [the] elder brother of the minors, was there and was old enough to look after them.

In two other cases custody was given to the maternal aunt and the uncle, respectively.[74] In the former case the father had filed a petition for custody of his son, who was living with his maternal aunt since he was only fifteen days old following the death of his mother. The court held that the mere fact that minor had attained the age of 7 years would not ipso facto entitle his father to his custody as

---

73 *Josip Stimac and others v. Melitta Syed Shah and others*, PLD 2009 Lah 393.

74 *Mst. Nighat Firdous v. Khadim Hussain*, SCMR 1998 1593, and *Karim Bakhsh v. Muhammad Bakhsh*, CLC 1997 316.

a matter of right. The court, emphasising the best interests of the child principle, stated that 'the right of father to claim custody of minor was not an absolute right and the father being lawful guardian of his minor child would be entitled to his custody, provided it was for the welfare of minor'. In the latter case the minor was not happy living with his father, who, on receiving his custody, had engaged him to earn a livelihood for his family members by working as laborer despite the main ground in his application for custody of the minor having been that he was not receiving an education. The Court held that the minor's welfare was not being served by living with his father and that his interest was instead best served while in the custody of his maternal uncle, where his grandmother was there to look after him; the minor had also expressed his willingness to live with his maternal relatives. Taking into consideration the child's wishes and his welfare, the High Court set aside the orders of the lower courts that granted custody of the minor to his father, and the minor child was allowed to live with his maternal uncle.

Habeas Corpus Petitions and Jurisdiction of the Court

In *Mst. Zohra Hilal v. Noor Sakht Shah*[75] the petitioner claimed that her minor daughter had been detained by the respondent/father of the minor improperly and illegally. The court dismissed the petition on two grounds: firstly, in the trial court the minor, when given the choice, opted for living with her father; and secondly, the court held that as it was a case of child custody arising out of a marital dispute, it should be decided in the court of the Guardian Judge or Family Court and not as a habeas corpus petition under Section 491 of the Cr.PC. In a similar case in 2005, the court refused to decide the case under Section 491 Cr.PC (*habeas corpus*) and held that 'this power being extraordinary in nature, should be sparingly used because paternal jurisdiction in the matter rested under Guardians and Wards Act, 1890'.[76] The court further held that the Superior Courts had exercised jurisdiction under Section 491 Cr.PC only in cases of real urgency, and such powers were exercised when the minor was of tender age. The court further held that 'the interest of suckling baby would be best served if he/she was handed over to mother as the life, health, or upbringing of the minor was in serious jeopardy'. The court refused to give custody to the mother on the grounds that the minors were well-settled; they attended their school regularly; the school fees, which were approximately Rs. 5,000 for 2 months for three minors, were being paid by the father of the minors without any default; the academic results of the minors were exceptional, and their attendance was maximum; and if the minors were removed from the school, their education was likely to suffer adversely. Keeping in view the age, welfare, education, and prevailing circumstances of the case, no justification existed to interfere in the custody of the minors.

[75] *Mst. Zohra Hilal v. Noor Sakht Shah*, PLD 2009 258.

[76] *Mst. Tasneem Fatima v. Arshad Mehmood and another*, YLR 2005 883.

Conversely, in *Mst. Moomal v. Jumo Salaro Mir Khan and another*[77] the habeas corpus petition of the mother of the minors under Section 491 was allowed, and the High Court permitted petitioner/mother to take the minors with her in order to ensure their welfare. In this case the children stated before the court that their father was being abusive to them. He had been extending threats to them, and on a number of occasions had also frightened them by pointing a gun towards them. In view of the statements of the minors the Court concluded that

> even if respondent/father of minors was not detaining them illegally ... he was keeping them in his house improperly and restraint on two minors was patently unjust, cruel and not in the best interest of two minors and their welfare and proper upbringing would be adversely affected[;] therefore custody must be awarded to the mother.

Custody Issues in Polygamous Marriages

In *Mst. Jamila Begum v. Mirza Muhammad and 2 others*,[78] where the father had contracted polygamous marriages the court awarded the custody of children back to the mother, who had been deprived of her children by concurrent orders of two courts on the sole ground of poverty. The High Court held that the courts misread the evidence, wherein it was categorically stated that the children in custody of the mother were happy and were receiving proper education. Evidence also showed that the father of the minor children was a crane operator who had contracted two other marriages, and in his meagre pay he could not be expected to send his children to a high standard educational institution. The Court further held that due to his polygamous marriages,

> the welfare of the minors in the presence of two step-mothers in the same house could not be stated to be more safe than in the custody of their real mother who after divorce neither had contracted [a] second marriage nor her character and occupation was such that custody of minors could be refused to her.

Child Abduction Cases

In the recent past, two French mothers (Ingrid Brandun Berger in 2012 and Peggy Collins in 2009) were allowed to take their children back to France after a struggle in the Pakistani higher courts. Their battle to secure the custody of their children was an onerous task but a successful one.[79] In both cases the grounds advanced by the fathers for retaining their children were based on religious and moral concerns.

In Berger's case, the father of the child claimed that he was his daughter's rightful custodian based on his religious beliefs. He argued that he brought his

[77] *Mst. Moomal v. Jumo Salaro Mir Khan and another*, PCr.LJ 1998 1535.

[78] *Mst. Jamila Begum v. Mirza Muhammad and 2 others*, YLR 2003 1337

[79] Ingrid Brandun Berger is an unreported case, but some information on this case is available in Childabductionrecoveryinternational 2014.

daughter to Pakistan and kept her there because both father and daughter are Muslims, and he wanted his daughter to live in Pakistan. The girl's grandfather also wished not to see his granddaughter 'growing up as an infidel' in a Western liberal culture. The case of Peggy Collins was similar, in which the father retained his 9-year-old son in Pakistan, and he argued—referring to several judgments given by the Supreme Court, the Mohammadan law, and *Hedaya*—that the custody of the child should not be given to an alienated non-Muslim mother who would encourage the boy to deviate from his father's religion. Such arguments, based on the mother's religion or culture, were not taken into account by the Pakistani courts.[80] In both cases, the judges made their decision according to logic, justice, good conscience, and the child's best interests. In Berger's case especially, the court observed that the father did not give any consideration to the mother's religion when he married her. His ex-wife's religion, culture, or nationality obviously did not matter when he fell in love and married her. According to the court, accepting arguments such as faith, nationality, and culture would have been adverse to justice, equity, and good conscience. In both cases, the child's best interests were the courts' primary consideration in granting custody of these minors to their mothers. Moreover, the Pakistani judges respected foreign court orders. Those stated that the fathers had broken some foreign laws, resulting in a deprivation of education and proper welfare for their children.

In another unique case, Roshni Desai, a Canadian national of Indian origin, came to reclaim the custody of her three-and-half-year-old son and filed a habeas corpus application under Section 491 of the Cr.PC before the Lahore High Court.[81] The father argued that, according to the Islamic laws, a Muslim child could not be entrusted to a non-Muslim mother. Since the child was born out of wedlock, the court drew attention to the fact that not only was it difficult to determine which parent should be granted custody of the child, but that living in the Pakistani culture would also prove troublesome for the child due to his illegitimate status. The court allowed the mother to take the child back to Canada and stated that Islamic law does not allow a father to keep custody of his illegitimate child. In such situations, the custody can only be given to the mother. The court further observed that: 'Under Islamic laws, the bond between a mother and her illegitimate child is stronger than the bond between this child and his/her father. And a father cannot become guardian of his illegitimate child.' The judge ruled that, as a single mother, she had the exclusive right of custody.

In the case of 12-year-old Scottish-Pakistani girl Misbah Rana, the girl's mother, Louise Campbell, approached the High Court of Lahore and filed a lawsuit against her ex-husband and Misbah's elder sister, both of whom had illegally taken Misbah to Pakistan.[82] She claimed that Misbah should be sent back to Scotland and the custody matter decided by the relevant court in Scotland, as per

80 *Peggy Collins v. Muhammad Ishfaque Malik* (2009) PLD 48 Lahore High Court, para 4.

81 *Roshan Desai v. Jahanzeb Niaz* (2011) PLD 423 Lahore High Court.

82 *Louise Ann Fairley v. Sajjad Ahmad Rana* (2007) PLD 300 Lahore High Court.

the UK-Pakistan Protocol. Louise Rana was worried that Misbah would be forced to marry at her early age, whereas Misbah consistently denied, through a news conference, that her Pakistani family was trying to force her into such a union. After listening to both parties' arguments, the Court ordered that Misbah should be handed over to the British High Commission within seven days so that the case could be decided as per the Protocol and the custody issue heard in Scotland's relevant court. Upon hearing that she would be handed over to her mother, Misbah protested against the Court's decision and expressed her desire not to go back to Scotland. On appeal, the Supreme Court of Pakistan set aside the judgment of the High Court of Lahore and mediated a settlement between the parties. Misbah herself stated that she did not want to reside with her mother because she forbade her from practicing her faith, gave her *haram* food, and was living with a man outside of marriage. Owing to Misbah's wish to stay with her father, the court allowed Misbah to stay with her father and granted access to her mother so that she could visit her daughter under certain conditions.

In Misbah's case, the court respected Misbah's point of view, as envisaged in Articles 12 and 9(2) of the UNCRC: 'In any proceedings …, all interested parties shall be given an opportunity to participate in the proceedings and make their views known.'

7.4.4.2 Evaluation

The review of these cases shows that by taking a proactive approach the superior judiciary in Pakistan has moved away from the traditional Islamic classical law on custody and guardianship and has applied the 'best interests of the child' principle by using judicial discretion. One example of exercising judicial discretion is the Lahore High Court decision in *Munawar Jan v. M Afsar Khan* case,[83] in which the court declared that the welfare of the child should take precedence over the personal law. The court held that: 'If there is a conflict between the personal law to which the minor is subject and considerations of his or her welfare the latter must prevail'. This shows that even in the presence of classical Hanafi Muslim personal law, the courts have given preference to the best interests of the child and on that basis have given custody to the mother. Additionally, the Courts have also used various frames of reference to ascertain this principle; for instance, a failure to provide maintenance has been a ground for not giving custody to the father, and wealth of the father was also not considered as a ground to give him the custody of children. Similarly, maternal relations have been given preference over the father in the absence of a natural mother of the minor if the father has failed to provide maintenance to the minors. The court has also considered the views of the child in deciding custody matters. At the same time, remarriage and the weak financial position of the mother were grounds for not awarding custody to the mother as this

[83] *Munawar Jan v. M Afsar Khan*, PLD 1962 Lah 142.

would have an impact on the best interests of the child. It has also been observed in the review of the cases that the personal situation of the parents matter, as a mother was awarded custody of male child because she was well-educated and in a financially stable position to support the male child. From the cases discussed above it has also become clear that the courts can decide against a parental agreement on custody if, according to the court, the agreement contradicts the interests of the child.

It is also interesting to note that the judgments given by the lower courts reflect a more conservative approach. The decisions of the lower courts show that classical Hanafi law as interpreted in *Hedaya*, societal norms, and the patriarchal structure of the society are some of the influential factors that have an impact on the decisions. By contrast, the decisions of the superior judiciary are more enlightened and reflect that the superior judiciary has made decisions on the basis of the principles of equity, justice, and good conscience. The review of judgments from Pakistani courts reveals, however, that there do not appear to be readily available examples of court cases where the judges have used or applied the CRC or other relevant international instruments. At the same time, in a few cases of child abduction we find references to the UK/Pakistan Judicial Protocol. One obvious reason for this could be that under Pakistani law courts are not bound to apply international law principles.

In Child abduction cases, Pakistani parents who abduct their child (usually the fathers) often base their decision on moral grounds, as they fear that the religion of the mother and the immorality of Western cultures may taint their children and render them immoral. Such claims or arguments based on religion or culture have been rejected by Pakistani courts; instead, the best interests of the child principle has been upheld and non-Muslim mothers have been given the custody of their children.

7.5 Conclusion

This study has shown that centuries of Muslim rule and British colonial domination in the Indian sub-continent has resulted in a cross-fertilization of religious and Common Law principles. This is reflected in the constitutional and legislative frameworks adopted in Pakistan. Further, by ratifying the UNCRC, Pakistan has undertaken the international obligation of bringing its laws in consonance with international human rights standards. However, ratified international instruments do not automatically have the force of law in Pakistan and must be incorporated through implementing legislation. In the absence of implementing legislation, provisions of international treaties, including the UNCRC, are addressed throughout national legislation in a piecemeal, subject-by-subject manner.

From the review of case law it has become evident that in its decisions the superior judiciary has avoided the rigid application of the principles of established Muslim jurisprudence and shifted family law from the realm of the civil to that of the Common Law. The 'welfare or best interests of the child' has been the guiding factor in deciding on the custody of children, and personal law based on classical Islamic principles has remained subordinate to such consideration before the courts. Thus, the sole criteria which must prevail is always the welfare of child, and overall custody is perceived foremost as a right of the child. To conclude in the words of Cassandra Balchin, 'Courts in Pakistan have succeeded in making inroads into established Muslim Jurisprudence and have at times over ridden [sic] express provisions of law to safeguard the best interest of the child.'[84]

References

Ali SS (2012) Navigating Religion, Politics and Cultural Norms: the Arduous Journey toward Domestication of CEDAW in Pakistan. JPCD 19:43–60

Ali SS, Azam N (1998) Custody and Guardianship Case Law 1947–1997. In: Shaheed F et al (eds) Shaping Women's Lives, Laws, Practices and Strategies. Shirkat Gah, Lahore

Ali SS, Jamil B (1994) The United Nations Convention on the Rights of the Child, Islamic Law and Pakistan Legislation: A Comparative Study. Shaheen Publications, Peshawar

Ahmad K (1959) Marriage Commission Report X-Rayed. Chiragh e Rah Publications, Lahore

Ahmad M (1993) The Muslim Family Laws Ordinance of Pakistan. IJWP 10:37–46

Baillie NB (1957) A Digest of Moohummudan Law, Part I. Premier Book House, Lahore

Balchin CA (1994) Handbook on Family Laws in Pakistan. Shirkatgah, Lahore

Bilimoria P (n.d.) Muslim Personal Law in India: Colonial Legacy and Current Debates. http://aannaim.law.emory.edu/ifl/cases/India.htm. Accessed 15 Oct 2014

Childabductionrecoveryinternational (2014) Parental Child Abducion [sic] Pakistan. Posted on 21 February 2014. https://childabductionrecovery.wordpress.com/2014/02/21/parental-child-abducion-pakistan. Accessed 19 Nov 2015

Coulson NJ (1957) Reform of Family Law in Pakistan. SI 7:135–155

Critelli FM (2012) Between Law and Custom: Women, Family Law and Marriage in Pakistan. JCFS 43:673–693

Davis MF (1985) Child Custody in Pakistan: The Role of Ijtihād. BCTWLJ 5:119–127

Haider N (2000) Islamic Legal Reform: The Case of Pakistan and Family Law. YJLF 12:287–341

Hamilton C (1982) The Hedaya or Guide: A Commentary on the Mussulman Law. Premier Book House, Lahore

Hussain F (2011) The Judicial System of Pakistan. www.supremecourt.gov.pk/web/user_files/File/thejudicialsystemofPakistan.pdf. Accessed 25 Oct 2014

Mahdi Z, Malek NA (1998) The Concept of Custody in Islamic Law. Arab Law Quart 13:155–177

Mulla DF (1938) Principles of Mohammadan Law. Eastern Law House, Bombay

Nasir JJA (2009) The Islamic Law of Personal Status. Brill, Leiden

Pearl DS (1969) Family Law in Pakistan. JFL 9:165–189

Rahim A (1911) The Principles of Muhammadan Jurisprudence According to the Hanafi, Maliki, Shafi'i and Hanbali Schools. Luzar & Co, London

Rehman T (1991) Majmua Qawaneen e Islam. IRI 2:886–887

Yefet KC (2009) What's the Constitution Got to Do With It? Regulating Marriage in Pakistan. DJGLP 16:347–377

---

[84] Balchin 1994, p. 164.

Chapter 8
Qatar

Anver M. Emon

Abstract This chapter provides an overview of provisions found in Qatar's 2006 Family Law Code that pertain to child custody and its related issues. The analysis situates the Code provisions within the institutional context of Qatar's judiciary and examines the limited number of recent Court of Cassation decisions on various provisions.

Keywords Qatar · Child custody · *Wilāya* · *Ḥaḍāna* · Islamic law · Legislation

Contents

8.1 Introduction

The State of Qatar is an unusual country in the Gulf. Though its neighbors such as Saudi Arabia are often associated with highly patriarchal forms of Islamic law and practice, Qatar has created a reputation for bucking certain trends. With its

The author is Professor of Law and Canada Research Chair in Religion, Pluralism and the Ruleof Law at the University of Toronto Faculty of Law.

A.M. Emon (✉)
Faculty of Law, University of Toronto, 84 Queens Park, Toronto, ON M5S 2C5, Canada
e-mail: anver.emon@utoronto.ca

N. Yassari et al. (eds.), *Parental Care and the Best Interests of the Child in Muslim Countries*, DOI 10.1007/978-94-6265-174-6_8

backing of *al-Jazeera*, its efforts to host international conferences, its investment in education and research development, and its initiatives to engage the international community,[1] it sits in an uneasy position as a country that negotiates between traditional attitudes and cultures on the one hand, and a cosmopolitan outlook on the other. And in the area of women's rights, some even view Qatar as a 'beacon of light … in the Middle East.'[2] As Lynn Welchman has written, new family law statutes in the Middle East and North Africa, such as Qatar's, have sought to extend a woman's custodial rights beyond what were provided in traditional Islamic legal doctrines (*fiqh*). In other words, as much as they may draw upon the premodern, Islamic legal doctrine, Qatar's legislative efforts extend the scope of women's custodial rights. 'In addition, they have increasingly included statutory references to the concept of the "interest of the child" on which the judge may modify … parts of the law, including primary allocation of custody rights.'[3] This short country study will review the constitutional and statutory framework that introduces aspects of Islamic family law into the Qatari legal system and explore recent decisions from the Court of Cassation that highlight the judicial approach to certain provisions of the 2006 statute.

8.2 Islamic Law, the Constitution and the Culture of (In) Equality: Between the Formal and Informal

Under the Constitution of Qatar (issued in 2004), Islamic law is an official source of law for legislation (Article 1). But what this means, as would be the case in any constitutional provision, is a subject of further analysis into legislative and judicial determinations. In other words, this provision by itself means very little and cannot be taken on face value to imply anything with respect to whether or not the full scope of premodern *fiqh* rules are or are not incorporated into the state's legal infrastructure.[4] Article 35 of the Constitution provides for the equality of people before the law, regardless of gender, origin, language or faith. Indeed, the theme of equality between men and women was a theme expounded upon by Shaykha Mu'za bt. Nasser al-Misnad, the wife of the former emir of Qatar, Hamad b. Khalifa Al Thani,

[1] In fact, Article 7 of Qatar's Constitution provides 'The foreign policy of the State is based on the principle of strengthening international peace and security by means of encouraging peaceful resolution of international disputes; and shall support the right of peoples to self-determination; and shall not interfere in the domestic affairs of states; and shall cooperate with peace-loving nations.' For the Constitution, see http://portal.www.gov.qa/wps/wcm/connect/5a5512804665e3afa54fb5fd2b4ab27a/Constitution+of+Qatar+EN.pdf?MOD=AJPERES (accessed 1 August 2014).

[2] Dye 2006–2007, p. 747.

[3] Welchman 2010, pp. 163–78.

[4] For studies on constitutional provisions that include such language, see Emon 2008, pp. 258–86; Lombardi 2006.

who together in 2013 handed leadership to their son Shaykh Tamim b. Hamad Al Thani. As Bahry and Marr have said, Shaykha Mu'za played a

> pivotal role in improving conditions for Qatari women, especially in education. Most important, she has provided an example of a woman who is gradually stepping out into the public domain … to participate in turning Qatari society in a more modern and liberal direction.[5]

Moreover, under the reign of the previous Emir, the legal system was reformed in various ways to create a more egalitarian image of the state.

Whether this image of a liberalizing regime exists only on paper or goes deep into the culture is a separate matter that requires further examination on an issue-by-issue basis. For example, sports is an area where the Qatari government is trying to ensure equality of participation counter to the tendencies of a conservative culture that might otherwise impede the participation of women athletes. As Barbara Surk reported in 2011, Qatar's government supported women athletes from Qatar to compete internationally. These formal legal efforts arose in a context of a conservative culture that operated informally in society against the interests of women who wished to participate athletically in a domestic and global environment. Surk wrote that

> [t]here are no written laws in Qatar … that ban and restrict women from participating in sports. Rather, the stigma of female athletes is rooted in conservative traditions and religious views that hold giving freedom of movement to women would make them vulnerable to sins.[6]

Whether religion or culture informs these conservative tendencies, the government of Qatar's formal efforts often work against the informal customary norms of society. Consequently, one cannot quickly characterize Qatar's treatment of women without first accounting for the difference between the efforts of the formal state and the predilections of the informal customs that pervade society.

8.3 The Qatar Family Law of 2006

8.3.1 General Considerations

Among the formal developments in Qatar are a series of reforms (legislative and institutional) to the regime of family law.[7] Prior to 2006, parties to a marriage would have taken their family disputes (e.g. divorce and custody) to a court of first

---

[5] Bahry and Marr 2005, p. 107. See also Dye 2006–2007, p. 750.

[6] Surk 2011, C3.

[7] Surprisingly, these reforms have gone unnoticed by various watch-dog agencies such as Human Rights Watch. Its 2012 country survey of Qatar made no mention of these reforms and instead held that all family law matters are decided in religious courts pursuant to Islamic legal interpretations, Human Rights Watch 2012, p. 615. This is, in fact, incorrect. Likewise, a UNICEF

instance (*al-maḥkama al-ibtidāʾiyya*), which, under Law No. 10 of 2003, had jurisdiction over family law matters (*masāʾil al-usra*).[8] However, in 2006, Qatar issued its first family law statute. Many of its provisions parallel those found in the model Personal Status Law issued by the Gulf Cooperation Council, known as the Musqat Document (*wathīqat musqat*).[9] Qatar's Family Law Act, Law No. 22 of 2006 (QFLA), represents its first attempt at a comprehensive family law statute. Drafted in 2000 by a committee led by Qatar's Sharia court, with the support of the Supreme Council for Family Affairs,[10] the QFLA was promulgated in 2006 after considerable debate on its various provisions. According to Qatar's report to the 57th session of the Convention on the Elimination of All Forms of Discrimination Against Women, 'no law has ever been discussed as extensively as the Family Act.'[11] Lynn Welchman noted that Qatari women were actively involved in the act's development:

> In Qatar, where the drafting committee was constituted of judges, the circulation of the resulting draft provided a forum for review and intervention *inter alia* by Qatari women, with the governmental National Committee for Women's Affairs submitting amendments for the consideration of the drafting committee.[12]

Footnote 7 (continued)

report states that despite the new reforms, a woman's testimony is in some cases worth half of a man's, as per pre-modern Islamic law, UNICEF 2011. This statement, though, is misleading. As a Freedom House report on Qatar shows, that is the case in only limited circumstances. Article 36 stipulates that two men must witness a marital contract and testify about its validity. Women are not permitted to do this as the provision specifically refers to two male witnesses (*shāhidayn rajulayn*). Furthermore, Article 93 requires either two men or one man and two women as witnesses (Freedom House 2009, p. 69). But that requirement pertains to determinations of kinship (*nasab*). It is followed by Article 94, which states that evidence about the birth itself can be established by a single witness, whether male or female. The report further states that no such gendered prejudice exists in the criminal or civil codes (Freedom House 2009, p. 69). These examples illustrate the need for careful research to guard against the intrusion of easy prejudice and stereotype when characterizing the laws of countries in the Middle East and North Africa.

[8] Article 11 Law No. 10 of 2003 Promulgating the Law on Judicial Authority (*iṣdār qānūn al-sulṭa al-qaḍāʾiyya*), www.almeezan.qa/LawArticles.aspx?LawTreeSectionID=13437&lawId=4052&language=ar (accessed 12 November 2014).

[9] *Wathīqat musqat*, http://sites.gcc-sg.org/DLibrary/index.php (accessed 25 July 2014). This document can be found on the GCC website, whose history extends back to 1996.

[10] The Supreme Council for Family Affairs was created in 1998 as a high-level and independent organization, one that would support the role of families in Qatari society and 'formulate and follow up on the implementation of strategies, policies and plans.' See Qatar, Consideration of Reports Submitted by States Parties Under Article 18 of the Convention on the Elimination of All Forms of Discrimination Against Women—Initial Report of States Parties, UNCEDAWOR, 2012, UN CEDAW Doc C/QAT/1.

[11] Qatar, Consideration of Reports Submitted by States Parties Under Article 18 of the Convention on the Elimination of All Forms of Discrimination Against Women—Initial Report of States Parties, UNCEDAWOR, 2012, UN CEDAW Doc C/QAT/1 at para 413–414.

[12] Welchman 2012, p. 373.

The 2006 law contains 301 articles[13] and covers issues including: marriage, dower, maintenance, separation, custody, and wills and inheritance.[14] As part of the institutional setting for the new personal status legislation, a court of first instance would be designated as a 'family court' (*maḥkamat al-usra*) and have the authority to hear cases related to 'marriage, divorce, maintenance, inheritance, custody of children, administration of the estates of minors, and other marital and family disputes.'[15] To understand the implication of this special designation, it is important to understand how the 2003 legislation set up the judiciary generally. Law No. 10 of 2003 presumed at the outset that courts would be centered in Doha. However, Article 5 of that law also allowed the court of first instance to be present in various parts of the country, effectively creating circuits or departments of the court of first instance (*dawāʾir al-maḥkama al-ibtidāʾiyya*). In the 2006 QFLA, therefore, when the legislation designates the courts that hear family law matters, it states that one or more circuit courts of the court of first instance (*dāʾira aw akthar bi-l-maḥkama al-ibtidāʾiyya*) (as well as the appellate court) could hear cases on family law matters, and that these courts would be called Family Courts (*tusmā maḥkamat al-usra*).[16] In other words, it would seem that specialized courts focusing on family law exercise jurisdiction on matters that fall under the act.

Article 3 QFLA provides that the dominant position (*al-raʾy al-rājiḥ*) of the Hanbali school of law[17] is to be followed when the statute is silent on a personal status issue. However, if no prevailing Hanbali position exists on the issue under consideration, the judge may apply rules from the other Sunni schools of jurisprudence.[18] Moreover, as will be discussed concerning judicial analyses of the statute, the Cassation Court makes reference to the four Sunni schools of law as well as to the Shia Ja'fari school of law when analyzing contentious matters under the QFLA.

Interestingly, the QFLA applies only to 'those subjected to the Hanbali school of law' (*ʿalā man yuṭabbiqu ʿalayhim al-madhhab al-ḥanbalī*). Others, including Muslims subscribing to other schools of jurisprudence and non-Muslims, do not

---

[13] Welchman 2012, p. 378.

[14] For an English translation of the Qatari Family Law Act, Law No. 22 of 2006 (hereinafter QFLA), see the online version: Al Meezan—Qatary Legal Portal (trans.), Law No. 22 of 2006 Promulgating 'The Family Law' 22/2006. www.rwi.uzh.ch/oe/cimels/law/countries/qatar/Law_22_2006_2558.pdf. Accessed 31 July 2014. All translations of the QFLA in this chapter are by the author working from the original Arabic version.

[15] Qatar Politics: Family courts set up 2006.

[16] Article 2 QFLA.

[17] Article 3 QFLA. Qatar is the first of the Middle Eastern countries to have based its personal status laws on the Hanbali school.

[18] Article 3 QFLA. The legislation does not specify the order in which the other Sunni schools of jurisprudence ought to be followed. If the four Sunni schools of jurisprudence are silent or inconclusive on the issue under consideration, the judge may employ the various interpretive principles (*al-qawāʿid al-fiqhiyya*) of the Islamic legal tradition.

fall under the purview of the QFLA.[19] Non-Muslims, in particular, have special provisions on family law issues. That said, 'the provisions of the [*Family Act*] apply if the parties so request it or if they do not share the same religion or denomination.'[20] How and to what extent Muslims following other schools of jurisprudence may opt out of the Family Act's provisions is unclear.[21]

8.3.2 Child Custody

Custody in Qatari law involves both physical custody (*ḥaḍāna*) and guardianship (*wilāya*). The former concerns the custodial parent who has physical custody of the children. The latter involves overall responsibility for the wellbeing of the children, in particular financial responsibility. The latter is generally granted to the father while the former is subject to a more complex regulatory framework under the QFLA. The QFLA defines custody (*ḥaḍāna*) in terms of preserving and supporting the child (*ḥifẓ al-walad*), raising and educating him (*tarbiyyatuhu wa taqwīmuhu*), and caring for him in terms of what upholds his interests (*ra'āyatuhu bi-mā yuḥaqqiqu maṣlaḥatahu*).[22]

The QFLA provides that custody lies with the mother until her children reach certain stipulated ages. For boys, the age is 13 years old; for girls, it is 15 years old (Article 173). However, though the mother's presumptive custody ends once her children reach these ages, she can nonetheless retain custody for a period of years thereafter. Article 173 provides that even after children reach these ages, a judge may award the mother continued custody of her children if doing so is in their best interests (*maṣlaḥat al-maḥḍūn*). This extended custody will continue for boys until they reach 15 years of age and for girls until they marry. Alternatively, with the approval of the disputing parties, the judge can allow the children to choose their custodial arrangement.

This article was at the center of a 2007 Court of Cassation decision, specifically case no. 8 of 2007. The case began in 2005 with a claim by the custodial mother for a greater amount of child support from the non-custodial father, namely an increase to 3000 riyals per month in addition to other custodial costs (e.g. house servant and chauffeur). The couple finalized their divorce in proceedings occurring in 2001, which granted her 1000 riyals per month for the care of her two children. In this 2005 case, the non-custodial father counter-claimed for custody of the two

[19] Article 4 QFLA.

[20] Article 4 QFLA. See also Qatar, Consideration of Reports Submitted by States Parties Under Article 18 of the Convention on the Elimination of All Forms of Discrimination Against Women—Initial Report of States Parties, UNCEDAWOR, 2012, UN CEDAW Doc C/QAT/1, para 416.

[21] Welchman 2012, p. 375. Welchman says that further research on this issue is required.

[22] Article 165 QFLA.

children on different grounds, only one of which is relevant for this analysis. In particular, the father claimed that the eldest child was already near the age at which *ḥaḍāna* would end, and thus the father should be able to exercise custody.[23] The court awarded the custodial mother 2000 riyals per month to be applied in equal parts to the two children. Moreover, they granted her additional sums for custodial costs, including domestic servant and chauffeur costs. The father appealed this decision. While there were various subsidiary issues at the appellate and cassation level about financial support payments, the key issue here concerns whether the lower court acted contrary to the law when it continued to invest the mother with ongoing custodial authority of the eldest child. The Cassation Court noted that Article 173 stipulates the mother's *ḥaḍāna* ends when a boy-child reaches 13 years of age and when a girl-child reaches 15 years of age. However, the provision also grants courts the discretionary authority to extend the maternal *ḥaḍāna* period if, in the court's analysis of the circumstances, to do so would be in the child's interests (*ba'd al-taḥqīq fī maṣlaḥat al-maḥḍūn*). In such cases, the *ḥaḍāna* would extend to 15 years of age for boy-children and, in the case of girl-children, until they wed. Moreover the courts can allow a child to make a determination whether maternal custody should end or continue upon reaching the statutorily designated default ages. The Cassation Court read this provision as granting the Court of First Instance the license (*amr jawāzī li-l-maḥkama*) to grant children this choice, upon reviewing the suitability of the two contending parties. The Cassation Court, in other words, upheld the underlying decision on the grounds that the lower court had the authority to make such a determination under the law, and there was therefore no error in law to reverse.[24]

8.3.2.1 Custodial Condition: Limitation on Remarriage

For the mother to retain custody, she must fulfill certain conditions. The statute lists various conditions that anyone (male or female) must satisfy in order to exercise *ḥaḍāna,* such as having reached the age of majority (*bulūgh*), being mentally competent (*al-'aql*) and in good health, and so on.[25] But a woman exercising *ḥaḍāna* must also meet an additional condition, one that is taken straight out of the premodern *fiqh* tradition. Namely, she must not remarry someone who would fall outside the requisite scope of her children's kinship network (*zawj ajnabī 'an al-maḥḍūn*).[26] Interestingly, however, the statute does allow a court to make an exception to this condition, where doing so supports the child's interests (*khilāf*

---

[23] Court of Cassation (Qatar), case no. 8, 2007, para 1.

[24] Court of Cassation (Qatar), case no. 8, 2007.

[25] Article 167 QFLA. See also Court of Cassation (Qatar), case no. 104 of 2013, for its reference to Article 167 and these various factors.

[26] Article 168 QFLA.

dhālik li-maṣlaḥat al-maḥḍūn).[27] Moreover, the QFLA stipulates that if a male exercises *ḥaḍāna*, he must share the child's faith, and that he must share his custodial responsibilities with a woman from his family who can assist in fulfilling the various requirements of exercising *ḥaḍāna*.[28]

8.3.2.2 Custodial Conditions: Religious Identity

The premodern tradition revealed a dispute about whether the custodial mother also had to be Muslim if she were to exercise *ḥaḍāna* over a Muslim child. The QFLA preserves a woman's custodial authority *even if she is not a Muslim*. Article 175 states that as long as she is not an apostate from Islam (*murtadda*), a non-Muslim woman retains her claim to *ḥaḍāna*. However, echoing one aspect of premodern *fiqh* analysis, the non-Muslim mother's period of *ḥaḍāna* is determined by reference to when the child develops the capacity to understand what faith and religion mean (*ḥattā yaʿqilu al-ṣaghīr al-adyān*). In other words, once a child acquires the requisite mental ability to understand what faith is, the non-Muslim custodial mother's presumptive custodial authority ends. She can still retain custody under the statute, which grants courts the power to allow the non-Muslim custodial mother to retain *ḥaḍāna* of a child beyond this age as long as there is no fear that the child might pursue a faith other than Islam. In either case, though, her custodial authority does not exceed the child's seventh birthday.[29]

8.3.3 Best Interests of the Child

Notably, the above discussion of the QFLA showcases how the language of 'best interests of the child' finds its way into modern legislative enactments in the region. Indeed, this focus on the child's interest is among the novelties of the QFLA. As Welchman has written, consideration of the child's interests 'is also increasingly required in codifications across the region in assessing the otherwise normative assignment of the function—or right—of custody to an identified succession of relatives.'[30] The emphasis on the child and his or her best interests is further evident in Article 166, which provides that 'custody is a right shared between the custodial agent and the child, but the right of the child is stronger' (*al-ḥaḍāna ḥaqq mushtarak bayna al-ḥāḍin wa-l-ṣaghīr wa-ḥaqq al-ṣaghīr aqwā*).[31] Indeed, as the Court of Cassation has remarked, *ḥaḍāna* involves protecting the

[27] Article 168 QFLA.

[28] Article 168 QFLA.

[29] Article 175 QFLA.

[30] Welchman 2010.

[31] Article 166 QFLA.

child, educating him and generally undertaking all measures that inure to his benefit (*wa-l-qiyām bi-jamīʿ shuʾūnihi allatī bihā ṣalāḥ amrihi*).[32] Even without reference to the 2006 Family Law Act, the Court of Cassation had already viewed the premodern *fiqh* rules on custody as framed around the best interests of the child. For instance, concerning an appeal about the grant of custody to the mother, the Cassation Court briefly reviewed the four Sunni and the Shia Jaʿfari schools of law on the age ranges for *ḥaḍāna.* Noting the differences between the schools, the Cassation Court concluded that the dominant rule among the various *madhhabs* was in fact aimed at fulfilling the best interests of the custodial child (*al-rājiḥ fī fiqh al-sharīʿa qāṣidan maṣlaḥat al-maḥḍūnīn*).[33]

8.3.3.1 Considering the Best Interests of the Child

When applying the best interests of the child in custody determinations, the QFLA offers statutory guidance to the judge. Article 170 provides that to uphold the interests of the child (*maṣlaḥat al-maḥḍūn*), the judge must consider, for instance:

- The custodian's affection (*al-shafaqa*) for the child and ability to raise him or her;
- The provision of a sound environment in which the child can be brought up and 'protected from delinquency';
- The ability to provide the best education and medical care; and
- The ability to prepare the child in terms of morals and customs for the time that he or she is ready to leave the custody of women (*ʿinda bulūghihi sinn al-istighnāʾ ʿan ḥaḍānat al-nisāʾ*).[34]

8.3.3.2 Problematizing Best Interests: The Relocation and Re-marriage Regulations

The interests of the child feature prominently in two provisions of the QFLA concerning relocation of the child and the remarriage of the mother, which refer to each other in limited cases. Consequently, both are addressed together in this section. Article 180 defines the custodial residence (*makān al-ḥaḍāna*) as the town of the one who exercises *wilāya* (as opposed to *ḥaḍāna*) over the child (*balad walī al-maḥḍūn*). As the Court of Cassation has noted, the reason for this provision is to allow the *walī* the necessary and easy access to the child to prepare the child for his or her future (*iʿdādihi li-l-mustaqbal*).[35]

---

[32] Court of Cassation (Qatar), case no. 104 of 2013.

[33] Court of Cassation (Qatar), case no. 30 of 2006.

[34] Welchman 2010, translating Article 170 of Qatar's Law No. 22 of 2006. See also Article 170 QFLA.

[35] Court of Cassation (Qatar), case no. 104 of 2013.

The exception to this domicile rule is the situation of the custodial mother (or other female custodian)[36] who remarries but nonetheless resides in Qatar. In such a case, the judge has the discretion to preserve the mother's custody over the child, as long as doing so upholds the interests of the child.[37] In other words, as long as the parties remain in Qatar, the woman exercising custody can still do so even if she remarries someone, whether or not he is within the prescribed kinship relations of the child. This provision is a departure from much pre-modern *fiqh*, which considers the mother's remarriage to a non-*maḥram* man as grounds for losing her custodial authority over her young children.

Article 183, however, addresses the instances when a person's custodial power will be rescinded. Of the three situations, the third is of particular interest here. It provides that custodial authority shall be rescinded when the father or *walī* is unable to uphold his responsibilities toward the child (*wājibāt al-maḥḍūn*), such as education and training, because the mother (i.e. *ḥāḍina*) has, without the *walī*'s permission, taken up residence with the child in a town (*balad*) that is hard to reach. However, given that even in this case the parties are all in Qatar, it ought not be surprising that a judge can still uphold the mother's *ḥaḍāna,* as long as the custodial arrangements inure to the child's benefit (*maṣlaḥat al-maḥḍūn*).[38]

Thus far the analysis has focused on a dispute between people who live in Qatar but relocate to different regions *within* the country. The law takes a stricter approach when considering international travel by either the *walī* or the custodial parent, and of course by the children. To control such travel, the statute stipulates in Article 176 that the legal guardian (*walī*) is to keep and hold the child's passports (*li-l-walī al-iḥtifāẓ bi-jawāz al-safar*).[39] When the *walī* is the non-custodial father when the children are young, this provision balances between the custodial mother's day-to-day control and oversight of the children, and the non-custodial father's concerns about domestic access to his children. But it also creates a moral hazard problem in cases when the father refuses to allow the custodial mother to travel internationally with her children. In such cases, the mother would need to petition the court, which in turn may permit the custodial mother/woman (*ḥāḍina*) to hold the passports if the *walī* stubbornly refuses to give them to her when she needs them.

To be clear, Article 176 does not suggest that a child cannot travel or that a mother exercising *ḥaḍāna* cannot travel with her children. But its protection of the *walī* non-custodial father is not equally extended when the circumstances are reversed. For instance, as the children get older, and the *walī* father is also the

---

[36] There are a wide range of possible custodians for children, with the mother taking priority. The statutory language applies to any woman, but for ease of analysis, the discussion herein will focus on mothers.

[37] Article 180 QFLA.

[38] Article 183 QFLA.

[39] Aside from the passports, though, the woman exercising custody holds all other papers and documents that are specific to the child, such as the birth certificate and so on, Article 176 QFLA.

custodial parent, this provision works against the non-custodial mother's interest in domestic access to her children. If the provision were meant to balance the interests between custodial and non-custodial parents' interests in ongoing access, one would expect the provision to say that the non-custodial parent or guardian holds the passports. But instead of using custody as the relevant variable for allocating possession of the children's passports, the provision grants a near-exclusive authority to the *walī* to hold the children's passports.

Moreover, the provision on passports raises a further question about who has the greatest license to travel with children: the father or mother, a male guardian or a female custodian? Article 185 addresses specifically the situation of a mother who wishes to travel with her children. As long as her reasons for doing so are reasonable (*sabab ma'qūl*), she should be free to do so, unless there is possible harm that might fall upon the child (*ḍarar bi-l-maḥḍūn*).[40] If the *walī* prevents her from such travel, she can petition a court, which can grant her the permission to travel if it seems that the *walī* has exercised his authority recklessly or unjustly.[41] If the woman exercising custody (e.g. a mother) is a foreigner (*al-ḥāḍina ajnabiyya*), and her travel is temporary (*'araḍī*) and not for establishing residence in her own country (*li-ghayr iqāma ilā waṭanihā*), then the judge can seek a guarantor who can ensure that she will return with the child. But if the *walī* has reasonable grounds (*mubayyin asbāb ma'qūl li-dhālik*) to fear that the foreigner exercising custody and traveling abroad might not return with the child, a court can prevent her from traveling with the child.[42]

The above analysis has focused on custodial mothers. The male guardian, on the other hand (e.g. the father or grandfather) can travel with the boy-child who has reached the age of seven for a reasonable amount of time. If the *walī* and custodial agent (e.g. mother) disagree on the amount of time, they can petition the court to decide the matter.[43] But other than the father and grandfather, no other *walī* or paternal relative can travel with the child during the period of *ḥaḍāna* without the custodial parent's permission. If the custodial parent refuses, a judge has the authority to override the custodial parent's wishes if there are good reasons to do so.[44]

40 Article 185 QFLA. Of particular concern with respect to the various legislative presumptions and guidelines is the discretion placed in the judge at the Court of First Instance—the court charged with making findings of fact in relation to the law. As various Court of Cassation decisions have indicated, there is great deference on appeal to factual determinations made at lower judicial levels. See, for example, Court of Cassation (Qatar), case no. 104 of 2013. If lower court decisions, which blend findings of fact with applications of law, reflect options articulated in the statute itself, appellate courts will not easily overturn those decisions.

41 Article 185 QFLA.

42 Article 185 QFLA.

43 Article 185 QFLA.

44 Article 185 QFLA.

In other words, if a Qatari mother wants to travel with her child, she needs to get permission from the child's father, who is the presumptive *walī.* If the father wants to travel with his son, who is above the age of seven (and thus still under the custodial care of his mother), the father can do so regardless of the mother's disagreement. All that she can do is complain about the duration of the travel period.

8.4 Conclusion

This chapter has outlined the basic provisions in the Qatar Family Law Code of 2006 that pertain to child custody. The provisions certainly track premodern Islamic *fiqh* traditions, but they also depart from those traditions in important ways. As much as the Hanbali legal school remains a primary source of reference, it is filtered through novel language about the best interests of the child. The consistent legislative reference to this idea reveals an important development in the family law regimes informed by Islamic law. The historical tradition, to the extent it is present in these legislative vehicles, is framed and often tempered by reference to this phrase—a standard that places in the judiciary a more robust role in assessing custody conflicts. For this reason, the reorganization of the judiciary speaks to state efforts to ensure that judicial oversight of family law cases involves a higher degree of specialization than was once the case in many regimes in the region. While the statute certainly draws inspiration from the historical *fiqh*, the differences between statutory provisions and the historical *fiqh* reveal a degree of flexibility in the formulation of the law. That degree of flexibility should not be overstated or misconstrued as a gesture toward substantive equality, given the continued gendered paradigms still present in the statute. But the developments are nonetheless noteworthy and require specialists in the field to continue exploring the implications of this statute on legal education and judicial practice.

References

Bahry L, Marr P (2005) Qatari Women: A New Generation of Leaders? Middle East Policy 12(2):104–119

Dye MB (2006–2007) Qatar: The Pearl of the Middle East and Its Role in the Advancement of Women's Rights. Univ Detroit Mercy Law Rev 84:747–763

Emon AM (2008) The Limits of Constitutionalism in the Muslim World: History and Identity in Islamic Law. In: Choudhry S (ed) Constitutional Design for Divided Societies. Oxford University Press, Oxford, pp 258–286

Freedom House (ed) (2009) Women's Rights in the Middle East and North Africa: 2009 Gulf Edition. Freedom House, New York

Human Rights Watch (2012) World Report 2012. www.hrw.org/sites/default/files/reports/wr2012.pdf. Accessed 15 Dec 2012

Lombardi CB (2006) State Law as Islamic Law in Modern Egypt. Brill, Leiden

Qatar Politics: Family Courts Set Up (2006) The Economist Intelligence Unit Views Wire, 10 Oct 2006, C3

Surk B (2011) Qatar Women Home To Make History at 2012 Games, Los Angeles Times, 25 Dec 2011

UNICEF (2011) MENA Gender Equality Profile: Qatar. www.unicef.org/gender/files/Qatar-Gender-Eqaulity-Profile-2011.pdf. Accessed 15 Dec 2012

Welchman L (2010) Gulf States: Bahrain, Qatar, United Arab Emirates: First Time Family Law Codifications in Three Gulf States. In: Atkin B (ed) International Survey of Family Law. Jordan Publishing, London, pp 163–178. http://eprints.soas.ac.uk/10899. Accessed 15 Dec 2012

Welchman L (2012) Gulf Women and the Codification of Muslim Family Law. In: El-Azhary Sonbol A (ed) Gulf Women. Bloomsbury Qatar Foundation Publishing, Doha, pp 367–406

Chapter 9
South Africa

Najma Moosa

Abstract This chapter on South Africa critically analyses the evolution of the concept of the best interests of the child, and specifically how it pertains to the fields of care (custody), contact (access), guardianship and maintenance (support), which are all part of parents' responsibilities and rights, and impact on the legal position of Muslim children. This chapter compares and contrasts Muslim Personal Law (MPL) and practices pertaining to children with those of South African law in order to ascertain whether they comply with, conflict with or compromise the 'best interests' concept paramount in, and permeating, South African law in general and international and regional instruments. In doing so, the chapter reviews the position of Muslim children and the milestones in child law in South Africa prior to and since democracy with a focus on three pieces of legislation since democracy: the Constitution (1996), the Children's Act (2005) and the Muslim Marriages Bill (MMB) (2010).

Keywords Parental responsibilities and rights · Care (custody) · Contact (access) · Guardianship · Maintenance (support) · Best interests of the child · Muslim children · South Africa · Muslim Personal Law

---

BA LLB LLM LLD (UWC); Professor of Private Law, Faculty of Law, University of the Western Cape; Dean of the Faculty of Law, 2002–2008; Advocate of the High Court of South Africa; Committee Member, South African Law Reform Commission Project (2003), 59 (Islamic Marriages and Related Matters), 1999–2003.
I wish to acknowledge, with thanks, the permission of the publisher, Juta & Co Ltd, of the book *The Law of Divorce and Dissolution of Life Partnerships in South Africa*, Moosa (2014), to use part of my contributing chapter (8), 'The Dissolution of a Muslim Marriage by Divorce', pp. 281–354, as a basis for especially Sect. 9.3.4 of this chapter. I have, however, revised and updated the information for purposes of this chapter. I thank Prof I. Leeman for his editorial assistance.

N. Moosa (✉)
University of the Western Cape, Private Bag X17, Bellville 7535, South Africa
e-mail: nmoosa@uwc.ac.za

N. Yassari et al. (eds.), *Parental Care and the Best Interests of the Child in Muslim Countries*, DOI 10.1007/978-94-6265-174-6_9

Contents

9.1 Introduction

The brief of this chapter for South Africa is to critically analyse the evolution of the concept of the best interests of the child, and specifically how it pertains to the fields of care (custody), contact (access), guardianship and maintenance (support), which are all part of parents' responsibilities and rights, and impact on the legal position of Muslim children. This chapter compares and contrasts Muslim Personal Law (MPL) and practices pertaining to children with those of South African law in order to ascertain whether they comply with, conflict with or compromise the 'best interests' concept paramount in, and permeating, South African law in general and international and regional instruments. In doing so, the chapter reviews the position of Muslim children and the milestones in child law in South Africa prior to and since democracy. There will be a focus on three pieces of legislation since democracy: the Constitution,[1] the Children's Act[2] and the Muslim Marriages Bill (MMB).[3]

Section 9.2.1 provides a general setting of the position in South Africa and briefly situates the historical position of Muslims in South Africa. While Sect. 9.2.2 outlines the position of children in South African law, Sect. 9.2.3 examines the impact of marriage laws and the status of (hitherto formally unrecognised) religious marriages generally and Muslim marriages particularly in a current context, on child law in a plural South African legal system. Sections 9.3.1 and 9.3.2 highlight that although in terms of South African law (a mixture of Roman-Dutch and English law), the best interests standard formerly was both vague and indeterminate and subject to interpretation in specific situations and with reference

1 Constitution of the Republic of South Africa 1996 ('the Constitution').

2 The Children's Act No 38 of 2005 ('Children's Act').

3 See General Notice 37 GG 33946 of 21 January 2011. The 2010 MMB is available at www.justice.gov.za/legislation/bills/2010_muslim-marriages-bill.pdf (accessed 9 February 2015).

to particular cultural and religious settings, since democracy the position is quite different.

In order to give a broad historical perspective of the evolution of the current South African rules on custody and guardianship, Sect. 9.3.3 provides an analytical overview of the legal consequences flowing from the application of the best interests concept to all (including Muslim) children, and Sect. 9.3.4 examines how it is proposed to apply it specifically to the Muslim child (which may also include dependant adult children) in terms of the MMB once it is enacted. The MMB is based on both Islamic law and South African law. Sections 9.3.3 and 9.3.4 focus on the position of minors and dependant Muslim children with regard to guardianship (*wilaya*), care or custody (*hadana*), contact or access, and maintenance or support (*nafaqa*). The position under traditional Islamic law (Shari'a) forms the focus of a separate chapter, and this chapter excludes detail of the general operation and application of both Islamic and South African law. The chapter follows an integrated approach when dealing with South African law, Islamic law and the proposed MMB, which has inevitably resulted in some overlap and repetition. While this is, for example, evident from the brief summary of the South African law provided in Sects. 9.3.3 and 9.3.4 which deals with the MMB in a comparative context, the overlap and repetition are kept to a minimum since Islamic law is only elaborated upon to elucidate provisions in the MMB based on it. Fortunately, child law, unlike many other more complex Shari'a issues, is less contentious although some of its provisions are of a gender sensitive nature.

9.2 Historical and Demographic Setting

9.2.1 General Setting

The initiation of the Max Planck Research Group's Project on Child Law in 2014 was particularly timely for three reasons. First, it coincided with the commemoration of 20 years since the advent of democracy in South Africa. Secondly, it also coincided with the twenty-fifth anniversary of the adoption in 1989 of the United Nations Convention on the Rights of the Child (CRC), which South Africa signed on 29 January 1993 and ratified on 16 June 1995 without recording any reservations. In South Africa 16 June is a national public holiday, Youth Day, which commemorates the violent uprisings which led to the loss of the lives of children, including Muslim children, during the struggle for liberation from apartheid (politically motivated racial segregation). Thirdly, 2014 also marked the first 'born free' election in South Africa in which youth aged eighteen (legal age of majority and minimum voting age), who were born after apartheid ended in 1994, voted for the first time in a presidential election.

The 2011 (latest) Census estimated the total South African population to be 51.8 million,[4] but excluded religious affiliation. However, data captured by the 2001 Census[5] highlight that Christianity (79.8%) was the dominant religion. African traditional beliefs, Judaism, Hinduism, Islam and other faiths together accounted for 3.7%, of which Muslims were estimated to constitute 1.5% (654,064), the largest of these groups, followed closely by Hindus (1.2%).[6] Children account for a substantial proportion of the nation. In mid-2012 children constituted 36% (18.6 million) of the total population.[7]

South African born Muslims do not constitute one homogeneous community, either in terms of origin and culture or ideological and political expression. They have both experienced, and fought against, colonialism and apartheid, and have a long history in South Africa dating back to the mid-17th century. They arrived here, at first involuntarily as slaves, indentured workers and political prisoners from the Far East (mainly Indonesia), and then voluntarily as traders from India, during the periods that South Africa was subject to colonial rule, first by the Dutch, and then by the British.[8] Muslims have since then played an active role in the struggle for liberation and to end apartheid imposed by a minority white government.

9.2.2 Children in South African Law

Prior to 1994 there were already several laws and international conventions in place that impacted on the lives of children. However, with democracy, it became clear that these laws were not able to protect and support all the children of the rainbow nation, nor were they deemed adequate. Thus, since 1994 child law has undergone dramatic change and developed exponentially so that today there are various pieces of legislation which specifically aim to protect and promote the rights and best interests of children. Foremost among these are the Constitution and the Children's Act. Section 28 of the Constitution deals with children: section 28(2) guarantees the paramountcy of the best interests of the child as a principle, and section 28(1) provides for independent rights within the Bill of Rights which, like all its other rights (such as, freedom of religion (section 15), association (section 18) and equality (section 9)) which may also apply to children, may be subject to limitation (section 36). Nonetheless, through section 28 the Constitution makes separate and dedicated provision for the rights of children and contains, as it were, a separate 'charter of children's rights'. The Children's Act

[4] See Statistics South Africa 2012.

[5] See Statistics South Africa 2004.

[6] Statistics South Africa 2004, p. 28.

[7] Hall et al. 2014, pp. 90–93.

[8] For detail see Moosa 2011, p. 146.

also contains a dedicated section 9 dealing specifically with the paramountcy of the 'child's best interest'. More importantly, the Children's Act does so in the context of a (first such legislated) guiding list of factors, relevant to the 'best interests of the child' standard (section 7), which is both flexible and not exhaustive. Section 7 provides the courts with a clear standard to guide them in the implementation of the constitutional injunction (section 28(2)) that the child's best interests are of paramount importance in all matters affecting children.

However, the Constitution and the decisions of the Constitutional Court (referred to below) primarily indicate the correct way to approach the application and evaluation of this standard and its content in the Children's Act. The Constitution makes it clear that the field of application of the best interests standard in the Children's Act is not restricted to proceedings under its own children's rights section (section 28).

The Children's Act resulted in the streamlining or replacing of some laws. International human rights instruments ratified by South Africa motivated many of the national reforms found in contemporary child law, including the Constitution and the Children's Act. As detailed in Sect. 9.3.3, as a consequence of a long process of review and consultation, the Children's Act and the Children's Amendment Act[9] were passed. On 1 April 2010 the Children's Act[10] eventually came into full force along with Regulations to the Act. This explains both why some of its main provisions (discussed below) were already in effect from 1 July 2007 and why the impact of the new provisions of the Children's Act on case law and emerging jurisprudence is still relatively new. The consolidating Children's Act is ranked, after the Constitution, as the most important piece of legislation on children's issues in South Africa. Despite its division into nine provinces, South Africa has a single national court system. Magistrates' Courts are the lowest level of the court system. In terms of the Children's Act,[11] every Magistrates' Court is a Children's Court. There are also special Maintenance Courts at every Magistrates' Court. This essentially simplifies access to justice for children. However, the Child Justice Act[12] deals separately with children who are in conflict with the law. In the hierarchy of courts, the Magistrates' Courts are followed by the provincial divisions of the High Court (formerly known as the Supreme Court); the Supreme Court of Appeal (SCA), formerly known as the Appellate Division (AD) and until 1994 the highest court in civil and criminal cases; and the Constitutional Court, established in 1994 as the highest court in constitutional matters.

The Constitution draws a clear distinction between children and adults so that child law in South Africa generally pertains to everyone under the age of eighteen and therefore excludes the unborn from the ambit of its protection. Support for the definition of a child as a person under the age of 18 years is found in both the

[9] Act No 41 of 2007.

[10] As amended by the 2007 Children's Amendment Act.

[11] Section 42.

[12] Act No 75 of 2008.

Constitution (1996),[13] the Children's Act (2005),[14] the CRC,[15] and the African Charter on the Rights and Welfare of the Child (ACRWC) of 1999,[16] all of which link the definition of a child to this age. The definition of a child in the Children's Act was amended to accord with that in the Constitution. While the South African approach that a child (a 'minor'), male or female, becomes a 'major' upon reaching the age of 18 years appears to be in line with the CRC provision, the latter is much wider. It appears to open the door to allow for legal discrimination between Muslim children of different sexes on the basis of their religion. While the CRC, because it is an older UN instrument, may itself be in need of revision, Muslim States have recorded reservations both to it and the 1979 UN Convention on the Elimination of All Forms of Discrimination Against Women (CEDAW).[17] Thus, unlike the position in many Muslim States, the legal position of Muslim children in South Africa, although considered by many to be a Third World country and still developing, is both different and unique and probably on a par with, if not better than, that of most children in the Western First World. Regrettably, this status may be true more in theory than in practice, especially since it may be mired in adverse socio-economic realities and practical implementation constraints with which the majority of South Africa's disadvantaged children, including many Muslim children, have to contend.

The Children's Act came about as a result of a law reform initiative (Project 110 of the South African Law Reform Commission (SALRC)) in 1998 which dealt with a review of the then existing Child Care Act (1983).[18] Unsurprisingly, given the differences between South African law and Islamic law (Shari'a) rules and the different perspectives of Muslims regarding children, of all the religions in South Africa discussed, it was only the section of the SALRC's Issue Paper 13 that dealt with the position of Muslim children that 'elicited strong and forceful responses'. The Child Care Act which governed the position of children was

---

[13] Section 28(3).

[14] Section 17. 'The common law term "minor" has always been used in South African law as a term of art; its antonym is a "major". In the absence of any statutory definition … a minor is understood to mean every person who is not yet a major. This usually means every person who is younger than eighteen years.' Schäfer 2011, pp. 11–12.

[15] Article 1: 'For the purposes of the present Convention, a child means every human being below the age of 18 years *unless under the law applicable to the child, majority is attained earlier* (my emphasis)'.

[16] Article 2. This Convention was adopted in 1990 and entered into force on 29 November 1999. Although it was signed by South Africa on 10 October 1997, a few months after the Constitution had come into effect (4 February 1997), it was only ratified much later on 7 January 2000.

[17] Although South Africa signed both the CRC and the CEDAW on 29 January 1993, it only ratified the CEDAW on 15 December 1995, some 6 months after the CRC and without also recording any reservations.

[18] Act No 74 of 1983. I contributed a chapter entitled 'Religious Laws Affecting Children: Muslim law', see Moosa 1998a, pp. 123–132, starting from note 215. This submission was subsequently published as 'Muslim Personal Laws Affecting Children: Diversity, Practice and Implications for a New Children's Code for South Africa', see Moosa 1998b, pp. 479–492.

replaced by the Children's Act. Although the Children's Act only came into full force on 1 April 2010, all the most important provisions pertaining to parental responsibilities and rights (which include access to, and the custody, guardianship, and maintenance of, children) and the best interests of a child came into effect on 1 July 2007. The term 'custody' has been replaced with 'care', and the term 'access' (or visitation rights) with 'contact'. As Muslim countries still refer to concepts like 'custody' (which is also treated as a form of guardianship) and 'access' in their traditional meanings when referring to Islamic law in State legislation pertaining to children, and, as indicated in Sect. 9.3.4 below, this is also the case in South Africa in the MMB, these terms will be used interchangeably in this chapter for the sake of convenience. Given that 2014 has marked 20 years of democracy in South Africa, the Children's Act is a relatively new statute. However, this does not detract from the fact that it was a long time in the making and was given priority treatment.

9.2.3 *Impact of Marriage Laws on Child Law in a South African Pluralistic Legal System*

At the time of the review of the Child Care Act, a parallel law reform initiative (Project 59 of the SALRC), which dealt with the recognition of Muslim marriages, was also in progress.[19] Although much progress has been made in this regard and the process has culminated in the MMB, also in 2010, the process has unfortunately stalled. The fact that there have thus far been three versions of the MMB, highlights that the Bill is in a constant state of flux and that the latest version may not be the final version and is still subject to change. The most recent step in the direction of recognition was initiated by the Women's Legal Centre, a feminist organisation situated in the Western Cape, on 3 March 2015 when it lodged an application urging the President of South Africa, among others, to enact the MMB into law within a year.[20] While the hearing of the application was postponed until June 2015, the main proceedings are expected to begin in May 2016.[21]

For Muslims, especially women with minor children, this effectively means that the ravages of apartheid still continue in their private lives, because their purely religious marriages, as is the case with all other religious marriages that are also not civilly entered into, still remain formally unrecognised. The religious or Islamic law (Shari'a) marriages of Muslims are still regarded as common law

[19] For a detailed history of the protracted process, the South African government's engagement with Islamic law, and the draft legislation, see Moosa 2011, pp. 143–162.

[20] See *Women's Legal Centre Trust v. President of the Republic of South Africa*, Case No 22481/14, [2014] ZAWCHC (17 December 2014); Bernardo 2015.

[21] See Isaacs 2015.

marriages in which parties are deemed to be living together without being legally married. A civil (secular) marriage is a registered marriage that has taken place before a magistrate or a minister of certain religions, including imams, rabbis and Hindu and Christian priests. A civil marriage can only be terminated by a divorce granted in the High Court.[22] In terms of the Marriage Act it has always been possible for imams to become civil marriage officers. In fact, many imams chose to participate in a 2013 government initiative which took place whereby a large number of imams received formal accreditation as civil marriage officers in 2014. However, this means that, if after entering into a Muslim marriage, the couple enters into a civil law marriage, the marriage is a civil law marriage and not a religious one regardless of the fact that the appointed marriage officer (celebrant) may also be an imam. Many Muslim men (mainly breadwinners) may prefer this status quo, while vulnerable Muslim women (mainly housewives) and their children who face practical hardships pertaining to their status and maintenance, stand to benefit most from formal statutory recognition of Muslim marriages.

Currently in a plural South Africa there are three types of marriages that are formally recognised: (1) heterosexual, monogamous civil marriages in terms of the Marriage Act,[23] which is the main or 'default' marriage and is still decidedly Christian in nature; (2) since 1998, monogamous or polygamous African customary marriages; and (3) since 2006, monogamous same- or opposite-sex civil unions. However, since 1994 the secular courts and the legislature have increasingly, albeit indirectly and in a piecemeal fashion, recognised some of the legal consequences of civil marriages in the context of purely religious Muslim marriages, regardless of their (monogamous or polygynous) nature and without recognising them as valid marriages. While it will remain the role of the legislature to directly and formally recognise Muslim marriages and to resolve interpretational complexities that may arise, judges have always made rulings in the context of non-recognition of Muslim marriages and have therefore justified avoiding any 'interpretation' of Islamic law, though not necessarily precluding it. Until the passage of the Children's Act in 2005, children born of such religious marriages were deemed to be born 'out of wedlock' and were treated by the law as de facto illegitimate. The progress that has been made in child law therefore benefits Muslim children, and will remain the position even if Muslim marriages are not formally recognised. It is both anticipated and inevitable that religion will probably feature more frequently as a (contested) factor in custody and access disputes. However, given the 'newness' of the Children's Act and the case law and jurisprudence based on it, the emphasis on the best interests of the child principle in South African law implies that there can be no generic recipe that is suitable for all children, and that each case has to be assessed on its own merits.

However, although judicial precedent may be foreign to Islamic law, given that the doctrine of '*stare decisis et non quieta movere*, which means that one stands by

[22] See Divorce Act No 70 of 1979.

[23] Act No 25 of 1961 (Marriage Act).

decisions and does not disturb settled points ...'[24] is part of South African law, this may imply that there is little room for flexibility. Nonetheless, the Preamble to the Constitution, although it holds little legal value, encourages the South African people to be 'united in our diversity'. The Constitution furthermore guarantees freedom of religion, and of association, and equality, among other rights, and makes provision for the recognition of religious marriages. It is therefore contended that if a custody dispute pursuant to a purely religious divorce arises, judges and judicial officers would be expected to be 'flexible' and display some 'judicial activism' in their application of the concept of the best interests of the child even if it may mean having to deviate from previous decisions. This will allow the accommodation of differences in religious rules regarding the custody (care) of a Muslim child, rather than to treat them as 'foreign', and to do so in ways that do not seek to further prejudice South African women whose rights may already have been curtailed by MPL.

For example, should it be deemed to be in the best interests of the child that the mother, rather than the father (the Islamic law default), be accorded guardianship or increased periods of custody after a Muslim divorce (which may even have occurred without her knowledge or consent), given that both her period of custody and post-divorce maintenance are limited (the Islamic law default) and her rights to marital property severely curtailed, it does not necessarily have to follow that she would also be expected to assume additional (or equal, in terms of South African law) maintenance obligations which are attributed to the father in terms of Islamic law precisely because they offset and compensate for the above inequities. Support for the above contention may also be found in the following facts: A uniform, Western or individualistic understanding of the best interests of the child concept may be considered to be 'foreign' to, and at odds with, the different norms and practices of the various multi-cultural and multi-faith communities that form part of a diverse South African society. South Africa is a developing country still faced with social and economic problems that, realistically, limit the application of the best interests of children in custody decisions, among others. Applying the best interests of the child principle in ways that seek to further prejudice women already prejudiced by religion could also be deemed to be discriminatory and unconstitutional. This implies that the provisions of the MMB, once enacted, given different perspectives on, and interpretations of, Islamic law, may be subject to constitutional challenge and further amendment.

In a plural and secular South Africa, the Constitution uniquely makes allowance for formal legal recognition of hitherto unrecognised religious marriages and/or personal laws of its minority (mainly, Hindu, Muslim and Jewish) religious

[24] See the comment of the Constitutional Court per Kriegler J in *Ex Parte Minister of Safety and Security and Others: In re S v. Walters and Another* 2002 (4) SA 613 (CC), p. 644 [para 57]. See also the approach adopted by the Constitutional Court in *AD and Another v. DW and Others* 2008 (3) SA 183 (CC) where Sachs J endorsed the view that the best interest of minors should not be '... held to ransom for the sake of legal niceties [p. 5 at para 10] (and further that) ... best interests should not be mechanically sacrificed on the altar of jurisdictional formalism [p. 16 at para 30].'

communities. Section 15(3)(a) does not constitutionalise the right to have MPL recognised, but provides for the enactment of legislation recognising '(i) marriages concluded under … a system of religious, personal or family law; or (ii) systems of personal or family law … adhered to by persons professing a particular religion'. A court therefore cannot deem (discriminatory) religious family law as inherently in violation of the Constitution's freedom of religion clause (section 15(1)). However, a court, relying on the provisions[25] of the Constitution, can require that MPL be consistent with the Constitution and its Bill of Rights, and therefore be subject to other constitutional rights, especially equality (section 9) and human dignity (section 10).

While little progress has been made concerning the recognition of Hindu and Jewish marriages, Muslims have opted for a draft statement dealing only with the recognition of Muslim marriages and related matters, rather than a 'code' of MPL. The MMB has been framed so that it can satisfy and synthesise both diverse Muslim (ideological) perspectives and the relevant constitutional commands (guarantees of religious freedom and equality). As alluded to in the Introduction, while the government has encouraged the formal statutory recognition of Muslim marriages as part of its law reform initiatives, it has been dragging its feet since the process started in 1999.

The main (civil) Marriage Act will not be amended to accommodate Muslim marriages. Instead, formal statutory recognition of such marriages will take place separately by adjusting South African law, which is already recognised as a hybrid or mixed legal system, because of the formal recognition of two other types of marriage. The proposed legislation is therefore intended to co-exist alongside the mainstream (civil) law rather than to form an integral part of it. Nonetheless, just as there is no strict separation between (the secular) State and religion in the Constitution, at present there is also no strict separation between some of South Africa's statutes and religious law; thus there already is an overlap between the two systems. This has mainly occurred since 1993 because of judicial and statutory interventions which have recognised Muslim marriages for certain purposes. Judicial intervention at the level of the Constitutional Court has occurred after test cases were brought by, or on behalf of, Muslim women and their children, who remain most affected by the consequences of non-recognition of Muslim marriages, upon the divorce or death of their spouses or fathers, respectively. The legislature has in most cases therefore been forced by the judiciary to amend certain laws to make allowance for the rights of Muslim women and children. However, there are many instances where the legislature has been proactive and amended the law of its own accord. A typical example is the Children's Act. The government, as it did with Muslim marriages, accorded children's rights a high priority by making that part of its law reform initiatives in 1998, although, as indicated, the Children's Act was only introduced a few years after a Project Committee of the SALRC had dealt with a review of the Child Care Act.

---

[25] Sections 15(3)(b) and 39(3) (interpretation clause).

This reform initiative overlapped with that pertaining to Muslim marriages, which, the Committee noted, would necessarily include the position of Muslim children within its ambit. As will be detailed in Sect. 9.3.4, the provisions of the MMB relating to custody, guardianship and maintenance largely conform to Islamic law and have therefore created little contention by according rights and protection to women and children and regulating the corresponding duties of men. Furthermore, given that the principle of best interests straddles both legal systems, until the recognition of Muslim marriages occurs, South African law and this principle remain the norm by which Muslim children's rights are judged.

As a first step to seeking recourse, many Muslims in purely religious marriages, especially women with children, seek the assistance of essentially conservative male religious authorities (*ulama*). These basically adhere to two (namely, the Hanafi and Shafi'i schools) of the four main Sunni schools of law and mediate (rather than arbitrate)[26] and resolve disputes of a religious nature or grant a religious divorce (*talaq* or *faskh*) in several informally constituted religious tribunals. The *ulama* have varying degrees of status based on their formal training and qualifications. Since their decisions do not have legal binding force, getting their decisions enforced by recalcitrant parties may be difficult. If unsuccessful or dissatisfied, these parties will often then seek resolution and relief from secular courts. To date, all such significant test cases were brought by or on behalf of Muslim women. If a religious divorce has, for example, been obtained, and should one party appeal to the secular (High and Divorce) courts (as upper guardian of all children) for a custody order, the standard of the best interests of the child would be applied regardless of any clash with the values of the religion that may be involved. For example, the fact that Islamic law may give preference to the mother (similar to the 'tender years' principle) would be deemed as discriminating between parents on the basis of gender in terms of section 9 (equality clause) of the Constitution.

With recognition of Muslim marriages it is envisaged that MPL matters will continue to be primarily adjudicated in secular courts where judges are not necessarily Muslim, and with religious authorities playing a more minor role than previously envisaged. The MMB is essentially a Shari'a compliant 'code' which is partly based on progressive interpretations of rules, developed by the Sunni schools of Islamic law, as they are currently understood and implemented in practice in the Muslim world. Once enacted, the MMB will be able to guide judges who interpret and apply Islamic law principles. Given that the 'code' is little more than a statement of law and does not contain intricate details of Islamic law, *ulama* and other experts are therefore still expected to give an interpretative and advisory input since there have been cases where secular judges have misinterpreted Islamic law, albeit in a well-intended effort to provide Muslim women with relief. Although judges cannot change Islamic law, the 'code' will at least provide them with a starting point and guide which they currently lack.

---

[26] Although it can be criticised for clearly being out of touch with current needs, the provisions of the Arbitration Act No 42 of 1965, for example, Section 2, do not make it conducive to mediating personal law matters.

9.3 The Best Interests of the Child as a Determining Factor in South African Law

9.3.1 Judicial Analysis of the Application and Evaluation of the Provisions Pertaining to the Best Interests of the Child in South African Legislation

That the best interests of the child should be the determining factor in decisions relating to guardianship, contact (access) and custody (care) of children is well established in South African private law. The rule has also been entrenched in the Constitution because the best interests of the child also form a key or guiding principle of the CRC (Article 3). The same can be said of Article 4 of the ACWRC, which deals with the 'primacy' of the best interests of the child because; although its ratification (2000) followed the coming into operation of the Constitution, it nonetheless preceded the Children's Act.

Section 28(2) of the Constitution states that '[a] child's best interests are of paramount importance in every matter concerning the child'. Skelton aptly describes how the Constitutional Court views section 28(2) as both a principle (standard) and an independent right when she states that '… [it] is not only a principle that helps interpretation of other rights. It is a right in itself'.[27] Unfortunately, since the Constitution does not define what exactly it means by this standard, it has given rise to varied judicial interpretations by the High Court and the Constitutional Court, as detailed below.

In fact, the best interests of the child principle (standard) is not a new concept in South African law as it was already established in an Appellate Division case (*Fletcher*) in 1948.[28] However, the Court in this case did not articulate what would constitute the best interests of a child nor did it set out any particular criteria to be considered. In 1994 the Cape Supreme Court (*McCall*),[29] in the context of the custody of a child, set out an extensive list of some thirteen (a–m) criteria which should be taken into account in determining the best interests of the child. Not only did the list clearly make reference to religion as a consideration ('the ability of the parent to provide for the educational well-being and security of the child, both religious and secular' (factor f)), but the last factor (m) was flexible enough to include religion in that it made provision for '*any other factor which is relevant to the particular case with which the Court is concerned*'. That list was accepted as a guide in custody cases in a number of High Court decisions. Furthermore, these factors were also subsequently statutorily recognised, with minor differences, in section 7 of the Children's Act (as will be detailed below). However, the formal incorporation of a guiding standard (section 7) in the Children's Act, although

27 Skelton 2013, p. 619.

28 *Fletcher v. Fletcher* 1948 (1) SA 130 (A).

29 *McCall v. McCall* 1994 (3) SA 201 (C) at 204 J-205F.

similarly expansive in that it lists some fourteen factors, regrettably does not contain a flexible criterion similar to the stated factor (m).

The influence of the best interests principle was initially limited to family law and care proceedings. What is new is that, apart from a (non-exhaustive) range of other rights contained in section 28(1)[30] and in the rest of the Bill of Rights that contextually also provide protection to children, the 'best interests' principle has also been specifically included, through section 28(2), as one of the fundamental human rights that constitute the Bill of Rights, and has, through it, been expanded to include all aspects of law affecting children. As Skelton points out and details in two recent sources, the Constitutional Court has therefore 'drawn',[31] although it has not necessarily uniformly dealt with[32] or applied it, the 'best interests' principle into several cases that not only pertain to the right to family or parental care (custody),[33] which is the focus of this chapter, but also to a range of other issues,

---

30 Section 28(1), which is also not exhaustive of children's rights, lists nine (a–i) specific rights which include the right '(*b*) to family care or parental care, or to appropriate alternative care …'.

31 See Skelton 2013, p. 620.

32 See Boezaart 2014, p. 174.

33 In *Bannatyne v. Bannatyne* 2003 (2) SA 363 (CC) the Court held that the best interests requirement obliged parents to properly care for their children, but also obliged the State to provide the necessary legal administration to ensure appropriate care—which in this case related to the payment of maintenance; In *S v. M (Centre for Child Law as Amicus Curiae)* 2008 (3) SA 232 (CC), which is also reported as *M v. S* 2007 (12) BCLR 1312 (CC) (see also note 35 below), the Court considered the best interests principle together with the right to family and parental care in a situation where children might be deprived of such care if their primary caregiver (in this case an unmarried mother) was imprisoned. The Court found (at para 30) that 'section 28 requires the law to make best efforts to avoid, where possible, any breakdown of family life or parental care that may threaten to put children at increased risk. Similarly, in situations where rupture of the family becomes inevitable, the state is obliged to minimise the consequent negative effect on children as far as it can'. In *C v. Department of Health and Social Development, Gauteng*, 2012 (2) SA 208 (CC) the Constitutional Court found the lack of a provision for automatic review of the removal of children from their parents to be an unconstitutional infringement of their best interests. Although not a Constitutional Court case, the criminal law case of *S v. Petersen* 2008 (2) SACR 355 (C) elicited much interest in the local community because the appellant, Nejwa Petersen, was the wife of a famous Muslim theatre personality, Taliep Petersen. She was, along with two co-accused, convicted in the Cape High Court of his murder and sentenced to 28 years imprisonment. Given that at the time she was the mother of the couple's minor daughter, Zaynab, the Court (at para 44) considered the position of the child in the context of her best interests in terms of section 28(2) of the Constitution and with reference to the then recent Constitutional Court case of *M v. S* (2007) referred to above. In so doing the Court recognised the rights and interests of children of perpetrators. After finding that the appellant was not the primary caregiver, the Court nonetheless went on to address the matter of the minor child's care as follows (at para 76): 'I am quite satisfied that she is presently in excellent hands, under the supervision of persons who love and care for her and have voluntarily undertaken this duty since the appellant's incarceration, if not already from the time of the death of the deceased. Zaynab is, in my view, in more than appropriate alternative care, as envisaged by section 28(1)(b) of the *Constitution*.' Such a ruling would satisfy Islamic law requirements since it typifies what would ordinarily be expected to happen in a similar case in the context of extended Muslim families.

for example, international child abduction and adoption by unmarried fathers, same-sex couples, and foreign couples. Furthermore, the 'best interests' principle may be of 'paramount importance' but, like every other right in the Bill of Rights, it may also be subject to limitation in terms of section 36 (general limitation clause). Therefore it does not enjoy any special hierarchic position in the Bill of Rights, nor does it automatically trump the rights of other interested parties, like parents or the State. Therefore, although section 7(1) of the Children's Act ought to be read in conjunction with the interpretation and context of section 28(2) of the Constitution as adduced from the Constitutional Court cases,[34] the Court has in more recent cases conceded that section 28 may also be used to limit rights and, as a right, is therefore also subject to limitation.[35]

Clearly modelled on section 28(2) of the Constitution, Chap. 2 of the Children's Act also contains a section (section 9) dealing specifically with the paramountcy of the best interests of a child as follows: 'In all matters concerning the care, protection and well-being of a child *the standard* that the child's best interest is of paramount importance, must be applied' (my emphasis).

Bosman-Sadie and Corrie[36] explain that in this section '"[p]aramount" means supreme or of utmost importance [and that] … [a]ccording to this section, the "best interests of a child" standard is the single most important principle to be considered in this entire Act'.

Bosman-Sadie and Corrie[37] also give an impressive list of some forty cases, starting with *Fletcher* (1948 in the Appellate Division) and ending in 2012[38] in the Constitutional Court, 'that tracks the development of the current best interests of the child standard over the last 60 years'. However, despite all this development, it is clear that currently '[w]hat is considered in the child's best interest has proved confusing. This difficulty is compounded by different and rapidly changing social standards and values of our diverse society'.[39]

Given its historical context, it is not surprising that the 'best interests' principle has often been referred to as the 'golden thread'[40] that permeates all law in South Africa when decisions affecting children are under consideration. Further

---

[34] For detail see especially the judgments of Goldstone J referred to in note 42.

[35] The limitation of the paramountcy of the 'best interests' principle is explained in the following cases: *Centre for Child Law v. Minister of Justice and Constitutional Development* 2009 (6) SA 632 (CC), per Cameron J, at para 29 and *De Reuck v. Director of Public Prosecutions (Witwatersrand Local Division) and Others* 2004 (1) SA 406 (CC), para 55, per Langa, DCJ. Similarly, the Constitutional Court expanded on the meaning of paramountcy in a later case, *M v. S* 2007 (12) BCLR 1312 (CC), p. 1324 at paras 23 and 26 of the judgment by Sachs J. The approach of this case was in turn applied in a subsequent Constitutional Court case, *Van der Burg v. National Director of Public Prosecutions* 2012 (2) SACR 331 (CC).

[36] Bosman-Sadie and Corrie 2013, p. 30.

[37] Bosman-Sadie and Corrie 2013, pp. 29–30.

[38] *CM v. NG* (2012) 3 All SA 104 (CC).

[39] Van der Walt 2009, p. 238.

[40] See *Kaiser v. Chambers* 1969 (4) SA 224 (C) at 228 E-G.

corroboration and guidance as to what is meant by this principle, and the factors that must be taken into account in giving effect to its application, are also found in section 7 (titled 'Best interest standard') of the Children's Act.

The principle of the best interests of the child must always be considered when making decisions about children. Section 7(1)(a–n) sets out a lengthy, though not exhaustive, list of fourteen factors for courts to consider when determining a child's best interests under the Act (the 'best interests of the child standard' is also referred to in section 9 of the Children's Act detailed below) and under the Constitution. These factors are:

(1)(*a*) the nature of the personal relationship between—(i) the child and the parents … and (ii) … care-giver;

(*b*) the attitude of the parents … towards—(i) the child; and (ii) the exercise of parental responsibilities and rights in respect of the child;

(*c*) the capacity of the parents … to provide for the needs of the child, including emotional and intellectual needs;

(*d*) the likely effect on the child of any change in the child's circumstances, including … separation from (i) both or either of the parents; or (ii) any brother or sister or other child, or any other care-giver or person …, with whom the child has been living;

(*e*) the practical difficulty and expense of a child having contact with the parents … on a regular basis;

(*f*) the need for the child—(i) to remain in the care of his or her parent, family and extended family; and (*ii*) to maintain a connection with his or her family, extended family, *culture or tradition*;

(*g*) the child's—(i) age, maturity and stage of development; (ii) gender; *(iii) background; and (iv) any other relevant characteristics of the child*;

(*h*) the child's physical and emotional security and…social and *cultural development*;

(*i*) any disability that a child may have;

(*j*) any chronic illness from which a child may suffer;

(*k*) the need for a child to be brought up within a stable family environment and, where this is not possible, in an environment resembling as closely as possible a caring family environment;

(*l*) the need to protect the child from any physical or psychological harm that may be caused by (i) subjecting the child to maltreatment, abuse, neglect, exploitation or degradation or exposing the child to violence or exploitation or other harmful behaviour; or (ii) exposing the child to [such behaviour] …;

(*m*) any family violence involving the child or a family member of the child; and

(*n*) which action or decision would avoid or minimise further legal or administrative proceedings in relation to the child (my emphasis).

Although culture and tradition (which may be linked with religion) are specifically mentioned in factor f (ii), and although factors g (iii–iv) and h may allude to it, it is a pity that section 7 does not specify religion in its list of factors or contain a useful flexible provision, similar to criterion (m) in the *McCall* case (as detailed above), from which to have inferred it.

However, ultimately, judges, because the court acts as the 'upper guardian' in *all* disputes concerning children, exercise discretion when determining what is, or may be, in a particular child's best interests. As will be detailed in Sect. 9.3.3.4 below, section 33(3) of the Children's Act, in the context of a parenting plan, makes provision for 'any matter' (including religion) to be catered for. As alluded to above, judges have expressed different views as to what section 28(2) (best interests standard) entails. For example, although the High Court may have deemed this section merely to be a 'general guideline',[41] the Constitutional Court has subsequently interpreted this provision as being both 'independent' of other rights contained in the Constitution and as an 'expansive guarantee'. In other words, given that both were never given 'exhaustive' content, section 28(2) is not limited by the list of rights enumerated in section 28(1) of the Constitution or the list of factors contained in section 7(1) (the best interests standard) of the Children's Act.[42]

Chapter 1 of the Children's Act, in the section dealing with its Objects, states that one of its goals is 'to give effect to the [above] constitutional rights of children, namely … that the best interests of a child are of paramount importance in every matter concerning the child …'.[43]

9.3.2 International and Regional Instruments

The Preamble to the Children's Act, which holds little legal value, sets out two of its purposes as according added significance to the best interests of the child (section 28) and South Africa's commitment to both regional and international human rights instruments which protect such interests. A clear goal of the Children's Act is 'to give effect to the Republic's obligations concerning the well-being of children in terms of international instruments binding on the Republic …'.[44] The section of the Constitution[45] dealing with the application of international law states:

> When interpreting any legislation, every court must prefer any reasonable interpretation of the legislation that is consistent with international law over any alternative interpretation that is inconsistent with international law.

---

41 See the judgment of Van Dijkhorst JP in *Jooste v. Botha* 2000 (2) BCLR 187 (T), p. 198.

42 See Chaskalson P at p. 1360 para 9 in *Fraser v. Naude and Others* 1998 (11) BCLR 1357 (CC); Goldstone J in *Minister for Welfare and Population Development v. Fitzpatrick and Others* 2000 (7) BCLR 713 (CC), pp. 719–720 and again Goldstone J in *Sonderup v. Tondelliand and Another* 2001 (1) SA 1171 (CC) which is also reported as *LS v. AT and Another* 2001 (2) BCLR 152 (CC), p. 162 at para 29 of the judgment.

43 Section 2(b)(iv).

44 Section 2(c).

45 Section 233.

Although the interpretation clause of the Constitution[46] states that a court, tribunal or forum 'must consider international law' and 'may consider foreign law' when interpreting the Bill of Rights, this consideration does not mean that it is obliged to 'apply' the provisions of international human rights instruments unless South Africa has also ratified them.

As indicated in Sect. 9.2.2, South Africa has both signed and ratified a range of regional and international instruments affecting women and children. These include the ACWRC, the CRC and the CEDAW, all of which enshrine the principle of the 'best interests' of the child. This therefore means that the provisions of these instruments must be taken into account when dealing with section 28 of the Constitution or any other relevant provision in it pertaining to a child. For example, Article 3(1) of the CRC provides:

> In *all* actions concerning children, whether undertaken by public *or private social welfare institutions*, courts of law, administrative authorities or legislative bodies, the best interests of the child shall be ***a*** primary consideration (my emphasis).

While section 9 of the Children's Act is modelled on section 28(2) of the Constitution, the latter clearly appears to have been modelled on Article 3 of the CRC. Although Article 3 can be construed to include unofficial religious bodies within its ambit, it appears that in South Africa the application by such bodies of Islamic law and custom governing Muslim marriages does not provide for a child's best interests being of paramount importance in every matter concerning the child, as provided for in the Constitution.

Article 16(1) of the CEDAW states:

> States Parties shall…ensure, on a basis of equality of men and women:
> (d) The same rights and responsibilities as parents, irrespective of their marital status, in matters relating to their children; *in all cases the interests of the children shall be paramount*;…
> (f) The same rights and responsibilities with regard to guardianship, wardship, trusteeship and adoption of children, or similar institutions where these concepts exist in national legislation; *in all cases the interests of the children shall be paramount*…(my emphasis).

When compared with the CRC, the following two provisions of the ACWRC appear to offer all South African children increased, and their best interests more emphatic, protection.

Article 1(3) of the ACWRC, which deals with the obligation of States Parties, expressly provides:

> *Any custom, tradition, cultural or religious practice* that is *inconsistent* with the rights, duties and obligations contained in the present Charter shall to the extent of such inconsistency be *discouraged* (my emphasis).

Article 4(1) of the ACWRC, which is dedicated to dealing with the best interests of the child, provides:

> In *all* actions concerning the child undertaken *by any person or authority* the best interests of the child shall be ***the*** primary consideration (my emphasis).

---

[46] Section 39(1)(a) and (b).

The conservative understanding and interpretation of the law has been, and is still being, developed to align with the provisions of the Children's Act and the guidance it provides. It is also clear that the formulation of Article 3 of the CRC which deals with the 'paramountcy' of the best interests principle has both led to and influenced the formulation of section 28(2) of the Constitution, which in its turn has influenced the incorporation of the best interests principle into national legislation in section 9 of the Children's Act. As indicated in Sect. 9.3.1, the same can be said of Article 4 of the ACWRC which deals with the 'primacy' of the best interests of the child.

The interpretation clause of the Constitution[47] further states:

> When interpreting any legislation, and when developing the common law or customary law, *every* court, *tribunal or forum* must promote the spirit, purport and the objects of the Bill of Rights (my emphasis).

Chapter 2 (General principles (sections 6–17)) of the Children's Act contains several important provisions pertaining to the best interests of children. One of its central foci is:

> All proceedings, actions or decisions in a matter concerning a child must respect, protect, promote and fulfil the child's rights set out in the Bill of Rights, the best interests of the child standard set out in section 7 and the rights and principles set out in this Act, subject to any lawful limitation.[48]

Finally, the Children's Act has incorporated the following three major international Conventions into South African law (and dedicates a specific chapter to each: the Hague Convention on Inter-Country Adoption of 1993 (Chapter 16); The Hague Convention on (the Civil Aspects of) International Child Abduction of 1980[49] (Chapter 17); and the UN Protocol to Prevent Trafficking in Persons, supplementing the UN Convention against Transnational Organized Crime of 2000 (Chapter 18). However, it appears that although the three Conventions are therefore enforceable in South African courts, that this may not be sufficient in itself.[50] The operation of the Hague Convention on International Child Abduction has amended South African law in respect of custody and access rights since 1997. South Africa does not appear to be a signatory or party to either the 1996 Hague Child Protection Convention[51] or the 2007 Hague Child Support Convention and Protocol.[52]

---

[47] Section 39(2).

[48] Children's Act No 38 of 2005, section 6(2)(a).

[49] This Hague Convention was adopted by South Africa in 1996 and has since the date of its entry into force (1 October 1997) been applicable between South Africa and several other contracting States. Cases decided before the Convention's incorporation by the Children's Act are therefore still of relevance.

[50] For detail see Schäfer 2011, p. 55.

[51] See www.hcch.net/index_en.php?act=conventions.text&cid=70 (accessed 26 May 2015).

[52] See www.hcch.net/index_en.php?act=conventions.status2&cid=131 (accessed 26 May 2015).

9.3.3 Parental Responsibilities and Rights in the Children's Act

With the introduction of the new Children's Act in 2005, South African law has moved its focus away from the concept of parental power or authority which constituted the sum total of the *rights and duties* of parents with regard to their children. The Children's Act places the emphasis on parental *responsibilities and rights* (in that reverse order of precedence), which include caring for, maintaining contact with, acting as guardian for, and contributing to the maintenance of, the child. Although, as indicated, the Children's Act only became fully operational on 1 April 2010, most of the provisions dealing with the acquisition of parental responsibilities and rights have been in operation since 1 July 2007. As indicated in Sect. 9.2.2 above, the term 'custody' has been replaced with the term 'care', and 'contact' is similar in meaning to 'access'. Guardianship may also be co-exercised or shared by parents.[53]

Parents who are legally (civilly) married to each other, and live together, are automatically and equally the guardians of their (biological) minor children born of the marriage. Equal guardianship rights would also apply to Muslim parents who have entered into both a religious marriage and a civil marriage. If for some reason a guardian is unable to, or fails to, perform his or her duties, the court may appoint a 'legal' guardian for the children. The High Court is itself ultimately the 'upper' guardian of all minor children.

9.3.3.1 The Marital Status of Parents and the Distinction Between Legitimate and Illegitimate Children

As will be detailed in Sect. 9.3.4.6 below, prior to the Children's Act, the law unjustifiably distinguished between illegitimate (born out of wedlock) and legitimate (born in wedlock) children. In this sense it accorded with Islamic law which still draws such a distinction. Although it did away with classifying children born of religious marriages, including Muslim ones, as 'illegitimate', it continued to categorise such children, although born of religious marriages, as born 'out of wedlock'. Thus, although in terms of section 1(c) of the Child Care Amendment Act No 96 of 1996 the term 'illegitimate' was replaced by the term 'out of wedlock', the substantive legal status of, for example, children born of marriages carried out in accordance with religious rites remained unaffected. The Children's Act, fortunately, no longer draws a distinction between legitimate and illegitimate children and simply refers to them as children born of married and unmarried parents, respectively.

---

[53] See Chapter 1, section 1 (interpretation) and Chapter 3, section 18(2) (parental responsibilities and rights) and section 18(3) (shared guardianship) of the Children's Act.

9.3.3.2 The Legal Duty of Maintenance

As guardians, both parents not only have joint custody and guardianship of their children but also have a legal duty to support (maintain) them. Furthermore, both the Children's Act and the Maintenance Act[54] provide for equal rights and duties of parents of children born of religious marriages regardless of the fact that such marriages are not legally recognised (or that in terms of Islamic law only a father has maintenance responsibilities, as will be detailed in Sect. 9.3.4.5 below).

The legal duty of parents to support their children usually terminates when the children become independent, for example, when they marry or when they become self-sufficient. If the children are not living with the mother or the father, the persons who are looking after them, for example, their grandparents (without distinction between maternal or paternal grandparents, as is the case in Islamic law), are able to apply for maintenance from the parents through the children's court. Section 22 of the Children's Act makes it possible for both sets of grandparents or other family members to become 'co-holders' with parents of parental responsibilities and rights through a written agreement registered with a family advocate or made an order of court (similar to a parenting plan referred to in Sect. 9.3.3.4 below). If the parents are themselves destitute and in need of support, they may apply for a State child support grant (CSG), or for a care dependency grant (CDG) if they have a child with a disability who may be in need of special care. A State foster care grant (FCG) is also available for children deemed to be at risk and who therefore have been placed in the care of foster parents (who are not the biological parents) by a children's court. Although the grants for the children are paid to the parent or person who has to take care of them, it is the children who have the right to the grants and not the parent or caregiver. Section 1 of the Children's Act generically defines an 'orphan' as 'a child who has no surviving parent caring for him or her'; children who have lost only one parent are excluded from the definition and may suffer prejudice as a result even though the Children's Act (section 150(1)(a)) is in the process of being further amended.[55] The households of many poor (especially black) families in South Africa are also headed by children ('child-headed households')[56] or grandparents due to the ravages of HIV/AIDS, poverty and the scourge of apartheid. The State currently carries the financial responsibility of providing grants to millions of destitute and needy children that are in more dire straits than their Muslim counterparts.

In terms of Islamic law a father is only responsible for maintaining his legitimate children. Where both parents are unable to support their children, the paternal grandfather may be expected to assist. The position is different in terms of South African law: both maternal and paternal grandparents of children born in wedlock may have an obligation to maintain them when necessary. In 1930, before

---

[54] Act No 99 of 1998.

[55] For a detailed critical discussion see Jamieson et al. 2014, pp. 18–19.

[56] See the Children's Act, section 137.

the concept of best interests started to play a role in court cases, the Appellate Division, in *Motan v. Joosub*,[57] drew a distinction between children born in and out of wedlock. The Court, per Wessels JA, upheld a Supreme Court (now High Court) decision that South African law did not recognise the right of a Muslim mother (who was equated to a concubine in this case) of four minor children born out of wedlock (because they were born of an unrecognised Muslim marriage and deemed to be 'illegitimate') to claim maintenance for them from their paternal grandfather. In the case of an extra-marital child whose parents were unable to support the child, the South African law, as interpreted in the *Motan* case, provided that only the maternal grandparents had a duty of support towards the child. It mattered little to the Court that the grandfather (the defendant in the case) had admitted that a Muslim marriage had existed between the children's mother and his son, and it appears that aspersions were instead cast on the mother's morality because of a remote possibility that the children might not be his grandchildren. Not surprisingly, the *Motan* ruling has, albeit only recently in 2004, been rejected as unconstitutional in yet another case involving Muslim parties, but which this time involved an illegitimate child. In *Petersen v. Maintenance Officer, Simon's Town Maintenance Court and Others*,[58] the applicant, a young single female, had been unable to secure from the child's biological father, who had admitted paternity, a contribution to the maintenance of their child. The applicant and her parents (the child's maternal grandparents) were supporting the child from straitened means. The High Court recognised the liability of paternal grandparents for the maintenance of a child who in this case was born out wedlock, since there was no question of any marriage.[59] The applicant's Muslim attorney argued that the law as interpreted in *Motan* was contrary to the best interests of the child.

9.3.3.3 Co-holders of Parental Responsibilities and Rights

Children born through artificial insemination to a childless couple or a lesbian couple in a (same-sex) civil union[60] or through surrogacy where at least one of the parents has contributed an ovum or sperm[61] are similarly (to children born of the marriage) also referred to as biological children because of the genetic link. However, adopted children are regarded as the 'natural' children of adoptive parents.[62]

The fact that the Children's Act permits legal adoption means that Muslim couples are able to adopt children in South Africa even though Sunni Islam is deemed

---

57 1930 AD 61. See especially p. 65 of the judgment.

58 2004 (2) SA 56 (C).

59 See van Schalkwyk 2009, p. 45.

60 Chapter 3 of the Children's Act.

61 Chapter 19 of the Children's Act.

62 Chapter 15 of the Children's Act.

not to permit adoption. However, section 234 of the Children's Act does make allowances for an 'open adoption', albeit in the context of formal adoption where the child's identity is fully absorbed into that of the adoptive family. The adoptive and biological families can enter into a 'post-adoption agreement' which makes provision for the right of the child and his or her biological family to retain contact with each other. As with formal adoption, Sunni Islam does not permit surrogacy for various reasons, which include implications of adultery (*zina*) and that a child's legal mother is deemed to be the birth mother. Support for the Islamic view against surrogacy can also be inferred from the MMB with its emphasis on children born of 'marriage'[63] since it implies that (biological) paternity is the consequence of a licit (legal) sexual relationship. Should a constitutional challenge arise in South Africa with regard to such an assisted reproductive technology (ART), it could raise questions pertaining to, in addition to status, the child's maintenance; inheritance; dignity; contract (womb rental); or even polygyny (such a marriage could, for example, be 'creatively' envisaged with a surrogate purely for the purpose of 'procreation', and just as easily terminated thereafter).

9.3.3.4 Parenting Plans

In South Africa custody (and therefore the best interests of children) usually only becomes a litigious issue once the marriage breaks up. When couples separate or divorce the court usually grants (physical) custody to one parent and general access to the other. In terms of section 1 of the Children's Act,

> 'contact' [or access], in relation to a child, means-
>
> (*a*) maintaining a personal relationship with the child; and (*b*) if the child lives with someone else—(i) communication on a regular basis with the child in person, including—(*aa*) visiting the child; or (*bb*) being visited by the child; or (ii) communication on a regular basis with the child in any other manner, including—(*aa*) through the post; or (*bb*) by telephone or any other form of electronic communication.

However, through the vehicle of a parenting plan newly introduced by the Children's Act,[64] there has been a shift from the idea of sole custody to joint custody in the best interests of children. Furthermore, courts can only be approached once parties have first sought to iron out such issues with the assistance of available expertise and/or through such a parenting plan. Although section 33(2) provides some guidelines as to the issues which may be dealt with in a parenting plan, which is usually helpful when divorce is in issue, it does not preclude parties from tailoring such a parenting plan to suit their culture, customs and religion, as long as they do not conflict with the best interests of the child standard detailed in section 7 of the Act as elaborated below. In terms of section 10 of the Children's Act

---

[63] See text to note 80.

[64] Sections 33(2) and 33(5).

(and as envisaged by Article 4(2) of the ACWRC and Article 12(1) of the CRC), the child's input and views (where maturity provides for it) may also play a role, as explained below. However, nothing precludes parties, who may as yet not have marital problems but want to be pro-active in avoiding co-parenting issues that may cause problems in the future, from also drafting such a parenting plan to help them deal with these issues within an existing marriage. In terms of section 33(3) of the Children's Act the content of a parenting plan may deal with '***any matter***' that may relate to 'co-parenting' or co-exercising or sharing of their parental responsibilities and rights, and with which they may be struggling. It may, for example, range from working out a fair division of labour if both couples work and co-contribute to income earned and how to deal with interfering in-laws; and it may include, where parents subscribe to different religions (in the case of inter-faith marriages) or different schools of Islamic law, what religion should be followed or what school should be attended by the child etc. As indicated, prior to seeking the intervention of a court, parties must, as a first step, seek the assistance of either a family advocate[65] or a social worker or a psychologist, or a suitably qualified person who can help mediate in order to reach agreement on disputed issues pertaining to care (custody), contact (access) and guardianship. A family advocate often works in collaboration with the expertise provided by these other specialists. A family advocate may, for example, facilitate the drafting of a parenting plan which in terms of section 33(4) of the Children's Act 'must comply with the best interests of the child standard set out in section 7'. Even though the Children's Act itself (as is the case also with all other legislation in South Africa) ultimately defers to the Constitution since it is the highest or supreme law, section 7 of the Children's Act, as detailed in Sect. 9.3.1, pays more attention to the child's best interests than section 28(2) of the Constitution, by detailing a list of factors for courts to consider and be guided by when ascertaining what may be in a child's best interests under both the Children's Act and the Constitution.

Section 34(1)(a) of the Children's Act prescribes the formalities with which the parenting plan must comply, for example, that it be in writing and signed. In terms of section 34(1)(b) a parenting plan may be legally enforceable either if registered with a family advocate or made an order of court. If, however, consensus cannot be achieved by the parties, a family advocate may make a recommendation to the court, always acting in the best interests of the child. This recommendation merely assists the court in reaching a decision and is therefore not binding until the court

[65] The Office of the Family Advocate, although established prior to democracy by section 2(1) of the Mediation in Certain Divorce Matters Act No 24 of 1987 (in terms of which litigants are now obliged to mediate their disputes before resorting to litigation), has expanded significantly with the implementation of the Constitution and the Children's Act. The responsibilities of family advocates are not limited to assisting with divorce matters in the Divorce Court, but also include matters heard in Children's Courts, mediation in domestic violence issues, and assisting in Maintenance Courts. The Office of the Family Advocate is a neutral institution which, because it is less formal than a court, is 'child-friendly' and affords both parents and children an opportunity to be heard. The family advocate is paid by the State which offers this service at no cost to parties. For more information see Department of Justice and Constitutional Development 2015.

deems it so. A parenting plan may be amended or terminated either by the Office of the Family Advocate (section 34(4)) or by a court (section 34(5)), as the case may be. A child (or his or her representative) may also approach the court for such amendment or termination. Section 35 deals with refusal of access or refusal to exercise parental responsibilities and rights. Section 35(1) makes it a criminal offence for one parent to deny access to a parent who has access in terms of section 22(4) of the Children's Act (that is, through a registered parental plan or one made an order of the High Court). In terms of section 305(4) the failure to honour an obligation to maintain a child is an offence. As indicated in Sect. 9.3.4.2, although the issues of access and maintenance may appear to be unrelated, the father's failure to maintain his child will often result in the mother denying him access, with the result that it is ultimately the child that gets 'punished'.

More often than not, and similarly to Islamic law, the mother is awarded custody by the court. However, there have been cases where awarding the father custody has not only been deemed to be in the best interests of the children but may also have been at their request or in accordance with their wishes. In terms of section 1(a–j) of the Children's Act, custody or 'care' is interpreted to include a host of factors, such as, providing a child with basic day-to-day necessities, such as, a suitable home, nutrition, financial support and education (including cultural and religious education), and, very importantly, '(*j*) generally, ensuring that the best interests of the child is the paramount concern in all matters affecting the child'.

However, quite unlike Islamic law where the father is deemed the sole guardian, given that normally the mother and father have joint guardianship of their children, they are expected to jointly make decisions in this regard. For example, section 18(3) of the Children's Act provides that a person who acts as a guardian must:

> (*a*) administer and safeguard the child's property and property interests; (*b*) assist or represent the child in administrative, contractual and other legal matters; or (*c*) give or refuse any consent required by law in respect of the child, including—(i) … marriage; (ii) … adoption; (iii) … departure or removal from the Republic; (iv) … child's application for a passport; and (v) … alienation or encumbrance of any immovable property of the child.

Nothing therefore precludes Muslim parents from utilising the tool of a parenting plan as long as it is in accordance with South African law. However, unlike civil (legal) marriages, which are dissolved in secular divorce courts and matters pertaining to the care, contact and maintenance of children are sorted out before a divorce is granted, the issue of how Muslim parents will exercise their religious parental responsibilities regarding their children, let alone their secular law responsibilities, does not automatically ensue when unrecognised Muslim marriages are terminated by divorce (whether by unregulated unilateral *talaq* by the husband or regulated *faskh* granted by a religious tribunal to either the husband or wife). Recalcitrant fathers often fail to uphold the legally non-binding decisions of *ulama* bodies when such a dispute has been decided in favour of mothers. As indicated, this has often left Muslim women with little option but to approach the secular courts for relief.

While, similarly to Islamic law, parents may still have many important rights over children, for example, the right to moderately chastise them, these rights do not necessarily take precedence over the rights of children. The rights and best interests of children may take precedence over those of parents regardless of any religious law or practice which may conflict with such rights, for example, when it may not allow for a medical blood transfusion to save the life of the child[66] or regarding a child's participation in religious activities in a particular church.[67] The rights of Muslim children, as those of all other children in South Africa, are currently protected from 'sabotage' under the guise of religion. Under normal circumstances, the roles of parent and child are expected to be both complementary and balanced so that children, as long as they are minors (or 'majors' in some instances) incapable of taking care of themselves, have the right to be reared jointly by both parents in a caring environment, and vice versa when parents reach old age. However, this ideal does not reflect current reality where parents get divorced or remarry or enter into polygynous marriages so that children are forced to live in 'blended' families with children from a previous marriage of the wife, husband, or both, or are orphaned when both biological parents die and are then often left to the mercy of welfare.

9.3.3.5 Capacity of Minors to Enter into Marriage

As eighteen is the legal age of majority, it is also the legal age to enter into marriage. A minor under eighteen, who has not been previously married, needs the written consent of both parents.[68] If parents unreasonably refuse their consent or there is sufficient evidence that getting married is in the best interests of the minor, consent can be requested from a judge of the High Court. Minors (those under the age of eighteen) require parental consent to marry. In addition, a boy under the age of eighteen or a girl under the age of fifteen will need the consent of, for example, the Minister of Home Affairs.[69] If a minor manages to get married without consent while under the age of eighteen, his or her parents can seek to have the marriage dissolved.

---

66 *Hay v. B and Others* 2003 (3) SA 492 (W), pp. 494–495.

67 *Kotze v. Kotze* 2003 (3) SA 628 (T), pp. 630–631. See text to note 78.

68 See the Marriage Act 1961, sections 24(1) and (2).

69 See the Marriage Act, section 26(1). If ministerial consent was required but not obtained, the minor's marriage will be deemed null and void. However, the Minister may also, in terms of section 26(2) read together with section 26(3) of the Marriage Act (dealing with the possibility of retrospective consent), subsequently declare the marriage 'valid' if 'desirable and in the interests of the parties in question'. It can therefore be deduced from the above that there appears not to be a set age below which it can be said with any certainty that a minor cannot enter into a marriage. A minor who enters into a valid civil marriage before attaining the age of eighteen acquires the status of majority.

In terms of Islamic law, the ages of marriage for girls and boys are even lower, and they are usually marriageable at the onset of puberty. Although they vary between the schools of law, the age of puberty for girls is lower than that for boys. South African law may penalise civil marriages entered into by underage couples, but the Muslim marriage per se is not secularly recognised. While it may be questioned whether or not a young (pubescent) girl is able to give 'full and free' consent to marriage as required in terms of international human rights instruments,[70] if Muslim children enter into such marriages in South Africa their religious validity will not be affected. Furthermore, given that there is no national register of Muslim religious marriages, it is difficult to ascertain the extent of such child marriages in South Africa. Of course, nothing will preclude an imam from officiating at the marriage of such children in terms of an Islamic *nikah* only, and thereafter, when both are of civil marriageable age, for them to enter into a civil marriage in terms of South African law, and, moreover, to even do so with a different imam who is also a registered civil marriage officer.

The MMB differs from the Marriage Act in this regard as follows. Unlike the position in respect of a civil marriage, clause 5 of the MMB, which deals with the requirements for the validity of Muslim marriages, does not set a minimum marriageable age. Instead, clause 5(4) of the MMB makes provision for a *wali* (guardian) of a minor to conclude a marriage on behalf of that minor.[71] Implicit in the application, and paramountcy, of the 'best interests' principle in South Africa is the power to curtail any rights that a *wali* may enjoy over minor children. Since there is no default guardian in terms of the MMB, and given that both Islamic law and South African law will be taken into consideration, this implies, especially since nothing precludes such an interpretation, that a mother may act as a *wali* even in such a case. However, the MMB makes it clear that the father retains the Islamic law financial obligations associated with guardianship although, strictly speaking, the application of the relevant provisions of the Children's Act may mean that both parents share in this responsibility, as will be detailed below. Given that the best interests of a child come into play only after a mother's official Islamic law period of custody (which is her right) ends, this would presumably also be the case if the mother were to be awarded custody beyond the (official) period in terms of a *khul* (divorce) arrangement. In other words, while the mother may decide to waive any compensation due to her in order to secure such a divorce, the father will not be absolved from his maintenance obligations towards the child. Furthermore, clause 5(5) of the MMB allows a Muslim person or body designated by the relevant Minister to authorise a marriage between minors. Activists have voiced concern that these provisions may encourage, rather than

---

[70] See Article 16 of the Universal Declaration of Human Rights (UDHR) (1948), which South Africa has not signed or ratified and whose provisions it may therefore not be obliged to apply.

[71] Although there are exceptions, a Muslim woman is usually not present at (her) the *nikah* (actual marriage) which takes place in a mosque. She is represented by a male guardian (father or brother) and signs the marriage register beforehand. In most cases, where she is present in the mosque, she is merely an observer and sits separated from the men.

deter, child marriages and that marriages without the knowledge and consent of the bride and groom could occur. The content of both these concerns would be contrary to the best interests of such children.

9.3.4 Parental Responsibilities and Rights in the Muslim Marriages Bill (MMB)

This Section will highlight that in terms of the provisions of the MMB, regard was had to the fact that in terms of Islamic law effective custody and guardianship ultimately remain vested in the (ex-)husband, whose financial and maintenance obligations to the (ex-)wife, though generous upon and during marriage, are severely curtailed upon and after divorce. Hence clause 10 (dealing with custody or guardianship of, and access to, minor (and major) children) and clause 11 (dealing with their maintenance) of the MMB regulate the usually limited consequences that flow from Muslim marriages and synthesise them with the provisions of South African law. In doing so, the MMB succeeds in making generous provision for children.

As indicated in Sect. 9.2.3, while the present version of the MMB may still undergo further revision, it is contended that, since it largely complies with Islamic law, the revisions, if any, will be minimal. This section therefore critically analyses clauses 10 and 11 of the MMB and does so in the context of South African law.

As indicated in Sect. 9.2.3, Muslim marriages are currently only recognised in terms of, and for the purposes set out in, several Acts including the Children's Act which comprehensively deals with the protection of the rights of a child. In terms of section 1(1) of the Children's Act:

> 'marriage' means a marriage (*a*) recognised in terms of South African law … or (*b*) concluded in accordance with a system of religious law subject to specified procedures, and any reference to a husband, wife, widower, widow, divorced person, married person or spouse must be construed accordingly.

9.3.4.1 Custody (*Hadana*) or Guardianship (*Wilaya*) of and Access to Children

Clause 10 of the MMB deals with the custody or guardianship of, and access to, children as follows:

> (1) In making an order for the custody of, or access to a minor child, or in making a decision on guardianship, the court must, ***with due regard to Islamic law*** and the report and recommendations of the Family Advocate, which must take into account ***Islamic norms and values, consider the welfare and best interests of the child.***

(2) … the non-custodian parent must be afforded reasonable access to a child.
(3) In the absence of both parents, for any reason … the court must, in accordance with Islamic law, in awarding or granting custody (*al-hadānah*) or guardianship (*al-walāyah*) of minor children, award or grant custody or guardianship to any person as the court deems appropriate, in all the circumstances.
(4)(a) An order regarding the custody or guardianship of, or access to, a child made in terms of this Act, may … at any time be rescinded or varied or, in the case of access to a child, be suspended by a court on good cause shown.
(b) If an enquiry is instituted by the Family Advocate … the court must consider the report and recommendations of the Family Advocate ***concerning the welfare of minor children in accordance with Islamic Law*** before making an order … (my emphasis).

Muslim children begin their first (natural) phase of life under female custody. Once this (limited) period terminates, they enter into a new phase under male guardianship. Having regard to both the Islamic and South African law contexts, clause 10(1) of the MMB, although clearly taking into consideration the best interests of the child, does not specify which parent, if any, is to be awarded custody or/and guardianship nor does it stipulate the period of such custody and/or guardianship. It can, therefore, be inferred that either parent (therefore equal rights), both parents, neither parent, or someone other than the parents can be granted custody and/or guardianship since the term 'parent' is not used. While Islamic law is not spelt out in the MMB, it is also important that any decision in terms of the MMB be guided by considerations and interpretations of Islamic law. However, Islamic jurisprudence recognises only the father as the guardian of his minor children and provides that divorced fathers (and relatives) of children generally have both more (albeit supervisory) guardianship rights and more (financial) duties than their (caretaker) divorced mothers (and relatives). Women are usually accorded the initial (and, therefore, also limited) and natural role of having custody of children.

Islamic law, rather than necessarily distinguishing between the terms 'custody' and 'guardianship', effectively treats custody *as* (a form of) guardianship. The mother's (right to and *duty* of) custody of her child during the early years of its life is, therefore, limited and is regarded as one (usually the first) of three categories of guardianship of the child. However, this does not mean that Muslim women and men have equal rights in this regard. The other two categories of guardianship, namely, with respect to the education and property of the child, are usually entrusted to the father (or other male relatives). Paradoxically, the fact that the mother may be financially competent and is allowed by Islamic law to own property and to control her own assets unaided, is of little consequence. The mother of the child, whether married to or divorced from the father, always has the first claim (and duty) to custody of her (infant) child. Although not explicitly stated and with due regard to the father's unilateral duty to support his children and the mother's initial right to custody, it seems that the MMB also supports the Islamic law view that custody be awarded to the wife (mother) in the first instance, as well as in the case of interim custody.[72] Custody may, however, be entrusted to someone other

[72] Muslim Marriages Bill, clauses 10(1) and (2) read with clauses 11(2)(c)(ii) and 9(3)(g)(i) (interim custody).

than the mother, and this person may also be the father. In terms of the MMB, in the absence of both parents, a court must also consider Islamic law when awarding custody or guardianship to anyone else.[73]

9.3.4.2 Practical Challenges: Access, Maintenance and Paternity Leave

It becomes apparent from Sect. 9.3.4.1 that Islamic law appears to promote the 'maternal preference' or 'tender years' principle in custody matters, which often implies the absence of fathers in the lives of young children. However, this principle has been challenged in the courts,[74] which have emphasised that parenting is a gender-neutral function. Although this therefore implies that both parents have equal rights in raising their children, practical reality appears to dictate otherwise. For example, access, maintenance and paternity leave are not necessarily unrelated factors in South Africa. The Maintenance Act (1998) provides socio-economic relief for children who have been neglected by their parents and responsible guardians. It places a responsibility on the parents to support the child financially and to ensure that they have basic nutrition and shelter. If they fail to do so, the State may be obliged to step in. The Department of Justice has recently concluded the process of amending the Maintenance Act. Legislation[75] to deal with maintenance defaulters hopes to enable credit bureaux to track them down and black-list them. Fathers who default in paying child maintenance are often denied access and visitation rights by mothers. South African law only provides for maternity leave and makes no provision for paternity leave. This state of affairs is currently being challenged[76]—about half of South Africa's over eighteen million children grow up without a father (who may be alive), and one of the main reasons cited for absent fathers not being involved in the lives of their children is a lack of money.

9.3.4.3 Re-marriage, Inter-religious Marriages and Sexual Orientation

It appears that although Islamic law may be interpreted to imply that a mother may lose her limited right to custody if she marries a man who is a stranger (that is, not a blood relative) to the child, it is doubtful that such rule will withstand constitutional scrutiny, especially if it would not be in the child's best interests that

73 Muslim Marriages Bill, clause 10(3).

74 See *Potgieter v. Potgieter* [2007] SCA 47 (RSA), pp. 16–17 [para 26].

75 The Maintenance Amendment Bill 2014 [B 16—2014] was tabled in Parliament on 5 November 2014. It was subsequently (on 7 September 2015) signed into law by the President as the Maintenance Amendment Act No 9 of 2015.

76 See Sosibo 2015, p. 16.

the mother be so debarred. Islamic law entitles a mother to custody irrespective of her Christian or Jewish (*kitabi*) religion in the case of inter-religious marriages. However, in South Africa, inter-religious marriages, although only permitted for Muslim men, do occur among Muslims of both sexes, as do gay marriages (to a lesser extent). It is anticipated that with recognition of Muslim marriages some discrimination is inevitable because of the nature of religious law, despite the guarantee of the rights to equality based on sexual orientation or religious freedom. It may, for example, be argued that while the MMB is only available to heterosexual Muslim couples, that nothing would preclude same-sex Muslim gay or lesbian couples and inter-religious couples (where the man is not Muslim or the woman is a follower of a religion other than Christianity or Judaism) from entering into a *nikah* (Muslim marriage) and thereafter legally entering into a civil union or marriage in South Africa, thereby deriving civil benefits and protections. However, I am doubtful that if a custody challenge is, for example, brought by a Muslim woman in an inter-religious marriage with a non-Muslim man who has not converted to Islam, or who has herself converted from Islam to, especially, another *kitabi* religion, that a gender-stereotyping disqualification of this nature would survive a constitutional challenge.

Furthermore, Muslim children usually follow the faith of their father upon birth. Although the MMB[77] defines a 'Muslim' as '… a person who believes in the oneness of Allah and who believes in the Holy Messenger Muhammad as the final prophet and who has faith in all the essentials of Islam …', and although Islam may be inferred from the application of Islamic law therein, the MMB does not give a clear indication of the child's religion. In the *Kotze* case,[78] although the parents were in agreement, the Court, as upper guardian of the child, refused to sanction their joint wishes contained in a settlement agreement in a secular divorce with regard to the (Christian) religious education of their 3-year-old son. It is contended that although both Article 14(1) of the CRC and section 15 of the Constitution assure children a choice of religion and section 18 assures everyone (including children) the right to freedom of association, the outcome of a similar case could be different today. The *Kotze* case preceded the Children's Act and, in addition, once religious (Muslim) marriages are formally recognised and end in divorce, it will be even more complicated for the courts to determine in an inter-faith marriage (regarding which the MMB strategically remains silent) the possibly competing claims of the parents as to whose religion their children will follow.

---

77 See clause 1.

78 *Kotze v. Kotze* 2003 (3) SA 628 (T), and see text to note 67.

9.3.4.4 Access, Periods of Custody and Guardianship

Section 10(2) of the MMB provides for the non-custodian parent to have reasonable access to the child, subject to a court's decision in that regard which must have been made considering the welfare and best interests of the child (section 10(1)).

The provisions of the MMB do not specify the periods of custody and guardianship and, therefore, guidance must be sought in Islamic law rulings which may also vary according to the school of law. This leaves much room for leeway because the mother's period of custody of her child, in respect of which there is no limitation in the Qur'an and Sunna, has been determined as a result of the *ijtihad* (independent reasoning or interpretation) of early jurists who also held different views in this regard. According to these views, although women are usually denied custody of their children beyond a certain age, depending on the gender of the child and the school(s) of law (*madhhabs*) to which the family (or each parent) subscribes, the child's wishes are also taken into consideration.

While the guardianship rights of the father are often viewed as depriving a woman of the right to bring up her children as an equal parent, the reality is that there are many Muslim women who are forced to, or may even choose to, leave their children with their father upon divorcing him or re-marrying. These women, instead of blaming themselves, could view this 'freedom' from, or 'rejection' of, 'natural' parental responsibilities and duties as a guilt-free re-balancing of priorities and a redressing of past inequalities rather than reverse discrimination, or even as being liberated from a burdensome role. Women in South Africa who are delaying motherhood, or deciding against it altogether, because of career options and the patriarchal nature of current unequal maternity and paternity laws, may find leaving children with fathers to be a better option. Parenting plans (detailed in Sect. 9.3.3.4 above) in South Africa can be tailored so that women can have the best of both worlds.

9.3.4.5 Maintenance (*Nafaqa*)

Clause 11 of the MMB deals with the maintenance (*nafaqa*) of children as follows. The Islamic law understanding is that *nafaqa* covers maintenance generally owed by a man to his dependants, and it is also understood as such in terms of the MMB. Clauses 11(2)(a) and (b) of the MMB expressly stipulate that the provisions of the Maintenance Act apply, 'with the changes required by the context' (clause 11(1)), if a Maintenance Court makes a maintenance order. This means that a court must take into consideration the Islamic law provisions in this regard and as outlined in clause 11(2) of the MMB. In a nutshell, upon the termination of his marriage, the obligations of a father with regard to his children do not also come to an end. In terms of the MMB, a father is obliged to maintain his daughters 'until they are married' (clause 11(2)(b)(i)), and his sons 'until they reach the age of majority or otherwise for the period that they are in need of support' (clause 11(2)(b)(ii)). This would include a divorced daughter (presumably until her re-marriage) and an adult male child who may, for example, be chronically ill, both of whom may be in need of further support. In accordance with the broader guardianship rights and duties of the father, more generous provision is made for support of children in the MMB, which stipulates that his duty to maintain children born of any marriage continues when the marriage ends and '… includes the provision of food, clothing, separate accommodation, medical care and education' (clause 11(2)(c)(iv)). In terms of the MMB the amount of maintenance for which a father is responsible will vary from case to case and 'must be' determined in a 'fair and just' (clause 11(3)) manner and with due regard to 'his means' and the special 'need of support' for older male children (clause 11(2)(b)(ii)) and older daughters. This would, therefore, also exclude the child who is in possession of his/her own wealth. While a father, for example, may himself suffer from a chronic illness which may prevent him from providing maintenance, it is expected that he make a concerted effort to ensure that he acquires the means to be able to earn a living when he is not so incapacitated.

9.3.4.6 The Marital Status of Parents and the Maintenance and Guardianship of Children Born in and Out of Wedlock and Post-divorce

As indicated in Sect. 9.3.3.1, prior to the Children's Act, children born of couples married only in terms of religious laws or rites, given that these marriages were (and still are) unrecognised, were accorded the status of 'illegitimacy'. It is only since 2005 that Muslim children in South Africa are no longer labelled as 'illegitimate' even though their parents may be only religiously married to each other and these marriages still remain unrecognised. Their parents are referred to simply as being 'married' or 'unmarried'. In terms of section 20 of the Children's Act (section 1 of which broadly defines 'marriage' to include Muslim marriages), a child is regarded as being born of married parents 'if the biological parents were legally married to each other at the time of the child's conception, or at his or her birth, or at any time between conception and birth'.[79] In terms of section 38 of the Children's Act, even if parents marry each other at any time subsequent to the birth of the child, the child will still be regarded as being born of married parents. The Children's Act has not only removed the status of 'illegitimacy' accorded to Muslim children in the past, but also accords both parents a legal duty to support them. Two practical questions that, therefore, arise concern, first, the legitimacy of a child conceived during marriage where the ex-wife's pregnancy is only ascertained during her mandatory waiting period (*idda*) after she has been irrevocably divorced, and, secondly, the legal position of the unmarried father and his illegitimate child. In the first case, the child is technically born 'out of wedlock' but in reality it is assumed that the child is her husband's especially since she may also

[79] See also Boezaart 2010, pp. 94–95.

not re-marry during the *idda* period. This of course does not rule out the possibility of pregnancy resulting from a sexual encounter with somebody else. In the event of a divorce, the MMB clearly limits the husband's duty to support, and issues of interim custody or access, to a 'child born of the *marriage*'.[80] Maintenance and guardianship of such children is, therefore, also not directly provided for in the proposed MMB and its recognition of Muslim marriages. In the event of a dispute of this nature arising after an irrevocable separation, Islamic law provides that the parentage of children of spouses, besides being established through marriage, may also be established through acknowledgement by the father or evidence (for example, through paternity testing or the witnessing of the birth by a midwife).[81]

Regarding the legal position of unmarried fathers in the second practical question, prior to the Children's Act, unmarried fathers had the right to go to court to ask for access to, and custody or guardianship of, their children.[82] In terms of the Children's Act, fathers, whether regarded in law as married or unmarried, automatically have parental responsibilities and rights if certain specified conditions are present. With its new provisions on the parental responsibilities and rights of unmarried fathers relating to access to, and the custody or guardianship of, their children, section 21 of the Children's Act, which deals with parental responsibilities and rights of unmarried fathers, merely *aims* to, but does not categorically, give unmarried fathers the same parental responsibility that biological mothers have. For example, if an unmarried father was residing with the biological mother of his child at the time of its birth, they will have equal rights (section 21(1)(a)); if not, the father is able to obtain such rights through his consent to be identified as the child's father (section 21(1)(b)(i)). An opinion[83] has been expressed that, in spite of the increased recognition afforded biological fathers as legal parents, this may not be enough because the Children's Act still draws a distinction between biological mothers and biological fathers as far as the automatic allocation of parental responsibilities and rights is concerned, and that therefore an argument for an equalisation of their legal positions is both constitutionally justifiable and ultimately in the best interests of their child.[84]

Regarding the legal position of illegitimate children in the second practical question, Muslim children that are illegitimate (born out of wedlock) because of

---

80 My emphasis. See, respectively, clauses 11(2)(c)(iv) and 9(3)(g)(i). See also text to note 63.

81 Nasir 2002, pp. 145, 150. See also section 21 of the Children's Act.

82 The Natural Fathers of Children Born out of Wedlock Act No 86 of 1997. This Act has been repealed by the Children's Act.

83 Louw 2010, pp. 156, 195.

84 In *S v. J* (695/10) [2010] ZASCA 139 (judgment delivered on 19 November 2010) the Supreme Court of Appeal held that the appellant, the father of a child (a girl) born out of wedlock (her mother had died shortly after her birth), had full parental responsibilities and rights in terms of section 18 of the Children's Act. The Court further held that the child should permanently reside with her father and that her (maternal) grandparents were entitled to have regular contact with her.

the unlawful sexual intercourse (*zina*) of their parents continue to be socially discriminated against and legally (financially) prejudiced because of traditional, but popular, interpretations of Islamic law to their detriment. Islamic law does not allow such children to be legitimated by the subsequent marriage of their parents. Furthermore, Islamic law also does not recognise any ties of maintenance between an illegitimate child and its putative father (or his relatives), placing this burden on the mother (and her relatives) as the child is considered to be related only to her.[85] It is contended that, although the MMB is silent on such children and places an emphasis on children born of a 'marriage', as indicated above, emphasis should shift from the status of illegitimate children to their best interests for the following reasons: they are born through no fault of their own; South African law no longer discriminates between legitimate and illegitimate children and emphasises the best interests of all children; and the father has to take some, even if only financial, responsibility for his role in the child's conception.

Clause 11(2)(c)(iii) of the MMB provides, in accordance with Islamic law, that, following the birth of her child, a divorced mother may breastfeed her baby for the duration of the nursing ('fosterage') period (which can be for up to 2 years) regardless of whether she is irrevocably divorced from the child's father. She is entitled to separate remuneration while she breastfeeds her own child. Clause 11(2)(c)(ii) of the MMB provides that during the nursing period following an irrevocable divorce, the father must maintain and house both the child and mother.

It is clear that the areas of guardianship, care, access and maintenance in relation to children often overlap, and for this reason it is also very difficult to strictly separate the position of the mother from that of her children. For example, while maintenance for the child is theoretically generously provided by the father, such maintenance ought to be inextricably linked with that given to the mother during the post-divorce period that their children are in her custody, and this symbiosis ought to lead to an increase of the usually limited amount and period of post-divorce support for the mother. It is, however, contended that, with some exceptions, the inference that mothers may stand to substantially benefit through children in their care is currently unfounded in South Africa. Although the Islamic ideal, this is simply not a material reality for many South African Muslim women who, instead, often have to step into the shoes of the father when he reneges on his duties in this regard. It is, therefore, hoped that the provisions of the MMB will be able to rectify this.

In accordance with the trend already established by South African courts in terms of Rule 43 concerning interim maintenance, but more strictly in accordance with Shari'a, the MMB provides that, following the registration of an irrevocable divorce[86] and after failed attempts at compulsory mediation,[87] in the event of a

---

[85] Nasir 2002, pp. 145–146, 150–151.

[86] In the form of a repudiation (*talaq*) (clause 9(3)(g)) or judicial divorce (*faskh*) (clauses 9(5)(b) and (c)).

[87] See Muslim Marriages Bill, clause 12(1) together with clauses 4, 9(3)(e) and 9(5)(b).

dispute and before the adjudication thereof by the court, given the urgent nature of these cases, spouses may make an application to seek interim relief pending litigation (*pendente lite*) in matters pertaining to interim custody of, or access to, minor children of the marriage or '*for the payment of maintenance*' (clause 9(3)(g)(i)), a contribution to costs (clause 9(3)(g)(ii)), and maintenance for the wife during the *idda* period (clause 9(3)(g)(iii)). I have emphasised 'for the payment of maintenance' to highlight the fact that, given the Islamic law unilateral duty of the father to provide maintenance for his children, and the initial right of custody on the part of the mother, it is contended that if a court grants the mother interim custody, the father is not only responsible for the child's maintenance but also for remuneration of the mother who has custody during this period and, further, that this is separate from and in addition to the *idda* maintenance of the wife.

9.3.4.7 How Is the Best Interests Rule to Be Applied When Muslim Marriages Are Recognised?

It is a fact that all rights, including competing rights like freedom of religion and equality, although guaranteed in the Bill of Rights, may be limited. Section 12 of the Children's Act allows, but regulates, social, cultural and religious practices, such as those relating to the marriageable age. It is also a fact that the legal age of marriage in South Africa, not only differs from Islamic law but that Islamic law also differs from it in allowing a guardian to contract the marriage of a minor as explained in Sect. 9.3.3.5 above. There is no doubt that each system can defend the legality of its rules in this regard. I contend that the solution does not lie in trying to prove that it would be in the Muslim child's best interests that his or her rights be judged according to Islamic law and not according to South African law, as has been proposed by Vahed.[88] This would merely amount to abstractly or clinically pitting the competing South African and Islamic law rules against each other to see which one may be in the child's best interests. The way to use this test when the MMB does become law is, first, to ask whether regard was had to the best interests concept and, secondly, whether it was applied in determining whether (in our example) a minor child of a particular age can marry and whether there were any other motivating factors that supported the need for an early marriage. For example, although sex outside of marriage is not permitted in Islam, South African law allows minors (between 12 and 16 years of age) to have consensual sex. If, as a result, the child becomes pregnant, she may not want an abortion for religious reasons although it may be legally permitted for minors in South Africa to have one on request.[89]

---

[88] Vahed 1999, p. 375.

[89] See section 129(1) of the Children's Act and section 2(1)(b)(i–iv) of the Choice on Termination of Pregnancy Act No 92 of 1996.

Although South African law no longer discriminates between legitimate and illegitimate children, the minor mother wants her unborn and herself to be protected from further societal and religious stigmatisation and may therefore opt for early marriage instead. Imams are already officiating at such early 'MGM' (must get married) marriages of pregnant teenagers.[90] In addition, early marriage may be encouraged to prevent MGM marriages. Heaton,[91] in a contribution dealing with the approach that should be adopted when applying the concept of 'the best interests of the child' and evaluating the individual factors that are used in determining what is in the child's best interests, gives sound advice in support of such an approach when she proposes that:

> … an individualised, contextualised and child-centred determination of the child's best interests is required. In view of our constitutional values of tolerance of and respect for diversity and pluralism, it is further submitted that we must move away from a mainly Judaeo-Christian, Eurocentric interpretation of 'the best interests of the child' to an approach that takes the cultural and religious circumstances, interests and needs of the individual child into account. It is concluded that all factors that are shown to be relevant because they have, or could have, a negative or positive impact on the individual child should be taken into account in a contextualised child-centred way without reducing other constitutionally-protected rights and interests to nothing.

9.4 Conclusion

Today, a post-apartheid and democratic South Africa can boast of having a Constitution and a Children's Act that are among the most progressive in the world, and which benefit all of the country's children, including Muslim children. As a consequence, the concept of the 'best interests of the child' is a decisive factor in all legislation, including the proposed legislation on the recognition of Muslim marriages, where the welfare of the Muslim child is paramount.

The position of a Muslim child in South Africa is therefore unique. The Constitution and Children's Act, with the favourable interpretation of their provisions by the courts, including the Constitutional Court, assure a Muslim child of the secular protection of the law, whether or not the religious (monogamous or polygynous) marriage(s) of his or her parents will be formally recognised or he or she is born in or out of wedlock (illegitimate). The MMB has ensured that the limited rights guaranteed to children in terms of Islamic law will be utilised optimally, and in so doing will allow Islamic law rights to be upheld secularly with the force of law and with the co-operation of religious authorities. If the legislature fails to enact the MMB, it will mean that, for the children and their mothers for whom the MMB is intended to be of most benefit, the *status quo* of non-recognition will

[90] See Moosa 2009, p. 81.

[91] Heaton 2009, pp. 1–18.

remain. However, this does not detract from the fact that the reality for Muslim men and women is that they live in a democratic South Africa, and as citizens have recourse to the secular laws of a State which already incorporates Muslim marriages within its protective ambit. With or without recognised MPL, Muslim women and their children have been accorded relief when seeking redress for the hardships caused by the consequences of the non-recognition of their Islamic marriages which have ended in death or divorce. Children, if they cannot depend on their parents' protection, can independently invoke the aid of the courts, whose judges are expected to act as their upper guardian, and can also rely on State protection. Ultimately, their best interests, a principle that permeates all law, must prevail. The MMB, if and when enacted into law, must defer to the provisions of the Constitution as the supreme law, as must the Children's Act. Although all three laws emphasise the paramountcy of the best interests of the child, the Constitution treats the best interests of the child as a principle and as an independent human right within the 'mini-charter' of children's rights that it contains, while the Children's Act goes further by providing interpretative guidelines through its own best interests standard. While the interpretation of the provisions of the MMB will therefore benefit from, and be guided by, recent case law and jurisprudence based on the Children's Act, this does not detract from the value of the case law that preceded it. Greater judicial flexibility and activism on the part of the courts is also anticipated with the formal recognition of Muslim marriages, and this will hopefully add a further unique dimension to the existing law. Ultimately, when a court sits as the upper guardian of minor children in custody matters, it is both duty bound, and has wide powers, to establish what is or is not in the best interests of minor or dependent children. Furthermore, without in any way diminishing the value of the recommendations made by the family advocate or expert evidence in assisting the court with ultimately determining the best interests of a child, it is submitted that when dealing with custody (care) cases involving Muslim children, given diverse Islamic law interpretations and perspectives, just as the courts are not bound to act in accordance with a family advocate's recommendation, decision-makers should remain neutral and impartial when it comes to questions of religion. They should guard against the following: projecting their own value systems into their decisions and evaluations when they consider the effects of the beliefs of parents belonging to religious minorities; by using the best interests standard unfairly prejudicing children of parents who are observers of minority faiths; and according the value judgments of religious experts and the evidence of Muslim religious experts undue weight when they are called upon to act as witnesses (which they will be because the MMB does not spell out what the Islamic law entails). Support for such a view can be adduced from a case[92] that was

[92] See *Potgieter v. Potgieter* [2007] SCA 47 (RSA), p. 11 [para 16].

decided before the coming into operation of section 7(1) (best interest standard) of the Children's Act.

Finally, Sachs J, in his judgment in *S v. M*,[93] eloquently sums up what to my mind is an ideal South African position as follows:

> Every child has his or her own dignity. If a child is to be constitutionally imagined as an individual with a distinctive personality, and not merely as a miniature adult waiting to reach full size, he or she cannot be treated as a mere extension of his or her parents, umbilically destined to sink or swim with them. The unusually comprehensive and emancipatory character of section 28 presupposes that in our new dispensation the sins and traumas of fathers and mothers should not be visited on their children.

Although the SALRC initiative regarding children overlapped with that regarding Muslim marriages, the former has resulted in a new Children's Act while the latter has not as yet led to any Act. Given that there is judicial support to ensure that the presidency and related bodies uphold their end of the legislative bargain, it is hoped that legislation will soon follow.

References

Bernardo C (2015) Womens' rights body compared to pet cat, IOL News, 2 December 2015. www.iol.co.za/news/crime-courts/womens-rights-body-compared-to-pet-cat-1954233#.Vl-PRKmukdQ. Accessed 27 Feb 2016

Boezaart T (2010) Law of Persons, 5th edn. Juta, Cape Town

Boezaart T (2014) The Position of Minor and Dependent Children of Divorcing and Divorced Spouses or Civil Union Partners. In: Heaton J (ed) The Law of Divorce and Dissolution of Life Partnerships in South Africa. Juta, Cape Town, pp 171–227

Bosman-Sadie H, Corrie L (2013) A Practical Approach to the Children's Act, 2nd edn. LexisNexis, Durban

Department of Justice and Constitutional Development (2015) The Office of the Family Advocate. www.justice.gov.za/FMAdv/f_main.htm. Accessed 28 Feb 2015

Hall K et al (2014) Demography of South Africa's Children. In: Mathews S et al (eds) South African Child Gauge 2014, part 3: Children Count - The Numbers, Children's Institute, University of Cape Town, Cape Town, pp 90–93. www.ci.org.za/depts/ci/pubs/pdf/general/gauge2014/ChildGauge2014.pdf. Accessed 25 Feb 2015

Heaton J (2009) An individualised, contextualised and child-centred determination of the child's best interests, and the implications of such an approach in the South African context. Journal for Juridical Science 34(2):1–18

Isaacs R (2015) MMB laws contradict Shari'ah: attorney. VOC News, VOCFM, 6 March 2015. www.vocfm.co.za/mmb-laws-contradict-shariah-attorney. Accessed 6 March 2015

Jamieson L et al (2014) Legislative Developments 2013/2014. In: Mathews S et al (eds) South African Child Gauge 2014, part 1: Children and Law Reform, Children's Institute, University of Cape Town, Cape Town, pp 13–20. www.ci.org.za/depts/ci/pubs/pdf/general/gauge2014/ChildGauge2014.pdf. Accessed 25 Feb 2015

Louw A (2010) The constitutionality of a biological father's recognition as a parent. Potchefstroom Electron Law J (PER/PELJ) 13(3):156–206

[93] In *S v. M (Centre for Child Law as Amicus Curiae)* 2008 (3) SA 232 (CC), p. 11 [para 18].

Moosa N (1998a) Religious Laws Affecting Children: Muslim Law. In: South African Law Commission, Issue Paper 13, Project 110: The Review of the Child Care Act, First Issue Paper, 18 April 1998, pp 123–132. www.justice.gov.za/salrc/ipapers/ip13_prj110_1998.pdf. Accessed 25 Feb 2015

Moosa N (1998b) Muslim Personal Laws Affecting Children: Diversity, Practice and Implications for a New Children's Code for South Africa. S Afr Law J 115(3):479–492

Moosa N (2009) Polygynous Muslim Marriages in South Africa: Their Potential Impact on the Incidence of HIV/AIDS. Potchefstroom Electron Law J (PER/PELJ) 12(3):65–95

Moosa N (2011) Unveiling the Mind: The Legal Position of Women in Islam - A South African Context, 2nd edn. Juta, Cape Town

Moosa N (2014) The Dissolution of a Muslim Marriage by Divorce. In: Heaton J (ed) The Law of Divorce and Dissolution of Life Partnerships in South Africa. Juta, Cape Town, pp 281–354

Nasir JJ (2002) The Islamic Law of Personal Status, vol XXIII. Arab and Islamic Laws Series, 3rd edn. Kluwer Law International, The Hague

Schäfer L (2011) Child Law in South Africa - Domestic and International Perspectives. LexisNexis, Durban

van Schalkwyk N (2009) Maintenance for Children. In: Boezaart T (ed) Child Law in South Africa. Juta, Cape Town, pp 38–61

Skelton A (2013) Children. In: Currie I, De Waal J (eds) The Bill of Rights Handbook, 6th edn. Juta, Cape Town, pp 598–623

Sosibo K (2015) One man fights for all fathers. Mail & Guardian 31(22):16 (29 May 2015)

South African Law Reform Commission (2003) Project 59: Islamic Marriages and Related Matters, Report, July 2003. www.justice.gov.za/salrc/reports/r_prj59_2003jul.pdf. Accessed 9 Feb 2015

Statistics South Africa (2004) Census 2001: Primary tables South Africa Census '96 and 2001 compared, Report No. 03-02-04, statssa 2001, p 25. www.statssa.gov.za/census01/html/RSAPrimary.pdf. Accessed 9 Feb 2015

Statistics South Africa (2012) Statistical release (Revised) P0301.4 2011, statssa 2012. www.statssa.gov.za/Publications/P03014/P030142011.pdf. Accessed 9 Feb 2015

Vahed MA (1999) Should the question: "What is in a child's best interests?" be judged according to the child's own cultural and religious perspectives? The case of the Muslim child. Comp Int Law J S Afr (CILSA) 32:976–990

van der Walt G (2009) Children's rights. In: Govindjee A et al (eds) Introduction to Human Rights Law. LexisNexis, Durban, pp 231–238

Chapter 10
Tunisia

Souhayma Ben Achour

Abstract Tunisia has long occupied a special position among the family law regimes of Muslim jurisdictions. The legal reforms introduced upon the initial codification of personal status law in the 1950s have brought about a departure from Islamic legal doctrine in many areas of family law. While the earliest legislative steps initially focused on questions of marriage and divorce, parental care has also seen far-reaching reforms, especially in the 1960s when the best interests of the child was elevated to the paramount consideration in awarding custody following a divorce. Ever since, judicial practice has echoed the focus on the best interests of the child and has not only applied the concept consistently, but also developed it further. At the same time however, Tunisian statutory law also remains faithful to Islamic legal tradition in that, in certain aspects of both custody and guardianship, it upholds a gendered division of parenting functions and defines the right to custody within the limits of guardianship. In 1993, the decision to grant the majority of guardianship powers to whoever serves as the child's custodian was therefore considered a significant step in the country's parental care regime and an advancement for the rights of mothers. Finally, in questions of cross-border family disputes and private international law, while courts do in general adhere to the significance of putting the child's best interests first, a certain hesitance can still be detected especially when it comes to enforcing foreign custody orders because of their alleged incompatibility with Tunisian public policy.

Keywords Best interests of the child · Custody · Guardianship · Tunisia · Legal reform · Private international law

The editors of this book wish to thank Global Affairs Canada for providing a first translation of this originally French text and Tess Chemnitzer and Shyam Kapila who have revised and edited this translation.
The author is Professor of Law at the Faculty of Law and Political Sciences in Tunis.

S. Ben Achour (✉)
Faculty of Law and Political Sciences, Université de Tunis El Manar, Tunis, Tunisia
e-mail: benachoursouhayma@ymail.com

N. Yassari et al. (eds.), *Parental Care and the Best Interests of the Child in Muslim Countries*, DOI 10.1007/978-94-6265-174-6_10

Contents

List of Main Abbreviations Used

AJT	Actualités juridiques tunisiennes (Tunisian legal news)
Bull. civ.	Bulletin des arrêts de la Cour de cassation, chambres civiles (Bulletin of the judgments of the Court of Cassation, civil divisions)
JCL	Jurisclasseur
JOT	Journal officiel tunisien (Tunisian Official Gazette)
JORT	Journal officiel de la République tunisienne (Official Gazette of the Tunisian Republic)
RCDIP	Revue critique de droit international privé (Critical review of private international law)
RIDC	Revue internationale de droit comparé (International Journal of Comparative Law)
RJL	Revue de jurisprudence et de législation (Journal of jurisprudence and legislation)
RTD	Revue tunisienne de droit (Tunisian law journal)
TPI	Tribunal de première instance (Court of First Instance)

10.1 Introduction

10.1.1 The Relationship Between Islamic Law and Positive Law

'It is an acknowledged fact that personal status is intimately connected to the mores, mentality, culture and civilization of each people or nation or even larger communities such as Islam. It is rooted in the depths of the people's soul.'[1] Family law in most Arab-Muslim countries has remained relatively faithful to the prescriptions of Islamic law.

[1] Déprez 1990, p. 35.

Tunisian law constitutes an exception. On 13 August 1956, the young Tunisian legislature promulgated an innovative Personal Status Code which deviated from the traditional solutions of Islamic law.[2] The legislature prohibited polygamy and made it a criminal offence. It abolished the institution of the matrimonial guardian and required the consent of both spouses. It prohibited repudiation and imposed the judicial dissolution of marriage on a totally egalitarian basis.

The reform then continued in small steps. The Law of 1 August 1957[3] made the marriage contract a solemn act. The Law of 4 March 1958[4] allowed adoption and made it a privileged way of protecting the child lacking a family. The Law of 3 June 1966[5] repealed the order of custody devolution directly derived from Maliki rite and made the child's best interests the sole criterion for its award. On 28 October 1998, a law was promulgated which made way for natural filiation in Tunisian law, allowing proof of paternity based on the genetic finger print test and without any bond of marriage.[6]

At the time of its promulgation, the Code was hailed in the West. It was considered a legislative monument[7] and a model for social progress,[8] and perceived as ushering the first signs of an Arab Spring.[9]

In the Arab-Muslim world, it has been received in a more moderate way. In Tunisia, it has not been well accepted by a large segment of the population. Some traces of Islamic law, however, subsist in Tunisian family law. The Personal Status Code maintained the inequality in inheritance between brother and sister. Islamic law still permeates the rules governing the relationship between parents and children. Guardianship is exercised primarily by the father. The mother cannot be the marital guardian of her minor children. The jurisprudence sometimes deals with any silence of the Code or its lacunae by turning to Islamic law.[10]

---

[2] Decree of 13 August 1956 Promulgating the Tunisian Personal Status Code, JOT No. 104 of 1956, p. 1742.

[3] Law No. 57-3 of 1 August 1957 Regulating Civil Status, JORT No. 2 and 3 of 30 July and 2 August 1957.

[4] Law No. 58-27 of 4 March 1958 Concerning Public Guardianship, *Kafāla* and Adoption, JORT No. 19 of 1958, p. 236.

[5] Law No. 66-42 of 3 June 1966 Amending the Personal Status Code, JORT No. 24 of 1966, p. 880.

[6] Law No. 98-75 of 28 October 1998 Concerning the Allocation of a Patronymic Family Name to Abandoned Children and Those of Unknown Parentage, JORT No. 87 of 30 October 1998, p. 2119.

[7] Colomer 1957, p. 117.

[8] Ben Achour Y 1992, p. 203.

[9] Benoist-Mechin 1958.

[10] On the relationship between Islamic law and Tunisian law, see Belknani 2010, pp. 79 and 99; Ben Achour S 2011, p. 17; Ben Halima 2000, p. 107; Ben Jemia 2008, p. 261; Ben Jemia 2012, p. 154; Bostanji 2009, p. 7; Bouguerra 2000, p. 7; Charfi 1973, p. 11; Charfi 1983, p. 405; Ladjili 1972, p. 25; Mellouli 2010, p. 79; Mezghani 1975, p. 53; Mezghani 2008, p. 345; Meziou 1984, p. 253; Meziou 1992, p. 247.

10.1.2 The Integration of International Standards

Notably, the framework of international human rights is the source of the Tunisian law. Two United Nations conventions are of particular interest in this study: that of 18 December 1979 on the Elimination of All Forms of Discrimination against Women and that on the Rights of the Child of 20 November 1989. Both have been ratified by Tunisia.[11] This shows a willingness to adhere to the universal values espoused by the two conventions.

But this accession was made with a certain distrust in the conventional standards. The Tunisian government, in ratifying the Convention of 18 December 1979, had issued numerous reservations. These reservations particularly concerned Article 16, whose purpose is to encourage the States to undertake to ensure equality between parents in their relationships with their children.[12]

An important step has since been taken by Tunisian law. Indeed, the reservations that the Tunisian government had made upon the ratification of the Convention, notably towards Article 16, have been lifted by the Decree-Law of 24 October 2011.[13]

The reservations and declarations formulated by Tunisia concerning the principles prescribed by the UN Convention on the Rights of the Child of 20 November 1989 also show some resistance to international standards. Upon ratification of the Convention, Tunisia had entered reservations and a declaration. According to the declaration, 'the Government of the Republic of Tunisia declares that it shall not,

[11] The Convention of 1979 on the Elimination of All Forms of Discrimination against Women has been ratified by Law No. 85-68 of 12 July 1985, JORT No. 54 of 1985, p. 915. It has been published by Decree No. 91-1821 of 25 November 1991, JORT No. 85 of 1991, p. 1956. The United Nations Convention on the Rights of the Child has been ratified by Law No. 91-92 of 29 November 1991, JORT No. 82 of 3 December 1991, p 1890. It has been published by Decree No. 91-1865 of 10 December 1991, JORT No. 84 of 10 December 1991, pp. 1946–1952.

[12] Indeed, according to Article 16(1)(d) 'States Parties shall take all appropriate measures to eliminate discrimination against women in all matters relating to marriage and family relations and in particular shall ensure, on a basis of equality of men and women … [t]he same rights and responsibilities as parents, irrespective of their marital status, in matters relating to their children; in all cases the interests of the children shall be paramount.' According to Article 16(1)(f) 'States Parties shall take all appropriate measures to eliminate discrimination against women in all matters relating to marriage and family relations and in particular shall ensure, on a basis of equality of men and women … [t]he same rights and responsibilities with regard to guardianship … [and] trusteeship … where these concepts exist in national legislation; in all cases the interests of the children shall be paramount.' On this Convention, see La non-discrimination à l'égard des femmes entre la Convention de Copenhague et le discours identitaire, colloque, Tunis, 13–16 janvier 1989, UNESCO-CERP (Centre de recherches, d'études et de publications) Imprimerie officielle de la République tunisienne, 1989; Chekir 2000.

[13] Decree-Law of 24 October 2011, JORT No. 82 of 2011, p. 246. However, the general declaration has been maintained. The notification of reservations to the Secretary-General of the United Nations was first frozen by the governments of Hammadi Jebali and Ali Larayedh. The notification of reservations was unfrozen in April 2014 under the government of Mehdi Jomaa.

in implementation of this Convention, adopt any legislative or statutory decision that conflicts with the Tunisian Constitution.' This reference to the old Constitution was presumably directed at its Article 1, which stated that Islam is the state religion.[14] Several decisions emanating from the Tunisian courts were based on Article 1 of the former Constitution in asserting that a child born to a Muslim father must be raised in the religion of his father.[15] Islam, as the religion of the state, was also considered the religion of the nation and the individuals who constitute it. This seemed to mean that it was obligatory to raise a child born to a Muslim father in the Muslim religion of his father.

The examination of the declaration shows some willingness on the part of the Tunisian government to resist the principles prescribed by the Convention, notably the principle of freedom of conscience and religious liberty of the child.[16]

It should be noted, however, that the Tunisian government reversed its position: the declaration was withdrawn under the Law of 9 June 2008.[17] That is to say that Tunisian law is no longer attached, as in the past, to the obligation to raise the child in the religion of his father.

A direct consequence of the Tunisian ratification of the UN Convention on the Rights of the Child was the adoption of the Child Protection Act by the Law of 9 November 1995.[18] Inspired by Article 3 of the Convention,[19] the Act states in Article 4 that 'the best interests of the child must be a major consideration in all actions taken in respect of the child by the courts, administrative authorities or public or private institutions of social protection.' It prescribes the taking into account of the 'emotional, affective and physical needs of the child, his age, his state of health, his family environment and the different aspects concerning his situation.'

The Child Protection Act has two main components. It prescribes, first, measures intended to protect children in danger, that is to say children in situations that may threaten their health or physical or mental integrity, such as the loss of the parents, abandonment, neglect, maltreatment, sexual exploitation, economic

[14] Article 1 of the new Tunisian Constitution of 27 January 2014 retained the content of the old Article 1 of the 1959 Constitution and reinforced it by stipulating that it 'might not be amended'. Proceeding from a different philosophy, Article 2 of the new Constitution declares that 'Tunisia is a civil state based on citizenship, the will of the people, and the supremacy of law.'

[15] See infra.

[16] On this question, see Ben Jemia 2000, p. 274.

[17] Law No. 2008-36 of 9 June 2008 Approving the Withdrawal of Declaration No. 1 and the Reservations No. 1 and No. 3 Appended to Law No. 91-92 of 29 November 1991 ratifying the United Nations Convention on the Rights of the Child, JORT No. 49 of 2008, p. 1860.

[18] Law No. 95-92 of 9 November 1995 Concerning the Publication of the Child Protection Act, JORT No. 90 of 1995, p. 2095.

[19] Article 3 of the United Nations Convention on the Rights of the Child states that '[i]n all actions concerning children, whether undertaken by public or private social welfare institutions, courts of law, administrative authorities or legislative bodies, the best interests of the child shall be a primary consideration.'

exploitation or involvement in criminal activity. It later outlines specific measures intended to protect the child offender.

The dangerous situation in which the child might find itself may affect the regulation of custody and guardianship. Thus, maltreatment inflicted by the parent on the child may justify the implementation of one of the measures provided by the Child Protection Act, such as the child's placement in a foster family or a specialized social or educational institution.

This study will cover only the rules on custody and guardianship in 'normal' situations, outside any intervention of exceptional measures provided by the Act.

This study covers aspects of domestic law (Sect. 10.2) and aspects of private international law (Sect. 10.3). The rules applicable in domestic law and those concerning private international law remain influenced by Islamic law but are also calibrated according to the fundamental rights and the child's best interests.

10.2 Aspects of Domestic Law

The child's family protection is ensured by two different institutions in Islamic law: custody, on the one hand, and guardianship, on the other.

Custody can be considered a 'domestic' or internal protection of the child. Muslim authors define custody as the action of raising, educating and taking care of a minor unable to provide for his own elementary needs because of his low age. It involves housing and supervising the child and providing it with food, clothes, and body care.[20]

Guardianship, on the other hand, can be considered a 'social' or external protection of the child. It can be defined as the totality of rights and duties exercised by the legal representative of the child regarding its property and person.

The Tunisian law knows both institutions. The rules governing the award of custody and guardianship (Sect. 10.2.1) and their organization (Sect. 10.2.2) show that Tunisian law oscillates between fidelity to Islamic law and adherence to fundamental rights.

[20] On the definition of the notion of *ḥaḍāna* in Islamic law and positive law, see Béji 1977–1978, pp. 4, 5; Bousquet 1975, p. 17; Chammam 1982, p. 11; Charif Feller 1996, pp. 46–51; El Euch 1985, p. 43; Mechri 2002, p. 74; Sabbagh 1966–1967, p. 515; Sabbagh 1968, p. 617; Sabbagh 1969–1970, p. 49.

10.2.1 The Award of Custody and Guardianship

In a traditional conception directly inspired by Islamic law, custody is essentially a maternal prerogative for the protection of the child of low age, while guardianship is essentially a paternal prerogative.

> The pre-eminence of men becomes apparent in guardianship, while custody is preferably entrusted to women. This distinction could be explained by the fact that guardianship governs the dealings of the minor with the outside, especially regarding its assets, while custody consists in ensuring the child's education and protection in his home. But the 'agnatic' idea seems to be the most suitable to account for the fundamental reasons for the distinction. Guardianship is usually exercised by the agnates, while custody falls upon the maternal family.[21]

For Muslims authors, *ḥaḍāna* is 'a right given to the mother, then to women with prohibited degrees, consisting in raising the child during the period when he cannot do without the care of women.'[22] '*Ḥaḍāna* is a purely practical task not connected with paternal power. *Ḥaḍāna* is a simple duty to fulfil in respect of the child of low age, a duty which, because of its nature, the father cannot undertake. It is the continuation of the breastfeeding duty.'[23] The Maliki school prolongs the *ḥaḍāna* until puberty for the boy and until the consummation of marriage for the girl.[24] In the other schools of law, custody ends at about the age of seven for boys and at about nine for girls.[25]

Guardianship or *wilāya* is a prerogative of the father or, alternatively, the agnates. From birth, the child is placed under the regime of paternal guardianship. We have seen that it lasts in the Maliki rite until puberty for boys and until the consummation of marriage for girls. There is no distinction between sons and daughters in the Hanafi rite since the guardianship lasts, in both cases, until puberty. In the event of death or absence of the father, guardianship has to pass on to others who are, in the Maliki rite, the testamentary guardian and the judge and, in the Hanafi rite, the parents of the male, the parents in the maternal bloodline, and, finally, the judge. Guardianship is first exerted on the person of the child. It contains, in particular, the right to educate and the right to impose marriage.[26]

> Within the Muslim family, the father in his lifetime is granted two important prerogatives regarding the person of his pre-pubescent child, on the one hand, the right to consent to the child's marriage or to compel him—this is the matrimonial guardianship—and, on the other hand, the right to educate the child morally and intellectually—this is the educational guardianship.[27]

---

21 Pruvost 1975, p. 299.

22 Abou Zahra 1957, p. 432.

23 Ladjili 1972, p. 25.

24 Béji 1977–1978, pp. 18, 19.

25 Bousquet 1975, p. 17.

26 Milliot and Blanc 1987, no. 525.

27 Ferchichi 1983, p. 245.

It is exerted subsequently on the child's property. The father manages the child's property. He may, under certain conditions, conduct legal acts in his name and on his behalf.[28]

This traditional conception no longer seems to influence the positive law in Tunisia regarding the award of custody (Sect. 10.2.1.1), but still impregnates the award of guardianship (Sect. 10.2.1.2).

10.2.1.1 The Award of Custody

Under Tunisian law, custody is exercised by both parents during the marriage.[29] In the original version of the Personal Status Code, upon the dissolution of the marriage, custody was exercised primarily by the mother and the maternal family. Former Article 57 set a predetermined and hierarchical order of custody devolution.[30]

Tunisian law has totally abandoned this traditional conception. Since the reform of 3 June 1966,[31] when a marriage is dissolved by divorce, custody is granted to one of the parents or to a third person in the child's best interests. If it is dissolved by death, custody is entrusted to the surviving parent.[32] The criterion of the child's best interests has thus replaced the predetermined order of custody devolution.

The Tunisian Court of Cassation shows great vigilance in the implementation of the child's best interests criterion for the award of custody. The choice among the father, the mother or a third party is, according to a consistent line of jurisprudence, based on the criterion of the child's best interests. The trial court, as does the Court of Cassation, draws on the evidence put before it to determine what this is.

Thus, one can cite a decision of 19 November 1981, in which the Court of Cassation[33] held that the Court of Appeal had violated the law when granting cus-

[28] Milliot and Blanc 1987, no. 526-8.

[29] Sabbagh 1968, p. 617; Sabbagh 1969–1970, p. 49.

[30] This text stipulated that 'in case of a marriage breakdown by divorce or death, custody devolves in the following order upon: the mother of the child, his maternal grandmother, his maternal aunt, the maternal aunt of his mother, the paternal aunt of his mother, his paternal grandmother, his father, his sister, his paternal aunt, the maternal aunt of his father, the daughter of his brother, the daughter of his sister, the testamentary guardian, his brother, his paternal grandfather, his maternal grandfather, the son of his brother, his paternal uncle, his paternal cousin. The full brother has priority over the uterine brother, the uterine brother over the paternal half-brother, in all possible degrees. In case of parity of those entitled to custody, it will be awarded first to the most deserving and then to the eldest. The agnatic relatives of the child must be of the same religion as the child.'

[31] Law No. 66-42 of 3 June 1966 Amending the Personal Status Code.

[32] Law No. 66-42 of 3 June 1966 Amending the Personal Status Code abolished the list of those entitled to custody in case of marriage dissolution by death or divorce.

[33] Court of Cassation, 19 November 1981, no. 6522, Bull. civ. 1981, p. 259.

tody of the child to the father without having conducted a preliminary investigation when the maternal grandmother had also claimed custody.

In another decision of 5 July 1983,[34] the Court of Cassation quashed the decision of the Court of Appeal, which granted custody to the father following the death of the mother, without commenting on the contentions of the maternal grandmother regarding the mistreatment suffered by the child and without seeking to determine what constituted its best interests.

In a decision issued on 22 April 1997,[35] the Court of Cassation considered that 'the best interests of the child should be the main, pivotal and unique criterion for the award of custody in accordance with Article 67 of the Personal Status Code.' Based on this parameter, the Court of Cassation decided that the trial court rightly awarded custody of the children to their mother following the dissolution of marriage by divorce, despite her being in ill health. The Court drew on a set of factors to determine the best interests of the children: their young age, the necessity of staying together, their need for their mother, and their emotional and psychological balance.

In a decision issued on 26 December 2003,[36] the Court of Cassation considered that 'custody should be awarded to one of the parents or to a third party on the basis of a single criterion, that of the best interests the child.' In the present case, the trial court had granted custody of a 17-year-old to his mother following the dissolution of the marriage. It drew on a set of facts to determine the child's best interests and, in particular, the 'emotional ties with his mother and her ability to educate and control him.' The trial court had also made its decision based on the opinion of the child. Indeed, the latter had clearly expressed his wish to remain with his mother. The father contested the decision before the Court of Cassation and declared that he was better able to ensure custody for the child. The Court of Cassation rejected his claims, supported the decision of the trial court, and maintained custody in favor of the mother.

In another decision issued on 6 March 2008,[37] the Court of Cassation drew on the child's best interests principle to justify the award of custody to the adoptive father after the death of the adoptive mother. Again, the Court drew on a set of parameters to determine the child's best interests, such as his close ties to his adoptive father, the lifestyle to which he was accustomed and the maintenance of a stable life.

---

34 Court of Cassation, 5 July 1983, no. 8625, RJL 1985, p. 82.

35 Court of Cassation, 22 April 1997, no. 57466, Bull. civ. 1997, p. 277.

36 Court of Cassation, 26 December 2003, no. 27602, Bull. civ. 2003, p. 414.

37 Court of Cassation, 6 March 2008, no. 20892, Bull. civ. 2008, vol. 1, p. 247.

10.2.1.2 The Award of Guardianship

A traditional conception of guardianship prevails even today in Tunisian law. Guardianship lasts until the age of majority, i.e. until the child is 18.[38] Guardianship is a mainly paternal prerogative under Tunisian law.

Prior to the reform of 1981, in case of death of the father, guardianship over the minor was ensured either by a testamentary guardian, i.e. a guardian the father had designated in his lifetime by will,[39] or by a judicial guardian the judge had to designate in the event that the father had not designated a testamentary guardian. Guardianship over the child could therefore be ensured by a person other than the mother, while the latter was still alive.

The reform of 18 February 1981[40] changed these solutions. In the event of death or incapacity of the father, the mother becomes the legal guardian of her children. The 1981 reform has prevented a third party, appointed testamentary guardian by the father or judicial guardian by the judge, from exercising guardianship while the mother is still alive. Article 155 of the Code (as amended in 1981) therefore provides that 'guardianship is exercised *de jure* over the minor child by the father, then the mother and then the testamentary guardian.' The testamentary guardian may exercise guardianship only in the event of death or incapacity of the mother. Similarly, the judge may appoint a judicial guardian only in the event of death or incapacity of both parents and in the absence of a will by the father designating a testamentary guardian.[41]

But the maternal guardianship is only a subsidiary guardianship. The mother becomes guardian only in the event of death or incapacity of the father. As long as he is alive and able to exercise them, she does not have the same duties and the same rights as the father. In fact, Article 154 of the Personal Status Code stipulates that 'the father is the guardian of the minor child and in the event of death or incapacity of the father, the mother becomes the legal guardian.'

In the matter of guardianship, therefore, the reform of 12 July 1993[42] strengthened the prerogatives of the mother, without making them equal to those of the father. This reform allowed the custodial mother to have certain prerogatives of guardianship in the event of dissolution of the marriage by divorce. It aims at avoiding the difficulties caused by the dissociation between custody and guardianship in the event of divorce. Para 4 of Article 67 of the Personal Status Code thus provides that 'when custody of the child is granted to the mother, she enjoys the prerogatives of guardianship with regard to the child's travels, studies and management of his financial accounts.'

---

[38] Article 157 Personal Status Code.

[39] According to Article 154 Personal Status Code, only the father is entitled to designate a testamentary guardian.

[40] Law No. 81-7 of 18 February 1981, JORT No. 11 of 1981, p. 334. On this law, see Meziou 1984, p. 253.

[41] Article 154 Personal Status Code.

[42] Law No. 93-74 of 12 July 1993, JORT No. 53 of 1993, p. 1004.

This text had awarded the mother certain prerogatives of guardianship. Notably, it allowed her to travel with the child without the authorization of the father-guardian. But this text failed to alter the practical consequences for custodial mother in the matter of the child's travels. Border police officers continued, despite the reform, to ask the custodial mother to produce a paternal authorization to travel with the child.

In reality, Article 67 para 4 could not apply to the issue of paternal authorization for the child's travels in the absence of a reform of the Law of 14 May 1975 on Passports and Travel Documents.[43]

A reform announced by the President of the Republic on 13 August 2015, a symbolic date marking women's day in Tunisia, will focus precisely on that law. A draft law approved by the Assembly of the People's Representatives on 19 October 2015[44] is of utmost importance. The text has not yet been enacted.[45] This draft law allows the child to travel with either parent's authorization if the spouses are married. If the spouses are divorced, the authorization of the custodial mother suffices.[46] The reform will chip away even more at the prerogatives of the father-guardian in favor of the mother and challenge the traditional division of roles between parents.

In addition, the judge may, in exceptional cases, appoint the mother, to whom custody has been entrusted following the divorce, as the judicial guardian granting her all the prerogatives of guardianship. This is what becomes apparent from para 5 of Article 67, according to which:

> the judge may entrust the responsibilities of guardianship to the mother who has custody of the child if the guardian is unable to ensure the exercise of them, demonstrates abusive behavior in the fulfilment of his task, fails to properly fulfil the duties arising from his task or absents himself from his home with unknown residence or for any cause prejudicing the child's best interests.

10.2.2 The Organization of Custody and Guardianship

The Tunisian legislature has remained relatively attached to a traditional conception of family relationships in regulating the organization of custody and

[43] Organic Law No. 1975-40 of 14 May 1975 on Passports and Travel Documents, JORT No. 43 of 1975, p. 1059, as amended by Organic Law No. 1998-77 of 2 November 1998, JORT No. 89 of 1998, p. 2180, Organic Law No. 2004-6 of 3 February 2004, JORT No. 11 of 2004, p. 252, Law No. 2008-13 of 18 February 2008, JORT No. 16 of 2008, p. 780.

[44] Draft Organic Law No. 2015-55, website of the Assembly of the People's Representatives, www.arp.tn, section draft laws, Journal La Presse of 19 October 2015.

[45] On the date of the final correction of this Article (2 November 2015).

[46] In the case of conflict between the parents concerning the travel of the child, the new text provides that the person who has an interest in it or the public prosecutor's office may submit a request to the judge who will rule on the issue by way of order on request taking into consideration the best interests of the child.

guardianship, but has largely adopted the principle of the child's best interests. This is what can be observed through the rules governing the relationship between custody and guardianship (Sect. 10.2.2.1), those regarding the conditions to be met by the holder of custody (Sect. 10.2.2.2), and those concerning his rights (Sect. 10.2.2.3).

10.2.2.1 The Relationship Between Custody and Guardianship

Guardianship and custody are regulated hierarchically in Tunisian law. Custody therefore remains confined within the limits of guardianship. This regulation reflects a marked influence of Islamic law.

In order to preserve the prerogatives of the father-guardian, Tunisian law has adopted a rule drawn directly from the Maliki rite, namely the prohibition of the custodial mother's moving away or relocating. Maliki classical authors, such as Khalil and Ibn Assem,[47] set the maximum distance that can separate the residence of the custodial mother from the residence of the guardian to six berids,[48] i.e. about 120 km.

The rule prohibiting the custodial mother from moving away or relocating[49] is enshrined in Article 61 of the Personal Status Code, according to which 'if the one who has custody of the children changes the place of residence and settles down at such a distance that prevents the guardian from fulfilling his duties towards his ward, he will be deprived of his right.' The different reforms that have since taken place have not modified this rule. The moving away or relocation of the custodial mother therefore leads to her forfeiting her right to custody. The father's moving away or relocation, on the other hand, does not lead to the forfeiture of the mother's right to custody. Under Article 62 of the Personal Status Code 'the father can only remove the child from the place of residence of the mother with the consent of the latter as long as she retains the right to custody, unless the child's best interests require otherwise.'

Article 61 of the Code seems incompatible with the conception that the Tunisian Personal Status Code adopts regarding custody. For Béji,

> the adoption of the child's best interests as the sole criterion for the award of custody … no longer allows one to proceed in an inflexible manner. Indeed, the custodian's change of residence and its establishment as far away as it may be, is not necessarily contrary to the child's best interests.[50]

---

[47] El Chafai 1986, pp. 166–77.

[48] One berid is equivalent to 20 km.

[49] Article 61 Personal Status Code uses in the Arabic version the term '*safar nuqla*'. The term 'journey' can thus be used (in this sense, see Ferchichi 1983, pp. 360–367). But it is, in reality, much more a move-away in view of a new settlement, or a one-way trip, than a journey in the sense of a return trip back to the departure point.

[50] Béji 1977–1978, p. 164.

After initially showing a certain severity in the application of this rule,[51] judges are now showing much more flexibility. This is apparent in particular from a decision issued on 26 December 2003 by the Court of Cassation.[52] In this case, the trial judges had granted custody of a teenager to his mother following the dissolution of the marriage. The mother had moved and had settled in a city distant from the one where the father lived. The latter then sought forfeiture of custody in accordance with Article 61 of the Personal Status Code. The trial court, supported by the Court of Cassation, considered that it was in the child's best interests not to deprive the mother of her right to custody. In this way they allowed the principle of the child's best interests to prevail over Article 61 of the Personal Status Code.

10.2.2.2 Conditions for the Exercise of Custody

Article 58 of the Tunisian Personal Status Code regulates the conditions for the exercise of custody. According to this text, the holder of custody must be capable of making reasonable decisions and of adult age. He also must be sane, honest, able to provide for the child, and free from any contagious disease.

Specific conditions are required of holders of custody (depending on their gender). Indeed, the male holder of custody must have available to him, according to Article 58, 'a woman who ensures the tasks of custody.' This stipulation reflects an old conception of custody as a 'mothering' of the child. The male holder of custody can only ensure custody of the female child if he is related to her in a prohibited degree, for example her father, grandfather, elder brother or uncle. This provision, which also contains an outdated conception of custody, is intended to prevent the holder of custody from sexually abusing the girl. It seems strange, insofar as a family relationship is never a guarantee against abuse!

Under the same law, the woman who ensures custody of the child, be it its mother or another person, must not be married. This condition can be bypassed in five cases: if the judge considers that the custody right of the married woman must be maintained for the child's benefit; if the husband is related to the child in a prohibited degree (the child's uncle, for example); if the husband is the guardian of the child; and if the holder of custody, i.e. the father, 'fails to claim his right in the year following the consummation of marriage'; if the woman is the wet nurse of the child; and if the custodian is both the mother and the guardian of the child. This text, poorly drafted, could simply have provided that the marriage of the

[51] Court of Cassation, 20 December 1965, RJL no. 3 of 1966, p. 46, and RTD 1966–1967, p. 193; De Lagrange, Case Note, Court of Cassation, 26 June 1967, RJL no. 3 of 1968, p. 51; Court of Cassation, 15 July 1969, Bull. civ. 1969, p. 88; Court of Cassation, 6 October 1987, Bull. civ. 1987, p. 207; Court of Cassation, 22 December 1992, Bull. civ. 1992, p. 167; Court of Cassation, 8 March 1994, Bull. civ. 1994, p. 284; on the whole question, see Ferchichi 1983, pp. 360 and 361.

[52] Court of Cassation, 26 December 2003, no. 27602, Bull. civ. 2003, p. 414.

holder of custody does not entail forfeiture if such a forfeiture would harm the best interests of the child.

Article 59 of the Personal Status Code reinforces this traditional conception. It provides that:

> the holder of custody of a confession other than the one of the child's father may exercise this right only until the child reaches the age of five and only if it is not to be feared that he will be raised in a religion other than the one of his father.

The text establishes an obligation to raise the child in the religion of his father. The same Article formulates an important reservation in favor of the mother. It provides that 'these provisions do not apply if the mother is custodian.'

Although Article 59 of the Tunisian Personal Status Code does not apply to the mother, Tunisian courts have sometimes subordinated the award of custody to the non-Muslim mother to the condition that she provide the child with a Muslim education. This is what emerges from certain old decisions issued within the framework of domestic relationships.[53] Article 59 has particularly been applied in relationships when the mother is foreign.[54]

An adjustment of custody by conventional means seems to be tolerated under Tunisian law, provided it is in the child's best interests. But the decisions issued on this subject remain scarce. Some old decisions emanating from the Tunisian courts have validated the agreements between spouses regarding custody in domestic relationships.[55] Such agreements also appear to have been accepted where the mother is foreign.[56] These agreements mainly aim at awarding, in advance, the custody of the child to the mother in the event of divorce.

10.2.2.3 The Rights of the Custody Holder

The Personal Status Code confers a number of rights on the holder of custody. Custody thus means that the custody holder has the right to keep the child at home. Article 62 of the Personal Status Code states that 'the father can only take the child out of the mother's place of residence with the consent of the latter as long as she has custody, unless the child's best interests require otherwise.'

---

[53] See Court of Appeal of Tunis, 23 December 1963, no. 56434, RTD 1967–1968, p. 198; Court of Cassation, 13 September 1972, no. 9393 (unpublished), cited in Chérif 1997, p. 162.

[54] On this question, see Ben Achour S 2004, p. 122.

[55] E.g. Tunis, 10 November 1965, no. 58-150, RTD 1966–1967, p. 188; Civ, 9 August 1978, no. 2651, RJL 1978, p. 54.

[56] Several decisions issued in 2000 accepted, indeed, parental agreements on custody in mixed relationships. These decisions are cited in Ben Abdelhamid-Dérouiche (2001), pp. 4 and 5.

Under Article 56 of the Personal Status Code, the father must also provide the child and the holder of custody with accommodation, where the latter does not have any. If he owns a home, he must put it at the disposal of the mother and children. If he does not own a home, he must rent accommodation for the mother and the children. This burden arises from the maintenance obligation the father has to bear.[57]

The Court of Cassation considered, initially, that this obligation vanishes if the mother resides with her own parents. This followed from a decision of 6 February 1979.[58] The court then changed that position by stating, in a decision of 12 January 2006,[59] that 'the fact that the custodial mother lives with her parents does not abolish her right to an accommodation allowance, as long as it is not proven that she owns a home.'

The Law of 4 March 2008[60] added a new Article 56a which introduced security of tenure in favor of the custodial mother when the father, as owner of the dwelling, is compelled to accommodate her with the child. This security of tenure does not get in the way of the father's right to sell the accommodation or mortgage it. However, he has to announce the security of tenure in favor of the custody holder and her child. Article 56a of the Personal Status Code establishes a penal protection of the security of tenure. In fact, it punishes (with a prison sentence of 3 months–1 year and a fine of 100–1000 dinars) the father who sells the accommodation or mortgages it without stating, in the title, the security of tenure.

If the father does not own a dwelling and is compelled to accommodate the holder of custody with the child, he is obliged under Article 56 to pay the rent. The penalties provided for in Article 56a apply if the father deprives the holder of custody and the child from occupying the dwelling thus rented by consciously cancelling the contract or by refusing to pay the rent due.

10.3 Aspects of Private International Law

We examine direct instances (Sect. 10.3.1) and exequatur instances (Sect. 10.3.2). The former cover cases where the parties directly address the judge, Tunisian in our case, to request the award of a right or the resolution of a dispute where the mother is foreign. The latter refer to cases where the parties submit to the judge a decision obtained abroad and request its recognition or execution.

57 In Tunisian law, the maintenance obligation is mainly borne by the father. This follows from Article 2 Personal Status Code that 'the husband, as head of the family, must provide for the needs of the wife and the children to the extent of his means and according to their condition, within the framework of the components of maintenance'. The wife must only 'contribute to the family expenses if she has property'.

58 Court of Cassation, 6 February 1979, no. 2567, Bull. civ. 1979, p. 63.

59 Court of Cassation, 12 January 2006, no. 5199, Bull. civ. 2006, p. 255.

60 Law No. 2008-20 of 4 March 2008, JORT No. 21 of 2008, p. 883.

10.3.1 Direct Instances

Where a case involves a foreign element, judges tend to apply directly the provisions of domestic law. A few old and rare decisions issued by the Tunisian courts have applied the rule set out in Article 59 of the Personal Status Code by refusing to grant custody to the non-Muslim mother (Sect. 10.3.1.1). More decisions have applied Article 61 of the Personal Status Code where the mother is foreign. But this trend seems to have been abandoned (Sect. 10.3.1.2).

10.3.1.1 The Refusal to Grant Custody to the Non-Muslim Mother

Although Article 59 of the Personal Status Code clearly provides that it does not apply to the mother, a few decisions have made it a condition of the award of custody to the foreign mother that she raise the child in the religion of his father.

It seems that only two decisions, issued with an interval of over 40 years between them, have expressly made this requirement.[61] The first decision was issued by the Court of Sousse on 7 November 1957.[62] In this case, the French courts had pronounced the divorce between a French woman and a Tunisian man who resided in France, awarded custody of the child to the mother and granted visitation rights to the father. The father took the child to Tunisia where he sought to obtain custody. An order dated 11 September 1957 transferred custody provisionally to the father. The mother then brought third-party proceedings. The Court of Sousse, ruling in summary proceedings, confirmed the father's provisional custody, stating that:

> if the mother took back her daughter and made her live with her in France, the father, who is a Muslim, would be unable to convince a court where most of the litigants are Christian that it is his duty to raise his daughter in accordance with Islamic principles and the Constitution of his country.

The second decision was issued by the Court of First Instance of Tunis on 20 April 1999.[63] In that case, a marriage had taken place between an Italian woman and a Tunisian man. A daughter was born in 1992. Subsequently, the husband filed for divorce and the custody of his daughter at the Tunisian courts. In response, the mother sought herself custody of her daughter.

The Court of First Instance of Tunis, after reminding itself that the provisions of Article 59 of the Personal Status Code do not apply to the mother, decided that:

---

[61] The Court of Appeal of Tunis, in a decision of 23 December 1963, RJL 1965, p. 59, has clearly stated that Article 59 Personal Status Code did not apply to a foreign mother who has been awarded custody. But the weight of this decision is reduced by the fact that both parents resided in Tunisia.

[62] President of the Court of Sousse, 7 November 1957, RCDIP 1959, p. 566 (case note by Jambu-Merlin).

[63] TPI of Tunis, 20 April 1999, no. 23-843 (unpublished).

> custody is awarded to the mother or the father according to the child's best interests. Despite the fact that Article 59 does not apply to the mother, it is not possible, in the present case, to award custody of the girl to the mother, because this contradicts the rules of Tunisian public policy of which Islam and Arabism are part. Islam and Arabism, incidentally, are the pillars of sovereignty according to the Constitution.

The Court adds that 'it is not excluded that the mother takes her daughter with her to Italy.' The Court of First Instance decided to grant custody of the child to her father and to give the mother limited visitation rights on Tunisian territory. In order to prevent the mother from removing the child from Tunisian territory, the Court authorized the air and border police to prohibit the child's travel.

These two decisions, which make the obligation to raise the child in the religion of his father a criterion for the award of custody, remain isolated in the Tunisian jurisprudence. Tunisian courts have chosen to invoke another rule, directly drawn from the Code of Personal Status, in relationships where the mother is foreign. This is the rule prohibiting the custodial mother from moving away or relocating.

10.3.1.2 The Rule Prohibiting the Custodial Mother from Moving Away or Relocating

Enshrined in domestic law, the rule prohibiting the relocation of the custodial mother has long prevailed in relationships where the mother is foreign (Sect. "The Consolidation of the Rule"). Today, it seems to be questioned by the Court of Cassation (Sect. "The Questioning of the Rule").

The Consolidation of the Rule

In terms of relationships where the mother is foreign, several decisions have supported the view that the mother forfeits her custody rights not only when she changes residence, but also when the father does so. The refusal on the part of the custodial mother to follow the father thus leads to the forfeiture of her right to custody.

The analysis of Tunisian jurisprudence shows that the two hypotheses are assimilated in instances where the mother is foreign in order to preserve the prerogatives of the father-guardian. Two situations may arise. First, some decisions have refused to grant custody to the mother if she resides abroad while the father resides in the country of origin, even if it is the father who moved away (Sect. (a)). Other decisions have granted custody to the mother when both parents are abroad, as long as the father can continue to exercise guardianship over the child (Sect. (b)).

(a) First case: the mother does not reside in the country of origin of the father

According to several relatively old decisions issued by Tunisian courts, custody cannot be granted to the mother if she does not reside in the country of origin of the father, as the latter will no longer be able to exercise guardianship over the child.

This is affirmed by a decision issued by the Court of Cassation dated 9 November 1982.[64] In that case, the Tunisian spouses resided in France with their children. The husband decided to return to Tunisia. The wife refused to follow him. He then filed before the Tunisian courts an action for divorce and, in addition, requested the award of custody of his children. The trial court awarded custody to the father and visitation rights to the mother. The mother then appealed against the decision. The Court of Cassation considered that the return of the father to Tunisia entailed, if she refuses to follow him, the forfeiture of the mother's custody rights. The Court confirmed the judgment of the Court of Appeal of Tunis, stating that 'the refusal of the wife to return to Tunisia, where her husband resides, harms the latter. Indeed, the fact that she resides in France makes her lose her right to custody, in accordance with Article 61 of the Personal Status Code.'

The same solution was adopted by the Court of Cassation in a decision dated 8 March 1994.[65] In this case, the Tunisian spouses resided in Germany. The couple's two children were born in Germany and attended school there. Following a serious conflict between the spouses, the father decided to return to Tunisia. The mother, who planned to stay in Germany with her children, brought an action for divorce before the Tunisian courts. In defense, the father sought the award of custody of the children. In a judgment dated 29 May 1992, the Court of First Instance of Sfax pronounced the divorce and granted the mother custody of the two children, and the father visitation rights. The Court of Appeal of Sfax upheld this judgment in a decision of 31 March 1993. The father then appealed against the decision. The Court of Cassation quashed the appeal decision, stating that:

> it follows from Article 61 of the Personal Status Code that the holder of custody forfeits his rights if he changes the place of residence and settles down at such a distance that prevents the guardian from supervising and controlling the child. The fact that the custodial mother decided to travel to Germany and refrained from returning to Tunisia where her ex-husband, the guardian of the children, resides, prevents the latter from supervising and controlling his two children.

It is clear that the Court of Cassation conflated the reasoning behind the law relating to the relocation of the custodial mother, stipulated by Article 61 of the Code, with that of the relocation of the guardian.

(b) Second case: both parents are residing abroad

According to some decisions, the parents' residence abroad permits the mother to keep custody. In fact, if the father resides abroad, custody can be awarded to the mother provided that she also resides abroad. In this case, the award of custody

[64] Court of Cassation, 9 November 1982, no. 6791, Bull. civ. 1982, p. 211.

[65] Court of Cassation, 8 March 1994, no. 38-798, Bull. civ. 1994, p. 284.

is possible because it does not affect the prerogatives of the father-guardian. The principle is established either explicitly or implicitly.

The condition of the confinement of custody within the limits of guardianship was explicitly set in the Ghani judgment issued on 26 February 1991[66] by the Tunisian Court of Cassation. Here, the Tunisian spouses resided in Germany. The husband filed before the Tunisian courts an action for divorce. The Court of First Instance of Tunis pronounced the divorce by application of Tunisian law and awarded custody of the child Ghani to his paternal grandmother, who resided in Tunisia. As the period for filing an appeal had lapsed when the wife returned to Tunisia, she could not contest this decision. She therefore brought a new action before the Court of First Instance of Tunis in which she requested that custody be awarded to her and that the paternal grandmother be deprived of her rights. In defense, the father argued that the mother worked in Germany and that the best interests of the child required that he be raised in Tunisia.

In a judgment dated 2 November 1987, the Court ruled in favor of the mother. It granted her the right to custody and the father visitation rights, specifying that:

> it results from the social investigation that both parents reside in Germany in the same city and that, therefore, no concerns exist regarding the award of custody of the child to his mother. His father may indeed visit him and control him. The child, given his very young age, needs his mother.

The father lodged an appeal against this decision. The Court of Appeal of Tunis confirmed the decision of the judges at first instance. The father then appealed against that decision. The Court of Cassation rejected the appeal, stating that 'custody is awarded to one of the parents according to the child's best interests which is the only criterion and the sole parameter to be considered.' But it added that, 'provided that both parents reside in Germany, no concerns exist regarding the award of custody to his mother. His father may indeed visit him and, as the guardian of the child, can exercise his control.'

Contrary to what the Court of Cassation said, the child's best interests did not constitute 'the only criterion and the sole parameter to be considered' for the award of custody. Certainly, it appears to have been in the child's best interests to reside with his mother and it cannot be said that the Court of Cassation has ignored the child's best interests. But the Court of Cassation added another criterion to the criterion of the child's best interests: that of the confinement of custody within the limits of guardianship. As Ben Halima[67] pointed out, the Court of Cassation could have contented itself with the child's best interests criterion, but it could not resist adding a second element based on the absence of any concern that custody be awarded to the mother provided she resides near the father-guardian. This second element was crucial and the solution would certainly have been

---

[66] Court of Cassation, 26 February 1991, no. 26-406, RTD 1995, pp. 119–143 (case note by Ben Halima).

[67] Ben Halima, Case Note, Court of Cassation, 26 February 1991, no. 26-406, RTD 1995, p. 136.

different if the father did not reside in Germany. Interpreted conversely, the Ghani judgment of the Court of Cassation means that custody could not have been awarded to the mother if her residence was distant from that of the child's father.

Some decisions can be interpreted as implicitly laying down a rule prohibiting the custodial mother from moving away. Thus, a decision issued by the Court of First Instance of Tunis on 9 November 1999[68] may be interpreted in this sense. Pronouncing the divorce between a Tunisian man and a Tunisian woman residing in Germany, the Court decided to grant custody to the mother and visitation rights to the father. The award of custody to the mother did not seem to pose any problem provided that it remained confined within the father's guardianship.

The Questioning of the Rule

The judgment issued on 21 May 2009 certainly marks a decisive turning point in Tunisian jurisprudence.[69] It challenges several decades of case law.

In this case, a Tunisian woman and an Egyptian man had married in 2004 and had settled in Egypt. When a conflict arose between them, the wife returned to Tunisia and sought divorce and the award of custody of the child from the Tunisian courts.

In a decision issued on 12 February, the Court of First Instance decided in her favor. Upon appeal by the husband, the Court of Appeal of Tunis affirmed the decision of the judges at first instance in a judgment of 12 November 2008.

The husband then lodged an appeal, in which he criticized, in particular, the Court of Appeal for having awarded custody to the mother. He argued that the award of custody to the mother prevented him from exercising the prerogatives of guardianship, since he lived in Egypt. The Court of Cassation rejected the appeal and said that 'the contested decision was based on the child's best interests.' For the Court of Cassation, 'the award of custody must take into account the child's best interests, not the best interests of the guardian, in accordance with Article 67 of the Code of Personal Status.'

The Court of Cassation confirmed this position in a particularly well-reasoned decision issued on 17 September 2009.[70] In this case, two Tunisians married in 2003 and settled down abroad immediately after their wedding. Following a conflict, the spouses filed for divorce before the Tunisian courts. In April 2008, the Court of First Instance of Sousse pronounced the divorce and awarded custody of the common child to the mother. This decision was confirmed by the Court of Appeal of Sousse in a decision of 13 February 2009. The father then appealed against this decision, requesting that custody be awarded to him. He invoked in particular Article 61 of the Personal Status Code.

---

[68] TPI of Tunis, 9 November 1999, no. 29-867 (unpublished).

[69] Court of Cassation, 21 May 2009, no. 32561, Bull. civ. 2009, p. 303.

[70] Court of Cassation, 17 September 2009, no. 35890, Bull. civ. 2009, p. 337.

The Court of Cassation, however, refused to follow his allegations and developed an interesting line of reasoning. It stated that:

> custody has been regulated by taking into account two rights: the right of the child to reside with the custodial mother so that he is not deprived of the ties with his mother and the right of the guardian to supervise the child's education. The guardian can exercise this right only provided that the child is near him. It is for this reason that Article 61 of the Personal Status Code forbids the custodial mother from travelling with the child.

Adopting an explanatory interpretation of Article 61, the Court of Cassation held that it does not apply to this case, because the text is aimed at cases where it is the mother who moves. For the Court, 'the situation is different when the custodial mother resided abroad after the marriage.' The Court then referred to the notion of the best interests of the child, which it set against the prerogatives of the father-guardian. It considers that:

> the legislature recommended the taking into account of the best interests of the child in all matters concerning him. If the child's best interests are opposed to those of the guardian, priority should be given to the former ... the prejudice suffered by the child because of his separation from his mother would be more important than the prejudice suffered by the guardian because of the remoteness of the child.

This decision is of considerable importance. It clearly gives precedence to the child's best interests over the prerogatives of the father-guardian and thus challenges several decades of jurisprudence.

10.3.2 *Exequatur Instances: The Foreign Decision in the Face of Public Policy*

Several decisions issued by both trial courts and the Court of Cassation in Tunisia have rejected the enforcement of foreign judgments on custody because of their incompatibility with Tunisian public policy.

The examination of these decisions shows that a debate of a confessional and cultural nature has taken place over several decades of jurisprudence (Sect. 10.3.2.1). But it can be argued that this jurisprudence has been questioned. The Court of Cassation today bases public policy on the child's best interests (Sect. 10.3.2.2).

10.3.2.1 The Lack of a Confessional and Cultural Community as a Basis for Invoking Public Policy Rules

Several decisions issued by Tunisian courts have refused to grant the enforcement of foreign decisions on custody rights for being contrary to Tunisian public policy.

The typical scenario with which Tunisian judges are confronted is that of a foreign judgment which awards custody to the foreign mother who resides abroad. The refusal of enforcement because of incompatibility with Tunisian public policy often comes from the Court of Cassation (Sect. "The Court of Cassation"), but sometimes also from the trial judges (Sect. "The Trial Judges").

The Court of Cassation

Many decisions issued by the Court of Cassation have objected to foreign judgments on custody on the grounds of public policy, because of the foreign jurisdiction's lack of a confessional nature.

In a case decided by the Court of Cassation on 15 May 1979,[71] a German judgment had pronounced the divorce between a Tunisian man and a German woman and had granted custody to the mother, who then sought to enforce the decision in Tunisia. The Court of First Instance of Tunis granted her request and awarded visitation rights to the father. That judgment was confirmed by the Court of Appeal of Tunis. On the husband's appeal, the decision was quashed. The Court of Cassation declared the German decision contrary to public policy, stating that:

> the compliance of the foreign judgment whose enforcement is sought with the rules of public policy is assessed in terms of the values contained in the Constitution and adhered to by the family and the society, notably religious and linguistic values and love of the homeland.

The same conception of public policy was adopted in a decision issued by the Court of Cassation dated 3 June 1982.[72] In that case, a French decision had pronounced the divorce between a Tunisian man and a French woman and had granted custody to the mother. The mother sought to enforce the decision at the Court of First Instance of Tunis. The trial judges granted it. Their decision was confirmed by the Court of Appeal of Tunis. On appeal by the father, the appeal judgment was quashed. The Court of Cassation declared the French decision contrary to public policy. It stated that:

> the assessment of the conformity of the foreign judgment whose enforcement is sought with the rules of public policy … is made on the basis of its lack of opposition to the essential attributes of the country, the most important of which, for Tunisia, are Islam and Arab authenticity.

The Court of Cassation added that:

> the uprooting of the child from the environment in which he grew up and of which he speaks and writes the language, from its customs and traditions as well as his detachment from his Arab and Muslim social environment are likely to make him a permanent exile, cut off from his religion and therefore an apostate. Such a judgment violates … the public policy of the country and opposes its Constitution.

[71] Court of Cassation, 15 May 1979, no. 2000, RJL no. 10 of 1980, p. 79.

[72] Court of Cassation, 3 June 1982, no. 7422, Bull. civ. 1982, p. 143.

The same arguments were accepted by the Court of Cassation judgments of 19 October 1985,[73] 4 January 1999,[74] and 22 September 1999.[75]

The Trial Judges

Concurring with the traditional position of the Court of Cassation, some decisions of the trial courts have been able to develop religious and cultural arguments to refuse the enforcement of foreign decisions because of their incompatibility with Tunisian public policy.[76]

This is, for example, the case with a judgment issued on 27 December 1996 by the Court of Appeal of Tunis.[77] In this case, a Tunisian man and a French woman were residing in France with their children. Following a conflict between the spouses, the father left France and settled in Tunisia with his children. The High Court of Nanterre, by a judgment of 26 May 1994, pronounced the divorce, granted parental authority to the mother, ordered that the two children reside with her, and awarded the father visitation rights. The mother sought to enforce the French judgment in the Tunisian courts. The Court of First Instance of Grombalia, in a decision of 8 May 1995,[78] granted the enforcement of the French decision and considered it consistent with public policy. The husband then appealed against this judgment. The Court of Appeal of Tunis declared the French decision contrary to public policy because:

> the two children are in Tunisia with their father who exercises the actual custody. They have become used to living in Tunisia, which allowed them to get used to the principles of Islam and its rules. To tear them away from their family environment would undeniably be very harmful to them. It is therefore appropriate to grant custody to the father.

10.3.2.2 The Child's Best Interests as the Basis of Public Policy

A significant turnaround has taken place regarding the conception of public policy in the field of custody since the 2000s.

The trend first of all affects the trial courts. Thus, a judgment issued by the Court of First Instance of Tunis on 19 June 2000[79] based public policy on the best

---

[73] Court of Cassation, 19 October 1985, no. 14220, Bull. civ. 1985, p. 61.

[74] Court of Cassation, 4 January 1999, no. 69523-98, RJL no. 1 of 2002, p. 167, and RTD 2001, p. 210 (case note by Ghazouani).

[75] Court of Cassation, 22 September 1999, no. 72212-99 (unpublished), cited in Ben Achour S 2004, p. 229.

[76] Court of Appeal of Sousse, 20 June 1995, no. 2412 and no. 2891 (unpublished).

[77] Court of Appeal of Tunis, 27 December 1997, no. 25429 (unpublished).

[78] TPI of Grombalia, 8 May 1995, no. 16790 (unpublished).

[79] TPI of Tunis, 19 June 2000, no. 34195, cited in Chedly and Ghazouani 2008, p. 256; on this decision, see also Meziou 2010, p. 59.

interests of the child. In the present case, the Libyan courts had pronounced divorce between a Tunisian woman and a Libyan man, finding the woman at fault, and deprived her of her right to custody. The judges refused to enforce the Libyan decision, stating that:

> the judgment emanating from a Libyan court, pronouncing divorce for fault of the wife and entailing forfeiture of all her rights, including custody, is a judgment contrary to the Tunisian public policy, the fundamental principles and the choice of legislative policy of the Tunisian system, which makes the best interests of the child the criterion for the devolution of custody.

The trend was then confirmed at the level of the Court of Cassation in a decisive judgment issued on 2 March 2001.[80] This decision undeniably constituted a notable change in the Tunisian jurisprudence.

In this case, the Court of Appeal of Tunis agreed to enforce a Belgian decision that had granted custody to the mother of a child born to a Tunisian father and a Danish mother residing in Belgium. The husband argued that the appeal judgment was contrary to public policy because 'custody should be granted in the best interests of the child. Now it is in the best interests of the child, who is Tunisian and Muslim, who lives in Tunisia and has known the national and family specificities of his country, to stay in Tunisia.'

The Court of Cassation dismissed the husband's appeal and did not declare the foreign judgment contrary to Tunisian public policy. The Court of Cassation considered that the foreign judgment fulfilled all the conditions required for enforcement. Analyzing then the conformity of the foreign judgment with Tunisian public policy, it decided that

> the Tunisian law takes into consideration the child's best interests for the award of custody … the trial judges have granted custody of the child to its foreign mother taking into account its best interests. Nothing in the foreign decision contradicts Tunisian public policy or Tunisian legislative policy. Only the child's best interests must be taken into account without any other consideration.

This is indeed the first time that the Court of Cassation did not adopt the classic line of reasoning. The Court of Cassation seemed to choose a new path. Rather than an assessment *in abstracto* based on general principles and impersonal directives, the Court of Cassation seemed to prefer an assessment *in concreto* based on specific circumstances and concrete data that allows the assessment of the best interests of the child. The best interests of the child presumably justified that custody be awarded to the Danish mother residing in Belgium and not to the Tunisian father residing in Tunisia.

The same conception of public policy, based on the sole criterion of the best interests of the child, emerges from the decision issued on 21 May 2009 by the Court of Cassation.[81] The case concerned a woman of Tunisian nationality, her

[80] Court of Cassation, 2 March 2001, no. 7286-2000, RJL January 2002, p. 183.

[81] Court of Cassation, 21 May 2009, no. 32561, Bull. civ. 2009, p. 303.

Egyptian husband and the custody of their child. The wife had sought from the Tunisian courts divorce and the award of custody. The trial judges had ruled in her favor. Before the Court of Cassation, as the husband argued that the award of custody to the mother would prevent him from exercising the prerogatives of guardianship, he submitted a decision issued in Egypt which awarded him custody of the child.

Based on Article 11 of the Code of Private International Law, the Court of Cassation refused to recognize the decision issued by the Egyptian courts, considering it contrary to Tunisian public policy. It reasoned that the Egyptian decision, which granted custody to the father, 'contradicts Tunisian public policy because it did not base itself on the child's best interests when granting custody.' For the Court of Cassation, the child's best interests required that custody be given to the mother.

References

Abou Zahra M (1957) Le statut personnel, 3rd edn. Al fikh al arabi, Cairo

Béji M (1977–1978) La garde de l'enfant en droit tunisien, DES thesis, Private Law, Faculté de droit, Tunis

Belknani F (2010) La jurisprudence civile et le fikh islamique. In: Cinquante ans de jurisprudence civile, 1959–2009, CPU, Tunis, pp 99-144 (in Arabic)

Ben Abdelhamid-Dérouiche I (unpublished) La loi applicable en matière d'obligation alimentaire et de garde, Mariage mixte et intérêt de l'enfant, conference organized by the École Supérieure de la Magistrature on 1 November 2001 (in Arabic)

Ben Achour S (2004) Enfance disputée, les problèmes juridiques relatifs aux droits de garde et de visite après divorce dans les relations franco-maghrébines. CPU, Tunis

Ben Achour S (2011) L'interprétation du droit tunisien de la famille: entre référence à l'Islam et appel aux droits fondamentaux. In: L'Interprétation de la Norme Juridique – Actes du colloque international organisé les 5 et 6 avril 2010 à Jendouba, Faculté des sciences juridiques, économiques et de gestion de Jendouba, pp 17–37

Ben Achour Y (1992) Politique, religion et droit dans le monde arabe. Cérès-CERP, Tunis, pp 203–225

Ben Halima S (2000) Religion et statut personnel en Tunisie, RTD 107–138

Ben Jemia M (2000) Ordre public, constitution et exequatur. Mélanges en l'honneur de Habib Ayadi. CPU, Tunis, pp 271–300

Ben Jemia M (2008) Non discrimination religieuse et Code du statut personnel tunisien. Droits et culture: Mélanges en l'honneur du Doyen Yadh Ben Achour. CPU, Tunis, pp 261–276

Ben Jemia M (2012) Le juge tunisien et la légitimation de l'ordre juridique positif par la charia. In: Dupret B (ed) La charia aujourd'hui, usages de la référence au droit islamique. La Découverte, Paris, pp 153–165

Benoist-Mechin J (1958) Un printemps arabe. Albin Michel, Paris

Bostanji S (2009) Turbulences dans l'application judicaire du Code tunisien du statut personnel. RIDC 61(1):7–47

Bouguerra M (2000) Le juge tunisien et le droit du statut personnel. AJT no. 14:7–181

Bousquet G-H (1975) Hadhāna. In: Encyclopédie de l'Islam, vol. 3, E. J. Brill, Leiden/ Maisonneuve & La Rose, Paris, pp 17–20

Chammam M (1982) Les dispositions de la ḥaḍāna, RJL 11–51 (in Arabic)

Charfi M (1973) Le droit tunisien de la famille entre l'Islam et la modernité, RTD 11–37

Charfi M (1983) Droits de l'homme, droit musulman et droit tunisien, RTD 405–423

Charif Feller D (1996) La garde (Ḥaḍanah) en droit musulman, dans les droits égyptien, syrien et tunisien. Librairie Droz, Geneva
Chedly L and Ghazouani M (2008) Code de droit international privé annoté, Tunis
Chekir H (2000) Le statut des femmes entre les textes et les résistances: Le cas de la Tunisie. Chama, Tunis
Chérif M-H (1997) Code du statut personnel annoté. Dar el mizen Linnachr, Tunis (in Arabic)
Colomer A (1957) Le Code du statut personnel tunisien, Revue algérienne, tunisienne et marocaine de législation et de jurisprudence 115–239
Déprez J (1990) Droit international privé et conflits de civilisations: Aspects méthodologiques. In: Académie de droit international de la Haye (ed) Recueil des cours 1988-IV. Martinus Nijhoff Publishers, Dordrecht et al, pp 9–372
El Chafai A-M (1986) Le divorce et les droits des enfants et des proches, études comparées entre les différents rites en droit musulman. Addar Al Jamiaia, Beirut (in Arabic)
El Euch H (1985) La garde en droit tunisien, RJL 43–59
Ferchichi B (1983) La tutelle des pères et mères sur leurs enfants mineurs dans les droits marocain et tunisien comparés, thesis. Université de Tunis, Tunis
Ladjili J (1972) Puissance des agnats, puissance du père: De la famille musulmane à la famille tunisienne, RTD 25–64
Mechri F (2002) L'enfant objet et sujet d'affection: Approche juridique et juristique des rapports parents-enfant en droit tunisien et en droit comparé. Tunis/Publisud, Paris, CPU
Mellouli S (2010) La problématique des sources, et la valeur du fikh islamique dans la jurisprudence civile. In: Cinquante ans de jurisprudence civile, 1959–2009, CPU, Tunis, pp 79-97 (in Arabic)
Mezghani A (1975) Réflexions sur les relations du Code de statut personnel avec le droit musulman classique. RTD 2:53–81
Mezghani A (2008) Religion, mariage et succession: l'hypothèse laïque. À propos d'une (R) évolution récente de la jurisprudence tunisienne. In: Droits et culture: Mélanges en l'honneur du Doyen Yadh Ben Achour, CPU, Tunis, pp 345–366
Meziou K (1984) Féminisme et Islam dans la réforme du Code du statut personnel du 18 février 1981, RTD 253–282
Meziou K (1992) Pérennité de l'Islam dans le droit tunisien de la famille. Le statut personnel des Musulmans: Droit comparé et droit international privé. Bruylant, Brussels, pp 247–274
Meziou K (2010) Les relations en droit international privé de la famille entre la Tunisie et les autres pays arabes. Le Code tunisien de droit international dix ans après, Première journée Mohamed Charfi de droit international privé, 21 et 22 novembre 2008. CPU, Tunis, pp 51–62
Milliot L, Blanc F-P (1987) Introduction à l'étude du droit musulman, 2nd edn. Sirey, Paris
Pruvost L (1975) Le statut juridique du mineur en Tunisie. RTD 1:281–334
Sabbagh R (1966–1967) L'enfant et la tutelle d'éducation, RJL 515-531 (in Arabic)
Sabbagh R (1968) La garde, RJL 617–627 (in Arabic)
Sabbagh R (1969–1970) L'évolution du droit de garde dans les pays du Maghreb, RTD 49-65

Chapter 11
Evolving Conceptions of Children's Rights: Some Reflections on Muslim States' Engagement with the UN Convention on the Rights of the Child

Shaheen Sardar Ali and Sajila Sohail Khan

Abstract The present chapter explores evolving perceptions of children's rights as reflected in Muslim state party practice in light of responses to the UN Convention on the Rights of the Child (CRC). The only human rights treaty making specific mention of Islam and ratified by all Muslim states, the CRC, also enjoys near-universal ratification by all UN member states (the only exception being the USA). But this unanimous ratification by Muslim states is accompanied by reservations, some of which have been entered in the name of Islamic law and sharia, raising questions of compatibility between the CRC and Muslims' perceptions of children's rights. Reservations to multilateral treaties such as the CRC are one of several indicators of Muslim state practice and of Islam's plural legal traditions in international law; others include, but are not confined to, country reports submitted to the CRC Committee, as well as a range of 'Islamic' human rights instruments. Assessing the first two indicators—reservations and country reports—against the backdrop of Islamic legal traditions and international conceptions of human rights, this chapter bears the following questions in mind: Does membership of the CRC *per se* constitute active engagement with and ownership of its provisions on the part of Muslim states? If so, is there a discernible or potential paradigm shift in perspectives in this area as a result of this engagement with the CRC as evidenced through reservations, withdrawals of reservations, and country reports? And to what extent do children's rights as set

Sajila Sohail Khan is a freelance consultant in gender and development, formerly a gender advisor with the International Labour Organization in Geneva, Switzerland. Views expressed in this chapter represent the author's personal views and do not express that of the organization.

Shaheen Sardar Ali is Professor of Law, University of Warwick, United Kingdom.

S.S. Ali (✉)
University of Warwick, Warwick, UK
e-mail: s.s.ali@warwick.ac.uk

S.S. Khan
e-mail: sajilasohail@gmail.com

N. Yassari et al. (eds.), *Parental Care and the Best Interests of the Child in Muslim Countries*, DOI 10.1007/978-94-6265-174-6_11

out in the CRC resonate with comparable conceptions within Islam's plural legal traditions—especially in relation to freedom of religion, thought, conscience, and the adoption of children? The chapter will focus on two of the CRC articles most widely reserved by Muslim states—Articles 14 (freedom of thought, conscience, and religion and 21 (adoption). It argues that children's rights are an evolving concept with changing content and connotations in classical Islamic law, in Muslim state practice, and in regional and international child rights instruments. Vague and fluid formulations of various aspects of children's rights both in the CRC and in classical conceptions of the Islamic legal traditions make it a malleable concept that enables diverse cultures and traditions to implement it in their particular contexts.

Keywords UN Convention on the Rights of the Child · Islamic law · Sharia · Adoption · *Kafāla* · Freedom of religion, thought and conscience · Country report · Reservations to treaties

Contents

11.1 Introduction

This chapter explores evolving perceptions of children's rights as reflected in Muslim state party practice in light of responses to the UN Convention on the Rights of the Child (CRC).[1] The only human rights treaty making specific mention of Islam and ratified by all Muslim states,[2] the CRC also enjoys near-universal ratification by all UN member states (the only exception being the USA). But this

[1] The CRC was adopted on 20 November 1989 and entered into force 2 September 1990, GA Res. 44/25 (1989), 1577 UNTS 3.

[2] 'Muslim state party' indicates a UN member state which is either a member of the Organization of Islamic Cooperation (OIC) or whose majority profess the Islamic religion.

unanimous ratification by Muslim states is accompanied by reservations, some of which have been entered in the name of Islamic law and sharia, raising questions of compatibility between the CRC and Muslims' perceptions of children's rights.

Reservations to multilateral treaties such as the CRC are one of several indicators in international law of Muslim state practice and of Islam's plural legal traditions; others include, but are not confined to, country reports submitted to the CRC Committee, as well as a range of 'Islamic' human rights instruments.[3] Assessing the first two indicators—reservations and country reports—against the backdrop of Islamic legal traditions and international conceptions of human rights, this chapter bears the following questions in mind: Does membership of the CRC *per se* constitute active engagement with and ownership of its provisions on the part of Muslim states? If so, is there a discernible or potential paradigm shift in perspectives in this area as a result of this engagement with the CRC as evidenced through reservations, withdrawals of reservations, and country reports?[4] And to what extent do children's rights as set out in the CRC resonate with comparable concepts within Islam's plural legal traditions—especially in relation to freedom of religion, thought, and conscience, and the adoption of children?

The chapter will focus on two of the CRC articles most widely reserved by Muslim states—Articles 14 (freedom of thought, conscience, and religion)[5] and 21 (adoption).[6] It argues that children's rights are an evolving concept with changing

[3] One of the earliest is the Universal Islamic Declaration on Human Rights, adopted by a group of Muslim scholars in 1981. This was followed by the 1990 OIC-sponsored Cairo Declaration on Human Rights in Islam. The 1994 Declaration on the Rights and Care of the Child in Islam and the 2005 Rabat Declaration on Child's Issues focused specifically on children.

[4] For a study of legislative reform in Muslim jurisdictions following CRC ratification, see Ali 2007, pp. 142–208.

[5] Article 14 runs thus: '1. States Parties shall respect the right of the child to freedom of thought, conscience and religion. 2. States Parties shall respect the rights and duties of the parents and, when applicable, legal guardians, to provide direction to the child in the exercise of his or her right in a manner consistent with the evolving capacities of the child. 3. Freedom to manifest one's religion or beliefs may be subject only to such limitations as are prescribed by law and are necessary to protect public safety, order, health or morals, or the fundamental rights and freedoms of others.'

[6] Article 21 runs thus: 'States Parties that recognize and/or permit the system of adoption shall ensure that the best interests of the child shall be the paramount consideration and they shall: (a) Ensure that the adoption of a child is authorized only by competent authorities who determine, in accordance with applicable law and procedures and on the basis of all pertinent and reliable information, that the adoption is permissible in view of the child's status concerning parents, relatives and legal guardians and that, if required, the persons concerned have given their informed consent to the adoption on the basis of such counselling as may be necessary; (b) Recognize that inter-country adoption may be considered as an alternative means of child's care, if the child cannot be placed in a foster or an adoptive family or cannot in any suitable manner be cared for in the child's country of origin; (c) Ensure that the child concerned by inter-country adoption enjoys safeguards and standards equivalent to those existing in the case of national adoption; (d) Take all appropriate measures to ensure that, in inter-country adoption, the placement does not result in improper financial gain for those involved in it; (e) Promote, where appropriate, the objectives of the present article by concluding bilateral or multilateral arrangements or agreements, and endeavour, within this framework, to ensure that the placement of the child in another country is carried out by competent authorities or organs.'

content and connotations in classical Islamic law, in Muslim state practice, and in regional and international child rights instruments. Vague and fluid formulations of various aspects of children's rights both in the CRC and in classical conceptions of Islamic legal traditions make it a malleable concept that enables diverse cultures and traditions to implement it in their particular contexts.[7] The 'headlines' of Muslim state practice regarding aspects of children's rights—observed as reservations to international treaties or in country reports—are not always reflected in the 'fine print'—i.e., application within Muslim communities and in state practice.

11.2 Islamic Law, Sharia, Human Rights Discourse, and the CRC: Backgrounds and Contexts

An analysis of reservations entered by Muslim states and of country reports to the CRC committee highlights the lack of homogeneity in positions adopted towards various articles. For an appreciation of the various viewpoints reflected in Muslim state practice, an overview of the sources of Islamic law and sharia is important in evidencing the plurality inherent within the Islamic legal traditions.

11.2.1 Sources of a Plural and Dynamic Islamic Legal Tradition

Sharia—a concept evoking radically different responses from different constituencies—is central to any discussion of the Islamic legal traditions. How sharia is understood and employed by Muslim states and governments, and in the lived realities of Muslims at an individual and collective level, varies greatly. Sharia may be described as the overarching umbrella of rules, regulations, values, and normative frameworks covering all aspects and spheres of life for Muslims as developed over time. It comprises elements informed by the religious texts of Islam, as well as human interpretations by generations of Muslim jurists and scholars. Sharia therefore denotes the *principles* of Islamic law rather than the law *per se*, encapsulating the rules of rituals and worship (*^{c}ibādāt*) and of social relations (*mu^{c}āmalāt*). Not all of sharia is legally enforceable in a court of law; some remains in the moral/ethical domain, and our human understandings of its requirements and our actions in relation to these are to be judged in the hereafter.

[7] For example, Article 1 states that '[f]or the purposes of the present Convention, a child means every human being below the age of eighteen years unless under the law applicable to the child, majority is attained earlier'.

An important reason for the fluidity, evolution, and plurality of sharia lies in the fact that its sources, too, demonstrate attributes of plurality in how they have been understood and applied over the centuries. Sharia (and its constituents, including Islamic law) is based upon primary sources—the Quran and Sunna[8]—and secondary sources including juristic consensus at any particular time on a question of law (*ijmāᶜ*) and 'deductive analogy' (*qiyās*).[9] But the story does not end there, for alongside the primary and secondary sources are the various juristic techniques of the Islamic tradition, which, again, allow for great fluidity and evolution. Briefly, if only to give a sense of the very broad possibilities inherent in Islamic jurisprudence, these consist of the following ideas:

Ijtihād is the exercise of independent reasoning to provide answers when the Quran and Sunna are silent on a particular issue. *Taqlīd*, generally considered the opposite of *ijtihād*, is the acceptance of the authority of a ruling through *ijtihād* without examining how it was arrived at; yet *taqlīd* still allows for choice from among the variant views of different schools of thought as recorded in authoritative texts. The juristic technique of *ikhtilāf* allows jurists to arrive at positions representative of diverse viewpoints; it is supported by a hadith: 'Difference among my community is a sign of the bounty of God.'[10] *Takhayyur* is used to consider possible alternatives from a range of opinions, with the intention of applying the least restrictive legal principle to an issue. *Talfīq* denotes the process whereby jurists construct rules through fusing opinions derived from different schools of thought. (A good example is the 1864 landmark case[11] in which an Indian girl, brought up within Shafi'i tradition, married without her father's consent. In court, she declared that she had chosen to adopt the Hanafi school's tradition, as this allowed an adult woman to marry without such consent.) *Maṣlaḥa* allows a deduction of law to be based on general considerations of the public good, and there is evidence that judges and jurists have employed *maṣlaḥa* to override problems arising out of adherence to strict doctrines enshrined in classical legal texts; in a modern context, jurists can reconcile modern cultural norms with the more 'traditional'. *Ḍarūra* can make what is prohibited permissible, for example, allowing the violation of a prohibition in order to avoid something which is contrary to *maqāṣid al-sharīᶜa,* i.e. the fundamental objective of the law. And this *maqāṣid al-sharīᶜa* itself is increasingly being invoked so as to overcome formalistic obstacles

8 The Sunna (the words and deeds of the Prophet Muhammad) is compiled from ahadith (singular hadith). A hadith is composed of the *matn* (text) and the *isnād* (the chain of transmitters).

9 As a source of law, *qiyās* comes into operation in matters that are neither expressly covered by the Quran or Sunna nor dealt with by *ijmāᶜ*: it is the law deduced by application of what has already been laid down by these three.

10 Coulson 1994, p. 102.

11 *Muhammad Ibrahim v. Gulam Ahmed* (1864) 1 BHC 236.

in implementing Islamic law. Last but certainly not least in the armory of juristic techniques is *ᶜurf*[12]: since what the people in general consider to be good is also considered to be good by Allah, long-standing and widely practiced custom—*ᶜurf*—can become acceptable in law.

Even to the casual observer of Islamic law, then, it should be clear that the manner in which law is generated within the Islamic legal traditions is most definitely pluralist, with the inherent capacity for alternative legitimate conceptions of what constitutes law and permissible action. Against this backdrop of the rich diversity of the sources of Islamic law and how it is understood by individual Muslims, states, governments, and communities, we can now briefly engage with perceptions of human rights in Islam and international law as manifested in treaties such as the CRC.

11.2.2 Human Rights in Islam and International Law: Some Observations on Ongoing Contestations

The drafting and adoption of international human rights treaties exemplify contestation among various constituencies of state and government as well as regional and international organizations. This contestation is also evident during the ratification process, when reservations and declarations are entered by some states and objections thereto registered by others. Despite the passage of almost a century since the term gained currency on the international law scene, 'human rights' discourse remains contested terrain, with debates mostly focusing narrowly on 'Western/non-Western' binaries (the 'non-Western' including 'Islamic' conceptions of human rights). Critiques include the charge of Eurocentrism or even of outright expressions of hegemonic impositions upon the postcolonial non-West.[13] 'Southern voices' presenting non-Western perspectives on human rights are comparatively rare in English-language literature.[14]

Human rights treaties speak to particular historical moments, reflecting dominant discourses that, nevertheless, evolve over time. The post-World War II era ushered in a host of Muslim states as UN members and as participants in the drafting of human rights instruments. A rich scholarship developed over the decades thereafter, presenting a wide range of perspectives and opinions on the relationship

[12] At times controversial, this source of law and juristic technique plays an important role in the growth of the Islamic legal tradition, as it speaks to the commonly held beliefs and convictions of communities. Thus some communities of South Asia rely upon *ᶜurf* to interpret Muslim laws of inheritance.

[13] Kavanaugh 2010, p. 17. Also see Mutua 2002; Spivak 2005, pp. 131–89.

[14] Twining 2009. On p. 1 he states that: 'The dominant Western scholarly and activist discourse on human rights has developed largely without reference to these other standpoints and traditions. Claims about universality sit uneasily with ignorance of other traditions and parochial or ethnocentric tendencies.'

between Islamic and international human rights law. Broadly defined, this discourse falls into two broad categories: those who adopt the compatibility/incompatibility approach, and those who find this distinction equally problematic and who argue for a shift in the way in which the debates are framed. Some scholars who advance the viewpoint that Islamic and international human rights law are incompatible offer historical, philosophical, and institutional grounds for their position. Jack Donnelly describes human rights as a 'set of social practices'[15] born out of necessities in the emerging modern societies[16] and not 'a timeless system of essential moral principles'.[17] He advances the view that most non-Western cultural and political traditions, 'like the pre-modern west, lacked not only the practice of human rights, but also the concept …. As for non-western societies, we cannot find the notion of natural law in Islamic, Indian and Chinese cultural traditions.'[18] Ann Elizabeth Mayer supports the view that Islamic and international human rights schemes have important points of divergence, especially with regard to women and minority communities. She is suspicious of Muslim scholars who 'put forward distinctive Islamic schemes of human rights' and in some cases 'seek to accentuate the formal resemblance between their schemes and the international ones even where that resemblance is misleading in terms of the actual protection they intend to provide.'[19]

On the other hand, there is an equally robust argument advanced by those Western and non-Western scholars who hold that human rights is a universal ideology that resonates with both Western and non-Western cultural and religious traditions.[20] Strawson, for instance, challenges the oft-repeated notion of human rights as emanating from a purely Western philosophy and tradition on two grounds: firstly, the existence of a single, homogeneous, monolithic, 'Western' human rights tradition is highly questionable; and secondly, the historical and philosophical roots of rights are distinctly discernible in non-Western cultural and religious traditions.[21] Baderin meanwhile has argued that 'the myth that the sharia is an

---

15 Donnelly 1989, p. 17.

16 Donnelly, cited in Afshari 2007, p. 6.

17 Lauren, cited in Afshari 2007, p. 6.

18 Afshari 2007, p. 6, citing Donnelly. Rhoda E Howard, B Lewis, and Daniel Pipes follow an almost similar trajectory of thoughts. See for instance Howard 1995, p. 67; Lewis 2005, p. 36; Pipes 2006; This view was earlier advanced by Pollis and Schwab 1979, pp. 1–18.

19 Mayer 2007, p. 57.

20 Morsink 1999; Weissbrodt 1988, p. 1; Vasak 1982, p. 672; Baderin 2005, p. 165. For a more detailed exposition of Baderin's views on the subject see Baderin 2003; Laqueur and Rubin 1979, p. 1. They argue that: 'Nor is it true that the idea of human rights is an invention alien to most non-western cultures and that it has been foisted on a more or less unwilling world. Even if there were no explicit covenants to that effect in traditional societies in Asia, Africa and Latin America, the idea of freedom was hardly alien to those civilizations.'

21 Strawson 1995, p. 2.

antithesis to … rights has been sustained for so long mainly due to the generalized and confrontational approach often adopted in comparison between Islamic law and international human rights law.'[22]

The CRC provides an example of the potential for transforming West-centric human rights to truly universal ones. By, for instance, acknowledging and protecting the rights to health, education, and clean drinking water, as well as protection from exploitation, the concerns of a truly universal constituency of children is addressed. After decades of wrangling over the question of whether or not Islam recognizes human rights, it would be more pertinent to pose the question thus: do the rights of the child as enunciated in the CRC resonate with comparable values within the Islamic legal traditions? This then opens the way to related questions, such as whether a Muslim intra-community dialogue employing the moral and ethical framework of the Quran might arrive at a notion of children's rights that reflects contemporary understandings of the concept?

Rajabi-Ardeshiri suggests that Muslim states, in an effort to own human rights as part of the Islamic traditions, have since the 1980s introduced alternative 'Islamic' human rights instruments, including those specifically addressing children's rights. Compared to the divergent notions of children's rights evident in the 1981 Universal Islamic Declaration on Human Rights and the 1990 Cairo Declaration on Human Rights in Islam, the 1994 Declaration on the Rights and Care of the Child in Islam and the 2005 Rabat Declaration on Child's Issues are visibly more convergent with the CRC.

11.3 'Constitutional Islamization' as Public Expressions of Plural Muslim Identities

In order to assess Muslim states' practice, a useful starting point is to capture some of the 'public' expressions of Islamic identity within and across these states, and see how they impact on positions adopted towards international human rights treaties including the CRC. One explicit expression of Islamic identity is how a national constitution describes any given Muslim-majority state. This approach, aptly described as 'constitutional Islamization',[23] might be evidenced by the insertion of an 'Islamic supremacy' clause (declaring sharia to be a, or the, principal source of legislation), a repugnancy clause (stating that no legislation may be adopted in contravention of sharia), a requirement that the head of state be Muslim, that persons holding public office take an Islamic oath, and so on. The usual diversity among Muslim jurisdictions is evident in the number and nature of Islamic clauses inserted.

[22] Baderin 2003, p. 167.

[23] Ahmed and Gouda 2015.

Expressions of how states present their public face to the international community vary, and they are not always reflective of the practices of communities on the ground. Posturing and positioning in public may be the result of political maneuvering at home or abroad, the compulsion of particular historical moments in time, or a 'playing to the domestic gallery'. In the context of Muslim jurisdictions, inserting clauses of constitutional Islamization is a public expression of Islamic identity.

There are significant differences in the way in which Islam is treated in the constitutions of Muslim countries,[24] 'especially in terms of its relationship to the state and public life',[25] and there is little uniformity in the number and substance of Islamic clauses inserted. For instance, it might be assumed that *all* Muslim jurisdictions would declare themselves to be an Islamic state, or declare Islam to be the state religion, or insert a repugnancy clause. Yet this assumption is incorrect: such clauses are in fact not the norm in the constitutions of Muslim-majority countries.[26] As shown in Table 11.1, Ahmed and Gouda analyzed the constitutions of 45 Muslim-majority countries[27] so as to inform some important questions: how prevalent is constitutional Islamization? What are the main Islamic clauses, and which countries have the most (and the least) Islamized constitutions?[28]

Table 11.1 Diversity of 'constitutional Islamization' among Muslim-majority states

Declare themselves to be Islamic states	Declare Islam to be the state religion	Have no constitutional declaration of 'Islamicity'	Declare themselves to be secular states
Afghanistan	Ten Islamic states plus:	Albania	Azerbaijan
Bahrain	Algeria	Gambia	Burkina Faso
Brunei	Bangladesh	Indonesia	Chad
Iran	Comoros	Lebanon	Guinea
Maldives	Djibouti	Sierra Leone	Kyrgyzstan
Mauritania	Egypt	Sudan	Mali
Oman	Iraq	Syria	Niger
Pakistan	Jordan	Uzbekistan	Senegal
Saudi Arabia	Kuwait		Tajikistan
Yemen	Libya		Turkey
	Malaysia		Turkmenistan
	Morocco		
	Qatar		
	Somalia		
	Tunisia		
	United Arab Emirates		

Source Table adapted from Stahnke and Blitt 2005; Ahmed and Gouda 2015, p. 1

[24] Abiad 2008, p. 34; also Stanke and Blitt 2005.

[25] An-Na'im 2001, p. 707.

[26] Abiad 2008, p. 34.

[27] Ahmed and Gouda 2015.

[28] Ibid., p. 2.

Islamization, then, is to be found in the constitutions of many but by no means all Muslim-majority nations. A number describe themselves as 'secular', while others are completely silent on the treatment of religion, declaring neither Islam nor secularism as a principle. Although almost 60% express some relationship to Islam in their constitutions, there is a tremendous variation in the degree and mode of Islamization. In terms of the number of Islamic clauses and their formulation, Iran appears to have the most Islamized constitution, followed by Saudi Arabia, the Maldives, Pakistan, Somalia, Afghanistan, Yemen, Bahrain, Iraq, and Algeria.

A popular clause is the 'state religion' clause: 10 countries explicitly declare themselves to be Islamic states, along with a further 15 which declare Islam to be the state religion (in the Maldives, for example, one must profess Islam in order to be a citizen). The constitutions of another 18 countries state that Islam will be a source of law, and six contain a repugnancy clause. The constitution of Iran states that judges should refrain from laws that violate Islam. The Saudi Arabian Basic Law of 1992 states that 'Judges bow to no authority' other than sharia. Fifteen constitutions require the head of state to be a Muslim, and some, including Iran and Yemen, also require this of the head of government. The Constitution of Pakistan requires members of parliament not to 'violate Islamic injunctions'. Pakistan, Mauritania, Morocco, Egypt, and Algeria provide for an advisory religious body (e.g., Pakistan's Council of Islamic Ideology), though in Iran this is not merely advisory but wields significant powers, including that of reviewing legislation to assess whether laws violate Islamic principles. The Pakistani constitution also provides for a Federal Shariat Court that can 'examine and decide the question whether or not any law or provision of law is repugnant to the injunctions of Islam', as laid down in the Quran and Sunna.

It is no surprise then that commentators have dismissed sharia provisions in Islamic constitutions as 'chiefly symbolic'[29] and unlikely to meaningfully constrain legislative activity. Some, however, are of the opinion that even simply privileging Islam as 'a' source of law, albeit the weakest formulation, makes it possible to argue that Islam forms the 'fundamental legal framework' of such constitutions.[30] This line of argument has been advanced at an international level by

[29] Hamoudi 2012, p. 431, citing Feldman N and Martinez R, Constitutional Politics and Texts in the New Iraq: An Experiment in Islamic Democracy, Fordham L. Rev. 75:903.

[30] Brown and Sherif 2004, p. 63.

'objecting states' in the face of 'blanket' reservations by some Muslim states to UN conventions including the CRC.[31]

Having analyzed the varying positions adopted by Muslim states in the extent to which they self-identify as Islamic, we now turn to how this variation plays itself out in reservations entered to the CRC.

11.4 Reservations to the CRC by Muslim States: 'Islamic' Interpretative Plurality or Autonomous State Practice?

Along with CEDAW, the CRC has attracted the highest number of religion-based reservations by Muslim states.[32] And like CEDAW, the pattern and trends of reservations is disparate. Amongst those entering reservations, some Muslim states specifically mentioned Islam and Islamic law as their reasons, while others did not. Some states entered reservations on specific articles of the CRC, whilst others did so on the convention as a whole. Table 11.2 demonstrates the diversity and interpretive plurality of the Islamic legal traditions. More so, this data is evidence of fluid and shifting positions adopted by Muslim states towards provisions of the CRC since a significant number of reservations including those entered in the name of Islam, have been subsequently withdrawn.

Table 11.2 Reservations (and their Withdrawals) entered by Muslim states to the CRC

Name of country	Date of ratification	Reservations entered/articles reserved	Withdrawn reservations
Afghanistan	28 March 1994	Reservations on all provisions of the convention that are incompatible with the laws of Islamic sharia and the local legislation in effect	
Albania	27 February 1992	No reservations	

(continued)

[31] For example, upon accession to CEDAW Libya stated that '[accession] is subject to the general reservation that such accession cannot conflict with the laws on personal status derived from the Islamic Shariah'; Iran, upon ratification of the CRC, entered the following reservation: 'The Government of the Islamic Republic of Iran reserves the right not to apply any provisions or articles of the Convention that are incompatible with Islamic Laws and the international legislation in effect.'

[32] See Hashemi 2007, p. 194.

Table 11.2 (continued)

Name of country	Date of ratification	Reservations entered/articles reserved	Withdrawn reservations
Algeria	16 April 1993	Interpretative declarations: 1. Article 14, paras 1 and 2 The provisions of paras 1 and 2 of Article 14 shall be interpreted by the Algerian government in compliance with the basic foundations of the Algerian legal system, in particular: – With the constitution, which stipulates in its Article 2 that Islam is the State religion and in its Article 35 that 'there shall be no infringement of the inviolability of the freedom of conviction and the inviolability of the freedom of opinion' – With Law No. 84-11 of 9 June 1984, comprising the Family Code, which stipulates that a child's education is to take place in accordance with the religion of its father 2. Articles 13, 16 and 17 Articles 13, 16 and 17 shall be applied while taking account of the interest of the child and the need to safeguard its physical and mental integrity. In this framework, the Algerian Government shall interpret the provisions of these articles while taking account of: – The provisions of the Penal Code, in particular those sections relating to breaches of public order, to public decency and to the incitement of minors to immorality and debauchery – The provisions of Law No. 90-07 of 3 April 1990, comprising the Information Code, and particularly its Article 24 stipulating that 'the director of a publication destined for children must be assisted by an educational advisory body' – Article 26 of the same Code, which provides that 'national and foreign periodicals and specialized publications, whatever their nature or purpose, must not contain any illustration, narrative, information or insertion contrary to Islamic morality, national values or human rights or advocate racism, fanaticism and treason. Further, such publications must contain no publicity or advertising that may promote violence and delinquency'	

(continued)

Table 11.2 (continued)

Name of country	Date of ratification	Reservations entered/articles reserved	Withdrawn reservations
Azerbaijan	13 August 1992	No reservations	
Bahrain	13 February 1992	No reservations	
Bangladesh	3 August 1990	[The Government of Bangladesh] ratifies the Convention with a reservation to Article 14, para 1. Also Article 21 would apply subject to the existing laws and practices in Bangladesh	
Bosnia and Herzegovina		The Government of Bosnia and Herzegovina made a reservation in respect of Article 9(1) of the Convention. The reservation reads as follows: 'The Republic of Bosnia and Herzegovina reserves the right not to apply para 1 of Article 9 of the Convention since the internal legislation of the Republic of Bosnia and Herzegovina provides for the right of competent authorities (guardianship authorities) to determine on separation of a child from his/her parents without a previous judicial review'	On 16 September 2008, the Government of Bosnia and Herzegovina informed the Secretary-General that it had decided to withdraw the reservation
Brunei Darussalam	27 December 1995	'The Government of Brunei Darussalam expresses its reservations on the provisions of the said Convention which may be contrary to the Constitution of Brunei Darussalam and to the beliefs and principles of Islam, the State religion, and without prejudice to the generality of the said reservations, in particular expresses its reservations on Article 14, Article 20 para 3, and Article 21 subparagraphs b, c, d and e of the Convention'	On 10 August 2015, the Government of Brunei Darussalam informed the Secretary-General that it had decided to partially withdraw its reservations to Articles 20(1), 20(2), and 21(a) made upon accession
Burkina Faso	31 August 1990	No reservations	
Chad	2 October 1990	No reservations	
Comoros	22 June 1990	No reservations	

(continued)

Table 11.2 (continued)

Name of country	Date of ratification	Reservations entered/articles reserved	Withdrawn reservations
Djibouti	6 December 1990	The Government of Djibouti shall not consider itself bound by any provisions or articles that are incompatible with its religion and its traditional values	On 7 December 2009 the Government of Djibouti informed the Secretary-General that it had decided to withdraw reservation made upon ratification to the Convention
Egypt	6 July 1990	Reservation on Articles 20, 21 which reads as follows: Since The Islamic Shariah is one of the fundamental sources of legislation in Egyptian positive law and because the Shariah, in enjoining the provision of every means of protection and care for children by numerous ways and means, does not include among those ways and means the system of adoption existing in certain other bodies of positive law The Government of the Arab Republic of Egypt expresses its reservation with respect to all the clauses and provisions relating to adoption in the said Convention, and in particular with respect to the provisions governing adoption in Articles 20 and 21 of the Convention	On 31 July 2003, the Government of Egypt informed the Secretary-General that it had decided to withdraw its reservation made upon signature and confirmed upon ratification in respect of Articles 20 and 21 of the Convention
Gambia	8 August 1990	No reservations	
Guinea	13 July 1990	No reservations	

(continued)

Table 11.2 (continued)

Name of country	Date of ratification	Reservations entered/articles reserved	Withdrawn reservations
Indonesia	5 September 1990	Initial reservations to Articles 1, 14, 16, 17, 21, 22 and 29 The reservation reads as follows: 'The 1945 Constitution of the Republic of Indonesia guarantees the fundamental rights of the child irrespective of their sex, ethnicity or race. The Constitution prescribes those rights to be implemented by national laws and regulations The ratification of the Convention on the Rights of the Child by the Republic of Indonesia does not imply the acceptance of obligations going beyond the Constitutional limits nor the acceptance of any obligation to introduce any right beyond those prescribed under the Constitution With reference to the provisions of Articles 1, 14, 16, 17, 21, 22 and 29 of this Convention, the Government of the Republic of Indonesia declares that it will apply these articles in conformity with its Constitution'	On 2 February 2005, the Government of Indonesia informed the Secretary-General that it had decided to withdraw its reservation made upon ratification on Articles 1, 14, 16, 17, 21, 22 and 29 of the 1989 Convention. 'With reference to the provisions of Articles 1, 14, 16, 17, 21, 22 and 29 of this Convention, the Government of the Republic of Indonesia declares that it will apply these articles in conformity with its Constitution'

(continued)

Table 11.2 (continued)

Name of country	Date of ratification	Reservations entered/articles reserved	Withdrawn reservations
Iran	13 July 1994	*Upon signature: Reservation:* 'The Islamic Republic of Iran is making reservation to the articles and provisions which may be contrary to the Islamic Shariah, and preserves the right to make such particular declaration, upon its ratification' *Upon ratification: Reservation:* 'The Government of the Islamic Republic of Iran reserves the right not to apply any provi sions or articles of the Convention that are incompatible with Islamic Laws and the international legislation in effect'	
Iraq	15 June 1994	Reservation in respect to article 14, para 1, concerning the child's freedom of religion, as allowing a child to change his or her religion runs counter to the provisions of the Islamic sharia	
Jordan	24 May 1991	The Hashemite Kingdom of Jordan expresses its reservation and does not consider itself bound by Articles 14, 20 and 21 of the Convention, which grant the child the right to freedom of choice of religion and concern the question of adoption, since they are at variance with the precepts of the tolerant Islamic sharia	
Kuwait	21 October 1991	Reservation of Kuwait to Article 21: The State of Kuwait, as it adheres to the provisions of the Islamic sharia as the main source of legislation, strictly bans abandoning the Islamic religion and does not therefore approve adoption	
Kyrgyzstan	7 October 1994	No reservations	
Lebanon	14 May 1991	No reservations	
Libya	15 April 1993	No reservations	

(continued)

Table 11.2 (continued)

Name of country	Date of ratification	Reservations entered/articles reserved	Withdrawn reservations
Malaysia	17 February 1995	Reservation: The Government of Malaysia accepts the provisions of the Convention on the Rights of the Child but expresses reservations with respect to Articles 1, 2, 7, 13, 14, 15, 28 para 1(a) and 37, […] of the Convention and declares that the said provisions shall be applicable only if they are in conformity with the Constitution, national laws and national policies of the Government of Malaysia Declaration: With respect to Article 28 para 1(a) of the Convention, the Government of Malaysia wishes to declare that with the amendment to the Education Act 1996 in the year 2002, primary education in Malaysia is made compulsory. In addition to this the Government of Malaysia provides monetary aid and other forms of assistance to those who are eligible	Articles 22, 28 para 1(b), (c), (d), (e) and paras 2 and 3, Article 40 paras 3 and 4, Articles 44 and 45 made upon accession
Maldives	11 February 1991	Reservations: '(1) Since the Islamic Shariah is one of the fundamental sources of Maldivian Law and since Islamic Shariah does not include the system of adoption among the ways and means for the protection and care of children contained in Shariah, the Government of the Republic of Maldives expresses its reservation with respect to all the clauses and provisions relating to adoption in the said Convention on the Rights of the Child (2) The Government of the Republic of Maldives expresses its reservation to para 1 of Article 14 of the said Convention on the Rights of the Child, since the Constitution and the Laws of the Republic of Maldives stipulate that all Maldivians should be Muslims' Reservations to Articles 14 and 21	
Mali	20 September 1990	The Government of the Republic of Mali declares that, in view of the provisions of the Mali Family Code, there is no reason to apply Article 16 of the Convention	

(continued)

Table 11.2 (continued)

Name of country	Date of ratification	Reservations entered/articles reserved	Withdrawn reservations
Mauritania	16 May 1991	In signing this important Convention, the Islamic Republic of Mauritania is making reservations to articles or provisions which may be contrary to the beliefs and values of Islam, the religion of the Mauritanian People and State	
Morocco	12 June 1993	Provisions of Article 14, para 1, of the Convention on the Rights of the Child in the light of the Constitution of 7 October 1996 and the other relevant provisions of its domestic law, as follows: Article 6 of the Constitution, which provides that Islam, the State religion, shall guarantee freedom of worship for all. Article 54, para 6, of Act 70-03 (the Family Code), which stipulates that parents owe their children the right to religious guidance and education based on good conduct. By this declaration, the Kingdom of Morocco reaffirms its attachment to universally recognized human rights and its commitment to the purposes of the aforementioned Convention. The reservation reads as follows: 'The Kingdom of Morocco, whose Constitution guarantees to all the freedom to pursue his religious affairs, makes a reservations to the provisions of Article 14, which accords children freedom of religion, in view of the fact that Islam is the State religion'	On 19 October 2006, the Government of Morocco informed the Secretary-General that it had decided to withdraw the reservation made with regard to Article 14 made upon ratification
Niger	30 September 1990	No reservations	

(continued)

Table 11.2 (continued)

Name of country	Date of ratification	Reservations entered/articles reserved	Withdrawn reservations
Oman	9 December 1996	(Initially, but later withdrawn) Articles 7, 9, 21 and 30 Reservations made upon accession read as follows: '1. … Article 9… 2. A reservation is entered to all provisions of the Convention that do not accord with Islamic law or the legislation in force in the Sultanate and, in particular to the provisions relating to adoption set forth in its Article 21 3. 3. … 4.… 5. The Sultanate does not consider itself to be bound by those provisions of Article 14 of the Convention that accord a child the right to choose his or her religion'	On 9 December 2014, the Secretary-General was notified of the Government of Oman's decision to withdraw the reservations to Articles 7, 9, 21 and 30 made upon accession. On 9 December 2014, the Secretary-General was notified of the Government of Oman's decision to modify the reservation to Article 14 made upon accession: The modified text is as follows: 'The Sultanate of Oman is not committed to the contents of Article (14) of the Convention, which gives the child the right to freedom of religion until he reaches the age of maturity'

(continued)

Table 11.2 (continued)

Name of country	Date of ratification	Reservations entered/articles reserved	Withdrawn reservations
Pakistan	12 November 1990	'Provisions of the Convention shall be interpreted in the light of the principles of Islamic laws and values'	On 23 July 1997, the Government of Pakistan informed the Secretary-General that it had decided to withdraw its reservation made upon signature and confirmed upon ratification
Qatar	3 April 1995	General reservation made upon signature and confirmed upon ratification to the Convention. The text of the general reservation reads as follows: '[The State of Qatar] enter(s) a general reservation by the State of Qatar concerning provisions incompatible with Islamic Law'	Council of Ministers decided at its fourth ordinary meeting of 2009, held on 28 January 2009, to approve the partial withdrawal by the State of Qatar of its general reservation, and informed the Secretary-General on 29 April 2009. The reservation shall continue to apply in respect of the provisions of Articles 2 and 14 of the Convention
Saudi Arabia	26 January 1996	[The Government of Saudi Arabia enters] reservations with respect to all such articles as are in conflict with the provisions of Islamic law	

(continued)

Table 11.2 (continued)

Name of country	Date of ratification	Reservations entered/articles reserved	Withdrawn reservations
Senegal	31 July 1990	No reservations	
Sierra Leone	18 June 1990	No reservations	
Somalia	1 October 2015	'The Federal Republic of Somalia does not consider itself bound by Articles 14, 20, 21 of the above stated Convention and any other provisions of the Convention contrary to the General Principles of Islamic Sharia'	
Sudan	3 August 1990	No reservations	
Syria	15 July 1993	Reservations: 'The Syrian Arab Republic has reservations on the Convention's provisions which are not in conformity with the Syrian Arab legislations and with the Islamic Shariah's principles, in particular the content of Article (14) related to the Right of the Child to the freedom of religion, and Articles 20 and 21 concerning the adoption'	On June 2012, the Government of the Syrian Arab Republic notified the Secretary-General of its decision to partially withdraw its reservations to Articles 20 and 21 of the Convention. The reservation to Article 14 continues
Tajikistan	26 October 1993	No reservations	

(continued)

Table 11.2 (continued)

Name of country	Date of ratification	Reservations entered/articles reserved	Withdrawn reservations
Tunisia	30 January 1992	Declaration: 1. The Government of the Republic of Tunisia declares that the Preamble to and the provisions of the Convention, in particular Article 6, shall not be interpreted in such a way as to impede the application of Tunisian legislation concerning voluntary termination of pregnancy 2. The Government of the Republic of Tunisia declares that its undertaking to implement the provisions of this Convention shall be limited by the means at its disposal Reservations: 3. The Government of the Republic of Tunisia enters a reservation with regard to the provisions of Article 2 of the convention, which may not impede implementation of the provisions of its national legislation concerning personal status, particularly in relation to marriage and inheritance rights. 4. The Government of the Republic of Tunisia regards the provisions of Article 40, para 2(b)(v), as representing a general principle to which exceptions may be made under national legislation, as is the case for some offences on which final judgment is rendered by cantonal or criminal courts without prejudice to the right of appeal in their regard to the Court of Cassation entrusted with ensuring the implementation of the law Declaration: 5. The Government of the Republic of Tunisia declares that it shall not, in implementation of this Convention, adopt any legislative or statutory decision that conflicts with the Tunisian Constitution 6. The Government of the Republic of Tunisia considers that Article 7 of the Convention cannot be interpreted as prohibiting implementation of the provisions of national legislation relating to nationality and, in particular, to cases in which it is forfeited	On 1 March 2002, the Government of Tunisia informed the Secretary-General that it had decided to withdraw declaration 2 and reservation 4 made upon ratification. On 23 September 2008, the Secretary-General received a notification from the Government of Tunisia that it had decided to withdraw the declaration and reservations made upon ratification at points 5 and 6

(continued)

Table 11.2 (continued)

Name of country	Date of ratification	Reservations entered/articles reserved	Withdrawn reservations
Turkey	4 April 1995	The Republic of Turkey reserves the right to interpret and apply the provisions of Articles 17, 29 and 30 of the United Nations Convention on the Rights of the Child according to the letter and the spirit of the Constitution of the Republic of Turkey and those of the Treaty of Lausanne of 24 July 1923	
Turkmenistan	20 September 1993	No reservations	
UAE	3 January 1997	Article 7 (nationality is an internal matter), 14 (tenor of this article to the extent that it does not conflict with the principles and provisions of Islamic law), 17 (country's traditions and cultural values are not violated), 21 (system of adoption)	
Uzbekistan	29 June 1994	No reservations	
Yemen	1 May 1991	No reservations	

While Table 11.1 reflected the diversity of positions adopted by Muslim states in how they self-identify as Islamic in their respective constitutions and other legal frameworks, Table 11.2 shows just how disparate their responses are to human rights treaties, as exemplified by their reservations to the CRC. Variously they cite national constitutions and laws, cultural practices, and religious injunctions as reasons for their reservations.

Analyzing Tables 11.1 and 11.2 together, some interesting facts emerge. Ten states ('a' in Table 11.3) self-identify as 'Islamic' in their constitutions; a further 15 (b) also declare Islam as the state religion; eight (c) make no declaration as to Islamic identity; and 11(d) identify themselves as secular. But this categorization does not necessarily match the reservations to CRC articles nor subsequent withdrawals, as demonstrated in Table 11.3. Please note that countries like Mali and Turkey are not mentioned as they did not fall into any of the categories below.

Table 11.3 Reservations and withdrawals by Muslim states at a glance

Article 14 reserved	Article 21 reserved	Both 14 and 21 reserved	Reservations invoking Islam	Ratified without reservations	Reservations withdrawn, in full/partial
Algeria (b)	Bangladesh (b)	Bangladesh (b)	Afghanistan (a)	Albania (c)	Brunei (a)
Bangladesh (b)	Brunei (a)	Brunei (a)	Algeria (b)	Azerbaijan (d)	Djibouti (b)
Brunei (a)	Egypt (b)	Indonesia	Brunei (a)	Bahrain (a)	Egypt (b)
Iraq (b)	Jordan (b)	Iran (a)	Djibouti (b)	Burkina Faso (d)	Gambia
Jordan (b)	Kuwait (b)	Jordan (b)	Iran (a)	Chad (d)	Guinea
Malaysia (b)	Oman (a)	Maldives (a)	Iraq (b)	Comoros (b)	Indonesia (c)
Maldives (a)	Somalia (b)	Oman (a)	Jordan (b)	Gambia (c)	Malaysia (b)
Morocco (b)	Syria (c)	Saudi Arabia (a)	Kuwait (b)	Guinea (d)	Morocco (b)
Oman (a)		Somalia (b)	Maldives	Kyrgyzstan (d)	Oman (a)
Qatar (b)		Syria (c)	Mauritania (a)	Lebanon (c)	Pakistan (a)
Somalia (b)		UAE (b)	Pakistan (a)	Libya (b)	Qatar (b)
Syria (c)			Qatar (b)	Niger (d)	Syria (c)
			Saudi Arabia (a)	Senegal (d)	Tunisia (b)
			Somalia (b)	Sierra Leone (c)	
			Syria (c)	Sudan (c)	
			UAE (b)	Tajikistan (d)	
				Turkmenistan (d)	
				Uzbekistan (c)	
				Yemen (a)	

Table 11.3, then, presents us with a complex picture of reservations and subsequent withdrawals in the light of the degree of Islamization of states' constitutions. Nineteen states ratified the CRC without entering any reservation to its substantive provisions on children's rights. Bahrain and Yemen, who constitutionally declare themselves to be Islamic states, ratified the CRC without reservation. Comoros and Libya, where Islam is also the state religion, ratified without reservation, whereas Bangladesh and Malaysia entered reservations without mentioning Islamic law and sharia as their reasons for doing so. Yet a close look at the reservations entered by Bangladesh reveals that its government cited 'existing laws and practices' as reasons for those reservations, not Islamic law and sharia as did other states. Indonesia, the country with the largest Muslim population in the world, also initially reserved Articles 1, 14, 16, 17, 21, and 29, but with no mention of religion.

On the other hand, Syria does not declare itself to be an Islamic state nor is Islam the state religion, yet its government entered reservations to Articles 14 and 21 citing Islamic law and sharia as reasons for doing so (see text of reservation below).

Twelve states have withdrawn their reservations (either partially or completely) since ratification. Of these, at least seven reservations were entered in the name of Islamic law and sharia, leading us to the conclusion that either sharia and Islamic law principles are dynamic, fluid, and evolving, allowing for reservations in the name of Islam to be withdrawn, or reasons for their entering and withdrawal were based upon fleeting assumptions with little to do with the Islamic religion or its legal traditions. Reservations might equally have been informed by the policies of governments who wished to highlight their Islamic identity and found this a useful way to do so.

An example of this can be found in the reservations entered by Egypt upon signature, confirmed upon ratification in 1990:

> Since the Islamic Shariah is one of the fundamental sources of legislation in Egyptian positive law and because the Shariah, in enjoining the provision of every means of protection and care for children by numerous ways and means, does not include among those ways and means the system of adoption existing in certain other bodies of positive law, the Government of the Arab Republic of Egypt expresses its reservation with respect to all the clauses and provisions relating to adoption in the said Convention, and in particular with respect to the provisions governing adoption in articles 20 and 21 of the Convention.

In 2003, however, Egypt informed the Secretary-General that it had decided to withdraw its reservation made in respect of Articles 20 and 21. No explanation was offered in the documentation as to how and why Egypt had changed its stated position whereby those articles were considered to be in conflict with sharia. Syria, similarly, entered the following reservations:

> The Syrian Arab Republic has reservations on the Convention's provisions which are not in conformity with the Syrian Arab legislations and with the Islamic Shariah's principles, in particular the content of article 14 related to the Right of the Child to the freedom of religion, and articles 20 and 21 concerning the adoption.

In response to German objections to these reservations, Syria declared that:

> The laws in effect in the Syrian Arab Republic do not recognize the system of adoption, although they do require that protection and assistance should be provided to those for whatever reason permanently or temporarily deprived of their family environment and that alternative care should be assured them through foster placement and *kafalah*, in care centres and special institutions and, without assimilation in their blood lineage (*nasab*), by foster families, in accordance with the legislation in force based on the principles of the Islamic Shariah. The reservations of the Syrian Arab Republic to articles 20 and 21 mean that approval of the Convention should not in any way be interpreted as recognizing or permitting the system of adoption to which reference is made in these two articles and are subject to these limitations only. The reservations of the Syrian Arab Republic to article 14 of the Convention are restricted only to its provisions relating to religion and do not concern those relating to thought or conscience. They concern: the extent to which the right in question might conflict with the right of parents and guardians to ensure religious education of their children, as recognized by the United Nations and set forth in article 18, paragraph 4, of the International Covenant on Civil and Political Rights; the extent to which it might conflict with the right, established by the laws in force, of a child to choose a religion at an appointed time or in accordance with designated procedures or at a particular age in the case where he clearly has the mental and legal capacity to do so; and the extent to which it might conflict with public order and principles of the Islamic Shariah on this matter that are in effect in the Syrian Arab Republic with respect to each case.

In 2012, nevertheless, Syria notified the Secretary-General of its decision to partially withdraw its reservations to Articles 20 and 21 (reservation to Article 14 continues).

Interestingly, where Bangladesh entered reservations to articles that other states reserved in the name of Islam, its government sidestepped objections by omitting mention of Islam or sharia: '[Bangladesh] ratifies the Convention with a reservation to Article 14, para 1. Also Article 21 would apply subject to the existing laws and practices in Bangladesh.' 'Practices' obviously alludes to customs, traditions, and cultures that include religious practices; was Bangladesh consciously avoiding mentioning Islam as it was bound to attract objections from some member states? Adopting a more politically savvy position, did its government circumvent controversy by omitting mention of religion, Islamic law, or sharia, even though those same articles were controversially reserved by other Muslim states because they were in conflict with Islamic law?

Indonesia initially entered reservations to a number of articles, but in 2005 its government withdrew them. It is pertinent here to note that Indonesia too had reserved Articles 14 and 21, but referred to its constitution rather than to Islamic law as its rationale.

Pakistan—a self-declared Islamic state with Islam as its state religion—initially entered a general reservation to the effect that: 'Provisions of the Convention be interpreted in the light of the principles of Islamic laws and values.' This reservation was taken by some other states parties, quite reasonably, as indicating that some provisions of the CRC were not entirely consistent with Islamic law and sharia. However, in 1997 Pakistan notified the Secretary-General that it had decided to withdraw its reservations.

A close analysis of the text of reservations made by Muslim states and their subsequent withdrawals underlines the main arguments advanced in this chapter—i.e., that the Islamic legal traditions are inherently plural; that Muslim state practice is not homogeneous; and that there is evidence of an evolving conception of children's rights. Why else would Muslim states reserve but then reconsider their position vis-à-vis substantive provisions of the CRC, and why would there be such a wide range of factors informing their varying positions, both initial and subsequent?

A further and more complex question is in order here: does the (near-)universal acclamation of the CRC denote universality of norms among states, and, despite disparate reasons for entering reservations, is some uniformity of perspectives evident not simply among Muslim states but among others as well? Contention ought not to come as a surprise, since some of the contentious issues debated during the drafting process and evident from a study of the *travaux préparatoires* reflect divergence in opinion among the representatives of the various states' parties. Indeed, it is those very issues, translated as 'difficult' provisions, that emerged as reservations in the post-CRC period and remain contested terrain.

In the early stages of the drafting process the 'North' was overrepresented, leading to fears that the treaty would be a 'heavily Northern-oriented text,'[33] but

[33] Steiner and Alston 2000, p. 513.

this was attenuated by active participation from a number of countries from the South, including many Muslim jurisdictions. Treaty formulations always entail protracted debate and controversy, and the CRC was no exception. What is relevant for the purposes of this discussion is the fact that those controversial provisions became the subject of reservations and thus impinged on the universality of the child rights norms espoused in the CRC.

One controversial question was the definition of the minimum age of the child—whether childhood started at conception or at birth—and the vague and fluid formulation of Article 1 was a compromise to overcome this difficulty. A second problem area was the extent and scope of Article 14, regarding freedom of religion. Initially modelled on Article 18 of the ICCPR, which included 'the freedom to have or to adopt a religion ... of his choice,' this article was reworded to address the strong objections articulated by representatives of Muslim jurisdictions, who pointed out that in the Islamic tradition a child born to Muslim parents does not have the right to change religion. Another area where Muslim states parties raised objections was the institution of adoption as conceptualized in the 'Western' legal tradition. A final example of such controversial issues was the age at which children should be permitted to take part in armed conflict.

Having looked at how public, constitutional expressions of Islamic identity were invoked in reservations, we can now assess whether or not similar approaches and positions were adopted in the country reports on the application of the provisions of the CRC. As will become evident, the varying and evolving notions of children's rights, especially in relation to Articles 14 and 21, are further demonstrated in Muslim states' country reports.

11.5 Article 14—Freedom of Religion, Thought, and Conscience: Balancing the Rights of Parents, States, and Children?

Framing and implementing the right to freedom of religion, thought, and conscience for a child raised in a predominantly (or uniquely) Islamic socio-religious environment is a difficult matter. In often predominantly patriarchal societies, the views of the father as head of the family might be authoritative in matters of religion, thought, and conscience, on the assumption that therein lie the child's best interests, as they are themselves unable to decide what is best for them. One of the challenges for implementing children's rights thus lies in posing the question: who is the repository of children's rights? Is it parents, society, state and government, or the child itself? Who decides what is in the child's best interest, and how do they arrive at that judgment? With such variable (and possibly irreconcilable) answers to such questions, it is unsurprising that Article 14 attracted one of the highest numbers of reservations.

Article 18 of the UDHR—a pre-cursor of similar rights in subsequent treaties—states that: 'Everyone has the right to freedom of thought, conscience and religion; this right includes freedom to change his religion or belief, and freedom, either alone or in community with others and in public or private, to manifest his religion or belief in teaching, practice, worship and observance.' Article 14 of the CRC (see footnote 5) similarly opens with a general statement protecting the right to freedom of religion, thought, and conscience. Some states parties have taken this to imply a unilateral right on the part of a child to exercise freedom of religion, including changing or renouncing the religion into which it was born. Yet the subsequent subsections of Article 14 (as well as the other instruments) neutralize this right and render it subservient to the rights of parents and guardians to bring up their children in the religion of their choosing. The final part of the article subjects the right to governmental limitations on public order. During drafting this proved to be one of the most contentious provisions, evoking an objection from the representative of Bangladesh, who stated that 'Article 7(bis) [Article 14] ... appears to run counter to the traditions of the major religious systems of the world and in particular to Islam. ... It appears to infringe upon the sanctioned practice of a child being reared in the religion of his parents.'[34]

At least insofar as no example has come into the public domain, a child's right to freedom of religion, thought, and conscience has never presented itself as an issue.[35] Pronouncements in various verses of the Quran versus actual Muslim practice and belief present us with an interesting observation in this regard: the Quran does not in fact favor children blindly following the religion of their parents, and thus would appear to uphold the right to freedom of religion.[36] Yet for centuries, changing one's religion has been deemed apostasy attracting the most serious punishment—the death penalty. How can this conflict of text and practice be understood? One explanation may lie in the separation of the Quranic text from the politics of survival of a new religious community, and an act of politics rather than a religious injunction. Once a person came into the fold of Islam, reverting to their old religion meant reinforcing the 'enemy's numbers' and strength.[37]

Based on the premise that parents as guardians know what is best for children who are not mature enough to make such important decisions, some non-Muslim states too have entered reservations and declarations to Article 14 and offered reasons that have similarities with those of Muslim states. For instance, the Netherlands' reservation declared that:

> It is the understanding of the Government of the Kingdom of the Netherlands that article 14 of the Convention is in accordance with the provisions of article 18 of the International

---

[34] Paper Submitted by the permanent representative of Bangladesh, U.N. Doc. E/CN.4/1986/39, Annex IV, at 2, quoted in Detrick 1992, p. 244.

[35] Hashemi 2007, pp. 215–216, observes that 'in practice there has never been a single case where a child changed his/her religion or where a child was punished for such a conversion.'

[36] See Quran 2:170; 5:104; 7:28; 10:78; 21:53 and 54; 26:74–76; 31:21; 43:22 and 23.

[37] See Hashemi 2007, p. 215 footnote 98.

> Covenant on Civil and Political Rights of 19 December 1966 and that this article shall include freedom of a child to have or adopt a religion or belief of his or her choice as soon as the child is capable of making such choice in view of his or her age or maturity.

Likewise, Poland made the following declaration:

> The Republic of Poland considers that a child's rights as defined in the Convention, in particular the rights defined in Articles 12–16, shall be exercised with respect for parental authority, in accordance with Polish customs and traditions regarding the place of the child within and outside the family.

The Holy See too entered a reservation:

> (b) That it interprets the articles of the Convention in a way which safeguards the primary and inalienable rights of parents, in particular in so far as these rights concern education (art. 13 and 28), religion (art. 14), association with others (art. 15) and privacy (article 16).

Both Muslim *and* non-Muslim states, then, appear to have made similar claims to the superiority of parental rights in matters of religion, thought, and conscience.

The country reports of Muslim states to the CRC committee also provide insights into how states understand, interpret, and respond to Article 14. While Bangladesh for example

> recognizes the right of the child to freedom of thought, conscience and religious practice, the society believes that a child, being immature by definition, is not in a position to consider such complex issues clearly and is consequently unable to make a free and voluntary choice of its own. The child, on the other hand, is likely to act in such cases under the influence, or even pressure, of others, neither of which is conducive to its normal, natural and healthy growth.

The Pakistan country report on Article 14 makes it clear that the exercise of the constitutional right to freedom of religion is subordinate to 'law, public order and morality'.

Saudi Arabia's response to Article 14, meanwhile, has become quite elaborate over the years and in successive reports. Its first country report on Article 14 stated that:

> Since Islamic law guarantees the right of the children to protection, and as children normally follow their father's religion, parents have the primary responsibility for the welfare development and protection of their children, especially in the light of their physical and mental immaturity.[38]

Its second periodic report covered Article 14 in identical words.[39] But the combined third and fourth reports of 2015[40] may be differentiated from the earlier reports in a number of ways. There is evidence of responsiveness to and engagement with the international human rights regime, in this case the CRC. Reporting

[38] CRC/C/61/Add.2, dated 29 March 2000.

[39] CRC/C/136/Add.1, dated 21 April 2005.

[40] CRC/C/SAU/3-4, dated 8 April 2015.

on Article 14, the Saudi government began by recalling the observations of the CRC committee on its second periodic report,[41] before responding that

> Saudi society is homogeneous in religion and language.... In spite of that, we would like to emphasize that the State respects the right of non-Muslim residents to their religious beliefs. It does not interfere in religious beliefs and rituals within the limits of personal practice that does not violate the rights of all members of Saudi society who profess Islam as a religion and belief. In accordance with this general framework, the State and Saudi families wish to bring up their children in the doctrine of the nation, with full freedom for non-Muslim families residing in the Kingdom to bring up their children according to their beliefs and religion. The state authorities have made strenuous efforts to promote religious tolerance and dialogue in society in a manner consistent with the principles of the Convention on the Rights of the Child.

Differing in their tenor and tone from the first two country reports, the authors of the combined third and fourth reports clearly ensured that the language was more in tune with what the CRC committee required.

Iran's Article 14 report is similar, stating that:

> According to Article 12 of the Constitution of the Islamic Republic of Iran, the official religion of Iran shall be Islam and the Twelver *Ja'fari* school. Other Islamic schools... shall be accorded full respect and their followers are free to act in accordance with their own jurisprudence in performing their religious rites. These schools enjoy official status in matters pertaining to religious education.... In regions of the country where Muslims following any one of these schools of *fiqh* constitute the majority, local regulations, within the bounds of the jurisdiction of local councils, are to be in accordance with the respective school of *fiqh*, without infringing upon the rights of the followers of other schools.

Indonesia's country reports are revealing, and are quite different from those of other Muslim states. The first, submitted in 1993,[42] placed implementation of Article 14 squarely within the context of Indonesia's laws regarding national education and individual development, rather than relating it exclusively to Islamic belief. The second report, in 2003,[43] observed that since 1993 questions had been raised 'regarding the difficulties experienced by children from families of the Baha'i faith/religion to freely study and practise their teachings and beliefs in schools in Indonesia', and that, in the light of concerns for rights and freedoms, measures had been implemented to guarantee the freedom to choose and practise religion. The third and fourth combined reports in 2012[44] went further, explicitly noting that children's freedom of religion and belief and their right to practise a religion according to one's religion and belief was by then guaranteed by law.

---

[41] 'In its observations issued following consideration of the second periodic report of Saudi Arabia, the Committee on the Rights of the Child referred to the right of the child to freedom of thought, conscience and religion, and to religious and school speech about religious minorities. In para 41 of its concluding observations, the Committee recommends promoting religious tolerance and dialogue in society.'

[42] CRC/C/3/Add.10, dated 14 January 1993.

[43] CRC/C/65/Add.23, dated 7 July 2003.

[44] CRC/C/IDN/3-4, dated 31 October 2012.

Syria likewise does not play the 'Islam' card, so to speak. Reporting on Article 14, its government declares its respect for religious diversity and

> guarantees to its citizens and anyone living in its territory the freedom to engage in religious practices in keeping with the teachings of religion and the laws specific to each religion. The Syrian Arab Republic earlier entered a reservation to Article 14 of the Convention on the Rights of the Child, concerning freedom of thought, conscience and religion. We emphasize here that children are not permitted under any legal system in the world to conduct financial or personal business or even to choose a partner in life. These are not matters to be elevated to the status of a conviction. To allow children the freedom to change or choose their religion as they wish would be incompatible with Article 18, paragraph 4, of the International Covenant on Civil and Political Rights adopted by the United Nations General Assembly, which provides for the liberty of parents to ensure the religious and moral education of their children in conformity with their own convictions. The same principle is articulated in the International Covenant on Social, Economic and Cultural Rights. How can it be, therefore, that this right is established for parents in these two international instruments and then subsequently denied under the Convention on the Rights of the Child? It is our hope that, for all of these reasons, the Committee appreciates why we continue to maintain our reservation to the above-mentioned article, while stressing that the reservation is limited to the right of the child to choose his or her religion. We say this because the Government is concerned not to undermine the freedom of parents with respect to their children's religious education and because it believes that this right may harm family cohesion, the solidity of which is regarded as a merit of Syrian society. To deny children the right to inherit from their parents would be damaging to them and would create conflict between them and family members, because of the legal principle that there can be no transmission by inheritance where the religion is different. Furthermore, it makes no sense to prevent children from disposing of their property because they have not reached the age of majority and yet allow them free rein in the matter of belief.

It is apparent, then, that there are plural responses across Muslim states to a child's right to freedom of religion, thought, and conscience. One point which is absent from the discussion, however, is what happens if the parents profess different religions. Article 14 does not establish the father's religion as superior to that of the mother, and this silence (as well as that in the country reports) serves to underline the fluidity and vagueness characteristic of human rights treaties.

As is evident from the literature,[45] freedom of religion for children of mixed-faith marriages is a challenge for Muslim states, with plural positions and outcomes ranging from denying custody and guardianship to a non-Muslim mother all the way through to a child choosing the religion of the non-Muslim mother. Case law is replete with examples where awarding custody of children has hinged on the faith of the mother, with non-Muslim women disadvantaged; exercising a true freedom of choice of religion by children is also restricted for practical reasons within jurisdictions where interpretations of classical conceptions of Islamic law declare that only a Muslim may inherit from a Muslim.

[45] For detailed discussions on this aspect see Gallala-Arndt 2015, pp. 829–58; Hashemi 2007, pp. 194–227; Rajabi-Ardeshiri 2009, pp. 475–89; Ali and Azam 1998, pp. 143–61.

11.6 Fossilized in History but Lost in Translation? *Kafāla* and Adoption[46] in the Islamic Legal Traditions and the CRC

Article 21 of the CRC talks of recognizing and/or permitting that a state's system of adoption 'shall ensure that the best interests of the child shall be the paramount consideration', yet few questions in Islamic law evoke a more unequivocal and emphatically negative response than 'does Islam permit adoption?' Adoption in the Western sense (non-biological parents taking a child as their own, giving it their name, and treating it the same as their biological children) is not permissible in Islamic law. Yet because traditional Islamic law prohibits adoption, it is therefore assumed that, by extension, Muslim states and communities follow that prohibition.[47] Fossilized in history with the revelation of the so-called 'adoption' verse (Quran 33:4), close jurisprudential interpretation and an evolution of text and context did not take place; the concept thus became fossilized. And a further reason for the scant discourse on this particular aspect of law has been the influence of 'Western' law and languages on non-Western socio-legal systems. Since the frame of reference became Western law and language, only the bare bones of concepts such as *kafāla* remained, rather lost in translation. With 'adoption' as defined in its Western sense not permitted, the term *kafāla* became synonymous instead with 'fostering', the literature on the subject trying then to equate the two.

In addition to reservations to Article 21 citing Islamic law and sharia as reasons (as we have seen), country reports too raise this issue. The approaches, however, are plural even between Muslim states, as the following examples demonstrate.

Saudi Arabia entered a general reservation to the CRC, making ratification subject to sharia, and this is the premise upon which its country reports are based. All three go straight to reporting on the local operation of the system of *kafāla*, with the first reporting that Saudi Arabia

> applies the *kafala* of Islamic law, which secures the child's right to life in conditions that guarantee freedom and dignity, promote the child's development and enable the child to manifest his or her talents in the future. The state has laid down, in compliance with Islamic Law, the conditions governing *kafala* and alternative families in a manner consistent with the best interests of the child as it requires that a woman or family wishes to assume a *kafala* should be of good reputation and health and sound social and financial standing.[48]

The following reports make similar points and go into further detail on, for example, funding and quality assurance with regard to *kafāla* arrangements. All of them emphasize the fact that *kafāla* is a system whereby orphans, abandoned children, and those from needy families are looked after in alternative family arrangements, the assumption being that only children in need of alternative family arrangements are the subjects of *kafāla*.

---

[46] For an excellent exposition and historical account of adoption within the Islamic legal traditions see Yassari 2015.

[47] Yassari 2015.

[48] First periodic report, CRC/C/61/Add. 2, dated 29 March 2000, pp. 43–44.

Unlike the Saudi country reports, which do not engage with adoption but simply replace it with *kafāla* as enunciated in Islamic law, Indonesia acknowledges adoption as stated in the CRC as a regime. In its first country report on Article 21, Indonesia noted that:

> Although a special law on adoption does not at the present exist in Indonesia, because of tradition and religion beliefs the adoption process has been carried out smoothly. To some extent, Indonesia has faced problems in inter-country adoption. To overcome this, a special regulation had been circulated under Supreme Court Circular No. 6, 1987. To prevent child abuse carried out though adoption, the minister of Social Affairs has appointed certain foundations and given them authority to handle inter-country adoption. To give assurance to children adopted abroad, Indonesia welcomes the European Convention on the Adoption of Children. However, the implementation of inter-country adoption will be carried out in accordance with the Indonesian Supreme Court Circular.

In its second report, however, it had the following to say:

> Based on observations by the Indonesian Supreme Court, there has been a change/shift in the practice of adoption in Indonesia. In the past, adoption of children was carried out in a traditional way, in order to obtain a child or for other reasons. According to Islam, if a child is adopted, the links between the child and his biological parents must not be broken. However, it is not uncommon that when a child is adopted, his adoptive parents keep the identity of the parents a secret from the child in order to make him believe that his adoptive parents are his biological parents. But, in general, this could be counterproductive, particularly once the child becomes an adult and learns about his real situation. As a consequence of Government Regulation No. 7 of 1997 concerning Civil Servant Salaries, which provides for benefits for civil servants adopting children through a court ruling, the practice of adoption with a court ruling has become more common.[49]

Indonesia's second country report also refers to the European Convention on the Adoption of Children as a source of 'inspiration' for Indonesian action in anticipation of the possibility of inter-country adoption. Yet such inter-country adoption and the acknowledgment of European laws on adoption is a notable departure from the general trend of Muslim states, which have displayed a reticence in joining the Hague Convention. Unlike Saudi Arabia and indeed most Muslim states parties to the CRC, the Indonesian reports do not discuss *kafāla* but confine their discussion and reporting to 'adoption'. Responding to questioning by the CRC committee, Indonesia recognizes that the 'not uncommon' practice of raising a child without telling him about his biological background can be counterproductive—an acceptance of how adoption is actually practiced in Muslim jurisdictions, rather than how it appears on paper.[50] Active engagement with and progressive implementation of Article 21 is evident in Indonesia's country reports: in the first, in 1993, no laws regulating adoption were available; whereas by the second, in 2012, laws had been developed at a national level, 'guided by the best interests of the child and in accordance with local customs and tradition and applicable to law'.[51]

---

[49] CRC/C/IDN/3-4, dated 31 October 2012.

[50] CRC/C/65/Add.23, dated 7 July 2003.

[51] CRC/C/IDN/3-4, dated 31 October 2012, p. 23.

Another Southeast Asian Muslim-majority country, Malaysia discusses adoption as well as *kafāla* in its reports: 'Adoption is allowed in Malaysia, and the legislation pertaining to adoption is aimed at protecting the welfare and best interests of the child.' It goes on to state that formal adoptions are monitored by the Department of Social Welfare but admits that there are many cases of informal adoptions which are arranged between adoptive and natural parents. This is an important point, indicative as it is of the actual practices of Muslim communities, going well beyond doctrinal Islamic law and often unreported and unacknowledged. The Malaysian reports also refer to *kafāla* as a Muslim practice recognized and implemented in Malaysian society. However, a distinction between adoption and *kafāla* is made:

> Kafalah is not adoption and creates no effect of 'parent-child' relationship. The child remains the obligation of the biological parent who remains the legal guardian. Kafalah does not make any child a family member of the custodian or appointed guardian (kafil). The child retains his natural parent's name, not affiliated to the foster father or mother and he is still able to inherit from his biological father or mother.

The Malaysian report also states that:

The fostered Muslim child is given the same rights as a natural child and may be entitled to benefit from the foster parents' property b-y way of gift (hibah) or the foster parents may devise not more than one third of their property by will (wasiat) to the child.[52]

The Indonesian and Malaysian reports on adoption and *kafāla*, then, present a more progressive and open approach to interpreting and applying Islamic law, as well as being more accepting of Islamic law as practiced on the ground. Both countries' reports present their cultures in a positive and inclusive light. Indonesia aptly describes Indonesian perspectives on its multi-ethnic and multi-religious polity by stating that 'there are five religions, namely Islam, Catholic, Christian, Hindu, and Buddhist. Although 90% of Indonesian citizens are Muslim, Indonesia does not accept a minority or majority concept.'[53]

This openness to other religious communities and cultures within their borders is certainly not replicated in Muslim countries such as Pakistan, however. Reporting on Article 21 in successive reports, the prohibition on adoption in its Western sense is explicit, without reference to those prevalent, informal arrangements by which childless Pakistani couples do adopt children: 'Foster placement is not recognized in Pakistan under any law. Adoption is also not permitted in Pakistan under Islamic law. Courts have given a ruling that there is nothing in Islamic law that is similar to adoption as recognized under Roman legal systems.'

In the combined third and fourth reports, at least, some slight evolution is visible regarding the long-term care of children in alternative family arrangements: 'The NCCWD is reviewing legal provisions for the long-term care of children including adoption, *kafala*, foster care and guardianship, but any provision must achieve the best interests of the child within *sharia* law.'[54]

---

[52] CRC/C/MYS/1, dated 22 December 2006, p. 26.

[53] CRC/C/3/Add.10, dated 14 January 1993.

[54] CRC/C/PAK/3-4, dated 19 March 2009.

Interestingly, Bangladesh (which until 1971 was part of Pakistan) adopted a different stance in its reservations and reports: while Pakistan initially cited religion as a factor inspiring its general reservation, Bangladesh justified its opposition to inter-country adoption with reference not to sharia but instead to the widespread abuse of the law in the wake of the country's war of independence in 1971, which left many war orphans.

Syria, in turn, presents an interesting example of a Muslim-majority country that initially entered reservations to Article 21 yet subsequently withdrew them. Reporting on Article 21, it observes that it

> withdrew its reservations to articles 20 and 21 [in] 2007. The only remaining reservation concerns article 14.... The reasons for this reservation are related to the religious teachings of Islam. The religion provides for the system of *kafalah* (guardianship) and placement in foster families, on condition that the filiation of the children concerned is not altered to prevent them from enjoying the right to know who their natural parents are (if their identity subsequently comes to light) and to rejoin them. It should be noted in this connection that adoption is permitted in Christian communities under their separate personal status codes.[55]

In its second report, though, Syria stated that:

> Adoption is not recognized in the Syrian legal system, and the Syrian Arab Republic expressed reservations concerning the right of adoption, which conflicts not only with the provisions of the Islamic Shari'a which prevail in the country but also with the provisions of national legislation for which Islamic legislation constitutes one of the principal sources, as stipulated in article 3, paragraph 2, of the Constitution. Although adoption is not recognized, Syrian legislation permits filiation. The concept of filiation is similar to the system of adoption, the difference between them lying in the fact that, under the adoption system, one or both of the parents must be known whereas, under the filiation system, the filiated child must be of unknown parentage or the offspring of an unlawful marriage.[56]

As will be clearly apparent, responses from Muslim states to Article 21 have highlighted once again a plurality of positions. This leads one to the understanding that, whilst some Muslim states continue to use Islamic law as the reason for not recognizing adoption as a mode of affiliation, others do nevertheless recognize it. The reason for this plurality in approach is difficult to state with certainty, and the answers may be more than one. The nation state and its policies are now driven by contemporary demands and informed increasingly by international law and policies; some Muslim states are courageously accepting the fact that adoption (in every sense of the term) exists, is practiced in their communities, and merits recognition; policy- and law-makers as well as scholars are giving closer scrutiny to the classical conceptions of Islamic law on adoption, including the Quranic verse on the subject, and are able to differentiate its essence. The evidence leads one to believe that it might be all of these, or simply the random repetition of historical and fossilized conceptions on adoption, which brings any given state to the position it holds.

---

55 CRC/C/SYR/3-4, dated 2 June 2010.

56 CRC/C/28/Add. 2, dated 14 February 1996.

11.7 Concluding Reflections

It is fair to state that the debate over Islamic and international human rights law remains inconclusive and as controversial as ever. Human rights concepts as they are currently formulated were not originally present in any legal or religious cultural tradition: the concepts of human rights as we see them expressed in covenants and conventions are, historically speaking, 'new' concepts both for the West and the non-West. True, they have antecedents in theology, philosophy, culture, and religious traditions, but individual human rights as they have come to be conceptualized since the UDHR and other human rights instruments are a new development. Just as Islamic conceptions of human rights are plural, so are those espoused within Western human rights traditions; Western and non-Western legal traditions are both pluralistic in their formulations. How else could we understand the outright refusal of the USA to ascribe to international human rights instruments including the CRC?

Subsequent developments in human rights treaties and discourse more broadly have brought Islamic law perceptions closer to those being canvassed at the international level. More and more Muslim jurisdictions are legislating for a higher minimum age in the fields of employment, marriage, and participation in armed conflict. Likewise, Western states are increasingly open to and making law acknowledging adopted children's right to know their biological parents. One persuasive approach to truly universalizing human rights norms is to accept the fluidity and evolving nature of human rights by identifying human suffering, impoverishment, vulnerability, and violations and offering support and solidarity. Who would have considered, a couple of centuries ago, that slavery would be universally prohibited as an abominable violation of human rights, despite its erstwhile presence in such widely disparate communities, cultures, and religious traditions? Likewise, perceptions of women's and minority rights are very different today and continue to change (albeit very slowly): neither violence against women nor the rights of lesbians were raised as burning issues during the CEDAW deliberative process in the 1970s; today, no international women's human rights conference would omit them. Female circumcision is now being challenged as against human dignity and bodily rights and as an issue of child rights as well as women's rights.

Application of the CRC in Muslim jurisdictions reflects their varied and complex socio-legal landscapes. Although some recognition of the CRC formulation is increasingly being reflected in national laws and policy, including the courts, translations of concepts into local parlance dilutes an already ambiguous meaning. The socio-economic, cultural, and political challenges of most Muslim jurisdictions cannot be separated from how children's rights are conceived and operationalized; hence the disparity between various countries. Simultaneously, and with increasing proactivity, 'Islamic' human rights instruments, including some focused on children, have been adopted by Muslim forums and organizations. To some these instruments appear as alternative human rights documents to those emanating from the UN and the international human rights regime. It may be argued though that these documents present an evolving Islamic human rights regime, reflective of convergence rather than diverging conceptions of human rights. In fact, it may be that the beginnings of a truly universal human rights regime is in the making—slowly but surely.

Children's rights as enunciated in the CRC are a relatively new phenomenon and unknown in their present formulations even a century ago. Historically, children across most legal and cultural traditions were not treated as individuals with a distinct legal personality and accompanying rights; but it was recognized that, along with women, the disabled, and the infirm, children formed a category of persons requiring protection and guardianship. The principle of what emerged in the twentieth century as the 'best interests of the child' is an evolving concept with a changing definition. It has become the most interesting yet challenging aspect of child rights discourse since its 'legalization' by inclusion in formal law at the national, regional, and international levels. As often transpires with other standard-setting concepts of rights, the 'best interests of the child' principle precedes its internalization and enculturation, not least due to the paradigm shift it requires within the relationships between children, adults, and institutions.[57]

Whilst it is recognized by diverse religious, cultural, and legal traditions that the best interests of the child is an overarching concept underlying all decisions arrived at relating to children, contestation between children and their parents or guardians may arise. For instance, are the best interests of the child determined by what a guardian or judge says they are, or are they where the child's interests will be best served?

There is an absence of a unified and homogeneous approach to reservations and to implementation of the CRC, as is clear from the country reports. Inferences however can be made.

As mentioned in the introduction to this chapter, the CRC has been ratified by all Muslim states, albeit with reservations, and detailed country reports outline implementation of its substantive articles. The tone and tenor of these country reports indicate the approaches adopted towards multilateral human rights treaties by Muslim states. The detailed information offered, as well as responses to additional questions posed by the CRC committee, is evidence, at least at a formal level, of the use of the CRC as an international bill of children's rights by these states.

There have also been improvements in the quality and detail provided in these country reports, albeit uneven. The country reports submitted to date by Saudi Arabia are an example. From a defensive position attempting to gloss over any 'difficult' areas, the combined third and fourth periodic reports reflect a significant change in language, content, and approach to children's rights. This 'change of heart', one hastens to add, does not necessarily imply change on the ground or among Saudi government and society; it might simply mean a better and more

57 For an interesting analysis see Garcia Mendez 2007, p. 106.

human-rights-literate author of the Saudi country report, since the expressions and language come close to those of a native English speaker.[58] In a similar vein, the successive country reports of Indonesia and Malaysia reveal an evolving legislative reform relating to laws regulating adoption as well as to laws for the protection of non-Muslim children.

Since its coming into force in 1990, the CRC has instigated legislative reforms in all member states including Muslim ones. What is more, Muslim forums have developed and adopted 'Islamic' human rights instruments, including children's rights. These developments, emanating from informal Muslim forums as well as from the OIC, demonstrate a positive engagement with the CRC.

There is no uniformity in the number of times Islam, Islamic law, and sharia are mentioned in country reports, though Saudi Arabia uses them most often. The very first word of the Saudi CRC country report is indeed 'Islam'.[59] The link made between Islam and concern for the welfare of children could scarcely be more emphatic: Islam, we read, 'advocates concern for the welfare of the family as the basic unit of society and pledges to provide it with all appropriate means to enable it to lead a decent life and to fully play its role in nurturing children and preparing them for life.' Application of Islam is, in essence, the very definition of the best interests of the child for the Saudis. The only use of the word sharia in the Pakistani report, by contrast, comes when it is conceptualized as being a paramount consideration when planning legal provision for the long-term care of children.[60] The 2012 Indonesian country report makes no mention of Islamic law or sharia; there, 'law', without exception, means statutory legislation rather than Quranic, sharia, or customary law.[61]

Another interesting outcome of the present enquiry has been the absence of correlation between states' positions and their schools of juristic thought in the Islamic legal traditions. Thus Malaysia and Indonesia, both Sunni and predominantly Shafi'i, had laws on the adoption of children, as did the predominantly Shia Azerbaijan. Iran on the other hand, with Shia Islam as its state religion, prohibits adoption, declaring it to be against the principles of Islamic law. Similarly Sunni, Hanafi Pakistan and Bangladesh have evoked quite distinct responses in their reservations to the CRC as well as their responses in country reports. National interests, policies, and historical moments all play a role in determining these positions, with Bangladesh recalling its wartime situation in its country report on Article 21.

The plurality of approaches to substantive provisions of the CRC by Muslim states is evidently mostly informed by national laws and societal practice. Although plurality within the Islamic legal traditions in the form of diverging

---

[58] It is common to hire the services of consultants who are adept at report writing, and having studied all the country reports for Saudi Arabia this is the conclusion I have arrived at.

[59] CRC/C/136/Add.1, dated 21 April 2005.

[60] Pakistan combined third and fourth reports, CRC/C/PAK/3-4, dated 19 March 2009, para 237.

[61] CRC/C/IDN/3-4, dated 31 October 2012.

schools of juristic thought may be a factor, this is not definitively verifiable as subtle variations remain. For instance, the Malaysian constitution pronounces a hierarchy of citizens, with the Malays as 'full citizens' and other religious/ethnic groups below that standard. On the other hand, Indonesia does not portray this differentiation between her citizens on the basis of religion and ethnicity.

In summation, and on the basis of the above discussion, it is fair to conclude that not only is there evidence of engagement with international human rights norms relating to children, but there is also a discernible paradigm shift in Muslim states' perspectives on children's rights. This is evident from the withdrawal of reservations by an increasing number of Muslim states parties, country reports and legislative reforms reflecting articles of the CRC as well as converging Islamic human rights instruments on children's rights.

References

Abiad N (2008) Sharia, Muslim States and International Human Rights Treaty Obligations: A Comparative Study. BIICL, London

Afshari R (2007) On the Historiography of Human Rights: Reflections on Paul Gordon Lauren's The Evolution of International Human Rights: Visions Seen. HRQ 29:1–67

Ahmed DI, Gouda M (2015) Measuring Constitutional Islamization: The Islamic Constitutions Index. Hastings Int'l Comp L Rev 38(1):1–74

Ali SS (2007) A Comparative Perspective of the Convention on the Rights of the Child and the Principles of Islamic Law: Law Reform and Children's Rights in Muslim Jurisdictions. In: Goonesekere S (ed) Protecting the World's Children: Impact of the Convention on the Rights of the Child in Diverse Legal Systems. UNICEF & Cambridge University Press, New York, pp 142–208

Ali SS, Azam MN (1998) Custody and Guardianship: Case Law 1947–97. In: Shaheed F et al (eds) Shaping Women's Lives, Laws, Practices and Strategies in Pakistan, Shirkatgah, Lahore, pp 143–161

An-Na'im AA (2001) Human Rights in the Arab World: A Regional Perspective. HRQ 23:701–732

Baderin MA (2003) International Human Rights and Islamic Law. Oxford University Press, New York

Baderin MA (2005) Human Rights and Islamic Law: The Myth of Discord. EHRLR 2:165–185

Brown NJ, Sherif AO (2004) Inscribing the Islamic Shari'a in Arab Constitutional Law. In: Haddad YY, Stowasser B (eds) Islamic Law and the Challenges of Modernity. Altamira Press, Walnut Creek, pp 55–80

Coulson NJ (1994) A History of Islamic Law. Edinburgh University Press, Edinburgh

Detrick S (1992) The United Nations Convention on the Rights of the Child: A Guide to the "Travaux Préparatoires". Martinus Nijhoff Publishers, Dordrecht/Boston/London

Donnelly J (1989) Universal Human Rights in Theory and Practice. Cornell University Press, Ithaca

Gallala-Arndt I (2015) The Impact of Religion on Interreligious Custody Disputes: Middle-Eastern and Southeast Asian Approaches. Am J Comp Law 63:829–858. doi:10.5131/AJCL.2015.0025

Garcia Mendez E (2007) A Comparative Study of the Impact of the Convention on the Rights of the Child: Law Reform in Selected Civil Law Countries. In: UNICEF (ed) Protecting the World's Children. Impact of the Convention on the Rights of the Child in Diverse Legal Systems. Cambridge University Press, Cambridge, pp 100–141

Hamoudi HA (2012) Repugnancy in the Arab world. Williamette Law Rev 48:427–450
Hashemi K (2007) Religious Legal Traditions, Muslim States, and the Convention on the Rights of the Child: An Essay on the Relevant UN Documentation. Human Rights Q 29(1):194–227
Howard RE (1995) Human Rights and the Search for Community. Westview Press, Boulder CO
Kavanaugh K (2010) Narrating Law. In: Emon AM et al (eds) Islamic Law and International Human Rights Law. Searching for Common Ground? Oxford University Press, Oxford, pp 17–51
Laqueur W, Rubin B (1979) The Human Rights Reader. New American Library, New York
Lewis B (2005) Freedom and Justice in the Modern Middle East. Foreign Affairs, May/June 2005. www.foreignaffairs.com/articles/middle-east/2005-05-01/freedom-and-justice-modern-middle-east. Accessed 23 Aug 2016
Mayer AE (2007) Islam and Human Rights: Tradition and Politics, 3rd edn. Westview Press, Boulder CO
Morsink J (1999) The Universal Declaration of Human Rights: Origins, Drafting and Intent. University of Pennsylvania Press, Philadelphia
Mutua M (2002) Human Rights. A Political and Cultural Critique. University of Pennsylvania Press, Philadelphia
Pipes D (2006) Cartoons and Islamic Imperialism. www.danielpipes.org/article/3360. Accessed 23 Aug 2016
Pollis A, Schwab P (1979) Human Rights: A Western Construct with Limited Applicability. In: Pollis A, Schwab P (eds) Human Rights: Cultural and Ideological Perspectives. Praeger, New York, pp 1–18
Rajabi-Ardeshiri M (2009) The Rights of the Child in the Islamic Context: The Challenges of the Local and the Global. Int J Child Rights 17:475–489
Spivak GC (2005) Use and Abuse of Human Rights. Boundary 2 32(1):131–189
Stahnke T, Blitt RC (2005) The Religion-State Relationship and the Right to Freedom of Religion or Belief: A Comparative Textual Analysis of the Constitutions of Predominantly Muslim Countries. www.uscirf.gov/sites/default/files/resources/stories/pdf/Comparative_Constitutions/Study0305.pdf. Accessed 23 Aug 2016
Steiner HJ, Alston P (2000) International Human Rights in Context: Law, Politics, Morals, 2nd edn. Oxford University Press, Oxford
Strawson J (1995) Reflections on the West's Question: "Is there a Human Rights Discourse in Islam?", paper presented at the Critical Legal Conference, University of Edinburgh, 8–10 Sept 1995
Twining W (2009) Human Rights, Southern Voices: Francis Deng, Abdullahi An-Na'im, Yash Ghai, and Upendra Baxi. Cambridge University Press, Cambridge
Vasak K (1982) Toward a Specific International Human Rights Law. In: Vasak K (ed) The International Dimension of Human Rights, vol 2. Greenwood Press, Westport/Connecticut, pp 671–679
Weissbrodt D (1988) Human Rights: An Historical Perspective. In: Davies P (ed) Human Rights. Routledge, London, pp 1–20
Yassari N (2015) Adding by Choice: Adoption and Functional Equivalents in Islamic and Middle Eastern Law. Am J Comp Law 63:927–962

Chapter 12
Synopsis

Nadjma Yassari, Lena-Maria Möller and Imen Gallala-Arndt

Keywords The best interests of the child · Parental care · Custody (*ḥaḍāna*) · Guardianship (*wilāya*) · Muslim jurisdictions · Comparative law · Cross-border disputes · Legal presumption in child law · Bilateral agreements · Hague Conference on Private International Law · Malta Process

Contents

N. Yassari · L.-M. Möller (✉)
Max Planck Institute for Comparative and International Private Law, Mittelweg 187, 20148 Hamburg, Germany
e-mail: yassari@mpipriv.de

L.-M. Möller
e-mail: möller@mpipriv.de

I. Gallala-Arndt
Max Planck Institute for Social Anthropology, Advokatenweg 36, 06114 Halle (Saale), Germany
e-mail: gallala@eth.mpg.de

N. Yassari et al. (eds.), *Parental Care and the Best Interests of the Child in Muslim Countries*, DOI 10.1007/978-94-6265-174-6_12

12.1 Introduction

In a way, parental care regimes in contemporary Muslim jurisdictions[1] lead a double life. On the one hand, they are firmly rooted in traditional Islamic legal doctrine in that they usually divide parenting functions into custody (*ḥaḍāna*) and guardianship (*wilāya*) and identify the former with the mother and the latter with the father. On the other hand, they have proven fairly flexible in recent decades and have witnessed some far-reaching reforms aimed at bringing family law in line with the evolving regulatory needs of society. In this regard, parental care regimes are exemplary for the dynamics and the development of Muslim family law in the 20th and 21st centuries.

The following synopsis will analyse the jurisdictions under review in this volume from a comparative perspective and will also discuss other Muslim countries approaches to regulating parental care where possible.

12.2 The Best Interests of the Child

Throughout the region, legislative reforms in the area of parental care have extended judicial discretion as regards the question of which parent is most suitable to act as custodian following a divorce. The most common concept that has been used to increase the leeway of judges is that of 'the best interests of the child' (*maṣlaḥat al-ṭifl*, *maṣlaḥat al-maḥḍūn*). By enshrining this principle into statutory law, legislatures have given it a prominent position which, in many instances, allows for a deviation from those rules that find their basis in Islamic jurisprudence (*fiqh*).[2] Yet, at the same time, the influence of the best interests of the child standard is not uniform in all aspects of parental care. Specifically, as has been argued elsewhere previously, *ḥaḍāna* has seen reforms that go significantly beyond those introduced in the area of *wilāya*.[3] The ten chapters collected in this volume all trace the introduction of the concept of the best interests of the child into the parental care regimes of selected Muslim jurisdictions. Many differences of course exist between the culturally and historically diverse jurisdictions that have been chosen for this study. Nonetheless, certain overarching trends and tendencies can be detected and are of particular interest as regards the overall trajectory of family law in the Muslim world.

---

[1] Throughout this contribution the terms 'Muslim jurisdictions' and 'Muslim countries' are defined as states with legislation reflecting or inspired by Islamic law. The term does not necessarily denote whether a particular country is composed of a majority or minority Muslim population or whether its self-image is that of a 'Muslim state/country'.

[2] On pre-modern rules of parental care see Ibrahim 2015, pp. 859–891.

[3] Möller 2015, pp. 893–925.

12.2.1 Custody

Custody, i.e. the physical caretaking and upbringing of the child, has by far seen the most significant modifications when compared to how it was regulated under pre-modern Islamic legal doctrine. The strict allocation of custody according to the age and gender of the child has been lifted in many jurisdictions and is now being regulated with a view to best serving the individual child's interests. This means that while we can still find statutory age limits associated with female custody in most jurisdictions, *ḥaḍāna* will no longer automatically revert to the child's father once the statutory age limits have been reached. Instead, many countries have handed over the power of custodial determination to the judge in that it will now be determined by a family court whether female custody should continue or whether a male caretaker would be the more appropriate choice. Similarly, many of the restrictions which affected the eligibility of mothers to act as their children's custodians, such as religious affiliation or remarriage, have been modified so as to allow for a more case-specific assessment of parental care.

Broadly speaking, one can identify three categories as regards the inclusion and the impact of the best interests of the child standard: First, jurisdictions in which the best interests of the child serves as an overriding principle to be considered in all decisions concerning parental care. Second, jurisdictions which have included the concept as a statutory exception in selected rules governing the allocation or revocation of custody. Finally, in some jurisdictions the best interests of the child principle has been employed to justify reforms despite not being referred to in the new regulations themselves.

12.2.1.1 The Best Interests of the Child as the Paramount Principle

The first category, i.e. the best interests of the child as an overarching principle governing all judicial decisions regarding custody, is best exemplified by the Tunisian legal system which, as illustrated in the chapter written by Souhayma Ben Achour, bases the allocation of *ḥaḍāna*, but not that of *wilāya*, exclusively on the best interests of the child. In consequence, Islamically inspired age and gender limits have been abolished entirely as determining factors and have instead been replaced by a process which gives family courts the discretion to allocate custody based on the specific interests of the individual child in question.

While an inner-Islamic comparison admittedly demonstrates that Tunisian reforms have gone the furthest, similar tendencies can be witnessed in other contemporary Muslim jurisdictions too. In their chapter on Pakistan, Ayesha Shahid and Isfandyar Ali Khan illustrate how custody has been reformed through case law which has given the best interests of the child an equally prominent position. In part, this development is owed to the fragmentary statutory basis for the adjudication of parental care cases in Pakistan. Specifically, the Guardians and Wards Act of 1890, inherited from colonial British India, mainly governs procedural aspects of parental care. The Act also applies regardless of the religious affiliation of either the child or the parents and is then supplemented by traditional Hanafi jurisprudence, Pakistan's dominant Sunni school of Islamic jurisprudence (*madhhab*). The Guardians and Wards Act facilitated Pakistan's reform-minded judicial approach to custody as, under the Act, the court is to 'be guided by what, consistently with the law to which the minor is subject, appears in the circumstances to be for the welfare of the minor.'

Although based on the same statutory legislation, i.e. the Guardians and Wards Act of 1890, judicial practice in India has taken a somewhat different route as Jean-Philippe Dequen argues in his contribution to the present volume. For Dequen, the status of Islamic law as a minority law in India has hindered the enforcement of the best interests of the child principle in legal practice as 'judges tend not to intervene within agreed-upon familial relations, especially when invoking personal law'. In consequence, while Indian law is similarly characterized by a strong potential for putting the child's best interests at the centre of custody disputes, Indian family courts have thus far been rather hesitant in comparison with their counterparts in neighbouring Pakistan. For Dequen, while this legal development is—as noted above—partially owed to Islamic law's status as a minority law in India, it can also be traced to the historical development of what came to be known as 'Anglo-Muhammadan law' in British India.

12.2.1.2 The Best Interests of the Child as a Statutory Exception

The second category of jurisdictions primarily comprises Arab states. The similarity of legal rules within the Arab world is largely owed to the fact that many Arab states modelled their personal status codes and family law provisions on one another.[4] Again, one of the main discernible trends in recent family law reforms in this region is the enhanced focus on the best interests of the child in the area of custody. Nevertheless, most countries have at the same time not yet followed the approach discussed above, instead choosing to incorporate the best interests of the child principle as an exception in different statutory rules governing the allocation or revocation of *ḥaḍāna*.

In consequence, we now find many provisions on custody that are clearly inspired or influenced by traditional Islamic jurisprudence, such as those prescribing age limits and gender differences for female custody as well as different conditions for female and male custodians to fulfil. At the same time however, many of the provisions also allow the judge to disregard the general rule and reach a contrary decision if such an exception is better suited to safeguarding the child's best interests. For example, Anver Emon, in his chapter on Qatar, highlights that there

[4] This is also illustrated by the existence of two so-called 'model codes', namely the Draft Unified Arab Law of Personal Status, prepared by the Arab League, and the Draft Law of Personal Status, issued by the Gulf Cooperation Council.

is almost no provision on the allocation or revocation of *ḥaḍāna* that does not refer to the best interests of the child. These statutory provisions oftentimes use the clause 'except for those cases in which the court, in considering the best interests of the child, decides to the contrary' (*'illā idhā qaddarat al-maḥkama khilāfa dhalika li-maṣlaḥat al-maḥḍūn'*), whereby the individual judge is empowered to disregard an Islamically inspired default rule and decide the custody case at hand based solely on the individual interests of the child.[5] A similar approach has been adopted in the recent family law codifications of Qatar's fellow Gulf Cooperation Council members Bahrain and the United Arab Emirates.[6]

While Qatari family law has incorporated such a statutory exception in different aspects of custody (such as age limits for female custody and remarriage of the mother custodian), most legislatures used this approach, first and foremost, in order to tone down strict age limits marking the end of a mother's entitlement to custody of her children. Interestingly, as a number of chapters collected in this book demonstrate, such an approach was, not infrequently, adopted in the early to mid-20th century before being done away with again at a later point.

Under Egypt's first legislative act dealing with aspects of custody (i.e. Law No. 25 of 1929), the judge, in considering the interests of the child, could extend the duration of female custody from 7 to 9 years for boys and from nine years to eleven years for girls. Similarly, in 1985, legal reforms prolonged the duration of female custody to ten years for boys and twelve years for girls with a possible extension (again if in the best interests of the child) to fifteen years for boys and until the girl is married. In 2005, however, as described in Jasmine Moussa's chapter on Egypt, while the duration of female custody was extended (to fifteen years for both boys and girls), the explicit reference to the best interests of the child standard was in fact dropped. Instead, it now falls solely upon the child itself to decide which parent he or she wishes to reside with once having reached the age of fifteen. Statutory law no longer envisions judicial consideration of the child's best interests.

Likewise, in 1951 Jordanian family law introduced a provision governing the duration of female custody and thereby for the first time introduced the concept of the child's best interests. The Jordanian provision, in both form and substance, is clearly based on Egypt's first legislative intervention in the area of custody. Consequently, the Jordanian legislature granted the individual family court judge the power to extend female custody from seven years to nine years for boys and from nine years to eleven years for girls if this was considered to serve the interests of the child. Yet in 1976, when the Jordanian legislature regulated custody in much more detail in a new family code, the reference to the best interests of the child was dropped. Instead, the age limits for female custody were raised but at the same time fixed without the possibility of a further extension based on the best

---

5 See also Möller 2016a, p. 100.

6 Möller 2016a, pp. 100 and 101.

interests of the child. Currently, Jordan, like Egypt, allows female custody until the child is fifteen, after which children have the right to choose which parent to stay with until they reach legal majority. As Dörthe Engelcke argues in her chapter on Jordan,

> [a]n analysis of the provisions introduced makes it clear that the concept of the best interests of the child is not the principal consideration when determining custody and visiting rights; rather, the interests and rights of the parents are paramount

Finally, in Lebanon's new Sunni Family Law of 2011, reference is similarly made to the best interests of the child as a statutory exception with regards to the duration of female custody. In this particular case, however, we find a use of the concept that affords judges further discretion in that they may consider the best interests of the child so as to either extend or reduce the duration of a mother's entitlement to custody depending on what they see fit in the individual case at hand.

The development of custody law regimes in Egypt and Jordan, in particular, alludes to the third and final category of how the best interests of the child standard is incorporated in Muslim family law. Specifically, instead of explicitly mentioning the principle as the paramount consideration or as a statutory exception, it has been used as an underlying consideration informing recent custody law reforms.

12.2.1.3 The Best Interests of the Child as an Underlying Consideration

In addition to Egypt and Jordan, we also find Iraq as a prime example of how considerations of preserving the child's best interests have shaped reforms in the area of custody law. As highlighted by Harith Al-Dabbagh, the Iraqi legislature explicitly referred to the best interests of the child principle as the leitmotif of the country's family law reforms as early as 1978. Specifically, according to the reformed code's explanatory memorandum, 'custody "has been entirely revised and its formulation has been simplified so that its provisions now stipulate that the basis of custody is the consideration of the interests of the minor" …'.

Interestingly, at the same time such an underlying consideration of the best interests of the child has oftentimes worked to the advancement of women's legal status (as mothers) too. In the case of Egypt, Jasmine Moussa argues that 'under Egyptian law … the child's best interests are considered synonymous with remaining in the custody of the mother and other female family members for the longest duration possible.' Similar observations have been made by Dörthe Engelcke for Jordan and by Marie-Claude Najm for Lebanon. In Iraq, the idea that women's rights can be improved through children's rights and vice versa is also evident in aspects of custody other than its mere duration. For example, since 1986, the mother's remarriage has no longer resulted in her loss of custody. This reform marks a clear shift away from the dominant position of pre-modern Islamic legal doctrine and constitutes an obvious advancement for Iraqi women's freedom to marry.

It can be noted from the foregoing that legislatures in countries such as Egypt, Jordan, and Iraq clearly acknowledged that decisions regarding custody should be generally informed by the best interests of the child. They have, however, partly removed the judicial discretion previously awarded to family courts when explicit reference was made to the concept as a statutory exception justifying a deviation from Islamically inspired default rules. Instead, by making the best interests of the child an implicit driving force behind family law reforms (and their outcomes in substantive law), the legislature has in a way reclaimed for itself the authority to determine what serves the child's interests best (such as remaining with the mother for the longest duration possible, despite her remarriage).[7] While this clearly results in an enhanced degree of legal certainty, it may simultaneously run the risk of children not being treated individually, but rather as categories determined by what the country in question perceives their general best interests to be.

12.2.2 Guardianship

As mentioned earlier, guardianship (*wilāya*) has witnessed less legislative intervention and reform than its custody counterpart. Similarly, the concept of the best interests of the child is not being employed as a technical term or overriding principle in the many rules governing the allocation and revocation of guardianship. Instead, the best interests of the child are overwhelmingly presumed to be embodied by the statutory provisions currently in force insofar as rather static presumptions exist about how a child's interests can be best safeguarded in the context of *wilāya*. These presumptions about guardianship can be seen as a mirror image of custody in that, for most legislatures, *wilāya* is best exercised by the father (or other male relatives) while, as discussed earlier, *ḥaḍāna* should be assumed by the mother (or other females relatives) for the longest duration possible. Such default rules on guardianship can be found in the vast majority of countries discussed in this volume. The only exception among the chapters is Tunisia, which has in fact modified the concept of guardianship significantly by aligning it with custody and thus has created a more unified concept of parental care whose main consideration is the best interests of the child.

[7] In Egypt, it is only under special circumstances that the best interests of the child serves as the paramount principle for awarding custody. As illustrated in Jasmine Moussa's chapter on Egypt, since 2000 the public prosecutor, but not the family court judge, has been authorized to carry out an investigation into the best interests of the child in order to grant interim custody to one of the disputing parents in advance of the final family court ruling resolving the matter.

12.2.2.1 Islamically Inspired Default Rules on Guardianship

In the majority of jurisdictions reported on in this volume, guardianship is awarded within the agnatic line, with the child's father usually assuming the position of default guardian. Guardianship, which consistent with traditional Islamic legal doctrine oftentimes comprises 'guardianship over property' (*wilāya ᶜalā al-māl*) and 'guardianship over the person' (*wilāya ᶜalā al-nafs*), has been influenced to a much lesser degree by the concept of individual child-specific rights and the necessity of case-by-case decisions. This is particularly significant given the scope of guardianship and the decision-making powers it comprises. In particular, guardianship over the person is closely connected with the upbringing and education of a child and thus overlaps considerably with the duties and responsibilities of a child's custodian. Yet we rarely find statutory provisions or case law which favour such an investigation into the child's best interests that also take into account where custody lies. Instead, guardianship over the person is usually awarded together with guardianship over property. Moreover, the main assumption underlying *wilāya ᶜalā al-māl* with respect to the child's best interests is that his financial rights need to be safeguarded and that, in consequence, financial transactions of significant value made by the guardian need to be approved by a court (cf. Egyptian, Indian, Jordanian, and Lebanese law).

Finally, in most jurisdictions, both the father (in his role as default guardian) as well as the court may theoretically grant guardianship to the mother by appointment. However, while such an appointment might be grounded in considerations about the child's best interests, it is not a paramount principle when allocating guardianship.

12.2.2.2 Putting the Child's Best Interests First

In a few countries, legislative steps have been taken to assure that guardianship is awarded with due regard for the child's best interests. This has usually been done not by including provisions to that effect into the rules governing *wilāya*, but by aligning some guardianship powers with custody. In Egypt, for example, a noteworthy legislative step was taken in 2008 that served to bridge the gap between custody and guardianship: According to the reformed Egyptian Children's Rights Act,[8] decisions regarding a child's education and schooling can now be made by the parent assuming custody and are thereby transferred from the father's authority as the child's guardian to that of the mother as the child's custodian during most of the child's school years. In combination with the custody reform of 2005 mentioned above, the modification of guardianship consequently allows for children

[8] Article 54 Law No. 12 of 1996 as amended by Law No. 126 of 2008 concerning the Amendment of Certain Provisions of the Child Law, the Penal Code, and the Civil Status Law, Official Gazette no. 24 (Suppl.) of 15 June 2008.

themselves to choose the parent responsible for their school careers by choosing whether they wish to reside with their mother or father once they have reached the age of fifteen.

The general idea of reforming parental care by aligning the functions of guardianship and custody has also been picked up by Tunisia. It should be recalled that Tunisian law does not privilege one parent over the other in the allocation of custody (following a divorce), but instead obliges the courts to award custody exclusively based on what is considered to be in the best interests of the child. Should a court award custody to the mother, however, she will also be entitled as a matter of course to assume guardianship regarding the child's travels and education as well as the administration of his assets. By doing so, the Tunisian legislature has not only transformed custody and guardianship into a de facto combined concept of parental care[9]; rather, in making the powers of guardianship subject to a judicial assessment of the child's best interests, it has also established the best interests standard as the paramount principle for allocating guardianship.

Finally, outside those countries covered in this volume, Tunisia's neighbour Algeria also introduced similar reforms in 2005. Algerian family law departs from the default rules on guardianship and makes its allocation a wholly judicial procedure since *wilāya* is necessarily granted to the parent awarded custody. As a result, considerations of the best interests of the child that affect the allocation of custody now have an impact on guardianship as well.[10]

Nonetheless, it should be stressed that by granting guardianship powers to the custodian, the legislature has avoided going so far as to make an assessment of the child's best interests a formal component of the guardianship decision. Rather, the principle is incorporated into guardianship determinations obliquely through its consideration in the judicial decision on custody.

12.3 Legal Presumptions in Custody Provisions

12.3.1 The Best Interests of the Child and Its Impact on the Legal Nature of Custody

The evolution of the conditions for the allocation of custody, from objective criteria such as age and gender to a subjective—albeit non-uniformly implemented—assessment of the individual needs of the child does not only illustrate the ability of Muslim jurisdictions to engage in family law reform in accordance with the

[9] But practical problems relating to a mother's travel with her children may arise (in Tunisia for example).

[10] Möller 2015, pp. 911–913.

perceived evolution of their society,[11] it also represents an important paradigm shift. The introduction of the best interests of the child in custody regulations—be it as the paramount principle, a statutory exception or an underlying consideration—represents a shift from stereotypes and cultural tradition to a consideration of the particular needs of the child at a given point in time in a given family,[12] thus constituting a shift from rules based on legal presumptions to a more flexible and fluid requirement demanding the individualization of each case. It thus necessitates the readiness of courts to consider each custody incident on a case-by-case basis rather than regarding children as a 'class or a homogeneous grouping with identical needs and situations'.[13]

Such a shift is, however, not self-fulfilling. If the introduction of the principle of the best interests of the child is to be taken seriously and implemented consistently, this new value must—ideally—be equally embraced by the specific provisions on the allocation, extension, and revocation of custody, and also by provisions on visiting rights as well as procedural rules surrounding custody proceedings. One has to bear in mind that the allocation of custody, while of acute importance when parents separate, is but the first step along a continuous process in which the custody arrangement will be steadily scrutinized according to the given circumstances until the child exits custody for good.

It is thus interesting to further investigate whether the detailed provisions on custody as well as their interpretation by the legal community are following this path and accompany the paradigm shift initiated by the inclusion of the principle of the best interests of the child. In this investigation, attention will be given to the question of which social and religious assumptions and—translating those—which legal presumptions inform the provisions on custody and their interpretation, and whether the introduction of the principle of the best interests of the child has changed the practice of custody.

12.3.2 Evolution of Custody Rules

A comparative analysis of the chapters shows a similar evolution in most countries as regards the allocation of custody: the first codifications of family law remained faithful to the pre-modern Islamic rules associated with the respectively prevailing school of law and replicated the custody allocation rules which were based on the age and gender of the children as well as on the gender, marital status and religion of the parents. In this étatisation process of pre-modern Islamic law, the idea that these rules were a manifestation of the best interests of the child[14] was left

[11] On the dynamics of legal change in family law see Yassari 2016.

[12] Kelly 1997, p. 385.

[13] Ibid.

[14] See Ibrahim 2015, pp. 859–891.

unarticulated, as the principle itself did not figure in the codes. Instead, the detailed rules—thought of as a display of that principle—were codified as objective, one-size-fits-all rules.

Further, custody was mainly codified in the section on divorce, insinuating that custody was a matter to be dealt with as a consequence of the dissolution of a parental marriage, and that the allocation of the child to one or the other parent was some kind of a 'collateral damage' caused by this dissolution that needed remedy. In most jurisdictions under review, this is clearly reflected in the legal terminology, where custody is described as the right or duty of one or the other parent, making the parents the centre of attention rather than the child. This preference is also illustrated in parental custody agreements, where the right of custody is traded in return for divorce or for relinquishment of the dower (*mahr*). In fact, the general system of family law in Islamic jurisprudence, particularly the web of interdependence between the personal and financial repercussions of marriage and divorce as well as the unequal access to divorce, created strong incentive for spouses and, by extension, for parents to accumulate bargaining power in order to reach their personal goals. Amongst these tools of power, the right to custody figured prominently: Iranian case law in divorce proceedings, for example, reveals how mothers would forfeit their dower to keep custody of their children beyond the statutory legal age[15] or how they would give it up to exit the marriage. Similarly, Tunisian women would renounce any financial claim available to them upon divorce to make sure that they would retain the right to care for their children.[16] Thus, as a matter of fact, custody was perceived of or at least used as a type of bargain between the parents. This enforced the perception that caring for a child was primarily the right of the caretaker, rather than being a right of the child as the one who is being taken care of.

Another important aspect, as shown in particular in the chapters on Jordan, Egypt, and Lebanon, is that the endeavours to reform family law, and the custody regulations that such legislation contains, were mainly directed at improving women's rights. The reforms in Jordan and Egypt, for example with regard to the extension of the mother's custody, were part of the reformist's agenda to strengthen the right of women/mothers vis-à-vis their husbands rather than striving to enforce the principle of the best interests of the child. Certainly, the reforms in custody law relied on the perception that the mother is better suited to care for small children;

[15] The practice of bartering parts of or the entire dower for the custody of the children is recognized by Iranian courts and sanctioned by the Legal Office of the Ministry of Justice, see statement no. 7/6664 of 10 October 2002, in Riyasat-i Jumhuri (2011) Majmu'ih-i Qanun-i Madani, 8th edn., Mu'avinat-i Tadvin-i Tanqih va Intisharat-i Qavanin va Muqarrarat, Tehran, Article 1169 Iran. CC, p. 382.

[16] Sabbagh 1969–1970, p. 63, who points to a 1966 Communiqué of the Tunisian Ministry of Justice that describes this situation, i.e. a renouncement of compensation in order to obtain custody, as one of the main reasons for lifting Islamic law's strict age and gender boundaries in custody matters.

however, the prolonged maternal custody period was meant in the first place to strengthen the position of women and mothers and thus provide a tool of empowerment.[17] As a consequence, under Egyptian Law for example, the automatic awarding of custody for small children to their mother is not checked against the formers' interests. Rather custody follows a strict objective rule dictated by age (and until recently by gender): in Egypt the period of maternal custody was steadily extended from seven for girls and nine for boys to fifteen for both genders, with further extension possible in accordance with the welfare of the child. In other words, it is not the specific needs of the child that are considered, but the child's presumed need to be nurtured and raised by the mother. Finally, the chapter on Lebanon also points to the fact that the extension of the mother's custody period was primarily meant to enhance the right of women and was advocated from a women's rights perspective, even if its final statutory version was linked back to the principle of the best interests of the child. Yet with the focus on the mother, the child's interests may get lost from view, potentially enforcing the idea that custody is basically a right of the mother to which the child must submit.

Shifting the focus on the interests of the child—as the paramount principle—disrupts this picture: Whereas the previously existing objective rules of custody were widely used in practice as a regulatory tool to balance the respective rights and claims of parents, the current approach—making custody a function of the best interests of the child—has a different focal point. The consideration of the child's interest means that custody is not contingent on statutory regulation or (unsupervised) parental arrangement, but is depending on the individual assessment of the welfare of the child by a more neutral authority, i.e. the courts. Where a court is to decide on the fate of a child to be cared for by one or the other parent, less room is given to the autonomy of the parents to negotiate custody between themselves and strike a deal—at the expense of their children. This shift has therefore great potential to change the perception of custody as a right of the parents to one genuinely seen as a right of the child.

12.3.3 Comparative Analysis of Custody Regulations: Presumptions, Myths and Realities

12.3.3.1 General Observation

As mentioned above, two Muslim majority countries stand out as to their position on the principle of the best interests of the child. One is Tunisia, which abandoned the pre-modern Islamic law rules on the allocation of custody through statutory reform as early as 1966, establishing instead the principle of the best interests of the child as the paramount principle. The second notable exception is Pakistan, where case law since the 1960s shows how the judiciary has developed the

[17] Cf. Möller 2016b.

principle of the best interests of the child into the paramount principle according to which, and even in contradiction to Hanafi rule, custody is to be awarded. The shift of focus from objective rules to subjective criteria has created considerable room to incorporate changed concepts of parent- and childhood and challenge existing ideas and stereotypes. The concern of the courts is no longer to balance all interests of the parties, but to serve the interests of the child, even if this means infringing on the rights of either parent. This is not to deny that the interpretation of the notion of the best interests of a child remains entrenched in the respective cultural context of each country. Tunisian and Pakistani law and judicial practice are—as in any given country—informed by traditional beliefs and assumptions regarding gender roles, children's needs and the eligibility requirements to be a custodian, as well as religious affiliation. This is even more pronounced in countries where the best interests of the child was not introduced as an overriding rule but was rather incorporated in selected provisions, adopted as a statutory exception or embraced as an underlying concept.

However some common trends can be detected in the region: The first observation is that in many countries the gender and the age of the children have been brought into line with each other. Even if these reforms have not remained unchallenged (as exemplified in the chapter on Iraq for instance), custody provisions today do not differ as regards gender and age of the children in Iraq, Iran, Indonesia, Lebanese Sunni law, Egypt, Jordan, or Morocco. Others have kept the distinction according to age and gender (such as Qatar, Afghanistan, Algeria, Bahrain, Kuwait, Syria) but have at the same time raised the mother's custodial period for both genders.

At the same time, provisions have been introduced in many countries that allow the child at a certain age to choose a custodian. Accordingly, after the prescribed custodial period of the mother or her substitute and that of the father (where applicable), the child is given the right to choose his custodian. This applies, for example, in Indian, Indonesian, Iraqi, Moroccan, Egyptian and Jordanian law, where pursuant to statute children can chose their custodian after reaching a certain age ranging from twelve to fifteen. However, it is not clear whether this option conveys a real decision-making power to the children, or whether it is understood as a right to be heard on their preferences, with the courts retaining the actual power to evaluate these preferences in accordance with the best interests of the child. Court decisions range widely on this matter and actual practice suggests that the autonomy granted to the child by law is not being fully implemented. The chapter on Indonesia points to the fact that despite the clear wording of the law, courts do not regularly give children a voice, and where they are heard their preferences are not automatically followed. This is mainly explained by the fact that children are considered to be opportunistic and tend to choose the more lenient parent. This is also illustrated in the chapter on Iraq, where the courts seem to hear the children but at the same time are not bound to follow their opinions and must consider their welfare. Under Lebanese Ja'fari law children must also be given a voice, but here again case law shows that the courts are not consistent in doing so. Qatari law is interesting, as the law permits a girl that has reached thirteen and a boy that has reached the age of fifteen to state a preference as to who the custodian should be as an alternative to the judge's decision on the custody.

The disconnect between the legal rights of the child and the actual practice of the courts sheds light on the perception of children as being inherently weak and unable to make decisions as to their own welfare. The perception of children in many countries revolves around stereotypes and a collective view of children: society at large does not afford great agency to children or to their ability to judge for themselves.[18] However, the sheer fact that such optional rights have been installed in statutes and case law might be indicative of a change towards a perception of children as mentally capable and self-determined individuals. At the same time, it needs to be discussed whether, and if so, how, further legal presumptions underlying the detailed rules of custody hinder or facilitate this evolution.

12.3.3.2 General Presumptions and Social Context

Custody as a Female Prerogative

What transcends all the jurisdictions under review is the so-called 'tender years doctrine'. This refers to the assumption that female custodians are better suited to care for very small children. This assumption is hardly checked against the individual interests of a given small child. Even in countries like Tunisia or Pakistan, where custody is to be awarded in the light of the child's best interests, courts widely abide by this assumption. Egyptian law takes this assumption even further. The gradual extension of the mother's custody period to fifteen years for both genders over the last hundred years indicate that the best interests of the child are considered to be synonymous with remaining in the custody of the mother (and other female relatives of the child) as long as possible, as shown in the chapter on Egypt.

The female prerogative in custody is in line with the concept of complementarity under pre-modern Islamic law, according to which women have a natural inclination toward caring and nurturing. Thus, women's emotional abilities, compassion and sensitivity qualify them best to fulfil the needs of a small child. Consequently, it is in the small child's best interests to be cared for by a female custodian. This assumption applies not only to the mother of the child, but also to the person to replace her if she fails to exercise custody. Thus, statutes in many countries provide for a list of subsequent female relatives that are to become custodians if the mother is absent or dismissed before the father is taken into account. This is true, for instance, under Lebanese Sunni and Druze law, Egyptian law and Jordanian law.

Also, where the father is awarded custody, in some jurisdictions the female priority still applies to a degree, requiring that the custodian father be assisted by

[18] See the Special Issue 'Children and young people in times of conflict and change: Child rights in the Middle East and North Africa' (June 2015) of Global Studies of Childhood 5:115–219. http://gsc.sagepub.com/content/5/2.toc (accessed 1 September 2016).

a female relative in the exercise of custody. This is true in Qatari or Tunisian law, where the custodian father must ensure that actual care is provided by a female. By contrast, Iranian, Iraqi, Moroccan or Algerian law, for example, give the father second rank after the mother, excluding other female relatives as primary custodian. Accordingly, the award of custody to the father does not require him to be assisted by a female. Interestingly, however, the idea persists to a certain extent and in court practice in Iran, for example, judges try to make sure during the proceedings that a female relative of the father is going to be incorporated into the day-to-day-care of the child, even though this is not a legal requirement.

Religion or Compassion?

Generally, children born to a Muslim father are considered to be Muslim by birth. As the marriage of a Muslim woman to a non-Muslim man is forbidden in most Muslim jurisdictions, religion can be an issue in cases where custody is at stake for a child born to a Muslim father and a non-Muslim mother. Another potentially problematic constellation would be the conversion of the non-Muslim father (and by extension his previously non-Muslim children) to Islam during the marriage and the consequent change of the applicable law, bringing up the question of the custody of the children following the divorce. Can a non-Muslim parent be the custodian of a Muslim child? The role of religious education as a key factor in the determination of the best interests of the child lies at the heart of this question. To avoid any deviation from the religion of the child, traditional religious doctrine holds that Muslim children ought to be and in fact can be properly raised in the Muslim faith only by a Muslim parent.

As a consequence, in some countries, such as Algeria, raising the child in the religion of his father is explicitly stated as being a duty of the custodian. In others, the non-Muslim mother will not be awarded custody of her children at all when the parents separate (such as in Iran, Bahrain as well as under Lebanese and Iraqi Ja‘fari law) or the general custodial time of the mother will as a rule be reduced to the child reaching his fifth or at the latest his seventh birthday (for example in Lebanese Sunni, Qatari, Egyptian and Jordanian law). Imposing a custody limitation at this early age is based on the assumption that a child is deemed to start developing a religious identity at that age and thus needs to be cared for by a Muslim custodian. Further, during her reduced custodial period the custodian non-Muslim mother still may lose custody if the father alleges that she turned the child away from Islam and taught the child her own religion. As in all cases of revocation of custody, the Muslim father has to sue for the custody of his child in court. However, the chapters suggest that claims of this nature will regularly be honoured and that in such cases judges have only minimal discretion to assess a change in custody under the best interests of the child standard.

Here a conflict arises between two opposing presumptions: on the one hand the presumption that the mother is best suited to bring up her small children and on the other the presumption that the Muslim child is in need of a proper religious upbringing and thus a Muslim parent. This conflict clearly swings in the vast majority of the cases to the benefit of religious education. In fact, the chapters show that the religious upbringing of the child is considered to be part of national public policy. In Indonesia, where statutory law does not point to the religion of the parent, case law reflects the same evaluation. The 2012 Feederika case is a perfect example of this attitude: the Indonesian Supreme Court upheld the lower court's decision revoking maternal custody because of the mother's conversion and rejected the petitioner's argument that Indonesian law specifies that child custody should solely be based on the principles of non-discrimination and the best interests of the child. Further, the chapter on Lebanon points to the fact that religion not only permeates the detailed provisions of custody but is also an underlying factor when interpreting the principle of the best interests of the child. In Lebanon this observation is not limited to the Muslim community; it can be observed in other communities as well since religion is an important factor in the country's identity politics as well as those of the region more broadly.

There are however some notable exceptions: in 2009 the Egyptian Supreme court ruled that a non-Muslim mother could keep custody of her children where her ex-husband had converted to Islam and by this act correspondingly changed the previous Christian religious affiliation of his children. In Tunisian law as well, the legislature has made an exception for non-Muslim custodian mothers: while the custodial period of any non-Muslim custodian is generally reduced, the rule does not apply to a non-Muslim custodian mother. She will not be subject to an automatic reduction of her custody period over her Muslim children, such a change occurring instead only where the interests of the child so require. And most recently, the right of a non-Muslim mother was honoured in an international dispute by Tunisian courts, as will be elaborated upon in more detail under Sect. 12.4.1.1.

The Evil Stepfather versus the Good Stepmother

Another contentious issue is the loss of custody by a custodian mother when she remarries. In a certain number of countries a custodian mother who remarries during her period of custody will lose her right to custody. The loss of custody of a remarried custodian mother is based on three assumptions: First it is believed that a stepfather has no natural inclination to care for a child with whom he is not genetically linked. Rather, the idea prevails that it is in the child's interests to live with his biological father and be taken care of by a female custodian since a stepmother, i.e. the new wife of the father, is—as a female—taken to have a natural biological inclination to care for children, regardless of genetic linkage. Thus a father's custodial rights are not affected by his marital status.[19]

[19] However in some jurisdictions, courts have taken into account the remarriage of the father as a factor amongst others not to award him custody (as in Jordan for example).

The second assumption is that a remarried mother, preoccupied with maintaining her new marriage, will not be able to properly care for her own children as her time is mostly consumed by her duties towards her new husband. And thirdly, the revocation of a married mother's custody is based on the assumption that abuse can be avoided and the welfare of the child (particularly a female child) better preserved if the child does not have to live with a male that is not a related to the child at a degree prohibiting marriage.

In some countries however, the principle of the best interests of the child is challenging these assumptions. Accordingly, the remarriage of a mother will not *ipso jure* affect her right to custody if remaining with the mother is in the best interests of the child. This applies pursuant to statutory provisions in Qatar, Morocco and Tunisia and based on case law in Jordan and Egypt, where courts have rejected fathers' efforts to revoke the custody of a remarried mother in view of the best interests of the child. In Iraqi law, the provision stipulating that a remarried mother will lose custody was abolished in 1986. Interestingly, the focus of the reform was less on the best interests of the child than on the right of the mother to 'a happy marital life'. Thus according to the new provision, a remarried mother only forfeits her right of custody if the court finds that the remarriage is *in concreto* harmful to the child.

Also the courts increasingly provide scope for a new husband to show his commitment to his wife and the children from her previous marriages. In Iraq for example, the courts ask the new husband to officially declare his good intention and his awareness of his moral duties to his new family. A similar path was taken by the Iranian legislature in 2013, albeit in a different setting. The new Adoption Law of 2013 gives single women the right to adopt a female child.[20] Further, the law determines that in the event of a subsequent marriage of an adoptive mother, her new husband has to commit to the care and protection of his stepchild.[21] The assumption that stepfathers are inherently hostile to their stepchildren is thus rejected and a certain degree of agency afforded to a mother's (new) husband. Finally, Pakistani law is an interesting example in this respect. On several occasions (and in different constellations) the courts held that the remarriage of any given parent was an important but not decisive factor in evaluating the interests of the child and assessing the proper custodian.

These decisions show how the focus on the child is allowing for a change in the evaluation of given ideas about parents and their qualification as custodians. When balancing the presumed harm possibly inflicted on the child by the presence of a new husband against the child's need to be cared for by his mother or to be

[20] The Iranian law does not use the word 'adoption' but the expression '*sarparastī*'. It has been argued in Yassari 2015, pp. 927–962, that under a functional perspective the *sarparastī* of orphaned children amounts to a functional equivalent to adoption.

[21] See Article 5(c) Law on the Protection of Unguarded and Ill-Guarded Children and Youth of 2 October 2013, Official Gazette no. 19997 of 28 October 2013.

cared for in a continuous manner, the latter is gaining strength. This also allows for more flexibility in reconsidering common gender roles in the cultural context of any given country.

Lifestyle as a Determining Factor

Generally, the statutory conditions for eligibility as custodian are termed in a gender-neutral way and apply to both parents (and any third party). In practice, in some countries these conditions are applied with regard to both genders (Iraq, Jordan), while in others the focus is rather on the mother. The common requirements found in all jurisdictions include that the custodian be of full age, reasonable and of sound character. Custody will not be awarded to a parent affected by certain diseases or physical disabilities and will be withdrawn where the child is being neglected. Whereas some of these conditions are objectively verifiable, the question as to the sound character of the parent (particularly for the mother) is more of an issue because it implies an assessment of how a woman's personal and social behaviour influences her ability to be a 'good' mother. Therefore the court's evaluation of this issue is very revealing as to the social understanding of motherhood.

To fill in the vague terminology, the courts have recourse to different frames of reference. More often than not—and unsurprisingly—these frames are shaped by religious and conservative values. What are the factors that, according to the courts, shape the character of a mother? The main factors found in the chapters revolve around her piousness, her social behaviour (in particular her interaction with men), and her employment status as well as the kind of employment she is exercising. Another issue often invoked is the question of fault and the marital dissent that caused the separation of the parents in the first place.

Here again, social assumptions play a significant role, as illustrated for instance by the chapter on Indonesia. Pursuant to statutory law, custody is awarded automatically to the mother until the children reach the age of twelve, and after that age children may choose their custodian. Although the law does not point to the principle of the child's best interests, courts consider it in both instances, i.e. during the custodial period of the mother and when deciding on the fate of a child that has reached the age of twelve. Additionally, the law does not specify what qualifications the custodian must fulfil; the clarification is left to the courts. The analysis of the case law in Indonesia shows a conservative approach to this issue: working mothers or mothers potentially considering remarriage have seen custody withdrawn from them. The general thread of these decisions reflects the assumption that their choices will divert them from their prime role as mothers. Considering remarriage or working outside the house tended to show that they had too little concern for the wellbeing of their children. These decisions did not consider the actual effects of the mothers' choices on the wellbeing of the children, but were made on an abstract general assumption regarding their potential effects on the children. The gendered aspect of these decisions is clearly shown by the fact that such concerns were not voiced, or only to a much lesser degree, where the father's custody was at issue, even though in most cases the fathers were working full-time and had much less time for their children.

12.3.4 An Incomplete Change of Paradigm

Custody and its allocation have undergone remarkable changes. The introduction of the principle of the best interests of the child has initiated a shift in focus from the prevalence of the needs and rights of the parents and general assumptions on the welfare of children as a group to a concrete consideration of the needs of individual children. This shift has not, however, been implemented consistently and reveals how underlying assumptions of mother- and fatherhood still permeate the specific custody provisions and the interpretation of the best interests of the child principle.

What does this imply for the nature of custody? The chapters reveal that custody has not yet shifted to become a genuine right of the child. Yet, the competition between parents has started to lose some of its most discriminatory edges, creating more room for new, more nuanced conceptions of parenthood and kinship relations. One notable change is the equalization of age categories or both genders; additionally, the right of children to choose their custodian is an important tool fostering their empowerment and emphasizing their centrality. The tender years doctrine has been retained by almost all jurisdictions, with a notable extension of maternal custody in some countries. At the same time this extension has not only increased the mother's right to care for her children but also her responsibility to do so. In most jurisdictions a mother cannot, unless for exceptional reasons, refuse to exercise custody. The refusal will be judged in view of the welfare of the child. Accordingly, a mother's bartering her right to custody in return for a divorce is not permissible in, among others, Iraq, Qatar, Afghanistan, Bahrain, or the United Arab Emirates.

With a focus on the mother and the child, the right of the father to custody is weaker. In most jurisdictions he must be assisted by a female relative or must first prove in court the inability of the mother to be installed as the custodian. This is true at every stage of the process of allocating custody: in a child's early years the mother is by law the custodian; after the expiry of her custodial period, however, the child is not transferred automatically to the father. Rather, this requires a court decision that generally considers the welfare of the child. That being said, in practice the courts do regularly transfer custody of the child to the father. However the structure of custody provisions and the chapters suggest that custody is presently understood as a right shared jointly by the female custodian and the child, with a slight leaning towards the child as the bearer of the right in some cases. Qatari law, for example, states that custody is a right shared between the custodian and the child, but it emphasizes that the child's right is stronger. Also, the general thread of the Iraqi and the Tunisian courts of cassation is that in custody cases the interests of the child must be given priority over the interests of the parties to the litigation. Finally, the legal department of the Iranian Justice Ministry has issued a statement specifying that custody is an inherent right of the child.[22]

The development of this trend, its impact and its reliability have yet to be fully traced, particularly in light of the intensification of migration since the second half of the 20th century and the occurrence of binational and interreligious marriages in the region. These families, often holding different nationalities or adhering to different religions, face specific challenges when family law disputes arise, disputes that intensify once children are born. An important and very contentious issue in this context is child abduction, where one parent wrongfully removes the child from his place of habitual residence. While domestic and international remedies for solving these problems include civil lawsuits or criminal proceedings,[23] private international law seeks to bridge the gap between the different legal systems involved through international conventions and bilateral treaties that determine the applicable law and arrange for the recognition and enforcement of foreign judicial orders. Legal difficulties are, however, intensified by the cultural and religious diversity inherent in cross-border cases. In his recent assessment of the difficulties faced in cross-border custody issues, Hans Van Loon, former General Secretary of the Hague Conference on Private International Law, identifies 'countries whose legal system is based on religious law, in particular Jewish and Sharia Law'[24] as causing the biggest problems.

Given the recent developments analysed here, this assessment needs a fresh evaluation: the introduction of the principle of the best interests of the child in Muslim jurisdictions has triggered new positions and a change of attitude, even though one cannot deny that legislation and case law still draw heavily on both Islamic legal doctrine and conservative assumptions regarding parenthood. In this, the prevailing laws certainly differ from the standards set forth in international conventions and in particular the laws of the founding countries of the Hague Conference. It is also certainly one of the reasons why many Muslim jurisdictions have refrained from ratifying the relevant conventions of the Hague Conference. As a consequence, a gap has appeared between the system established by the Hague Conference and the legal regimes of many Muslim jurisdictions. In the following section, the most contentious issues related to the adherence of Muslim jurisdictions to the Hague Conventions will be discussed and solutions will be sought to bridge this gap.

[22] Statement of the Legal Department of the Iran. Ministry of Justice no. 7/4771 of 4 February 1991, in Riyasat-i Jumhuri (2011) Majmu'ih-i Qanun-i Madani, 8th edn., Mu'avinat-i Tadvin-i Tanqih va Intisharat-i Qavanin va Muqarrarat, Tehran, Article Iran. CC, p. 381.

[23] Boykin 2012, p. 453.

[24] Van Loon 2011, p. 180.

12.4 Parental Care in Cross-Border Disputes

12.4.1 The Gap between the Hague Conference System and Muslim Jurisdictions

Although being a member of the Hague Conference does not entail an obligation to ratify the conventions drawn up by the Conference, it is still the case that only very few Muslim majority countries have even become members (e.g. Egypt, Jordan, Malaysia, Morocco, and Tunisia).[25] The Hague Conference has elaborated significant international instruments relevant to cross-border parental care issues. The most important among them are the Convention on Civil Aspects of International Child Abduction of 1980 and the Hague Convention on Jurisdiction, Applicable Law, Recognition, Enforcement, Co-operation in Respect of Parental Responsibility and Measures for the Protection of Children of 1996. Among Muslim jurisdictions, only Morocco and Iraq have ratified these instruments.[26]

The reluctance of Muslim countries to ratify these conventions can be primarily explained by the differences between the concept and the perception of parental care in the Hague conventions and the United Nations Convention on the Rights of the Child of 1989, on one hand, and the parental care regimes in jurisdictions having an Islamic legal tradition on the other hand. In fact, the founding countries of the permanent structure of the Hague Conference are mainly 'Western' European civil law countries.[27] Muslim jurisdictions thus consider that the ideas underlying this system and the standards it establishes do not take into consideration their laws and the founding principles of their legal orders.

The chapters collected in this volume reflect the conceptual difference between the Hague system and the general frame of reference for custody matters in Muslim jurisdictions as concerns chiefly two points: first, the religious foundation of parental care regulations, in particular the prerequisite of affiliation to Islam as a condition of eligibility to exercise parental care for a Muslim child, and secondly, the gendered division and hierarchy of parental responsibility. However, new trends on both the national and international level raise the prospect of surmounting discrepancies.

12.4.1.1 The Religious Foundation of Parental Care Regulations

Family and succession laws—including parental care regimes—in Muslim jurisdictions are rooted in traditional Islamic legal doctrine to varying degrees. In some

---

[25] See the official website of the Hague Conference www.hcch.net/en/states/hcch-members Accessed 1 September 2016.

[26] While Morocco has ratified both conventions relevant to cross-border parental care issues, Iraq is a member only to the Convention on Civil Aspects of International Child Abduction of 1980.

[27] Van Loon 2011, p. 175.

countries constitutional clauses require a reference to Islamic law (as in Egypt, Iran or Afghanistan for example), in others statutory law demands legal lacuna to be filled in through recourse to Islamic law (for instance in Qatar, Jordan or Syria), yet in others judicial practice refers regularly to Islamic ethical, moral and legal values (as exemplified in the chapters on Indonesia, Lebanon and Jordan). Also, in some Muslim jurisdictions personal status disputes featuring parental care matters are submitted to a religious court (sharia courts). This is true for example in Jordan, Lebanon, and Bahrain. Further, Islamic law still strongly influences substantive law and its interpretation. This applies also to countries such as Tunisia, where pre-modern Islamic law is a source of law in neither the Constitution nor in statutory law. In fact, the Tunisian Code of Personal Status departed from traditional Islamic law in many important aspects, as it explicitly prohibited polygamy and the husband's unilateral access to divorce. Also as regards custody, Tunisia was one of the first countries to abandon the Islamic criteria for the allocation of custody. Nevertheless, for decades Tunisian courts have continued to reflect religious legal doctrine in questions of parental care, and judges have interpreted ambiguous provisions of the Tunisian Code of Personal Status with reference to Islamic law, basing their reasoning in particular on Article 1 of the Tunisian Constitution that stipulates that Islam is the religion of the state.

However, Middle Eastern law is not static. Notwithstanding the strong hold of Islamic law and values in many aspects, judicial practice and legislation have been evolving in many countries, as shown above. As such, many countries have effectively abolished religious courts (Tunisia, Morocco, Egypt, Pakistan and Iran), and state courts are adjudicating family law instead. The attitude towards international disputes is also evolving. Where the courts have to balance the interests and the laws of several people and jurisdictions, some jurisdictions have shown more flexibility. Tunisia is a good example of this, where courts have undergone a clear change of course and moved towards the standards of the Hague conventions as regards claims for the recognition and enforcement of foreign custody decisions. For many years the Tunisian courts had refused to enforce foreign judicial decisions awarding child custody to a foreign (non-Muslim) mother, conveying the message that the protection of the Muslim and Arab identity was part of Tunisian public policy. However, public policy is a fluid notion, inherently subject to change. While early decisions from the 1950s through the 1970s saw religious values and the collective identity of the Tunisian state and society being given paramount importance in the rejection of enforcement orders, in the 1980s and 1990s the courts adopted new terminology and engaged in new argumentation: based on the principle of the best interests of the child the courts argued that the child's best interests required that he be raised in Tunisia as a Muslim. Over the course of time however, courts dissociated the best interests of the child from the notion of belonging to Islam or from the idea that the child's interests required that his religion be preserved. Rather the courts emphasized the concrete needs of the child himself. This led to the recognition of a series of foreign decisions, as exemplified by a 2001 case in which the award of custody to the Danish mother living in Belgium was recognized despite the objections of the Tunisian father who lived in Tunisia.

Similarly, in Egypt a decision was rendered in 2009 that, while not encompassing an international context, could nevertheless be seen as an indicator of change in international disputes. Specifically, the court ruled that the children of a Muslim father were entitled to remain in the custody of their Christian mother until they were fifteen, thus granting the Christian mother the same period of custody as Muslim mothers. In so doing, the Egyptian Supreme Court set a milestone on the road to dissociating the best interests of the child from the parents' faith. These examples show that vague legal notions in parental care and societal concepts of mother and fatherhood are evolving. Further, it illustrates the diversity between Muslim jurisdictions.

Notwithstanding these cases, in all other countries under review the obligation of the custodian to be a Muslim as a condition for his/her eligibility remains practically untouched.[28] Whereas other conditions for the eligibility of the custodian or the guardian have been reformed or applied with flexibility by the courts, the custodian's religious affiliation to Islam has been considered non-negotiable. Ensuring that a Muslim child gets a proper religious education from a Muslim parent is in those jurisdictions considered to be in the child's best interests.

It is thus safe to say that Islamically inspired perceptions of parenthood will continue to inform law and judicial practice in Muslim jurisdictions. Also, legislative reforms in parental care issues are, more often than not, framed in Islamic legal terminology and values and are portrayed as new interpretations of Islamic law. There seems to be a need to emphasize that new regulations are in conformity with religious law and thus the perceived cultural identity of the child. This is shown for instance by references made to Islamic law in the reform process, as discussed in the chapter on Iraq. Also the chapter on Egypt emphasizes that the Egyptian legislature secured support for its reform of the custodial period of the mother by commissioning the Azhar University with a fatwa as to the compatibility of the reform with Islamic tenets.

This is probably the most visible difference between the legal framework elaborated by the Hague Conference for parental disputes and those of Muslim jurisdiction: whereas the international conventions do not grant any space for the interests of any given community or religion to keep its believers together and guarantee an education in a particular religion, a Muslim upbringing remains part and parcel of the duties of parents and is considered a matter of public policy in (most) Muslim jurisdictions.

12.4.1.2 The Hierarchy and Gendered Division of Parental Responsibility

Another matter of contention and an important obstacle to Muslim jurisdictions embracing the Hague conventions is the gendered and hierarchical aspect of

[28] On this issue see Gallala-Arndt 2015, pp. 829–858.

parental regulation. This aspect is visible in the continued division of parental care into female custody and male guardianship as well as in the dominance of guardianship over custody. As a consequence, the rights of the custodian to choose a residence and to travel with the child outside the country mostly depend on the consent of the guardian and are therefore ultimately under his authority.

Algerian law makes a notable exception on this point. In 2005 the Algerian legislature combined the rights to custody and guardianship in a remarkable and completely new manner: Accordingly, after the separation of the parents, guardianship will automatically be awarded to the custodian parent, regardless of the custodian's gender.[29] This reform is particularly noteworthy as it essentially brings an end to the traditional division of parental care into guardianship and custody. Whereas courts previously refused to grant the mother custody if she did not live in the same country as the guardian, in 2008 the Algerian Court of Cassation held that it was in the best interests of the children to remain with their mother in France even though their father was living in Algeria.[30] This ruling was also grounded on a provision of the Algerian family code which allows the court to preserve the custodial status of a person who has established habitual residence outside the country.[31]

In the same vein, Tunisian courts have come to curtail the father's right to guardianship in application of the principle of the best interests of the child. In a case involving a Tunisian mother and an Egyptian father, the mother had filed for divorce and custody of their common daughter in Tunisia after she had left Egypt. The Tunisian Court of Cassation in its decision in 2009 held that the award of custody must take into consideration the interests of the child and not the interests of the guardian, and therefore rejected the father's argument that awarding the mother custody would prevent him from exercising his rights of guardianship over the child.

Again, notwithstanding these developments, the hierarchy between custody and guardianship is still a matter of conflict: this is true in a national context and it becomes even more complex in cross-border situations. The weight given to the fatherly supervision of the child as his guardian stands in opposition to the requirement of an individual assessment of the child's best interests in all matters related to the child, and thus it stands in opposition to the standards of both the UN Convention on the Rights of the Child as well as international Hague instruments.

---

29 Cf. Article 87 Algerian Family Code.

30 Decision of the Algerian Court of Cassation no. 457038 of 10 September 2008, RCS. 2008, p. 313.

31 Cf. Article 69 Algerian Family Code.

12.4.2 Can the Gap Be Bridged?

The foregoing analysis has shown that there are some encouraging developments in the region toward bridging the differences in the conception and perception of parental care. The chapters in particular demonstrate how parental care regulations in Muslim jurisdictions have evolved to incorporate more flexibility. Legislation and case law illustrate how a more individual approach to the allocation of custody is taking root, and the perception of the child as the subject and not the object of custody is evolving in statutes and legal practice. Correspondingly, on the level of public international law, the chapter by Shaheen Sardar Ali and Sajila Sohail Khan illustrates how Muslim countries endeavour to engage with the UN Convention on the Rights of the Child and details their growing readiness to adopt the standards set forth in the convention. Some Muslim jurisdictions offer additional mechanisms in their domestic laws which may be helpful in cases of cross-border child abduction. For instance in Pakistan habeas corpus applications have been successfully filed to recover a child unlawfully removed from the foreign parent. Equally, it is very important to keep in mind the differences amongst the Muslim jurisdictions, both between themselves and in their interaction with the system established by private and public international law.

A rapprochement between the systems set by international instruments and those of Muslim jurisdictions will however also require the willingness of the international community to acknowledge these developments and to show awareness of the concerns of Muslim countries in this area. The gap between Hague member states and Muslim non-member states is rightly explained to a large extent by the religious nature of the family laws in these countries. However, it is not religion as such that is the main obstacle, but rather the use of religion as an identity factor to block the introduction of legal instruments considered to be imports of Western legal tradition and thus manifestations of imperialism.[32] Interestingly, such a resistance can also be seen in secular legal orders such as in Japan, where the courts have been equally reluctant to let a child return to his habitual residence, arguing that it was in the child's best interests to hold the Japanese nationality and to be raised in Japan.[33]

Thus beyond the religious argument, other reasons must exist that prevent Muslim countries from adhering to the Hague instruments. In findings presented to the Canadian Standing Senate Committee on Human Rights—regarding research on the attitudes of Non-Hague Abduction Convention Muslim states—Anver Emon makes an interesting point: he emphasizes that the engagement of the international community with these countries must go beyond a discussion of religion and religion-based legal systems and investigate as well the role of sovereignty and the problems associated with 'states giving up claims on their national children'. Even if, as Emon points out, this will not be a magic solution for overcoming the resistance of Muslim

[32] Report of the Standing Senate Committee on Human Rights (July 2015) Alert: Challenges and International Mechanisms to Address Cross-Border Child Abduction, p. 27. www.parl.gc.ca/Content/SEN/Committee/412/ridr/rep/rep13jul15-e.pdf. Accessed 1 September 2016.

[33] Boykin 2012, p. 451 esq.

jurisdictions to ratifying Hague conventions,[34] taking the concerns of representatives of these countries seriously will pave the way for a rapprochement of the different positions.[35]

The overall aim must be to find common conditions and criteria applicable in international disputes, with the interest of the child in central focus. Here, we must mention some significant initiatives undertaken on the international level in order to bridge the gap, such as the Malta Process and the conclusion of bilateral agreements.

12.4.2.1 Malta Process

The Malta Process is a negotiation forum designed to bring together, on the one side, authorities and judges from states signatory to the Hague Abduction Convention and, on the other, the corresponding representatives from Muslim jurisdictions; the aim of the initiative is to fill the legal gaps resulting from the reluctance of Muslim countries to embrace the convention.[36] Representatives from both sides are meant to meet and exchange their views on the solution of cross-border child custody disputes in cases where the Abduction Convention does not apply.[37]

Three conferences have been convened in the framework of the Malta Process. The declarations issued after these conferences focussed on the importance for Muslim jurisdictions to understand the system and rules established by the Hague conventions. Additionally, the conferences encouraged direct judicial communication in concrete cases arising between the states.[38] The success of this process so far has been moderate; in practice this effort has brought little to the parents and their children who are party to cross-border disputes.[39] There is however room for hope. The process has facilitated diplomatic contacts between Hague system states and Muslim countries. Both sides have learned about their counterparts' legal systems and the challenges they are facing. And it should be recalled that the ratification of the Hague Abduction Convention by Morocco in 2010 can be directly attributed to the Malta Process.[40] Finally, it is a very positive sign that the number of the participants in the Process has been growing.[41]

---

[34] Report of the Standing Senate Committee, p. 27 (see *supra* n 32).

[35] For more details on Emon's work concerning the Hague Abduction Convention and Islamic Law see www.anveremon.com/projects/hague-abduction-convention-.html. Accessed 1 September 2016.

[36] Report of the Standing Senate Committee, p. 25 (see *supra* n 32).

[37] Report of the Standing Senate Committee, p. 25 (see *supra* n 32).

[38] Report of the Standing Senate Committee, p. 25 (see *supra* n 32).

[39] Report of the Standing Senate Committee, p. 26 (see *supra* n 32).

[40] Report of the Standing Senate Committee, p. 27 (see *supra* n 32).

[41] Report of the Standing Senate Committee, p. 25 (see *supra* n 32).

12.4.2.2 Bilateral Agreements

In addition, further negotiation and the conclusion of bilateral agreements could help to coordinate cross-border parental care disputes, in particular where such solutions cannot be reached on a more global level.[42] Such agreements have already been established, for instance, between France and Algeria (1981), Morocco (1981), Tunisia (1982), Egypt (1982) and Lebanon (1999).[43] Mention can also be made of the agreement concluded between Egypt and Australia regarding co-operation on protecting the welfare of children (2000). All agreements have similar goals and aspirations even though they differ as regards their implementation.[44]

In general, the following types of agreements can be distinguished: bilateral conventions on administrative and judicial cooperation, consular cooperation agreements and administrative agreement protocols. In the first category we can differentiate between agreements with a limited scope of cooperation and those modelled on multilateral conventions, such as the Hague Convention on Child Abduction and the European Convention on Recognition and Enforcement of Decisions concerning Custody of Children and on Restoration of Custody of Children.[45] The agreements inspired by these multilateral conventions have also established central authorities meant to ensure communication between the contracting states. As to the effectiveness of these bilateral instruments, an inquiry by the Permanent Bureau of the Hague Conference revealed the following problems: first, long delays in the starting of the judicial procedures requested and, second, a lack of communication as regards official documents, in particular as regards judgments and the whereabouts of the abducted child.[46] Agreements that do not include judicial cooperation but establish consultative committees often deal with specific custody cases and access to abducted children. However, a lack of financial means prevents those committees from meeting regularly.[47] Nevertheless they account for some success. For instance, after the mixed Franco-Lebanese committee met, many French mothers were allowed access to their children in Lebanon after long having been denied such access.[48]

One of the most successful bilateral agreements, considered as a model for further bilateral measures, was concluded in 2003 between the UK and Pakistan.[49] This agreement takes the form of a protocol coordinating judicial cooperation

[42] Gosselain 2002, pp. 4–5.

[43] For a comprehensive list see Gosselain 2002, p. 11.

[44] Gosselain 2002, p. 12.

[45] Available at https://rm.coe.int/CoERMPublicCommonSearchServices/DisplayDCTMContent?documentId=0900001680078b09. Accessed 1 September 2016; Gosselain 2002, p. 12.

[46] Gosselain 2002, p. 23.

[47] Gosselain 2002, p. 24.

[48] Gosselain 2002, p. 24.

[49] Report of the Standing Senate Committee, p. 29 (see *supra* n 32).

between the two countries. In the application of this protocol, liaison judges have been appointed to ensure direct contact between judges in both countries. The protocol is not legally binding, but it has been enforced in Pakistan on several instances, as shown by the chapter on Pakistan. According to the protocol, an abducted child should be returned to the country where he or she usually lives. In addition, the protocol provides that the courts of the country of the child's habitual residence have jurisdiction to decide on the case. The agreement intends to make the judges of both countries respect each other's custody orders. Interestingly, the examples highlighted in the chapter by Ayesha Shahid and Isfandyar Ali Khan show how Pakistani judges have departed from the regime set forth in the protocol and reached decisions that they consider more in favour of the child's wishes.

Perhaps one of the obstacles to these agreements is that there is an imbalance as regards the claims on the side of Hague member states as opposed to those of Muslim non-member states. In fact, in the overwhelming majority of the cases, it is Hague member states which are requesting access to the child and his or her return to a parent.[50] But even in cases where a Muslim non-member state is seeking to exercise a right of access in a European state, administrative problems remain, as it is difficult for nationals of many countries in the region to get a visa to enter European territory.[51]

To sum up, the bilateral agreements display some success but they do not suffice, and in practice the processes under those agreements are lengthy and require several attempts by the requesting state.[52] However, even if the immediate effectiveness of bilateral agreements is still problematic, they can offer a quicker channel of communication and help establish a dialogue between the judges of Muslim and non-Muslim jurisdictions.[53]

In the long run, a new tradition of coordination and effective cooperation between Hague states and Muslim jurisdictions will depend on reciprocal knowledge, the recognition of opposing legal and social structures, and a reliance on common targets. With these building blocks in place, a satisfactory resolution of cross-border custody disputes may follow.

References

Boykin M (2012) A Comparison of Japanese and Moroccan Approaches in Adopting The Hague Convention on the Civil Aspects of International Child Abduction. Family Law Quart 46:451–469

Gallala-Arndt I (2015) The Impact of Religion in Interreligious Custody Disputes: Middle Eastern and Southeast Asian Approaches. Am J Comp L 63:829–858

[50] Gosselain 2002, p. 25.

[51] Gosselain 2002, p. 25.

[52] Gosselain 2002, p. 24.

[53] Gosselain 2002, p. 27.

Gosselain C (2002) Child Abduction and Transfrontier Access: Bilateral Conventions and Islamic States. A research paper for the Permanent Bureau of the Hague Conference on Private International Law. https://assets.hcch.net/upload/abd2002_pd7e.pdf. Accessed 1 Sept 2016

Ibrahim AF (2015) The Best Interests of the Child in Pre-modern Islamic Juristic Discourse and Practice. Am J Comp L 63:859–891

Kelly JB (1997) The Best Interests of the Child: A Concept in Search of Meaning. Fam Concil Cts Rev 35:377–387

Möller L-M (2015) An Enduring Relic: Family Law Reform and the Inflexibility of Wilāya. Am J Comp L 63:893–925

Möller L-M (2016a) Struggling for a Modern Family Law: A Khaleeji Perspective. In: Yassari N (ed) Changing God's Law: The dynamics of Middle Eastern family law. Routledge, London/New York, pp 83–112

Möller L-M (2016b) Improving Women's Rights Through Children's Rights? The Reform of Custody Laws in Contemporary Muslim Jurisdictions. In Jänterä-Jareborg M, Tigroudja H (eds) Women's Human Rights and the Elimination of Discrimination/Les droits des femmes et l'élimination de la discrimination (Académie de droit international de la Haye). Brill, Leiden/Boston, pp 465–489

Sabbagh R (1969–1970) L'évolution du droit de garde dans les pays du Maghreb. Revue tunisienne de droit 49–65

Van Loon H (2011) Legal Diversity in a Flat, Crowded World: The Role of the Hague Conference. Int J Legal Inf 39:172–185

Yassari N (2015) Adding by Choice: Adoption and Functional Equivalents in Islamic and Middle Eastern Law. Am J Comp L 63:927–962

Yassari N (ed) (2016) Changing God's Law: The dynamics of Middle Eastern family law. Routledge, London/New York

FSC
www.fsc.org
MIX
Papier | Fördert
gute Waldnutzung
FSC® C083411

Kolibri 360 GmbH
Ferdinand-Jühlke-Straße 7
99095 Erfurt, Deutschland
produktsicherheit@kolibri360.de